EXPLORING THE ECONOMY OF LATE ANTIQUITY

This collection of essays, by leading historian Jairus Banaji, provides a stimulating rebuttal to the prevailing minimalism in late antique studies. Together, they strike a balance between the wide lens and more specialised discussion, expanding on the perspective and argumentation laid out in an earlier book, *Agrarian Change in Late Antiquity* (2001). Successive chapters discuss the scale of the late Roman gold currency, the economic nature of the aristocracy, the importance of trade, relations between state and ruling class and the problem of continuity into the early Middle Ages. A substantial introduction pulls together the themes of the book into a coherent synopsis, while the preface clarifies the broad aims behind the study. The book as a whole deploys a wide range of sources in various languages and is intended for ancient historians, students of late antiquity and economic historians more generally.

JAIRUS BANAJI is Research Professor at the School of Oriental and African Studies, University of London. He has published on a wide range of subjects and very different periods, and his last book, *Theory as History* (2010), won the 2011 Isaac and Tamara Deutscher Memorial Prize.

CAMBRIDGE
UNIVERSITY PRESS

University Printing House, Cambridge CB2 8BS, United Kingdom

Cambridge University Press is part of the University of Cambridge.

It furthers the University's mission by disseminating knowledge in the pursuit of education, learning and research at the highest international levels of excellence.

www.cambridge.org
Information on this title: www.cambridge.org/9781107101944

First published 2016

Printed in the United States of America by Sheridan Books, Inc.

A catalogue record for this publication is available from the British Library

Library of Congress Cataloguing in Publication data
Banaji, Jairus, 1947–
[Essays. Selections]
Exploring the economy of late antiquity : selected essays / Jairus Banaji.
pages cm
Includes bibliographical references and index.
ISBN 978-1-107-10194-4 (hbk)
1. Economic history–To 500. I. Title.
HC31.B36 2016
330.937′09–dc23 2015027881

ISBN 978-1-107-10194-4 Hardback

EXPLORING THE ECONOMY OF LATE ANTIQUITY

Selected Essays

JAIRUS BANAJI

CAMBRIDGE
UNIVERSITY PRESS

For Elio Lo Cascio

Contents

Preface

In the past three decades a wide range of disciplines and subdisciplines from numismatics and monetary history to ceramics, Byzantine papyrology, late antique/medieval archaeology and cultural and religious history have converged to revamp the history of the fourth to seventh centuries into a general picture of what Bryan Ward-Perkins has called 'the new Late Antiquity'. Since nothing in history stays new for long, this may not be the best expression to use to demarcate the model of a fascinating and vibrant period in human history, but it refers and is intended to refer, clearly, to the watershed that separates Rostozvteff from the kind of history and archaeology that saw a profusion of new scholarship especially from the 1980s on. Even as late as 1973 when Finley published *The Ancient Economy*, there was not a glimmer of the notion that late antiquity might be worth looking at in its own terms rather than the sombre images of the abridged paragraph that ends the (first edition of his) book. In 1969 Fausto Zevi and André Tchernia had published a seminal piece of research on the cylindrical containers at Ostia that were manufactured in the Sahel (Tunisia) and carried massive quantities of olive oil and other commodities to markets elsewhere in the Mediterranean.[1] And of course Peter Brown's *The World of Late Antiquity* appeared in 1971. What both works suggested in rather different ways was a world bubbling with vastly more energy, certainly 'less depleted by catastrophe' and more sophisticated and interesting for all sorts of reasons than whole generations of scholars had led themselves and others to suppose.

'Late antiquity' has thus become one of those great continents of history opened up to exploration only relatively recently. Moreover, historians of late antiquity have never had a wider range of resources to work with than in the past decade or two, with the explosion of archaeological sources

[1] F. Zevi and A. Tchernia, 'Amphores de Byzacène au Bas-Empire', *Antiquités africaines* 3 (1969), 173–214.

and a huge and rapid proliferation of secondary literature throughout the subject. Yet in one sense they remain *less* certain than ever about these centuries and it is worth noting this uncertainty because it resonates with ambiguity. Bryan Ward-Perkins constructs a narrative in which the collapse of Roman power inaugurates centuries of 'dramatic decline in economic sophistication and prosperity',[2] whereas in Michael McCormick's recent work the 'fall' of Rome is rapidly succeeded by the Middle Ages and a new surge of creativity, and this already by the fifth or sixth centuries.[3] It goes without saying that both scholars are talking about the west, the same set of territories over an identical time span.

Historians of late Rome have been well known to vacillate between two more or less distinct images of the late empire, either applauding its novelty and dynamism, as Mazzarino famously did in the 1950s, or foregrounding the mammoth state and its insatiable appetites, an 'omnipotent and obtuse colossus'[4] that stamped out the last traces of any economic vigour or capitalist drive (*philargyria*) Roman society may once have possessed. Thus when, in a seminal paper published in 1969, one medievalist argued that 'when the empire collapsed it released the tax-paying millions of western Europe from a paralysing oppression',[5] he expressed a view that stems from the idea, widespread in more conventional narratives, that the late Roman state absorbed a *disproportionate share of the national wealth* in the fourth, fifth and sixth centuries. This was basically A. H. M. Jones's view of the late empire, but its chief failing is that it radically misrecognises the subtle ways in which what Nicolas Oikonomidès called a 'curious mixture of free enterprise and state intervention' worked in reality and over a very long span of centuries. To take one rather dramatic example of this complexity, in a paper written shortly before she died in 2008 Angeliki Laiou had to point out that 'In the *Book of the Eparch* … the entire regulatory system is geared to free labourers and free manufacturers and traders.'[6] So this was not an economy where the state owned absolutely everything, not a *state* economy in the strong sense of that term;

2 B. Ward-Perkins, *The Fall of Rome and the End of Civilization* (Oxford, 2005), p. 183.

3 J. R. Davis and M. McCormick, 'The Early Middle Ages: Europe's Long Morning', in *The Long Morning of Medieval Europe: New Directions in Early Medieval Studies* (Aldershot and Burlington, 2008), pp. 1–10.

4 Peter Brown in his review of Jones and characterising the latter's depiction of the state.

5 A. R. Bridbury, 'The Dark Ages', *Economic History Review*, 2nd ser., 22 (1969), 526–37, repr. in *The English Economy from Bede to the Reformation* (Woodbridge and Rochester, 1992), pp. 43–55 (at p. 50).

6 A. Laiou, 'The Byzantine City: Parasitic or Productive?' in *Economic Thought and Economic Life in Byzantium*, ed. C. Morrisson and R. Dorin (Aldershot, 2013), no. XII, pp. 1–35, at 6.

indeed, far from it. Nor was it one in which private interests played a marginal role. Nothing undermines that notion more decisively than the unfettered domination of the fourth-century aristocracy over the City of Rome itself. But aristocracies did suffer major upheavals at various times and places between the fifth and seventh centuries and eventually disappeared even in the Byzantine heartland where the rupture is most marked by the emergence of a more militarised landed elite, the 'great families of the middle Byzantine period', in the eighth century.[7] These transformations were protracted over centuries and of course the whole debate has been about how much of a catastrophe they represented.

The 'mammoth state' view is simply the form that minimalism has tended to take in late antique history, the extreme position of *denying autonomy to economic forces* and seeing the late antique economy as an economy held together, essentially, by the state.[8] However, before saying what the chapters that follow set out to do in response to this and related ideas, it may help to start by listing the distinct varieties of catastrophism that permeate the historical literature on the end of Rome.

There are at least four that can be usefully listed, since each implies a different procedure of historical deduction and projects a distinctive set of emphases. 1) *The end of the Roman economy in the west.* The most powerful articulation of this variant is Bryan Ward-Perkins's book *The Fall of Rome and the End of Civilization.* He postulates a 'slow decline' starting in the fifth century and continuing into the seventh as successive regions were disrupted by invasion and their economies destroyed by the shock of external events. The catastrophe here is the dismemberment of the Roman state and the economic consequences of that. 2) *The Italian crisis.* This version, unsurprisingly, attracts mainly Italian scholars, both Roman and medieval (Carandini, Delogu), and a great deal of the argumentation is framed in terms of longer-term demographic collapse, settlement change and urban crisis. Italy's permanent economic decline becomes a sort of concentrated image of the wider economic decline. 3) *End of the Mediterranean exchange system.* This is the prime version to be found in Chris Wickham's work and probably commands near-universal assent. But even if we argue that

[7] C. Wickham, *Framing the Early Middle Ages* (Oxford, 2005), p. 236.

[8] Minimalists who 'characterize everything pre-industrial as primitive' (M. W. Frederiksen, 'Theory, Evidence and the Ancient Economy', *JRS* 65 (1975), 164–71, at p. 171) will naturally have an even bleaker picture of late antiquity. Catastrophism is not confined to their ranks, however. Late antique catastrophists can be modernists when it comes to the late Republic and early empire, but deeply pessimistic when they look at changes from the third century on. Rostovtzeff and Carandini are perfect examples of this combination.

Mediterranean-wide exchange networks broke down by stages starting as early as the fifth century, the final crisis is postponed to the end of the seventh century/early eighth. This is, moreover, the weakest form of catastrophism or not catastrophism at all *unless*, like Pirenne, one argues that pan-Mediterranean links were abruptly severed 'from the middle of the 7th century' by the Arab inruptions.[9] Finally, 4) *Catastrophe flips ('very sudden negative change' or rapid collapse)*. The great advantage of this form of catastrophism (Ken Dark, also Wickham) is that it can work as a description of local situations with no logical requirement that it must extend to any wider scale than that, such as the whole of the western empire. A maximal version of this model would count as the strongest (and probably least tenable) form of catastrophism, and basically it is some picture of this sort that underpinned much of the earlier, mainly pre-war historiography that lacked any real notion of late antiquity as a period (Weber, Rostovtzeff, Walbank).

It is not my intention to deny that each of these models or forms of description contains *some measure of truth*. The Roman economy *did* end in the western provinces (even if Roman-style estates certainly survived and Roman law left its permanent imprint on later social relations). Italian landscapes *were* gradually and in the end even dramatically transformed (though not everywhere), and Italian urban prosperity receded to a low point in the eighth century.[10] Major trading centres of the western Mediterranean 'vanished off the commercial map', as David Abulafia tells us,[11] and the Roman-imperial exchange system was radically reconfigured between the late seventh and ninth centuries. Catastrophe flips did occur in provinces like Britain that saw a sudden collapse of the Roman state. *And so on*. I also agree with the position averred by Ward-Perkins that 'there is a real danger for the present day in a vision of the past that explicitly sets out to eliminate all crisis and all decline'.

The aim behind these essays is not to deny these undeniable moments of truth but, with less sense of orthodoxy perhaps, (1) to defend the *sophistication* of ancient economic behaviour against a minimalism that downgrades it irredeemably; (2) to argue strongly for the sheer scale and *resilience* of the late antique economy against an oversimplified catastrophism; and (3) to canvas the need for historical models that can *integrate* ancient and medieval economic history the way Mickwitz dreamed of doing.

[9] H. Pirenne, *Mohammed and Charlemagne*, trans. B. Miall (London, 1939) p. 165.
[10] Wickham, *Framing the Early Middle Ages*, pp. 644–56.
[11] D. Abulafia, *The Great Sea: A Human History of the Mediterranean* (London, 2014), p. 256.

A word about each of these strands of argument may well be in order by way of an extended preface. In terms of the more classic periods of Roman history (the Republic and early empire) minimalism is probably linked to the idea that Roman society was largely dependent on slave labour and that slaveholders were incapable of a rational organisation of labour, let alone of any wider economic rationality.[12] This view denies any rational core to the Roman economy, by which I mean quite simply the Roman obsession with money-making (*quaestus, lucrum*), whether we describe this as 'capitalist', 'quasi-capitalist',[13] 'entrepreneurial' or in some other more neutral way. This aspect is strikingly evident in so many ways, from the remarkable sophistication of Roman commercial law and the sorts of business organisation it allowed for[14] to the purely economic dimensions of Roman control of the Mediterranean, Rome's capacity for organisation and technical inventiveness, the obsessive rationalisation of labour that runs through the agricultural writings,[15] etc. It is not in the least surprising that historical sociologists like Runciman should have characterised the Roman economy (Rome's 'mode of production') as *capitalist*; 'in every respect', as he says, except for its ostensible lack of any widespread employment of free labour.[16] Of course, this position has failed to win assent because it states its case too starkly. A more complex approach can still be structured as follows.

The advent of mass production in Rome's ceramic industries (the transition from craft-based to industrial modes of production reflected in the emergence of a widely distributed black-gloss ware dubbed Campanian A), which first appeared as early as the last two decades of the third century BC,[17] was both driven by a desire for economies of scale[18] and bound

[12] Contrast Oakes in his study of American planters, J. Oakes, *Slavery and Freedom: An Interpretation of the Old South* (New York, 1990), p. 54.

[13] W. V. Harris, 'Production, Distribution, and *Instrumentum Domesticum*', in *The Inscribed Economy*, ed. W. V. Harris (Ann Arbor, 1993), p. 189.

[14] F. Serrao, 'L'impresa in Roma antica', in *Impresa e responsabilità a Roma nell' età commerciale* (Pisa, 1989); A. Di Porto, 'Il diritto commerciale romano', in *Nozione formazione e interpretazione del diritto dall' età romana alle esperienze moderne*, vol. III (Naples, 1997), pp. 413–52.

[15] See my reference in Banaji, 'Modernizing the Historiography of Rural Labour: An Unwritten Agenda', in *Companion to Historiography*, ed. M. Bentley (London and New York, 1997) to 'such basic features of Roman estate organization as the continuous monitoring of labour costs, careful attention to optimal gang size (Columella, *RR* 1.9.7ff.), use of sample checks to control the intensity of labour, or formulation of performance standards to help owners define efficient manning ratios' (pp. 89–90).

[16] W. G. Runciman, 'The "Triumph" of Capitalism as a Topic in the Theory of Social Selection', *New Left Review* I/210 (1995), 33–47, at p. 37.

[17] A. Carandini, *L'anatomia della scimmia: La formazione economica della società prima del capitale* (Turin, 1979), pp. 192–3.

[18] M. Picon 'Production artisanale et manufacturière à l'époque romaine: À propos de *L'Histoire brisée* d'Aldo Schiavone', in *L'économie antique: Une économie de marché?*, ed. Y. Roman and J. Dalaison

up with export markets that presupposed an extensive operation of commercial capital.[19] Stated in a more general way this means that Italian domination of the Mediterranean at the purely *economic* level was founded not just or even primarily on 'Roman imperialism', but, in more specific and concrete ways (and perhaps more interestingly), on revolutionary changes in the scale of production, an increased industrial use of slavery and the enhanced grip of large-scale commercial enterprises whose networks straddled international markets. Rural estates (*villae*) producing wine, olive oil and so on were a sort of agrarian counterpart of these ceramic factories. These were all features that impressed Rostovtzeff no end. On the other hand, these were only the 'dynamic' sectors of the economy and Simon Swain is quite right in saying that 'no widespread capitalism emerged'.[20] This, arguably, is how we can and should *both* recover the affinity between the Roman world and our own thoroughly capitalist one as well as mark the distance that separates them. It is one way of breaking down the myth of the Chinese wall separating 'ancient' and 'modern'.

Did the Roman passion for business simply evaporate, then?[21] Were business groups and elites of various kinds not active throughout the centuries of late antiquity, now on the wider scale of a more provincial empire and one founded on a solid gold currency?

Catastrophist views of the period certainly imply this. But the extraordinary *volumes* of coinage and expanding *circulation* of gold both suggest otherwise. Moreover, Sasanian silver production shows that the surge in monetary economy was a feature more generally true of the late antique world, and not just of the Roman empire. Several chapters demonstrate the truly impressive scale on which both coinages circulated, most intensively within core regions but over vast geographical areas in any case. It would be not a little strange to imagine that the private economy withered at the precise moment when there was a massive surge in levels of monetary activity. Though Mickwitz himself never explicitly suggested that the Republic's tradition of aristocratic/upper-class involvement in business

(Paris, 2008), pp. 191–214, at 202–3 (on strategies more typical of industrial than craft-based producers).

19 J.-P. Morel, 'La produzione della ceramica campana: Aspetti economici e sociali', in *Merci, mercati e scambi nel Mediterraneo* (*Società romana e produzione schiavistica*, vol. II), ed. A. Giardina *et al.* (Rome and Bari, 1981), pp. 81–97, at 92–3; the best account.

20 S. Swain, *Economy, Family, and Society from Rome to Islam* (Cambridge, 2013), p. 168, later adding, 'the fact there was no general capitalism in antiquity does not mean there was no capitalist mentality' (p. 174), which I presume means that there were always a fair number of capitalists around!

21 Cicero, *Pro Sulla* 58: *negoti gerendi studium*, about the Campanian banker P. Sittius, cf. R. Syme, *Sallust* (Berkeley, etc., 1964), p. 101.

continued vigorously into the late empire, that perspective is certainly implicit in his argument that the *private* sector was the key driver behind the monetary economy of the fourth century.[22] Both the introductory essay and some of the chapters below are meant to show why we shouldn't see the public/private dichotomy as a zero-sum game and why it makes more sense to allow for a fluid integration between the two sectors, one that worked and manifested itself differently at different times and in different regimes (notably including the Umayyads and what Patricia Crone in *Slaves on Horses* calls their 'affinal state').

The thrust of this second strand of my argument is to *contest a simplistic reading of economic history in terms of 'political and military difficulties'*. The temptation to engage in a reading of this sort is strong because a lot of late Roman economic history (more indeed than any other period of Roman history) is written largely as a narrative of the state, so that the economy, inevitably, is framed as an extension of politics, moulded and driven by the state and crucially vulnerable to its crises.[23] This, it seems to me, is the wrong way of mapping the economy of the Roman world, because it focuses too narrowly on the demands and characteristics of state economy and does so not least because the bulk of our sources are documents emanating either directly from the state (the law codes) or from the interactions of taxpayers and the state (a lot of the papyrological evidence). There is a *huge* disproportion between this type of documentation and what survives in terms of private records from, say, the purely civilian and business sectors of the economy. To take an obvious example; there is a strikingly complete absence of any papyrological material from Alexandria, the commercial hub of the eastern Mediterranean, a major banking centre and a veritable base of what must have been a thriving 'private economy' generating hundreds of business papers (contracts, accounts, correspondence, etc.) on a daily basis. Of course, the same is true of the private records and papers of merchant diasporas *all over the Mediterranean* and deep into the hinterlands where traders and trading firms were active. This is precisely where the gap between the written sources and the ceramic evidence is most strident and extreme. What, for example, would be the

[22] G. Mickwitz, *Geld und Wirtschaft im römischen Reich des vierten Jahrhunderts n. Chr.* (Helsinki, 1932), ch. 5.

[23] The classic instance of this is a paper by Michael Hendy, 'From Antiquity to the Middle Ages: Economic and Monetary Aspects of the Transition', in *De la Antigüedad al Medievo, Siglos IV–VIII: III Congreso de Estudios Medievales* (León, 1991), pp. 323–60, where he ends by suggesting that the economy of late antiquity is probably best seen as an 'example of a categorical type of economy', presumably state economy.

impact on our vision of the economy if a late antique equivalent of the Cairo Geniza were discovered somewhere? Or if the powerful shipowners of Alexandria had left us with serial records of tonnages and merchandise similar to the records of the *Casa de Contratación* in Seville? It scarcely bears thinking about!

Finally, about the need (for *economic* historians) to break down the artificial divisions between late antiquity and the Middle Ages. If, as Perry Anderson says, 'the birth of *capital* also saw … the rebirth of antiquity',[24] it really would be counter-intuitive to argue that this happened as a purely legal and cultural inheritance without the remanence of *economic* institutions and practices that reflected the more subtle and magnetic ways in which ancient and late antique legacies were absorbed by Byzantium and Islam respectively and passed on, through them, into a wider medieval world that was being pushed into full throttle as the Levant trade picked up in the tenth century and the commercial revolution gathered momentum. Venice would become the incarnation of a vigorous mercantile capitalism that straddled the rest of the Middle Ages,[25] down even to the sixteenth century. In the same way, it seems to me, the 'strong Byzantine influence on Italian commercial and maritime institutions'[26] that historians have often drawn attention to implies a major element of continuity (one of those Braudelian *permanences*) between the Middle Ages and late antiquity. To direct research to these strands or elements of continuity is not tantamount to espousing some abstract, much less radical continualism. If the third quarter of the seventh century signalled a serious decline in the vitality of Marseilles as a major port, there are certainly enough signs that the seventh century *retained* much of its vitality at this level. Carthage was still trading actively with monasteries in Rome and with the Byzantine capital late into the century,[27] and early Islamic hoards from Spain suggest that 'merchants still traversed the length of the Mediterranean in the eighth century'.[28] Of course, the eighth century is more medieval than it is late antique, a world that has spun away from its Mediterranean core, dominated in the west by the Carolingians and their

[24] P. Anderson, *Lineages of the Absolutist State* (London, 1974), p. 422.

[25] G. Cracco, *Società e stato nel Medioevo veneziano (secoli xii–xiv)* (Florence, 1967).

[26] R.-H. Bautier, *The Economic Development of Medieval Europe* (London, 1971), pp. 67–8.

[27] In Marseilles itself excavations at the place Jules-Verne show that 'activity continued … into the later seventh century or even the early eighth', S. T. Loseby, 'Marseille and the Pirenne Thesis, II: "Ville Morte" ', in *The Long Eighth Century*, ed. I. L. Hansen and C. Wickham (Leiden, 2000), pp. 167–93, at 172.

[28] D. M. Metcalf, 'Monetary Recession in the Middle Byzantine Period', *Numismatic Chronicle* 161 (2001), 111–55, at p. 134.

northern orientations, further east by the new foundation of Baghdad, seat of an empire whose 'wealth and interests … poured eastwards'.[29] It is the *eighth-century gap* that historians and archaeologists will have to plug and will doubtless do so, gradually.

The essays deploy a fairly wide range of sources across the book as a whole, but I have desisted from any discussion of these *as sources*, especially those in Arabic that form the basis of Chapter 8, as this would require a very different book. The sheer cosmopolitanism of late antiquity is to me its most attractive feature, not least in intellectual and elite circles, both religious and secular. Ammianus Marcellinus wrote one of the longest and most brilliant histories of the empire in Latin but 'as a Greek'.[30] At the other end of late antiquity, a Christian Arab sat down to write his *Defence of Holy Images* at a Muslim court in the final years of Umayyad rule.[31] And between these framing images (Ammianus travelling west; John of Damascus taking on the Byzantine iconoclasts) lies the extraordinary spectacle of the last Sasanian king being buried by the bishop of Merv.[32] The chapters that follow are premised on this conception of 'late antiquity' as culturally and politically diverse – Sasanian and Umayyad as much as it was late Roman and Byzantine.

The bibliography is avowedly select, gathering mainly those items that I myself have found both illuminating and helpful, even when, of course, I disagree with some of them. The list includes works not especially related to late antiquity or the ancient world but which contribute decisively to our understanding of economic history and the many levels at which it can be pursued.

[29] P. Brown, *The World of Late Antiquity* (London, 1971), p. 202.

[30] Amm. Marc. 31.16.9.

[31] P. Brown, *The Rise of Western Christendom: Triumph and Diversity A.D. 200–1000* (Oxford, 2003), pp. 397–9.

[32] Al-Ṭabarī, *The Crisis of the Early Caliphate* (*The History of al-Ṭabarī,* vol. xv), trans. R. Stephen Humphreys (Albany, 1990), p. 89, calling the bishop *muṭrān* (metropolitan) of Merv.

Acknowledgements

Most of the chapters in this book were previously published in journals or collections that are not always easily accessible. I'm grateful to the editors and publishers below for allowing me to republish the papers in this volume:

Chapter 2 was published as 'Mickwitz's Modernism: The Writings of 1932–36', in *Gunnar Mickwitz (1906–40) nella storiografia europea tra le due guerre*, edited by Mika Kajava (Acta Instituti Romani Finlandiae, volume 34) (Rome, 2007).

Chapter 3 was published as 'State and Aristocracy in the Economic Evolution of the Late Empire', in *Production and Public Powers in Classical Antiquity*, edited by E. Lo Cascio and D. W. Rathbone (Cambridge: The Cambridge Philological Society, 2000).

Chapter 4 was published as 'Economic Trajectories', in *The Oxford Handbook of Late Antiquity*, edited by Scott Johnson (Oxford University Press, 2012).

Chapter 5 was published as 'Discounts, Weight Standards and the Exchange-Rate between Gold and Copper', in *Atti dell' Accademia Romanistica Costantiniana. XII Convegno Int. in onore di Manlio Sargenti* (Naples, 1998).

Chapter 6 was published as 'Precious Metal Coinages and Monetary Expansion in Late Antiquity', in *Dal Denarius al Dinar: l'Oriente e la moneta romana: atti dell'incontro di studio, Roma 16–18 settembre 2004*, edited by Federico De Romanis and Sara Sorda (Rome: Istituto italiano di numismatica, 2006).

Chapter 7 was published as 'Aristocracies, Peasantries and the Framing of the Early Middle Ages', *Journal of Agrarian Change*, 9(1) (2009), 59–91 (Special issue edited by Peter Sarris and myself).

Chapter 8 is a substantially revised and expanded version of a paper first written for a workshop organised by Richard Payne at the Institute for the Study of the Ancient World, New York, in April 2013 and subsequently presented to the 'After Rome' seminar at Trinity College, Oxford, in May 2013.

Chapter 9 was published as 'Late Antique Legacies and Muslim Economic Expansion', in *Money, Power and Politics in Early Islamic Syria*, edited by John Haldon (Ashgate, 2010).

Chapter 10 was published as '"Regions that Look Seaward" – Changing Fortunes, Submerged Histories, and the Slow Capitalism of the Sea', in *A Tale of Two Seas*, edited by Federico De Romanis and Marco Maiuro (Brill, 2015), 114–26, and is published here as well with William Harris's gracious consent.

Among my several debts of gratitude to those who in various ways made this book possible I'd specially like to thank Henry Bernstein, Glen Bowersock, Peter Brown, Federico De Romanis, John Haldon, Elio Lo Cascio, Marco Maiuro, Fergus Millar, Bernhard Palme, Peter Sarris, Brent Shaw and Chris Wickham. I'm lucky to have had the chance to work with the late Patricia Crone, who was ever so generous with her time and erudition and without whom Chapter 9 would have been impossible. And I'm no less grateful to Michael Sharp and Liz Hanlon for seeing the essays into production.

CHAPTER I

Mass production, monetary economy and the commercial vitality of the Mediterranean

The Roman economy

The Roman economy was as much a proto-industrial economy as an agrarian one.[1] It was characterised by an abundance of manufactured goods, competition within industries, widespread mass production and a massive, intensely structured exploitation of natural resources that reached staggering proportions with the opening up of Spain and North Africa to Roman imperial and business interests.[2] Tablewares, glass, nails, iron tools, bricks, marble, salted fish, olive oil, grain, wine, textiles were all mass-produced or produced in bulk to massive quantities for mass markets.[3] In the more purely industrial sectors such as pottery this implied standardisation. The single most widely produced Italian ware of the late Republic (Campana A) exemplifies mass production of a good-quality product at low cost. Standardisation, Morel argues, was linked to high productivity, a drive to structure labour processes to ensure a maximum

[1] K. R. Dark, 'Proto-Industrialisation and the End of the Roman Economy', in *External Contacts and the Economy of Late Roman and Post-Roman Britain*, ed. K. R. Dark (Woodbridge, 1996), pp. 1–21, and K. Dark, 'Proto-Industrialization and the Economy of the Roman Empire', in *L'artisanat romain: Évolutions, continuités et ruptures (Italie et provinces occidentales)*, ed. M. Polfer (Montagnac, 2001), pp. 19–29, are both seminal and should carry the debate forward. In the second of these papers he refers to the 'existence of a highly-developed Proto-industrial economy in the Early Roman Empire' (p. 25).

[2] E.g. A. Wilson, 'Machines, Power and the Ancient Economy', *Journal of Roman Studies* 92 (2002), 1–32, esp. pp. 17–23 describing the massive extraction of metal from mines in Spain and elsewhere.

[3] See A. I. Wilson, 'Large-Scale Manufacturing, Standardization, and Trade', in *Engineering and Technology in the Classical World*, ed. J. P. Oleson (Oxford, 2008), pp. 393–417, for most of these. A. Marzano, *Harvesting the Sea: The Exploitation of Marine Resources in the Roman Mediterranean* (Oxford, 2013) now deals with large-scale fishing operations; R. Étienne, Y. Makaroun and F. Mayet, *Un grand complexe industriel à Tróia (Portugal)* (Paris, 1994) calculate an annual export of 2 million Dressel 14 amphorae for one large salting complex in the Sado estuary, south of Lisbon (p. 164). G. Volpe, *Contadini, pastori e mercanti nell'Apulia tardoantica* (Bari, 1996), p. 168, estimates that the late Roman villa of San Giusto had an annual production capacity of 36,000 litres of wine, and Mattingly, 'The Olive Boom', *Libyan Studies* 19 (1988), 21–41, documents even larger production capacities in olive oil.

efficiency of labour power.[4] The samian potteries at la Graufesenque in southern Gaul were 'one of Europe's first large-scale manufacturing industries',[5] active from the earliest first century to the first third of the second century, with large-scale production based on a 'very strict division of labour'[6] and geared to a wide scale of exports throughout western Europe. Here individual workshops each produced millions of vessels, with total production running into 'probably tens of millions of vessels if not more'.[7] A striking feature of both Campana A and the French samian potteries is the sheer scale of production, which of course raises the pivotal issue of the economic structure of the industry – how was it organised? Who owned the potteries? Who made the commercial decisions? And, how important were those groups in shaping the nature of the Roman economy as a whole? In fact, how do we even begin to answer these questions if much of the argument is inferential or based on sources that *can* provide no answers? Ken Dark has noted that la Graufesenque was more advanced than the Staffordshire potteries of the early eighteenth century.[8] Maurice Picon has suggested that its manufacturing was organised on a capitalist basis.[9] Even if we agree with this (and I am inclined to), it does not follow that the investors who owned the massive furnaces at la Graufesenque also handled the marketing of their products, so we need a wider range of economic agents and crucially of course the sort of firms that could organise distribution and sales across vast areas of western Europe, namely, wealthy mercantile enterprises. This feature (of the intervention of merchant enterprise) is so unmistakeable in the Roman pottery industries that the 'merchant' emerges here as a more substantial figure than the commercial capitalists that Marx saw being subordinated to industrial capital in the late nineteenth century. Indeed, standardisation across whole swathes of the industry strongly implies the role of entities closer to the retail end of the trade. Thus Carandini in his most theoretical piece of writing referred

4 J.-P. Morel, 'La produzione della ceramica campana: Aspetti economici e sociali', in *Società romana e produzione schiavistica*, ed. A. Giardina *et al.* (Rome and Bari, 1981), vol. II, pp. 81–97, at 88.

5 M. Fulford, 'Gallo-Roman Sigillata: Fresh Approaches, Fresh Challenges, Fresh Questions', in *Seeing Red: New Economic and Social Perspectives on 'Terra Sigillata'*, ed. M. Fulford *et al.* (London, 2013), pp. 1–17.

6 A. Mees, 'The Internal Organisation of *Terra Sigillata* (Samian) Workshops', in *Seeing Red*, ed. Fulford *et al.*, pp. 66–96, at 66.

7 J. R. L. Allen, 'Some Potters of Samian Ware at la Graufesenque: Notes towards the Shape of the Industry', in *Seeing Red*, ed. Fulford *et al.*, pp. 49–65, at 50, 52.

8 Dark, 'Proto-Industrialization and the Economy of the Roman Empire', p. 23.

9 M. Picon, 'Production artisanale et manufacturière à l'époque romaine: À propos de *L'Histoire brisée* d'Aldo Schiavone', in *L'économie antique: Une économie de marché?*, ed. Y. Roman *et al.* (Paris, 2008), pp. 191–214, at 200–1.

to a type of production 'essentially subordinated to commercial capital',[10] and it is this nexus (of the domination of producers by merchants or their dependence on the latter) that Françoise Mayet and her colleagues have called 'commercial capitalism'. Of course, the relationship between merchants and producers would clearly have varied considerably, depending on who the latter were – the third-century aristocrats who dominated the massive trade in Libyan olive oil were at one end of this spectrum, the mass of *terra sigillata* producers conceivably at a very different end of it.

Both *terra sigillata* and the Roman brick industry have seen some exceptional work addressed to issues like the economic structure of the industry, the organisation of workshops (*officinae*) and the scales on which production occurred. The distinctive feature of much of this work is that the evidence is interpreted in terms of a model that is at least partly drawn from it, so that there is a close interaction between 'theory' and 'evidence' (a virtuous circle, if you like), much closer in fact than anything to be found in Moses Finley's deeply influential *The Ancient Economy*. Spanish *sigillata* was characterised by a handful of large firms plus a mass of small ones.[11] Rome's brick industry, by contrast, was almost entirely dominated by the city's aristocracy, which outsourced production to *officinatores* or 'workshop managers' who were actually entrepreneurs but in charge solely of the production end of the industry.[12] Control of the business itself lay firmly in the hands of the aristocracy (the *domini*, including members of the imperial family) and was doubtless just one of a fairly wide range of investments that typified the economy of Roman upper-class households. The repeated characterisation of the Roman aristocracy as a class of landowners is misleading *if* the suggestion is that it should be seen essentially as an agrarian class not fundamentally different from the Prussian junkers of the eighteenth century, or that 'agriculture' is where, say, 90 per cent of its economic interests lay. Apart from the cash-rich husbandry of suburban villas (*pastio villatica*) that was geared to extraordinary profits in super-rich markets[13] and the more widespread industrial-scale monocultures in wine

[10] A. Carandini, *L'anatomia della scimmia: La formazione economica della società prima del capitale* (Turin, 1979), p. 193.

[11] F. Mayet, *Les céramiques sigillées hispaniques* (Paris, 1984), p. 216, 'une foule de petits ateliers à côté de quelques grandes firmes'.

[12] This is basically the model Margareta Steinby develops, see M. Steinby, 'I senatori e l'industria laterizia urbana', in *Epigrafia e ordine senatorio* (Rome, 1982), vol. 1, pp. 227–37; 'L'organizzazione produttiva dei laterizi: Un modello interpretativo per l'*instrumentum* in genere?' in *The Inscribed Economy*, ed. W. V. Harris (Ann Arbor, 1993), pp. 139–44.

[13] Cf. Varro, *RR* 3.16.11, *ut magnos capiam fructus*, and see N. Purcell, 'The Roman *Villa* and the Landscape of Production', in *Urban Society in Roman Italy*, ed. T. J. Cornell *et al.* (London, 1995), pp. 151–79.

and olive oil, known senatorial investments at various times included warehouses, stone quarries, brick factories, mining contracts, financial investments in shipping and commercial enterprises[14] and all manner of speculation, not least in the hoarding of wine, foodgrains and so on. This characterisation of the Roman aristocracy carries over into the late empire where in fact it is much less visible except perhaps for the remarkably aggressive way in which it effected a wholesale takeover of the city's real estate market during the aristocratic housing boom of the fourth century.[15] Yet beyond the narrow circles of the aristocracy, Rome-based and provincial, lay a much wider group of business classes, from the powerful associations of wholesale merchants attested in the Foro delle Corporazioni at Ostia in the late second/early third centuries[16] to a mass of smaller entrepreneurs, in trade, construction, manufacturing, etc., who were the backbone of the urban economy in all periods of antiquity. If we view the Roman and Byzantine periods as a whole, from the late Republic to the last centuries of the Byzantine empire, this vitally important set of classes was never completely static in its composition and there is no obvious or unified terminology we can invoke either to refer to it or to latch on to as its official nomenclature. 'Businessmen' is Oikonomidès's loose translation of the Byzantine term *ergasteriakoi*, which he claims covered mainly merchants and artisans.[17] Indeed, much of the economic vitality of the late antique world, reflected in the radical changes to the configuration of numerous cities discernible from the fifth century (the economic saturation of town centres, the industrial reuse of public buildings and so on), was an expression of the expanded weight of these groups, and of the weight of the urban economy as a whole, in an empire now more dependent than ever on the east. Already in the fourth century the author of an anonymous tract had implied a broad division of the upper strata of late Roman society into bureaucrats, landowners and businessmen, describing the last group as *negotiatores mercium lucra tractantes*.[18] *Negotiator* was doubtless a generic term for the various business groups engaged in *large-scale* trade, banking and manufacture. It would have included the wholesale merchants involved in the Mediterranean wine trade, who were

[14] J. H. D'Arms, *Commerce and Social Standing in Ancient Rome* (Cambridge, MA, 1981), p. 39.

[15] See C. Machado, 'Aristocratic Houses and the Making of Late Antique Rome and Constantinople', in *Two Romes: Rome and Constantinople in Late Antiquity*, ed. L. Grig *et al.* (Oxford, 2012), pp. 136–58.

[16] G. Becatti, *Mosaici e pavimenti marmorei* (*Scavi di Ostia*, vol. IV) (Rome, 1961), pp. 64 ff.

[17] N. Oikonomidès, 'Entrepreneurs', in *The Byzantines*, ed. G. Cavallo (Chicago and London, 1997), pp. 144–71.

[18] Anonymous, *De rebus bellicis*, Praef. 6 (Thompson, p. 92).

organised in a *corpus* described as *splendidissimus*;[19] wholesale oil merchants like the Aelii Optati from Celti near Hispalis (Seville);[20] wealthy bankers like Julianus, one of many *argentarii* active in Ravenna in the sixth century; the money changers whose financial interests Symmachus defended in the 380s[21] – all of them wealthy commercial groups outside the main sector of the aristocracy proper. This, and the mass of smaller entrepreneurs known simply as *mercatores*, is the milieu least well attested in the literary sources (for obvious reasons perhaps) but massively presupposed in the archaeology where the growing weight of the 'productive and commercial middle classes'[22] is now seen as a major factor in the evolution of a new urban topography, or where the 'Byzantine shops' constructed in Sardis in the late fifth century, classic exemplars of the so-called 'encroachment of private enterprise ... upon the formerly public spaces of the town', were less retail outlets than quarters that integrated homes with small business premises owned by an industrious and at least moderately affluent middle class.[23] As the coercive weight of the fourth-century empire declined dramatically in the fifth, trade associations in all lines of business acquired considerable autonomy,[24] some even attempting to run price cartels,[25] while preachers as far away as Gaul could complain of the 'hordes' of businessmen ('all from the east') that now apparently dominated 'almost the greater part of all the cities in the world'![26]

In the late Republic and early empire the aristocracy had consistently used slaves and freedmen as fronts for business activity, exploiting the resources of a sophisticated private law system that contrived considerable flexibility for the organisation and conduct of business by owners of

[19] P. Baldacci, '*Negotiatores* e *mercatores frumentarii* nel periodo imperiale', *Rendiconti dell'Istituto Lombardo, Classe di Lettere* 101 (1967), 273–91, at p. 289; H. Bloch, 'Inedita Ostiensia I', *Epigraphica* 1 (1939), 37–40 (big wine merchants from the Sahel).

[20] S. J. Keay, *Roman Spain* (Berkeley and London, 1988), pp. 102–3.

[21] Symmachus, *Relatio* 29 (Barrow, p. 162).

[22] E. Zanini, 'Artisans and Traders in the Early Byzantine City', in *Social and Political Life in Late Antiquity*, ed. W. Bowden *et al.* (Leiden and Boston, 2006), pp. 373–411, at 405.

[23] A. Harris, 'Shops, Retailing and the Local Economy in the Early Byzantine World: The Example of Sardis', in *Secular Buildings and the Archaeology of Everyday Life in the Byzantine Empire*, ed. K. Dark (Oxford, 2004), pp. 82–122, at 116–17. Constantinople itself may well have anticipated the trend, cf. G. Dagron, *Naissance d'une capitale: Constantinople et ses institutions de 330 à 451* (Paris, 1974), p. 528.

[24] M. Bianchini, 'Controllo dei prezzi e autonomia delle associazioni di mestiere in *Nov. Iust.* 122', in *Studi in memoria di G. Tarello* (Milan, 1990), vol. 1, pp. 117–40.

[25] *CJ* 4.59.2 (483) with special mention of master builders and craftsmen in the building trades. See p. 44.

[26] Salvian, *de Gub. Dei* IV.69 (G. Lagarrigue, *Salvien de Marseille, Oeuvres*, vol. II (Paris, 1975), p. 288), esp. *negotiatorum et Syricorum omnium turbas*.

capital. Di Porto has shown in detail exactly how this was done.[27] And again, there is no reason to suppose that this culture of doing business (the aristocracy's reliance on the entrepreneurial skills and management of various employees) saw any dramatic decline in the late antique world. A passage in Firmicus Maternus' astrological work *Mathēsis* suggests otherwise. It refers to the *scribae* (secretaries or agents) employed by the aristocracy to manage its financial accounts, banking operations, branch businesses and commercial transactions.[28] Marble workshops, stone quarries, brick factories and commercial shipping are some of the areas directly attested for the fourth-century aristocracy.[29] At this level, agriculture too was basically a business, with some three quarters of the total income drawn by the great aristocratic families of the city from their estates accumulating as cash reserves, if Olympiodorus is to be believed. For example, in the deep south of southern Italy, in the southern part of Calabria south of Catanzaro, where the late antique period saw a renewed burst of vigour, wine emerged as the leading cash crop and was grown on massive estates (*massae*) on a productive model closer to the industrial monocultures of North Africa than anything to be seen in Italy itself.[30] The sheer scale of production involved in Calabria's wine business can also be inferred from the very wide distribution of Keay LII, an amphora type produced locally at Pellaro and other kiln sites in the countryside around Reggio, the main port from which these containers were shipped and the base, apparently, of a major salted fish industry as late as the seventh century.[31] This shows, by the way, that where the written sources are exiguous (a brief reference in the *Expositio* to the wine of the Bruttii as *multum et optimum*), the archaeology can make a dramatic difference to our assessments, as Filocamo shows in his monograph on Calabria and the Straits region.[32]

27 A. Di Porto, *Impresa collettiva e schiavo 'manager' in Roma antica (II sec. a.C.–II sec. d.C.)* (Milan, 1984).

28 Firmicus, *Math.* III.x.1 (P. Monat, *Firmicus Maternus Mathesis* (Paris, 1994), vol. II, p. 101); see ch. 4, this volume, n. 35.

29 As I note in Chapter 4, this volume, C. Caeionius Rufius Volusianus Lampadius, urban prefect in 365, had a marble workshop at Ostia, see G. Becatti, *Case ostiensi del tardo impero* (Rome, 1948), p. 31. For shipping cf. *IGR* I, no. 416 (Baiae), *Elpidios naukleros Symmachon ton lamprotaton enthade keitai*; for stone quarries, *CTh.* X. 19. 8 (376).

30 A. B. Sangineto, 'Trasformazioni o crisi nei *Bruttii* fra il II a.C. ed il VII d.C?', in *Modalità insediative e strutture agrarie nell'Italia meridionale in età romana*, ed. E. Lo Cascio and A. S. Marino (Bari, 2001), pp. 203–46, esp. 226ff., who describes the background to the new estates as a prolonged restructuring of the countryside that led to massive concentration (218ff.).

31 So I infer from a passing reference in L. Saguì, 'Roma, i centri privilegiati e la lunga durata della tarda antichità', *Archeologia Medievale* 29 (2002), 7–42, at p. 32.

32 A. Filocamo, *Anfore, palmenti, monete: Il vino nell'economia dello Stretto della tarda antichità* (Naples, 2013).

As Bryan Ward-Perkins notes, 'The minimalist, and predominantly pessimistic, view that [A. H. M.] Jones had of the late Roman economy was to a large extent possible because he *almost completely ignored archaeological evidence.*'[33] What struck Jones most about the later empire was the overwhelming pressure of the state. Looking for explanations of the 'decline' of the empire, Jones decided in 1959 that this had to be due to taxation. The late empire was an empire impoverished by 'over-taxation'. The peasantry was malnourished and the death rate amongst it was 'abnormally high'.[34] The only solid piece of evidence Jones used in this article was *P. Cairo Masp.* 67059, the great tax register from Antaeopolis dating to the time of Justinian. Yet, curiously enough, Jones himself, analysing the same data in 1951, drew the very opposite conclusion: 'The rate [of tax] per arura does not work out at a startingly high figure, about 3⅕ artabae if the whole tax burden is calculated in wheat, about 7⅔ carats if it is reckoned all in gold … in the sixth century Egypt was not grossly overtaxed.'[35]

Minimalism

Minimalism simplifies social structures, denies economic complexity to pre-capitalist societies, regards trade and money as of little or no significance in the history of such societies (for example, it downplays the economic role of coinage) and in general believes that no 'modern economic concepts' can be used to analyse the world before, say, the eighteenth century.[36] No plausible minimalist historiography can ever be constructed simply because it would simplify the fabric of history so radically that the most we would have is an impoverished image of it or a strangely distorted one. When applied to the late empire these assumptions generate a model where exaggerated importance is ascribed to the state and to taxation as a

[33] B. Ward-Perkins, 'Jones and the Late Roman Economy', in *A. H. M. Jones and the Later Roman Economy*, ed. D. M. Gwynn (Leiden and Boston, 2008), pp. 193–211, at 203.

[34] A. H. M. Jones, 'Over-Taxation and the Decline of the Roman Empire', in *The Roman Economy*, ed. P. A. Brunt (Oxford, 1974) pp. 82–9, esp. 88; first published in *Antiquity* 33 (1959).

[35] A. H. M. Jones, *Journal of Hellenic Studies*, 71 (1951) p. 271 (review of Johnson and West, *Byzantine Egypt*).

[36] 'Modern economic concepts': cf. the following from Hopkins in what looks like his last published paper: 'But I do still have colleagues (as well as the ghost of my teacher Moses Finley in my conscience) who believe that it is impossible or at least unprofitable to use modern economic concepts in order to analyse the pre-industrial embedded economy. *For them, the ancient economy was a cultural system, which was dominated by nonrational considerations of status and ritual* and so was immune to cold rational analysis', K. Hopkins, 'The Political Economy of the Roman Empire', in *The Dynamics of Ancient Empires*, ed. I. Morris *et al.* (Oxford, 2009), pp. 178–204, at 200; my italics.

driver of the economy, while the relation between 'private economy' and the state is construed in terms of an overpowering dirigisme. This is exactly the image of the late Roman economy that underlies much of the argumentation in McCormick's *Origins of the European Economy*, where the Roman economy is described as 'an economy dominated by annona transport' and we are told that 'the annona ... dominated all other forms of shipping in volume and importance'.[37] The simple answer to this is, how do we know? Do we have even the vaguest estimate of the total volume of business that flowed through the Mediterranean at *any* time between the first and the fourteenth or fifteenth centuries?[38] McCormick sets out to challenge 'the old vision of a stagnant and closed economy in northwestern Europe around 800 A.D.'[39] but leaves the old vision of 'late Roman economic decline' perfectly intact.[40] In particular, the one body of evidence that he completely ignores is data pertaining to the monetary history of the late empire and of late antiquity more generally. The same is true of Carandini. His views underwent a dramatic shift between the excellent introduction he wrote to the third volume of *Società romana e impero tardoantico* (1986) and the deeply pessimistic chapter in the corresponding volume of *Storia di Roma* published in 1993. In the first of these essays Carandini points out that Rome had been characterised by a 'commercial organisation' that was 'pre-industrial' but 'modern' all the same. The reference here was to Braudel's discussion of commercial capitalism in the early modern period and the distinction drawn there between types of markets according to the degree of domination exercised over them by, for example, large producers. Of particular interest in this essay was his critique of Whittaker (seen by Carandini as 'nullifying the market in favour of political dirigisme and pure subsistence', with theses described by him as 'primitivist') and the view, an exceptional one, that the state was not a burden on the economy but functional to its existence (this in a discussion of late Rome!).[41] In 'The Last Civilisation to be Buried', by contrast, late antiquity is viewed

[37] M. McCormick, *Origins of the European Economy* (Cambridge, 2001), at pp. 116 and 783 respectively.

[38] See Braudel's rough calculations of the total tonnage of Mediterranean shipping in *The Mediterranean and the Mediterranean World in the Age of Philip II* (London, 1975), vol. I, pp. 445 ff.

[39] McCormick, *Origins*, p. 6.

[40] McCormick, *Origins*, p. 119. Cf. 'The overall trend of the Roman economic world from c.200 to 700 was downward' (p. 30).

[41] A. Carandini, 'Il mondo della tarda antichità visto attraverso le merci', in *Società romana e impero tardoantico*, ed. A Giardina (Rome and Bari, 1986), vol. III, pp. 3–19, esp. 10ff. (Whittaker), 12 (Roman commercial organisation), 17 (state and economy).

less as a historical period (contrast Mazzarino, for example) than a state of entropy that moves relentlessly from Italy's advanced stage of decline in the third century to North Africa under the Vandals, and eventually the eastern provinces from the late sixth century.[42] The essay is replete with biological metaphors and an unmitigated catastrophism, with several arguments clashing directly with the archaeological evidence that began to be laid out in the 1990s and certainly by the 2000s.[43]

The spate of Italian journals that emerged between the late 1960s and the early 1980s under the patronage of prominent left-wing academics like Bandinelli and Canfora is symbolic of the seminal role of the sixties as an intellectual and academic watershed in Italy.[44] The 'materialist' turn to archaeology,[45] the renewed interest in Marxism and eventually the at least *stated* intent of integrating history and archaeology and of treating 'the archaeological documentation as a source for ancient economic history'[46] would find their true dénouement, however, not in the serried ranks of Italy's archaeologists and historians but in the work of a medievalist based, at least formally, in Britain. This refers of course to Chris Wickham's magnificent integration of history and archaeology in *Framing the Early Middle Ages*. What was remarkable here was the sheer weight of the archaeological evidence in establishing a much richer, more complex and nuanced *non-catastrophist* reading of the evolution of the early Middle Ages out of the dissolution of the late Roman empire which remains our best single account to date. The main limitation, however, was Wickham's decision not to include a treatment of money as one of the many strands in the general fabric of his analysis. Though he himself has explained this at least partly on formal considerations (an already extended treatment of exchange in chapter 11),[47] the deeper reticence may well stem from the peculiar tenacity of a specific model of the Roman monetary economy that distinguished British minimalism in the seventies and eighties. If models have to have a name, this one can perhaps be called the 'closed monetary circuit' model.

[42] A. Carandini, 'L'ultima civiltà sepolta o del massimo oggetto desueto, secondo un archeologo', in *Storia di Roma*, vol. III/2, ed. A. Schiavone (Turin, 1993), pp. 11–38, esp. 19–22.

[43] The most extraordinary case of this is the description of seventh-century Syria as more like Merovingian Gaul (whatever that means) than the Roman province of the fifth century. Contrast A. Walmsley, *Early Islamic Syria: An Archaeological Assessment* (London, 2007).

[44] *Quaderni di Storia* was founded by Canfora in 1975; Bianchi Bandinelli started *Dialoghi di Archeologia* in 1967; and *Opus* was established by Ampolo and Pucci in the early 1980s.

[45] Cf. Carandini, *Archeologia e cultura materiale* (Bari, 1975).

[46] From Ampolo and Pucci's manifesto to the first issue of *Opus*.

[47] C. Wickham, 'The Problems of Comparison', *Historical Materialism* 19/1 (2011), 221–31, at p. 229.

In *Agrarian Change in Late Antiquity* I suggested that the crux of any theory of a late imperial decline 'has always been some set of postulates about the monetary history of the fourth century'.[48] The chief example cited there was Michael Crawford's claim that, come the late fourth century, Theodosius I abolished the last vestiges of any taxation in money, since the monetary circle (as he calls it) 'simply became increasingly meaningless'.[49] This was said in 1975, the very year that saw a monograph by Cerati setting out to show the *exact opposite* through a careful sifting of the numerous legal texts on taxation.[50] But the early seventies were clearly the heady days of monetary minimalism, since they had started with a more famous paper by Crawford that planned to conclude that 'an economic and social system in which coined money played a major rôle as a means of exchange, although it existed in the Roman world, was not common'.[51] Here was an argument about the Roman coinage that was clearly designed (1) to minimise its function as means of exchange and (2) to limit the scope of the monetary sector of the economy to the extent possible. Not only was the 'use of coined money as a means of exchange' 'largely limited to the cities of the Empire', Crawford argues in this paper, but the 'cities of the Roman Empire *came only by accident to adopt coined money as their means of exchange*'.[52] Crawford flatly denied that 'coined money' had any economic reason for existence in the ancient world. It was issued solely to 'enable the state to make payments, that is, for financial reasons', and, 'Once issued coinage was demanded back by the state in payment of taxes.'[53] In his 1975 paper the model was more fully elaborated to read: 'in the early Empire, money flowed from the treasury to the soldiers and officials, from them to the peasants in payment for food, from the peasants back to the treasury in taxes'.[54] Of course, once the silver coinage was debased, repeatedly and substantially, in the course of the third century, 'the monetary circle simply became increasingly meaningless' and (a *major* leap here!) was 'doubtless completely abolished in the end by Theodosius I'.

[48] J. Banaji, *Agrarian Change in Late Antiquity*, 2nd revised edn (Oxford, 2007), p. 23.

[49] M. Crawford, 'Finance, Coinage and Money from the Severans to Constantine', *Aufstieg und Niedergang der römischen Welt*, 2/2 (1975), 560–93, at p. 571.

[50] A. Cerati, *Caractère annonaire et assiette de l'impot foncier au bas-empire* (Paris, 1975).

[51] M. Crawford, 'Money and Exchange in the Roman World', *Journal of Roman Studies* 60 (1970), 40–8, at p. 40.

[52] Crawford, 'Money', p. 45. For an early critique see E. Lo Cascio, 'State and Coinage in the Late Republic and Early Empire', *Journal of Roman Studies* 71 (1981), 76–86.

[53] Crawford, 'Money', p. 46. [54] Crawford, 'Finance', p. 571.

It was this *radical* monetary minimalism (based in Crawford's case on a huge abstraction from the decisive monetary changes of the fourth century) that soon passed into Michael Hendy's massive book on the Byzantine monetary economy, where it was called 'the monetary cycle'[55] and presumably meant to explain why late Rome and Byzantium had such vibrant monetary economies in the first place. In short, the tension at the heart of Hendy's picture of monetary relations in late antiquity and the Byzantine Middle Ages was, as Fergus Millar described it,

> a real contradiction ... between the numismatist's interest in the *minting* of coins and the historian's interest in the monetized economy, and indeed in the wider question of economic exchanges as a whole. For it is not in the least self-evident *how* important was the role played, even in the monetized section of the economy, specifically by *newly-minted* coins. To examine the limited concerns and objectives of the state in minting coins *is not identical with studying the economic functions, and the patterns of circulation, of the coins once minted.*[56]

The distinction implied in the quote from Millar is fundamental and has recently been restated by Michael Metcalf in the following way: 'Monetary history can be divided into two parts, namely, how and why coins were minted, and secondly what became of them after they had been put into circulation. The history of minting reflects government policy, whereas *monetary circulation often reveals wider economic trends that lay partly outside government control.*'[57]

It is these 'wider economic trends' that must inexorably lie at the heart of any economic history, whether of late antiquity or any other period. And if the archaeology has now made a decisive difference to the way economic histories should be written and to the assessments we form, so should monetary history. This was understood by Mickwitz as early as the thirties and led to a massive, fundamental re-evaluation of the late empire that broke decisively with the images of it transmitted in Rostovtzeff's writings from the late twenties. Gradual impoverishment, the decay of commerce, a state based on 'general ignorance, on compulsion and violence, on slavery and servility', a state that was a 'vast prison for scores of millions of men' were some of the more sombre ways in which Rostovtzeff characterised the political and economic regime from Diocletian onwards

[55] M. Hendy, *Studies in the Byzantine Monetary Economy c. 300–1450* (Cambridge, 1985), p. 606.

[56] F. Millar, *Journal of Roman Studies* 78 (1988), 198–202 (review of Hendy), at p. 199; last italics mine, all others Millar's. Millar also notes Hendy's debt to Crawford's *JRS* paper.

[57] D. M. Metcalf, *Byzantine Lead Seals from Cyprus* (Nicosia, 2004), p. 28; italics mine.

(as if he were actually describing the reactions of a deeply conservative 'liberal' to the emerging horrors of Stalinism).[58] The general move away from these stereotypes was a very gradual one, however, spanning whole decades from the thirties to the end of the sixties and punctuated by isolated if important contributions, at least till Peter Brown opened the floodgates.[59] But today the pendulum has swung so far the other way that scholars find it useful to remind us that there *were* discontinuities in 'political, administrative, military, social, and economic life',[60] the empire *did* disintegrate in the western provinces, and that the seventh century marked a major watershed in removing the richest eastern provinces from Byzantine control. These massive changes would eventually radically reconfigure the monetary map of Europe, depleting the west of its reserves of gold currency[61] and leading in Byzantium to a severe if temporally limited monetary recession from the late seventh century.[62] Yet down to these periods of abatement, the one gradual and irreversible, the other more sudden and compacted in time, monetary economy was the backbone of the late empire and the sheer scale on which gold circulated actively is surely the most telling sign both of the general nature of economic activity in these centuries (fourth to seventh) and of its staggering levels. The picture could scarcely be more different from the 'almost pure "house-economy"', the 'very primitive forms of economic life' posited by Rostovtzeff.[63] If anything, as one scholar noted, 'If monetization is a measure for the volume of trade in the Roman economy, then *the late Roman period should have rather more than less trade.*'[64]

Yet Hendy would have none of this. Vaguely aware, in the early eighties, that the 'New Archaeology' as he called it was starting to demonstrate substantial flows of commerce across the Mediterranean, he was frankly dismissive of the evidence.[65] In a tradition of history (Britain's) already marked by its self-assured minimalism, his must have been, arguably, the most extreme example of what Verboven describes as Finley's cultural

[58] Rostovtzeff, *The Social and Economic History of the Roman Empire*, vol. I, pp. 523–4, 531–2.

[59] Note Brown's description of *The World of Late Antiquity* (1971) as a 'book of the late 1960s', in P. Brown, 'The World of Late Antiquity Revisited', *Symbolae Osloenses* 72 (1997), 5–30, at p. 22.

[60] B. Ward-Perkins, *The Fall of Rome and the End of Civilization* (Oxford, 2005), p. 171.

[61] M. Blackburn, 'Money and Coinage', in *The New Cambridge Medieval History*, vol. II: *c.700–c.900*, ed. R. McKitterick (Cambridge, 1995), pp. 538–59, esp. 539ff.

[62] D. M. Metcalf, 'Monetary Recession in the Middle Byzantine Period: The Numismatic Evidence', *Numismatic Chronicle* 161 (2001), 111–55.

[63] Rostovtzeff, *Social and Economic History*, p. 532.

[64] H. Ziche, 'Integrating Late Roman Cities, Countryside and Trade', in *Ancient Economies, Modern Methodologies*, ed. P. F. Bang *et al.* (Bari, 2007), pp. 255–76, at 273.

[65] Hendy, *Studies*, p. 553.

determinism.[66] Here, in the face of his own evidence for a thriving monetary economy and a rigorously maintained gold coinage, was his own apriorism about how things really were: he argues, from a passage in Kekaumenos about the 'ideology of self-sufficiency' ('ideal' may have been more correct),

> [T]he existence of this ideological principle will have meant that what, apart from the state itself, were economically the most powerful classes in the empire will deliberately have restricted their involvement in monetary affairs to the purchase of what they and their households, which could be enormous, needed or desired, but could otherwise not provide themselves with ... and the accumulation of a necessary reserve.[67]

Here 'ideology' is made to carry a burden it cannot possibly bear, namely, of explaining the nature of an economy that in one form or another spanned the entire period from the fourth century to the fourteenth century and suggesting that the role of money within it (e.g. the vast coinage of the sixth century) was after all an aberration. There is a rough analogy here to the dilemma that Keith Hopkins too seems to have faced in what must have been the last paper he ever published, viz. his obvious admiration for the sheer scale of the Roman currency, the repeated reference to '[t]he huge growth in the Roman money supply under the emperors' or to 'a massive growth in money supply' followed by the claim that the emperors 'produced coins as economic objects for the facilitation of trade and taxation but *above all as symbolic objects of ostentation and political authority*'.[68]

The strength of private interests

Thus, next to mass production (Ken Dark's 'proto-industrial economy') and the widespread existence of commercial classes, money is the third element we need to integrate into a viable picture of the Roman economy, despite the astonishing claim that it lacked any specific economic function in the ancient world or the only slightly less incongruous assertion that it was produced *chiefly* as an object of ostentation. Rome, it is now widely acknowledged, had an 'intensely monetized economy'[69] and it seems unlikely that this was unrelated either to the relative sophistication

[66] K. Verboven, 'Cité et reciprocité: Le rôle des croyances culturelles dans l'économie romaine', *Annales HSS* 67/4 (2012), 913–42, esp. p. 919.

[67] Hendy, *Studies*, pp. 567–8.

[68] Hopkins, 'Political Economy', p. 202.

[69] E. Lo Cascio, 'The Function of Gold Coinage in the Monetary Economy of the Roman Empire', in *The Monetary Systems of the Greeks and Romans*, ed. W. V. Harris (Oxford, 2008), pp. 160–73, at 163.

of Roman financial instruments[70] or to the volumes of commercial activity and the 'passion for business'[71] that were both true of Roman economic and social history at various times. Like Roman private law or Roman debates about the nature of money,[72] these were all, absolutely, elements of proto-modernity, *anticipations of our own historical world*, even if it is misleading to characterise them as 'proto-capitalist', since that has an unmistakeable teleological charge and suggests that both class and economy as a whole were tending to a full-blown capitalism, which was so manifestly not the case that no one has ever argued it, least of all Rostovtzeff, for whom the late empire was, if anything, the graveyard of ancient capitalism. What *is* worth considering seriously is Ken Dark's suggestion that 'the Late Roman economy was industrialised more intensely than that of the late Middle Ages',[73] as well as the related ideas that the Roman world was more advanced technologically than entrenched orthodoxies have always implied[74] and that the mass markets that sustained production in a whole range of basic industries were not driven *solely* by aristocratic demand.[75] On the contrary, Angeliki Laiou's insistence that semi-luxury goods were a major segment of the market, certainly in the urban economy, suggests a wider spread of demand than that[76] and ties in perfectly with the kind of industrious and moderately affluent middle class that Anthea Harris finds in Sardis and that is presupposed in a wide range of urban centres throughout the Mediterranean, including of course Constantinople with its densely packed, multi-storied buildings, numerous workshops and 'vast population of inhabitants'.[77]

70 W. V. Harris, 'A Revisionist View of Roman Money', *Journal of Roman Studies* 96 (2006), 1–24.

71 Cicero, *Pro Sulla* 58: *studium negoti gerendi*. For late antiquity, cf. Salonius, *In parabolas Salomonis expositio mystica*, esp. *PL* 53.987C: 'The more wealth one accumulates, the more one is driven by the desire to keep expanding it'; or Ambrose's description of merchants as 'slaves to their capital', *De officiis* 2.67 (Davidson, vol. 1, p. 304).

72 E. Lo Cascio, 'Teoria e politica a Roma tra III e IV d.C.', in *Società romana e impero tardoantico*, ed. A Giardina (Rome and Bari, 1986), vol. 1, pp. 535–57, 779–801.

73 Dark, 'Proto-Industrialisation and the End of the Roman Economy', p. 14.

74 See Wilson, 'Machines' (n. 2); H. Schneider, 'Technology', in *The Cambridge Economic History of the Greco-Roman World*, ed. W. Scheidel *et al.* (Cambridge, 2007), pp. 144–71. Even jewellery was 'produced with the aid of mechanised techniques', see J. Campbell, *The Anglo-Saxon State* (London and New York, 2000), p. 72.

75 Cf. N. Purcell, 'Wine and Wealth in Ancient Italy', *Journal of Roman Studies* 75 (1985), 1–19, esp. pp. 13ff. on Italian mass markets for wine in the early empire.

76 See esp. A. Laiou, 'The Byzantine City: Parasitic or Productive?' in *Economic Thought and Economic Life in Byzantium*, ed. C. Morrisson and R. Dorin (Aldershot, 2013), no. XII, which starts with a critique of Finley.

77 Ammianus 31.16.7: *incolentium plebem immensam* (by 378!). The 'democratisation' of demand that Laiou discusses in a Middle Byzantine context was doubtless equally true of the fourth, fifth, sixth and seventh centuries, even given the ravages of the plague.

The idea that the economic life of these cities was shackled by some all-consuming *étatisme* is simply ludicrous, as Jean-Michel Carrié properly argues,[78] and stems from the stereotypes that I mentioned earlier. It is of course easy to read the late Roman legal sources in an uncritical way and extract a model of a *sistema vincolistico* that was so overwhelming in its scrutinies and controls that it led to a drastic reduction in the scope for a 'free' market, effectively killed such a market.[79] But this classically liberal, Enlightenment-driven picture of Rome's dark ages misses what was in fact central to the relationship between state and aristocracy in the late empire, namely, the enormous power of the aristocracy (much greater than anything known from previous centuries) and the numerous ways in which the state both reinforced that power[80] and encouraged the expansion of the aristocratic sector. The most striking case of this is the way the late Roman government encouraged the expansion of large properties by willingly privatising vast stretches of the *fundi patrimoniales*, sometimes auctioning off these estates.[81] But the same co-mingling of the public and private spheres can be seen in a host of other examples, including the return of private *domini* to the city's brick industry,[82] or the lavish benefactions that helped consolidate an aristocracy around the Constantinian household,[83] or the fact that government outsourced much of its own production, resources such as quarries, mines, etc. Indeed, in crucial ways there was *less* state control in the late empire, a stronger more widely accessible legal culture and a more subtle set of relationships between 'public' and 'private' such as we see emerging in a more complex and intricate form in Justinian's empire, notably in the peculiar nature of the *kommerkiarioi* as Oikonomidès understood them, viz. as businessmen drawn partly from the aristocracy trading in silk after successful bids for what were essentially commercial contracts at an auction where the state sold monopoly rights

78 J.-M. Carrié, 'Les échanges commerciaux et l'État antique tardif', in *Les échanges dans l'Antiquité: Le rôle de l'État* (St-Bertrand-de-Comminges, 1994), pp. 175–211.

79 F. Serrao, 'Il diritto e il processo privati', in *Storia di Roma*, vol. III/2 (n. 42), pp. 1011–34, seems to do precisely this, guided more by Carandini's catastrophism than his own good sense as a legal historian.

80 Take the fascinating example of family law discussed by J. Hillner, 'Family Violence: Punishment and Abuse in the Late Roman Household', in *Approaches to the Byzantine Family*, ed. L. Brubaker *et al.* (Aldershot, 2013), pp. 21–46, esp. 28ff.

81 *CTh.* 11.62.6 (384), 5.14.30 (387–8?), *CJ* 11.70.4 (395–402), *Nov. Val.* 10 (441), which between them refer to a right of control over estates by virtue of investments in barren land, donations by the emperor or purchases. *CTh.* 5.16.32 (408–11) suggests that sales were denuding the *domus divina* of its patrimony and should stop.

82 M. Steinby, 'L'industria laterizia di Roma nel tardo impero', in *Società romana e impero tardoantico*, ed. A. Giardina (Rome and Bari, 1986), vol. II, pp. 99–164, esp. 132–3, 157ff.

83 Anonymous, *De rebus bellicis* 2.1–2.

to the business in wide-ranging regional markets.[84] Here again, government was essentially *outsourcing* the production and trade in silk to private interests, thus expanding the scope of private business. If the *publicani* of the Republic were 'private entrepreneurs who lived in large part on the state',[85] the Byzantine *kommerkiarioi* were not vastly different. Certainly, the economy of the eastern empire in its essential nature was closer to the 'highly mercantile economy' reflected in the Geniza records[86] than it ever was to the economy of Russia under War Communism or, later, under Stalin.

Thus an *integration* of public and private business[87] would perhaps be a more precise way of characterising the relationship between private capital and the state sector than any of the standard clichés of dirigisme. The Roman and late Roman world presents us with a wide range of economic agents from bankers, manufacturers, wholesale merchants, building contractors, entrepreneurs, shipowners and so on to a mass of self-employed artisans and an even greater mass of wage labourers and slaves. Late Rome in the fourth century was a society still largely founded on slavery,[88] even if less vitally dependent on it than the Republic had been, and wage labour too was widespread. These tendencies of late Roman society re-emerge in an even purer form in the eastern empire, where the civilian character of the regime, its strong legal protections for the ordinary citizen[89] and very wide spread of jobs in the bureaucracy[90] *combined* with expanding cultivation and rural settlement to make the fifth and sixth centuries look not so different from the Golden Age of the Antonines. There was a great deal of building all over the eastern empire as provincial capitals proliferated and

[84] Most recently, N. Oikonomidès, 'The *Kommerkiarios* of Constantinople', in *Byzantine Constantinople: Monuments, Topography and Everyday Life*, ed. N. Necipoğlu (Leiden, 2001), pp. 235–44.

[85] W. V. Harris, 'The Late Republic', in *Cambridge Economic History of the Greco-Roman World* (n. 74), pp. 511–40, at 520.

[86] S. D. Goitein, *A Mediterranean Society, vol. i: Economic Foundations* (Berkeley, Los Angeles and London, 1967), p. 116.

[87] Cf. Procopius, *HA* xx.5 on Justinian's *monopōlia*, where the partnership is unmistakably implied.

[88] K. Harper, *Slavery in the Late Roman World, AD 275–425* (Cambridge, 2011).

[89] T. Honoré, 'Roman Law AD 200–400: From Cosmopolis to Rechtstaat?', in *Approaching Late Antiquity: The Transformation from Early to Late Empire*, ed. S. Swain *et al.* (Oxford, 2004), pp. 109–32. The great exception, of course, was that resident workers were more securely tied to estates than ever in the past. This didn't make them 'unfree' (as slaves were) but it did represent an attack on their civil freedoms.

[90] The Byzantine papyri are full of government employees with both rural and urban assets, e.g. the more affluent layers of the provincial bureaucracy owned orchards worth hundreds of solidi, cf. *P. Oxy.* LXIII 4394 (494–500), epitomising the business dealings of a coterie of public servants resident in Alexandria.

the urban centres themselves saw further expansion in the fourth and fifth centuries.[91] So too in the countryside where the construction of churches becomes, later, an obvious symptom of the vitality of civil society and where the sheer *wealth* of the countryside, even in remote rural villages such as those in the mountains of Lycia, is indicated by sporadic finds of church treasures, like the Sion Treasure dated to the sixth century.[92] Rostovtzeff's description of the 'commerce and industry' of the empire (in chapter 5 of *The Social and Economic History of the Roman Empire*) could easily be extended to late antiquity with the appropriate adjustments and a less dogmatic commitment to a classical Roman urban formalism. The dominance of wholesale merchants, the strong commercial edge built-up by traders from the east, the government's commitment to a 'policy of *laissez-faire*', the decentralisation of industry, the standardisation of goods, the emergence of mass markets and the wide spread of banking operations were *all* true of the late antique Mediterranean, even despite the disintegration of the western empire.[93] The banker Julianus' benefactions to various churches were in excess of 50,000 solidi, and that in a city (Ravenna) with an exceptional concentration of bankers in the fifth and sixth centuries.[94] Cosentino suggests that commissions on exchange transactions involving different currencies were where the *argentarii* made the bulk of their money, but the financing of maritime trade is another strong possibility, given the scale of Ravenna's traffic with the eastern Mediterranean via Classis. Again, Flavius Anastasius, the Constantinople banker from whom two leading villagers of Aphrodito borrowed the relatively small sum of 20 solidi in the year 541 expected repayment in his branch (*apotheke*) back in Alexandria.[95] For Mickwitz this was crucial evidence of the relatively advanced character of banking in the late antique world.[96]

91 E.g. C. Foss, *Byzantine and Turkish Sardis* (Cambridge, MA, 1976), p. 51.

92 S. A. Boyd, 'A "Metropolitan" Treasure from a Church in the Provinces: An Introduction to the Study of the Sion Treasure', in *Ecclesiastical Silver Plate in Sixth-Century Byzantium*, ed. S. A. Boyd and M. M. Mango (Washington, D.C., 1992), pp. 5–37, esp. 18 where she says, 'even these rather remote, rural villages must have been fairly wealthy'.

93 The list is extracted from Rostovtzeff, *Social and Economic History*, pp. 158 (wholesalers), 169–70 (competitive edge), 170 (laissez-faire), 173 (dispersal of industry), 175 (standardisation), 179ff. (banking).

94 S. Cosentino, 'Le fortune di un banchiere tardoantico: Giuliano argentario e l'economia di Ravenna nel VI secolo', in *Santi banchieri re: Ravenna e Classe nel VI secolo* (Milan, 2006), pp. 43–8, esp. 44 (largesse), 44–5 (concentration of bankers).

95 J. G. Keenan, 'A Constantinople Loan, A.D. 541', *Bulletin of the American Society of Papyrologists* 29 (1992), 175–82, discussing *P. Cairo Masp.* 67126.

96 G. Mickwitz, 'Die Organisationsformen zweier byzantinischer Gewerbe im X. Jahrhundert', *Byzantinische Zeitschrift* 36 (1936), 63–76, at p. 64 where the *apothēkē* is seen as a commercial branch ('die Filiale').

The Alexandrian traders based in provincial centres such as Oxyrhynchus were likewise probably local, branch representatives of Alexandrian firms dealing in commodities like flax.[97] In the late eleventh century Alexandria exported 5,000–6,000 tons of raw flax to markets in the Mediterranean.[98] When we turn to the late antique evidence, however, there is simply no way of telling how much flax was grown in Egypt, but it must have been substantial.

The most striking *economic* fact about late antiquity is that from the abundant numismatic and papyrological evidence and the written sources it is certain that there was an increase in the 'per capita value of the money stock',[99] more money in circulation *per head of the population* than at any previous time in Roman history, the bulk of this in the form of gold. And again, on broadly Rostovtzeffian lines, it would be plausible to argue that the basis of this expansion lay in a major growth of trade and manufacturing fuelled by increased urbanisation, growing populations (a net overall increase), successive construction booms, massive state spending, etc. In Justinian's reign the supply of grain from Egypt amounted to some 240,000 tons and even this staggering figure was probably less than 15 per cent of that country's gross production. Foodgrains, wine, olive oil, flax, wool, silk and other textiles, pottery, glass, metal, building materials, salt, spices, marinated fish, even jewellery and silver plate were all traded in huge quantities, often across a range of market segments. Manufacturing, trade and food processing were widely dispersed through the Mediterranean in all sorts of locations from the great markets of the eastern empire such as Constantinople and Alexandria to major urban centres, smaller towns, villages, estates, monasteries and isolated coastal sites. This is the only way of making sense of the archaeology as well as accounting for the huge commercial flows reflected in the 'thousands upon thousands of sherds of pottery' found all across late antique/early medieval sites.[100] The most recent synthesis of the ceramic evidence

[97] Most recently, *P. Oxy.* LXXII 4918 (March 494–6), involving the same local merchant ('from the great city of Alexandria') as does *P. Oxy.* VIII 1130 (484), both contracts using loans to secure supplies of flax.

[98] A. L. Udovitch, 'International Trade and the Medieval Egyptian Countryside', in *Agriculture in Egypt: From Pharaonic to Modern Times*, ed. A. Bowman *et al.* (Oxford, 1999), pp. 267–85.

[99] R. H. Britnell, 'Commercialisation and Economic Development in England, 1000–1300', in *A Commercialising Economy: England 1086 to c. 1300*, ed. R. H. Britnell *et al.* (Manchester and New York, 1995), pp. 7–26, esp. 12–13, and the paper by Mayhew, 'Modelling Medieval Monetisation', pp. 55–77.

[100] S. T. Loseby, 'The Mediterranean Economy', in *The New Cambridge Medieval History*, vol. I: *c.500–c.700*, ed. P. Fouracre (Cambridge, 2006), pp. 605–38, at 608; Ward-Perkins, *Fall of Rome*, pp. 88ff., describes the impression conveyed by 'massive quantities' of high-quality Roman pottery, and

for trade in the eastern Mediterranean suggests that contacts across the Aegean were sustained at least to the second half of the seventh century, that Constantinople retained its commercial links with Africa throughout the seventh century and indeed continued to 'drain eastern goods to the north' down the late seventh century.[101] And this takes us frontally to the great questions of 'continuity, "crisis" and decline', as Moses Finley once summed all this up in a paper in the pages of the Italian journal *Opus*.[102]

Economic cycles, institutional continuities

The most striking and in some ways perplexing feature of the *seventh* century is how differently the two main regional blocs of the eastern Mediterranean seem to have performed across its turbulent, politically fraught decades. The prolonged prosperity, under Umayyad rule, in Syria, Palestine and Egypt[103] could scarcely stand in sharper contrast to the 'two centuries of crisis' that engulfed the Byzantine heartland in its 'dark ages'.[104] The explanation for this remarkable divergence must lie, clearly, in the wider economic trends that came to characterise each of these large sets of territories. Both Byzantium and the new Islamic lands retained a functioning monetary economy throughout the seventh century, and permanently after that, but the late seventh century saw the Byzantine state plunge into what looks like a prolonged monetary recession that was bound to affect life at all levels, down to whether peasants had the resources to sustain taxation in money or at least substantial levels of it. By contrast, the Umayyads exacted vast sums of gold and silver from their subject populations (the former Sasanians included), while the Arab empire rapidly created a vast new economic space that stretched from the Indian Ocean to Spain, all along the southern rim of the Mediterranean, and north and east into the Central Asian land mass. If Byzantium languished in a protracted fiscal and economic *deflation* till the revival of

argues, 'If good-quality pottery was reaching even peasant households, then the same is almost certainly true of other goods, made of materials that rarely survive in the archaeological record … There is, for instance, no reason to suppose that the huge markets in clothing, footwear, and tools were less sophisticated than that in pottery' (p. 94).

101 C. Abadie-Reynal, 'Les échanges interrégionaux de céramiques en Méditerranée orientale entre le IVe et le VIIIe siècle', in *Handelsgüter und Verkehrswege*, ed. E. Kislinger *et al.* (Vienna, 2010), pp. 25–36, at 27, 28, 32.

102 M. I. Finley, *Opus* 1 (1982), pp. 208ff.

103 A. E. Laiou and C. Morrisson, *The Byzantine Economy* (Cambridge, 2007), p. 24.

104 C. Wickham, *The Inheritance of Rome: A History of Europe from 400 to 1000* (London, 2009), p. 554.

the later eighth or ninth century, the Near East was awash with liquidity, thriving levels of monetary and economic activity that reflected the burgeoning urban centres that spread across the caliphate and gave local economic life an altogether more vibrant quality.

Thus the first point about the seventh century is that it was a watershed into very different sorts of economic histories, and notions like continuity, crisis, decline and so on are just not sufficiently differentiated (not strong enough as *concepts*) to capture the divergent evolutions at work. Constantinople remained a major metropolis across the early Middle Ages, the islands were, arguably, vibrant exceptions to the 'Byzantine economic collapse', if one wants to call it that, and, as I just noted, a whole swathe of former Roman/Byzantine territory saw renewed economic expansion under Islam.[105] At any rate, the Mediterranean remained integrated for much of the seventh century[106] and regardless of the fiscal/monetary crisis that engulfed the Byzantine state, there were very substantial amounts of gold *in circulation* in the Mediterranean *throughout* the seventh century.[107]

Perhaps the best way of *re*-framing the problem of 'decline' and avoiding its catastrophist implications is to think of ancient economic history as marked by *cycles* (broad fluctuations across whole swathes of history) and to see the later seventh century as the start of a cyclical downturn that was, however, peculiar to the truncated Byzantine empire and not true of the territories under Arab control or of the Merovingian west. Despite the abysmal uncertainties of middle Byzantine economic history,[108] the general shape of Byzantium's economic trajectory now seems fairly well

[105] Islands: for example, L. Zavagno, 'At the Edge of Two Empires: The Economy of Cyprus between Late Antiquity and the Early Middle Ages (650s–800s CE)', *Dumbarton Oaks Papers* 65–6 (2011 –12), 121–56. 'Byzantine economic collapse': the phrase occurs in M. Whittow, 'Decline and Fall? Studying Long-Term Change in the East', in *Theory and Practice in Late Antique Archaeology*, ed. L. Lavan *et al.* (Leiden, 2003), pp. 404–23, at 407, who disagrees with it, of course, as would C. Lightfoot, 'Business as Usual? Archaeological Evidence for Byzantine Commercial Enterprise at Amorium in the Seventh to Eleventh Centuries', in *Trade and Markets in Byzantium*, ed. C. Morrisson (Washington, D.C., 2012), pp. 177–92. Expansion under Islam: more than any other scholar it was Maurice Lombard (1904–65) who picked up on this in a series of papers of astonishing creativity.

[106] Cf. the high percentage of amphorae of eastern origin in the end-of-seventh-century deposit at the Crypta Balbi in Rome, Saguì, 'Roma' (n. 31).

[107] C. Morrisson, V. Popović and V. Ivanišević, *Les trésors monétaires byzantins des Balkans et d'Asie Mineure (491–713)* (Paris, 2006), nos 60 (Varna, *c.*690), 133 (Athens/Acropolis, *c.*668), 314 (Antalya, *c.*685), 315 (Arkessini, *c.*674–7/8), 334 (Datça, *c.*641–68) and 344 (western Asia Minor, *c.*695) in their catalogue, substantial hoards with large numbers of solidi of Constans II and/or Constantine IV. Finds from elsewhere (Milazzo, Amorgos, Nikertai, etc.) reflect the same pattern.

[108] See Whittow's excellent survey, M. Whittow, 'The Middle Byzantine Economy (600–1204)', in *The Cambridge History of the Byzantine Empire c. 500–1492*, ed. J. Shepard (Cambridge, 2008), pp. 465–92.

established. The late seventh and eighth centuries were a demographic low-water mark,[109] also characterised by (seemingly) a less prosperous society that had seen the traumatic loss of the rich eastern provinces[110] and was now suffering a severe monetary deflation after the peak levels of the sixth and early seventh centuries. In this bleak landscape the mid-eighth century may well have been the trough, since this period of 'abatement' if one wants to call it that was followed by a gradual recovery from the late eighth into the tenth centuries and this in turn by the vigorous expansion of the eleventh and twelfth centuries, as Europe was hurtling through its 'commercial revolution'.[111] By the fourteenth century Byzantium seems, by all accounts, as close to its own forms of commercial and financial capitalism as it would ever get.[112] A sort of capitalist aristocracy had finally emerged, less powerful, it is true, than the Italian merchants who dominated the commercial capitalism of this age, but with commercial practices that were *no less advanced*.[113]

If we stand back from this trajectory for a moment, the chief lesson that seems to emerge from Byzantine economic history *which is more widely applicable* is its indelibly cyclical nature. The general shape of the curve reflects a series of interlocking cycles (demographic, monetary, economic). A phase of strong demographic advance in the fifth and sixth centuries that must have plateaued in the seventh was followed (not everywhere!) by sharp demographic contraction to a trough in the mid-eighth century, and this by strong (demographic) recovery and expansion from the ninth. As Alan Harvey argued, this Middle Byzantine demographic increase in turn fuelled an expansion of large estates because labour was more easily available now (large landowners brought land back into cultivation using available labour).[114] On a wider scale this resurgence of large private estates in the tenth century only replicates a process that had occurred centuries earlier, probably throughout the eastern Mediterranean, and that is best

109 E. Le Roy Ladurie, *The Peasants of Languedoc*, trans. J. Day (Urbana, Chicago and London, 1974), p. 14.

110 'Traumatic loss, etc.' from J.-C. Cheynet, 'Bureaucracy and Aristocracies', in *The Oxford Handbook of Byzantine Studies*, ed. E. Jeffreys *et al.* (Oxford, 2008), pp. 518–26, at 518.

111 The demographic recovery of Constantinople dates from the reign of Constantine V, cf. P. Magdalino, *Constantinople médiévale: Études sur l'évolution des structures urbaines* (Paris, 1996), p. 58.

112 See N. Oikonomidès, 'Byzantium Between East and West (xiii–xv Cent.)', *Byzantinische Forschungen* 13 (1988), 319–32, esp. pp. 327–9.

113 M. Balard, 'Les hommes d'affaires occidentaux ont-ils asphyxié l'économie byzantine?', in *Europa medievale e mondo bizantino*, ed. G. Arnaldi *et al.* (Rome, 1997), pp. 255–65.

114 A. Harvey, *Economic Expansion in the Byzantine Empire, 900–1200* (Cambridge, 1989), pp. 47–8, 60.

captured in the evidence from Egypt where a new eastern aristocracy, first emerging in the main part of the fifth century, came to control substantial properties based on the deployment of permanent workers, that is, a mass of landless peasants residing on the estate, a 'surplus' population that sought employment. Those estates were largely producing for the market (the Apion estate in the Oxyrhynchite was generating over 18,500 solidi in the 580s, from this one district alone),[115] which in turn suggests, as the ceramic evidence does, that markets were booming throughout the eastern empire, and that a wider process of economic growth was in play. So too in the tenth, eleventh and twelfth centuries, which of course were also periods of monetary growth and of major intellectual and social change in Byzantium.

If the transformations of the early Middle Ages are best disentangled from the once hugely popular problematic of the 'decline of empires' and seen in terms of the distinct dynamics at work in political history and economic life, the problem of continuity could likewise be framed in a less literal way. The major transformations that swept through the east Roman empire in the seventh century and the very real social changes they may well have brought about (an aristocracy is vaguely discernible again only from the middle of the eighth century) should not distract us from the essential continuity of economic relationships implied throughout Byzantine history, by which I mean continuity with the economic system of the empire as this had evolved by the sixth century. Just as much of the population of Constantinople had expanded through continuous migration from the countryside and elsewhere, the huge demographic losses sustained by it in the seventh and early eighth centuries may well have seen a massive reverse flow, with fewer jobs available and a fiscally depleted state. The dramatic decline in building activity in seventh-century Constantinople[116] certainly suggests that even skilled workers were no longer in demand. On the other hand, as Paul Magdalino argues, the fabric of the city itself remained essentially unchanged, the Constantinople that Justinian built surviving as the solid bedrock of the medieval city and the great palaces of the aristocracy often changing hands but otherwise physically intact.[117] This is a superb metonym for the wider relationships implied in the history

[115] See T. M. Hickey, 'An Inconvenient Truth? *P. Oxy.* 8.2196 verso, the Apion Estate, and *fiscalité* in the Late Antique Oxyrhynchite', *Bulletin of the American Society of Papyrologists* 45 (2008), 87–100.

[116] J. Bardill, *Brickstamps of Constantinople* (Oxford, 2004), vol. 1, pp. 39–42.

[117] Magdalino, *Constantinople médiévale.*

of the middle empire, namely, a profound institutional continuity with the past where both the essential nature of the Byzantine aristocracy and the commercial institutions and practices of urban economy 'survived' as the invisible grid of economic life, as did a strongly rooted Roman civil law tradition. Byzantium was the *only* medieval society that fully accepted the legitimacy of interest on loan capital, that is, of the right of money capital to a profit, grounding this in an absolute affirmation of the force of private contracts.[118] Given the rapid growth of Byzantine commercial capital in the eleventh and twelfth centuries, these debates about the nature of interest had a more than purely scholastic quality. But what they also reflected was the solid remanence of a legal tradition inherited from the past, a creation in fact of the Republic, just as the professional guilds regulated in the *Book of the Prefect* were at some level a throwback to the trade and professional associations of late antiquity, even if the glimpse afforded into Constantinople's business world reflects not the actual operations of that world (where are the sources for that?) but only the state's standpoint on its ideal regulation (though this shows that government sought to minimise competition within trades and to discourage vertical integration).[119]

What fascinated Mickwitz was the problem of continuity in this deeper sense, of how institutions inherited from the past could contain the seeds of potentially major new developments, as he suggested in his analysis of the Byzantine silk industry and his attempt to show that it was based on early forms of capitalist organisation.[120] Business partnerships are the other major inheritance from the Roman past that found a renewed resonance in the economic ferment of the eleventh and twelfth centuries, and even more so as the Byzantine empire became more deeply integrated into Mediterranean commercial capitalism after the twelfth century. These were not durable corporate entities like the later Venetian *compagnie* but temporary associations like their Roman exemplars, but their significance for economic history is to underline the complex ways in which the different global/economic regions emerging from a once-unified late

118 See A. Laiou, '*Nummus parit nummos*: L'usurier, le juriste et le philosophe à Byzance', in *Economic Thought and Economic Life in Byzantium* (n. 76), no. IV, where she argues that the Aristotelian doctrine of the sterility of money emphatically found no resonance among the Byzantines.

119 Oikonomidès, 'Entrepreneurs', pp. 154–7; cf. J. Holo, *Byzantine Jewry in the Medieval Economy* (Cambridge, 2009), pp. 153–4, contrasting the very different structure and management of Jewish businesses.

120 Mickwitz, 'Organisationsformen' (n. 96), pp. 70–6. On the further, distinctly *capitalist*, transformation of the provincial silk industry in the eleventh and twelfth centuries, see the brilliant case study in D. Jacoby, 'Silk in Western Byzantium before the Fourth Crusade', *Byzantinische Zeitschrift* 84/5 (1991–2), 452–500.

antique past were reassembling contacts and forms of integration in a sort of cross-fertilisation peculiar to the economic life of the Mediterranean. In 1929 Jacob Strieder had wondered if Italy's medieval capitalism was not in some sense an unmediated legacy of the traditions inherited from its Roman past, the 'forms of money and credit-economy inherited from the ancient world' that had '*kept their vitality*'.[121] In 1936 Mickwitz, who was certainly influenced by Strieder, asked if Byzantium ('wealthy Constantinople with its economic organisation inherited from antiquity') was not, at this level, the major transmission belt between antiquity and the Italian mercantile republics.[122] Oikonomidès later suggested on the same lines that the *chreokoinōnia*, a means of financing maritime trade attested by the seventh century, may well have been at the origin of the Italian *commenda*.[123] In fact, both Lopez and Udovitch had already wondered if the *commenda* did not derive, more plausibly, from the various forms of partnership that were widespread in the Islamic world throughout the centuries of Byzantine quiescence.[124] These are fascinating issues, all of them far from resolved, but what they do point to is an economic history where connectivity acquires a more elusive, subterranean meaning, a dimension of what Mickwitz called a 'problem of influence'.

As the Mediterranean embarked slowly on a new cycle of commercial growth from the later eighth century, what emerged most forcefully was the triangular trade between Constantinople, the Italians and the expanding cities of the Muslim world. The re-emergence of the Golden Horn as the commercial hub of Byzantium's trade was linked to the Italians establishing their trading quarters in the lower Golden Horn area (surely, *by* the ninth century) and choosing to do so, Magdalino has argued, because Perama had long been the location of one of the great clearing houses (*mitata*) used by the Middle Eastern merchants, major trading partners of the Italians.[125] The first large settlement of Italians in Constantinople was

[121] J. Strieder, 'Origin and Evolution of Early European Capitalism', *Journal of Economic and Business History* 2 (1929), 1–19, esp. pp. 4–5; my italics.

[122] G. Mickwitz, 'Un problème d'influence: Byzance et l'économie de l'Occident médiéval', *Annales d'Histoire Économique et Sociale* 8 (1936), 21–8.

[123] N. Oikonomidès, *Hommes d'affaires grecs et latins à Constantinople (XIIIe–XVe siècles)* (Montreal and Paris, 1979), p. 72, n. 107, describing it as 'assez générale pour qu'elle puisse être à l'origine de la *commenda* aussi bien que de la *societas maris* ou *colleganza*'.

[124] R. Lopez, 'Les méthodes commerciales des marchands occidentaux en Asie', in *Sociétés et compagnies de commerce en Orient et dans l'Océan indien*, ed. M. Mollat (Paris, 1970), pp. 343–8, at 345; A. Udovitch, *Partnership and Profit in Medieval Islam* (Princeton, 1970), p. 171.

[125] P. Magdalino, 'The Maritime Neighborhoods of Constantinople: Commercial and Residential Functions, Sixth to Twelfth Centuries', *Dumbarton Oaks Papers* 54 (2000), 209–26, esp. pp. 219–23 and the suggestion, 'If I am right in thinking that the Italians developed their business

by the merchants of Amalfi,[126] and if we wish to track the origins of the economic fortunes of the maritime cities of Byzantine Italy in the early Middle Ages, Amalfi is where we would have to start.[127] Amalfi's period of most rapid expansion coincided with the Arab conquest of Sicily in the early ninth century, but Citarella argues, crucially, that its trade with the Maghreb had certainly started by the eighth century, and that this was a commerce where timber and foodgrains mattered more than the human commodity and a commerce largely fuelled by the Arab urban revolution.[128] This picture is the *antithesis of Pirenne's thesis* and entirely in keeping with Lombard's vision of the Islamic world as the true catalyst of growth in a Mediterranean otherwise dependent solely on the forces of a depleted Byzantine state. 'Islam' accomplished what Justinian's reconquest of the west had signally failed to do (reunify the Mediterranean); welded together two massive economic zones (the Indian Ocean and the Mediterranean); traversed eastern and northern Europe with its commercial and monetary circuits; and contributed decisively to Byzantium's renewal (*renouveau*) from the ninth century.[129] Here then is a model where the less visible connectivity of the Mediterranean becomes fully intelligible, providing both a sort of prototype for Venetian commercial expansion to the east (in the shape of Amalfi's precocious contacts with the Arab world) and a concrete material setting within which a gradual and permanent osmosis between different commercial traditions was unfolding.

interests at Constantinople through association with the Arabs and their *mitaton* at Perama, they gravitated to the Golden Horn because this was the place for foreigners to trade' (p. 222). Cf. Magdalino, *Constantinople médiévale*, pp. 88–9, and the date proposed in Magdalino, 'Medieval Constantinople: Built Environment and Urban Development', in *The Economic History of Byzantium from the Seventh through the Fifteenth Century*, ed. A. F. Laiou (Washington, D.C., 2002), vol. II, pp. 529–37, at 532: 'the Arab *mitaton*, which must have been established in the late seventh century …'.

126 Cf. Oikonomidès, 'Entrepreneurs', p. 159.

127 'Amalfi is one of the great mysteries of Mediterranean history', D. Abulafia, *The Great Sea: A Human History of the Mediterranean* (London, 2014), p. 267, also noting, 'The label "Amalfitan" was really a brand name … the whole southern shore of the Sorrentine peninsula … was "Amalfi"' (p. 268).

128 A. O. Citarella, *Il commercio di Amalfi nell'alto Medioevo* (Salerno, 1977), pp. 43 (problem of origins), 45 (meteoric rise), 48–58 (trade with Muslim cities). Elsewhere Citarella wrote, 'We find them [Amalfitans] in large numbers throughout the agricultural centers of Puglia,' implying that Amalfi *dominated the grain trade of southern Italy* and made this central to its precocious ties with Muslim North Africa. See A. O. Citarella, 'Patterns in Medieval Trade: The Commerce of Amalfi before the Crusades', *Journal of Economic History* 28(4) (1968), 531–55, at p. 541.

129 M. Lombard, *Espaces et réseaux du haut moyen âge* (Paris and the Hague, 1972), pp. 41–4.

The crucial point was one made by Delogu:

> The Mediterranean did not become an underdeveloped area as a consequence of the disintegration of the Roman World. Although a contraction of social and economic life may have taken place on its shores in connection with the collapse of the Roman system ... from the end of the eighth century symptoms of new political and commercial vitality appear. The most evident of them is the resumption of Islamic expansion, now towards Italy, soon followed by new Byzantine enterprises.[130]

If the Lombard/Byzantine peace of 680 was the symbolic threshold to a new epoch, marked by numerous symptoms of renewal *already by the end of the seventh century*,[131] then 'dark age' Byzantium with its reduced energies and state of emergency[132] cannot be a model for all of the totalisations that traversed the 'practical field' of the Mediterranean in the seventh and eighth centuries. The eighth-century northern expansion *cannot* be pitted against a unified Mediterranean collapse in the seventh and/or eighth centuries, since no such *generalised* crisis or end-of-the-ancient-world scenario existed then. Imports from southern Italy and even from the east were widespread during the eighth and possibly part of the ninth century, both in the lagoon of Venice and that of Comacchio. The whole stretch of land between Ravenna and the Venetian lagoon *teemed* with new settlements like Comacchio that were both centres of trade and production, and invested in substantial trade infrastructures like harbour facilities and canals,[133] suggesting that northern Italy at least, like the southern ports, was part of the wider currents of exchange emanating from the southern and eastern Mediterranean. The more general point here is that the eighth century was, as Gelichi has argued, 'on an economic level, by no means a period of stagnation'.[134] The background to the gradual consolidation of Venetian dominance in the ninth century was, classically, the emergence, in the eighth century, in this north-western stretch of the Adriatic,

130 P. Delogu, 'Transformation of the Roman World: Reflections on Current Research', in *East and West: Modes of Communication*, ed. E. Chrysos *et al.* (Leiden etc., 1999), pp. 243–57, at 256.

131 P. Delogu, 'La fine del mondo antico e l'inizio del medioevo: Nuovi dati per un vecchio problema', in *La storia dell'Alto Medioevo italiano (VI–X secolo) alla luce dell'archeologia* (Florence, 1994), pp. 7–29.

132 M.-F. Auzépy, 'State of Emergency (700–850)', in *Cambridge History of the Byzantine Empire* (n. 108), pp. 251–91.

133 S. Gelichi, 'The Eels of Venice: The Long Eighth Century of the Emporia of the Northern Region along the Adriatic Coast', in *774: Ipotesi su una transizione* (Turnhout, 2008), pp. 81–117, esp. 92 (imports from east), 108–9 (harbour facilities).

134 Gelichi, 'Eels', p. 83.

of one of those many 'key economic areas'[135] that had always sustained and driven commercial cycles in the Mediterranean, simultaneously or in succession, from, say, central (Tyrrhenian) Italy in the middle/late Republic to southern Spain in the early empire to North Africa in the third and fourth centuries to the Levant and Egypt in the sixth (and much later again under the Fatimids). That Venice clinched her own domination of the eastern trade by competitive methods that were often ruthless, for example, driving out the competition of Jewish merchants through physical expulsions[136] or simply wiping out Comacchio,[137] is again reminiscent, finally, of a whole dynamic that had characterised the commercial life of the Mediterranean for certainly well over a millennium, in Rome's case ever since the Punic Wars.

Summary of select themes

It may help to say something briefly about some of the chapters that follow. With two exceptions they all postdate the first edition of my book *Agrarian Change in Late Antiquity* (2001) and proceed from its general understanding of the essential novelty of the late empire. Apart from the obvious feature of Christianity and what he called the 'democratisation of culture', Mazzarino identified that novelty with the radically new monetary system introduced by the 'revolutionary' Constantine and the deeper stratification of society that emerged along with it.[138] In line with these perspectives, seminal for their time, money, class and the sheer economic vibrancy of the late antique world form the major leitmotifs that run through much of this book and knit its chapters together. In particular, the scale of the currency, the strength of private economic interests and the commercial dynamism linked to them, the nature of the ruling class and the problem of continuity into and across the Middle Ages are some of the basic themes that unify the chapters that follow. The broad divisions are indicated in the way the chapters have been grouped together to start with a general mapping of essential features of the late antique economy (Chapters 2–4) before dropping the level of abstraction to examine factors connected with the dynamics of monetary circulation (Chapters 5–6); the

[135] Ch'ao-ting Chi, *Key Economic Areas in Chinese History as Revealed in the Development of Public Works for Water-Control* (New York, 1963), a reprint of the London edition of 1936.

[136] Citarella, *Commercio*, p. 44. [137] Gelichi, 'Eels', p. 102.

[138] A sense of this novelty was already apparent in some strands of historiography soon after the First World War, e.g. A. Rosenberg, *Einleitung und Quellenkunde zur römischen Geschichte* (Berlin, 1921), pp. 53–4 (on the 'solid new foundation' of Constantine's monetary system).

spectrum of aristocracies, structure of estates and nature of the rural labour force (Chapters 7–8); and, in the final section, the economic transformations which in different ways came to characterise developments within the early caliphate and on the much wider canvas of the Indian Ocean trade (Chapters 9–10).

The symbiosis of state and aristocracy in the eastern empire is a central argument of Chapter 3 and constructed largely as an alternative to Gascou's extreme view that the aristocracy and its estates were simply public or semi-public institutions deprived of any major economic decision-making of their own, as if constructing and expanding estates as the Apions did in Middle Egypt was simply a function of their liturgical obligations. A crucial document cited there, *P. Oxy.* 1829, has recently been discussed by Joëlle Beaucamp in terms of its underlying prosopography,[139] but as far as I know there has been no further discussion of the nature of the document itself or my suggestion that the transmission of the pagarchy within aristocratic families would have had to have some formal, legal expression. Chapter 4 underlines the commercial vitality of the east, a theme presupposed in the two chapters that follow it as well as in Chapters 9 and 10. Chapter 6 highlights the commercial function of the late Roman/Byzantine and Sasanian coinages against the widespread view that these coinages were essentially fiscal instruments. The Sasanians turned out what Philip Grierson called 'one of the hugest silver coinages known to history'[140] and the link between strictly commercial functions and both the scale and purity of the currency is especially clear in their case. Indeed, much of the silver that ended up in Scandinavia in the ninth century was recycled Sasanian silver.[141] On the other hand, I would be much less confident now about my suggestion that 'ships from China' might actually have meant Chinese merchants sailing to the Gulf.[142] Chapters 7 and 8 articulate a view of late antique/early medieval aristocracies as essentially

[139] J. Beaucamp, *Le statut de la femme à Byzance (4e–7e siècle), vol. ii* (Paris, 1992), p. 445, nn. 16 and 20.

[140] P. Grierson, 'The Role of Silver in the Early Byzantine Economy', in *Ecclesiastical Silver Plate in Sixth-Century Byzantium*, ed. Boyd *et al.* (n. 92), pp. 137–46, at 138.

[141] R. Naismith, *Money and Power in Anglo-Saxon England: The Southern English Kingdoms 757–865* (Cambridge, 2014), pp. 159–60.

[142] See Chapter 6, pp. 138–9. As Wolters pointed out, Ṭabarī's 'ships from China' 'can equally well mean "ships on the China-run" or, perhaps, ships with China-type merchandise', O. W. Wolters, *Early Indonesian Commerce: A Study of the Origins of Śrīvijaya* (Ithaca, NY, 1967), p. 146. In the twelfth century, when merchants from China did sail all the way, cargoes destined for Middle Eastern markets were transferred to smaller vessels at Quilon (*Ku-lin*), cf. A. Netolitzky, *Das Ling-wai tai-ta von Chou Ch'ü-fei: Eine Landeskunde Südchinas aus dem 12. Jahrhundert* (Wiesbaden, 1977), pp. 40–1, 55.

divided, ensembles as often characterised by fragmentation and internal conflict as any unifying political loyalties or class interests. The broader canvas here is the way what John Haldon calls the tributary mode of production allowed for a *wide range of relationships between ruler and aristocracy*, from the endemic tensions characteristic of Sasanian history or the fraught instabilities of Visigothic rule to the comparatively less violent history of the East Roman state under Justinian.[143] Thus Wickham's move from 'aristocracy' to 'aristocracies' is a welcome one, an invitation to write materialist histories in less abstract and dogmatic ways. The view in Chapter 7 that the seventh century should be seen as the start of a new cycle of growth in the Merovingian countryside is fully supported by the way Olivier Bruand constructs his argument in *Voyageurs et marchandises aux temps carolingiens*.[144] A paper by Margerete Weidemann that appeared at the same time as my own looks at some of the same issues of continuity in the organisation of estates and deployment of rural workers, but misses the crucial point that while the Merovingians continued basically late Roman models of estate organisation, the Carolingian manor cannot be deduced in a similar way from that earlier trajectory; far from it.[145] On the other hand, Neustria itself may well have been a 'laboratory' in which production and the organisation of labour *were* being reorganised as early as the seventh century, so that the manor was not a *complete* innovation.[146] Chapter 8 ends by suggesting that cash-cropping was a mainstay of Sasanian aristocratic estates and that the bulk of the canal-irrigated lands in southern Iraq had been parcelled out to sections of the aristocracy closest to the ruling family, a pattern soon to be replicated by the Umayyads. However, it should be added here that *having said this* it remains entirely unclear where the balance lay, at the *economic* level, between the traditional aristocratic families with their regional power bases and the commercial classes that pioneered the expansion of Sasanian trade to the north and east. Sasanian monopoly of the flow of silk from eastern sources implies a class of merchants that was both well resourced and extremely

[143] J. Haldon, *The State and the Tributary Mode of Production* (London, 1993).

[144] O. Bruand, *Voyageurs et marchandises aux temps carolingiens: Les réseaux de communication entre Loire et Meuse aux VIIIe et IXe siècles* (Brussels, 2002), esp. pp. 31 ff.

[145] M. Weidemann, 'Spätantike Traditionen in der Wirtschaftsführung frühmittelalterlicher Grundherrschaften', in *Von der Spätantike zum Frühen Mittelalter*, ed. T. Kölzer *et al.* (Ostfildern, 2009), pp. 287–317. Note Wickham's quite proper characterisation of the Merovingian economy as 'pre-manorial', C. Wickham, 'Rethinking the Structure of the Early Medieval Economy', in *The Long Morning of Medieval Europe: New Directions in Early Medieval Studies*, ed. J. R. Davis *et al.* (Aldershot, 2008), pp. 19–31, at 20.

[146] S. Lebecq, *Les origines franques (Ve–IXe siècle)* (Paris, 1990), pp. 140–1.

well organised. A striking example of these groups is the Nestorian merchant Gabriel son of Čahārboxt, who seems to have travelled to Mylapore (in what is today Chennai) some time in the second quarter of the seventh century, boarding ship, almost certainly, at Rev-Ardashir in Arrajān.[147]

Some concluding remarks, finally, about various arguments in Chapters 2, 5 and 9 in particular, especially as two of these have been highlighted in this introductory chapter. The most contentious part of Chapter 5 will remain my metrological reinterpretation of the so-called 'minus carats system', a form in which the money markets in Egypt and elsewhere regulated payments in gold coinage to allow for differences in local weight standards.[148] In *Du village à l'Empire* Zuckerman sticks fast to the conventional view that is attacked in Chapter 5, seeing expressions of this form, which refer to a weight standard, as involving an actual *deduction of value*. He dismisses my argument as 'extravagant',[149] as if to suggest that it is absurd to think that the expressions ζυγόν and σταθμός that occur in the context of monetary payments might have anything to do with the weights used for establishing the value of those payments and not be what they are for him (and other scholars before him), viz. code for an artificially complicated system of accounting that was supposed to enforce a 'surcharge' on payments in gold coin (and not, for whatever reason, on the base-metal currency as well). If the 'minus carats' system really did embody deductions of value and 'compensation for lack of weight' was at the origin of Aphrodito's alleged 2 carat charge,[150] then what Zuckerman would have to explain is why the *rate* of compensation would vary so dramatically between different localities. Why would the government be slapping a 'surcharge' on the Fayyum that exceeded 7 carats (!) but one of only 2 carats in Aphrodito? This makes no sense at all and shows how a whole tradition of scholarship in this field seems to lack even a rudimentary grasp of how markets work. Zuckerman

147 G. Gropp, 'Christian Maritime Trade of Sasanian Age in the Persian Gulf', in *Golf-Archäologie: Mesopotamien, Iran, Kuwait, Bahrain, Vereinigte Arabische Emirate und Oman*, ed. K. Schippmann *et al.* (Buch am Erlbach, 1991), pp. 83–8.

148 Local weights: e.g. A. Kushnir-Stein, 'Two Inscribed Weights from Banias', *Israel Exploration Journal* 45 (1995), 48–51, τὸ τρίτον τῆς λίτρης ἐντοπίας.

149 C. Zuckerman, *Du village à l'Empire: Autour du Registre fiscal d'Aphroditô (525/526)* (Paris, 2004), p. 78.

150 Zuckerman, *Du village à l'Empire*, p. 68 ('la compensation pour le manque de poids est à l'origine de la déduction', after he has just told us 'la soustraction de plusieurs carats sur chaque solidus encaissé ne peut pas être expliquée par le manque de poids', p. 67), cf. Keenan's clear summary of Zuckerman's argument in R. S. Bagnall, J. G. Keenan and L. S. B. MacCoull, *A Sixth-Century Tax Register from the Hermopolite Nome* (Durham, NC, 2011), p. 29, and in his review in *Bulletin of the American Society of Papyrologists* 42 (2005), 285–97, esp. p. 289: 'an advance, safe-side surcharge on payments in gold coins *in case they turned out to be underweight*'. The editors of the tax register rely too heavily on Zuckerman and ignore Hahn's more credible reconstruction of follis weights and exchange rates. After all, if the follis was worth 100 talents in money of account (as they surmise), then a carat worth 900 talents (*Sixth Century Tax Register*, p. 30) presupposes an exchange rate of 216 folles to the solidus (Hahn's rate), *not* 240 (Zuckerman's).

himself refused to engage with any of the evidence cited by me in the paper republished here as Chapter 5. I cite three papyri from *Sammelbuch* (*SB* 9772, 9280 and 9459) in all of which payments described as '*x* solidi minus *y* carats' are redescribed a few lines later as '*x* solidi'. To those three examples we can now add *P. Mich.inv.* 6642 (639), a lease where 4 solidi less 23 carats are redescribed as 'the same 4 solidi' with no reference to any missing carats, a fact that seems to have baffled its editor.[151] Metrology was fundamental to the monetary regimes of antiquity and it is staggering that scholars should be so dismissive of the subject, not least beause we have abundant evidence, both in the papyri and outside them, that weight standards varied between localities even down to the level of individual villages.[152] As Michael Bates points out, 'the monetary value of a payment was determined by its total weight'; 'since the monetary value of each coin was proportionate to its weight, the easiest way to make payments was by weighing the coins in bulk, basing the value of the payment on the total weight of the coins, not their number'.[153] But it follows that since payments were only transacted by weight, there had to be a precise indication of which weights were used in a given transaction. The term *parallelismos* was used to describe the process of adjustment between local weight standards. For example, the Ptolemaic *uncia* of *c.*439 grains (28.447 g)[154] would have made a full-weight solidus equal to 22.98 carats, which is why the 'Alexandrian' solidus is consistently described, in the Byzantine papyri, as 'of 23 carats'.[155] So too in Gaza where the same standard (23 carats) prevailed.

151 P. J. Sijpesteijn, 'Two Byzantine Papyri from the Collection at the University of Michigan', *Zeitschrift für Papyrologie und Epigraphik* 100 (1994), 275–82, at pp. 278–9; now *SB* XXII 15729. (Nick Gonis tells me that Sijpesteijn's reading of lines 22–23 is far from certain.) The assumption that actual values are being deducted when weight standards are used leads to repeated puzzlement among papyrologists, e.g. N. Kruit and K. A. Worp, *Tyche* 18 (2003), 52, note to l. 13, wondering why the contract says '1¼ solidi less 7¾ carats' when the scribe could just have said '20¼ carats'!

152 E.g. *P. L. Bat.* 25.18 (487/8) which describes the standard (*stathmos*) of the Hermopolite village of Pois as 'less 2½ carats'.

153 M. L. Bates, 'The Function of Fātimid and Ayyūbid Glass Weights', *Journal of the Economic and Social History of the Orient* 24 (1981), 63–92, at p. 76; Bates, 'Coins and Money in the Arabic Papyri', *Documents de l'Islam médiéval: Nouvelles perspectives de recherche*, ed. Y. Rāġib (Cairo, 1991), pp. 43–64, at 60.

154 W. M. Flinders Petrie, 'Glass Weights', *Numismatic Chronicle* 18, 4th ser. (1918), 111–16, at p. 114, esp. 'It is clear that the Alexandrian system produced a modified uncia'. Cf. G. C. Miles, 'On the Varieties and Accuracy of Eighth-Century Arab Coin Weights', in *L. A. Mayer Memorial Volume (1895–1959)*, ed. M. Avi-Yonah *et al.* (Jerusalem, 1964) pp. 78–87, at 84: 'The weight of the Egyptian *kharrūbah* or carob seed has generally been calculated to be approximately 0.195 or 0.196 grams ... I have now reweighed these seeds with much more accurate equipment and have arrived at a figure of 0.1957 grams.'

155 The reference to (full-weight) solidi described as 'each of 18 carats of Alexandria' (*P. Oxy.* 4930.13ff., dated 614) must refer to the Alexandrian *litra* of 363.83 grams, cf. M. Lang, 'A Roman Bronze Weight from Egypt', *American Numismatic Society Museum Notes* 7 (1957), 91–3.

Chapter 2 discusses the work of Mickwitz to try and reintegrate it into a modernist tradition against Finley's claim that the Finnish scholar was a harbinger of the sort of positions Finley himself came to advocate. Mickwitz contested the orthodoxy about the late empire as a sort of nebulous transition to the natural economy supposedly characteristic of the Middle Ages, citing Alfons Dopsch's work in medieval history, which he even described as 'epoch making', and noting that Dopsch had himself rejected a similar characterisation for late antiquity.[156] He was clearly deeply influenced by Dopsch, but so too was Pirenne, in the opposite sense that the latter's Carolingian pessimism was a reassertion of orthodoxy against the Austrian medievalist. Today, almost a century after Dopsch started laying into the isolationist dogmas of Weber, Sombart and others, one can scarcely be in two minds about which direction the historiogaphy has taken and where the balance lies today. Mickwitz also believed that there was no essential difference between ancient and medieval economic history.[157] This postulate, of an essential continuity between them, one that minimises any qualitative rupture between these periods of history, is entirely jettisoned by McCormick in *Origins of the European Economy*. At one point McCormick writes, 'Even if he [Pirenne] vastly underestimated the changes which had affected the Mediterranean economy of Gaul in the centuries preceding the Merovingians … Pirenne was right in focusing scholarly attention on *how different the economic age of the Carolingians was from that of late antiquity*.'[158] This strikes me as an odd way of saying that, like McCormick, Pirenne subscribed to a radical discontinuity between the two epochs, *given that* the signs are completely reversed between their respective arguments about those periods.[159] A final point: in many ways the heart of Chapter 2 is Mickwitz's fascination with business organisation and practices. The point worth making here is that *implicit* both in his discussion of the nature and evolution of the guilds and in a great deal of Roman economic history, not least the work of archaeologists who deal with ceramic assemblages, is the notion that in the strictly commercial sectors of the economy a conscious process of competition was at work. Industrial complexes like kiln sites and

[156] G. Mickwitz, *Geld und Wirtschaft im römischen Reich des vierten Jahrhunderts n. Chr.* (Helsinki, 1932), pp. 3–4.

[157] Notably, G. Mickwitz, 'Zum Problem der Betriebsführung in der antiken Wirtschaft', *Vierteljahrschrift für Sozial- und Wirtschaftsgeschichte* 32 (1939), 1–25, esp. pp. 1–2, 25.

[158] McCormick, *Origins*, p. 119.

[159] For Pirenne it was the eighth century that was the absolute low point, 'the state of economic regression' (H. Pirenne, *Mohammed and Charlemagne* (London, 1939), p. 246), while the Merovingians retained much of the *vitality* of the late antique world.

fish factories, port cities in proximity to one another like Narbonne and Arles, and even entire regions *competed* to retain, expand or conquer markets. The *garum* of Baetica disappeared from Mediterranean markets in the third century thanks to the competition of Lusitania.[160] If much of the late antique prosperity of the Levant was export driven,[161] the initial *breakthrough* occurred, as Paul Reynolds suggests, because 'major urban markets in the West' had 'temporarily lost their North African supply' around the second quarter of the fifth century.[162] Sasanian merchants consciously kept their Byzantine competitors at bay by buying up whole cargoes of Chinese silk in South Indian markets,[163] and in the better documented world of the Geniza, business houses like the Majjānīs, Stillman tells us, were in 'strong competition with other Tunisian business houses'.[164] This is a theme that runs through several chapters of this book, though none of them discusses it in an explicit way. The crucial point that deserves to be made is that unlike the nineteenth and twentieth centuries, this was a competition *between merchants more than producers.*

Chapter 9, finally. This and the final chapter begin to move beyond late antiquity, but without any sense of a sharp rupture. Ruling-class responses to the wave of invasions that spread across the Near East in the second quarter of the seventh century have hardly ever been documented, much less discussed, but what is so striking about them is their diversity. Flight and capitulation were certainly more widespread than any determined resistance, which may well be part of the explanation for the extreme rapidity of the Arab conquests. The sole exception to this pattern was the decimation of the Sasanian aristocracy in a series of major confrontations that ended abruptly in 642. The report in some Arabic authors that the vast sums of money paid in 647 to buy off the Arab advance into North Africa were largely funded by the export of olive oil to Byzantine markets speaks volumes for the continuing economic resilience of the seventh century.[165] North Africa at least still had active links across all sectors of the Mediterranean. However, the main argument in these pages is that there

[160] Étienne, Makaroun and Mayet, *Un grand complexe industriel à Tróia*, p. 165.
[161] See Chapter 4, this volume.
[162] P. Reynolds, 'Hispania in the Late Roman Mediterranean: Ceramics and Trade', in *Hispania in Late Antiquity: Current Perspectives*, ed. K. Bowes *et al.* (Leiden and Boston, 2005), pp. 369–486, esp. 438.
[163] See Chapters 6 and 10, esp. p. 131.
[164] N. A. Stillman, 'The Eleventh Century Merchant House of Ibn ʿAwkal (A Geniza Study)', *Journal of the Economic and Social History of the Orient* 16 (1973), 15–88, at p. 26.
[165] See E. Lévi-Provençal, 'Un nouveau récit de la conquête de l'Afrique du Nord par les Arabes', *Arabica* 1 (1954), 17–49, at p. 37.

was no break in the monetary economy of the Near East across the political watersheds of the seventh century and that it was this continued resilience that formed the true basis of Umayyad prosperity. This particular sense of the continuity between the Byzantine and Umayyad periods of the Near Eastern economy is strongest in the work of Alan Walmsley.[166] Both he and Jodi Magness have noted the absence of any archaeological evidence for widespread destruction during the successive conquests of the early seventh century.[167] Not cited in the chapter is a short but remarkable paper by Rebecca Foote that argued that Umayyad-period urban planning retained an earlier orthogonal tradition from the Roman period and sought to show that 'industrial productivity was a major aspect of urban activity' at sites like Baysan and Jarash.[168] The 'acquisitive aristocracy' of the Umayyad period that is foregrounded in that chapter, incarnated in elite figures like Maslama b. ʿAbd al-Malik and Khālid al-Qasrī, was, it is suggested, the perpetuation of a late antique tradition that was especially strong in the eastern provinces of the former Roman empire where there had been widespread aristocratic ownership of workshops and other industrial and commercial establishments. Maslama, according to a tradition reported by al-Madāʾinī, had textile factories (*maṣāniʿ*) constructed for his father ʿAbd al-Malik.[169] The ninth-century ʿAbbasid boom was in the end as much a product of these traditions as of the more immediate political and economic conjunctures that led to new investments in agricultural redevelopment and to expanding international trade.[170]

166 Walmsley, *Early Islamic Syria*, pp. 37ff.

167 J. Magness, *The Archaeology of the Early Islamic Settlement in Palestine* (Winona Lake, 2003), esp. p. 215.

168 R. Foote, 'Commerce, Industrial Expansion, and Orthogonal Planning: Mutually Compatible Terms in Settlements of Bilad al-Sham during the Umayyad Period', *Mediterranean Archaeology* 13 (2000), 25–38.

169 Yāqūt, *Muʿjam al-buldān*, ed. F. Wüstenfeld, *Jacut's geographisches Wörterbuch* (Leipzig, 1866–73), vol. 1, p. 649, cf. R. B. Serjeant, *Islamic Textiles* (Beirut, 1972), p. 36. His brother Hishām's 'great interest in business affairs' has recently been highlighted by E. Khamis, 'Two Wall Mosaic Inscriptions from the Umayyad Market Place in Bet Shean/Baysān', *Bulletin of the School of Oriental and African Studies* 64 (2001), 159–76, esp. pp. 175–6.

170 Cf. Wickham, *Inheritance of Rome*, pp. 360–2 (ninth-century boom). Already by the eighth century Iraq had a sophisticated system of commercial law, cf. B. Johansen, 'Le contrat *salam*: Droit et formation du capital dans l'Empire abbasside (XIe–XIIe siècle)', *Annales HSS* 61 (2006), 863–99.

PART I

Mapping the late antique economy

CHAPTER 2

Mickwitz's modernism
The writings of 1932–6

Readers of *The Ancient Economy* will recall that Moses Finley ascribed considerable importance to two papers that Mickwitz published in the late 1930s, dealing with the general issue of economic rationalism in antiquity.[1] Since then an impression has been created, which we mainly owe to Finley, that Mickwitz's essays arguing the absence of economic rationalism in antiquity were a powerful, self-consciously conceived argument in favour of the kind of positions that Finley himself came to endorse, and that Mickwitz can therefore be said, at the very least, to foreshadow a form of minimalism. This view, as implicit as it is widespread, radically distorts the style of Mickwitz's historiography, whose most obvious unifying characteristic was the sense of practising an essentially modern discipline, of *Wirtschaftsgeschichte* as irreducibly linked to the contributions of modern economic science and impossible without the concepts drawn from there. Later in this chapter, I shall deal with the middle period work that substantiates this in a fairly direct way, namely, Mickwitz's preliminary discussions of the 'problem of continuity', of the sense in which early capitalism built on legacies handed down, in an immediate or mediated form, from antiquity, and his superb monograph on the economic significance of the guilds. Finally, in the concluding section I shall stand back from Mickwitz and return to the issue of 'ancient capitalism', justifying this at least by reference to the scarcely noticed footnote where readers were told that he would at some stage deal with the issue of 'ancient capitalism' in a separate study. It is of course possible that the paper Mickwitz was referring to was in fact the one he published in the *Vierteljahrschrift für Sozial- und Wirtschaftsgeschichte* in 1939, but just as possible that he had a more substantial study in mind which he never completed.

[1] M. I. Finley, *The Ancient Economy* (London, 1975), pp. 110 f. with n. 43 (at 201), 116 with n. 57 (at 203).

Geld und Wirtschaft was a watershed in the historiography of the later Roman empire and was extremely favourably reviewed when it appeared. Marc Bloch called the book an 'excellent study' that would put Mickwitz into the top rank of economic historians working on antiquity. Yet despite the series of rave reviews, it took almost two decades for the full impact of Mickwitz's work to be assimilated into contemporary historiography. When Mazzarino published *Stilicone* in 1942, it was, as Giardina has reminded us,[2] still largely the influence of Rostovtzeff that helped to frame the 'problem' of the late empire.[3] But by 1951, Mazzarino had returned to Mickwitz and absorbed the full significance of his critique. The great political conflict of the third century, as Rostovtzeff had conceived this, now seemed a less natural framework for the reconstruction of the fourth than Mickwitz's demonstration of its monetary vitality and the related argument that much of the social and economic history of the new period was driven by a conflict between the bureaucracy and the landed classes. Mickwitz, it is well known, argued that conflicts over the form of payment (of both taxes and salaries) were largely shaped by the experience of inflation. The uncertainty caused by repeated bouts of inflation in the third and early fourth centuries inclined landowners to payments in money and government employees to salaries in kind. This was not an obvious interpretation of the written sources or the legal texts, and one presumes that Mickwitz's thinking was largely influenced by the example of Sweden. Mazzarino stood Mickwitz's essential thesis on its head, arguing that it was not the taxpayers but the bureaucracy that stood behind the movement for *adaeratio*. This was a crucial inversion. By linking the state to the forces of monetary expansion in this way Mazzarino had opened the way to a more nuanced vision of late antiquity, one which *absorbed* Mickwitz's 'optimistic' assessment (the term is Mazzarino's)[4] into a more complex historiography of the late empire that saw Constantine as a *revolutionary* and referred repeatedly to his monetary innovations as a monetary *revolution* with social consequences every bit as profound as the acceptance of Christianity.[5] This huge leap in the paradigm of late

[2] A. Giardina, 'Mazzarino e Rostovtzeff', in *Rostovtzeff e l'Italia*, ed. A. Marcone (Naples, 1999), pp. 115–29.

[3] S. Mazzarino, *Stilicone: La crisi imperiale dopo Teodosio*, new edn (Milan, 1990), p. 238, calling Rostovtzeff's great book 'the most recent and most penetrating study' (*l'indagine più recente e più profonda)* of the political crisis of the third century.

[4] S. Mazzarino, *Aspetti sociali del quarto secolo* (Rome, 1951), p. 24 ('un giudizio "ottimistico" sullo "stile" del basso impero'), p. 30 ('L'"ottimismo" di Mickwitz'); pp. 21 and 26 respectively of the new edition by E. Lo Cascio (Milan, 2002).

[5] E.g. Mazzarino, *Aspetti sociali*, pp. 109 (= p. 91), 131f. (= 110), 165 (= 137); Mazzarino, *L'impero romano*, 4th edn (Bari, 1990), vol. 2, pp. 666, 694; Mazzarino, 'Sull'epigrafe dioclezianea di Afrodisiade

antiquity which led from the 1960s into an absolute efflorescence of the subject was thus impossible without the 'negative' moment that absorbed and integrated Mickwitz's book into a more complex and creative vision of late antiquity than Mickwitz himself had.[6]

In reversing Mickwitz's hypothesis, Mazzarino had also undermined the least satisfying part of the argument in *Geld und Wirtschaft*, namely, its dualism. As Bloch remarked in one of the more perceptive reviews of the book, if the bureaucracy was so keen on payments in kind, how do we explain the fact that the more powerful landowners who were generally part of the same administration failed to show similar enthusiasm for such payments in their private transactions?[7] Mickwitz's dualism between a private economy based on a high level of monetary activity and a public finance system based on natural economy was almost certainly due to the influence of Heckscher and, through Heckscher, of Dopsch, for both of them rejected the evolutionist dogma that money economy and natural economy were chronological stages that succeeded each other in some sequence, arguing that every economy comprised elements of both. Dopsch was an important predecessor in several ways. He never accepted the theory of a reversion to natural economy in the third century which then supposedly dominated the whole subsequent epoch till well into the Middle Ages.[8] He also rejected the isolationism of Weber and Sombart, the idea that late Roman estates were structured on the model of a 'closed household economy'.[9] Weber's most forceful statement of this

"Bicharactam": Per l'interpretazione romana delle misure "inflattive"', in *Scritti sul mondo antico in memoria di Fulvio Grosso*, ed. L. Gasperini (Rome, 1981), pp. 333–70, at 368–9; Mazzarino, 'L'"erà costantiniana" e la "prospettiva storica" di Gregorio Magno', in *La società del Basso Impero: Guida storica e critica*, ed. D. Vera (Bari, 1983), pp. 116–37, at 129, and his description of Constantine as 'the greatest revolutionary of the imperial period' in *La fine del mondo antico* (Milan, 1959), p. 179.

6 The more thoroughgoing reassessment began with Peter Brown and was strikingly foreshadowed in his review of Jones, *The Later Roman Empire*, in *Economic History Review*, 2nd ser., 20 (1967), 327–43; repr. in P. Brown, *Religion and Society in the Age of Saint Augustine* (London, 1972), pp. 46–73.

7 M. Bloch, *Le Moyen Age*, 3rd ser., 7 (1936), 208–11, at p. 211: 'Enfin une question ne peut guère manquer de venir à l'esprit: à une époque où les fonctionnaires étaient si empressés, nous dit-on, à se faire payer en nature, comment expliquer que, dans les rapports de droit privé, un pareil souci n'ait pas été ressenti par quiconque se trouvait en mesure de dicter ses conditions à des personnages économiquement ou socialement plus faibles; que notamment, il ait manqué à inspirer les actes de ces grands propriétaires, dont beaucoup étaient, en même temps, à la tête des principales administrations? Je ne me charge pas de résoudre la difficulté.'

8 A. Dopsch, 'Frühmittelalterliche und spätantike Wirtschaft', in *Verfassungs- und Wirtschaftsgeschichte des Mittelalters: Gesammelte Aufsätze von Alfons Dopsch*, ed. E. Patzelt, 2 vols (Vienna, 1928; repr. Aalen, 1968), vol. I, pp. 219–34, a superb essay; so too in Dopsch, *Naturalwirtschaft und Geldwirtschaft in der Weltgeschichte* (Vienna, 1930), pp. 21, 244–5.

9 A. Dopsch, *Wirtschaftliche und Soziale Grundlagen der Europäischen Kulturentwicklung aus der Zeit von Caesar bis auf Karl den Grossen* (Vienna, 1924) vol. II, p. 408; also, *The Economic and Social Foundations of European Civilization* (New York, 1969), pp. 328–9, and Dopsch, *Naturalwirtschaft und Geldwirtschaft*, p. 83.

view was of course the Freiburg lecture of 1896.[10] It may be worth noting that the Freiburg lecture is never cited anywhere in Mickwitz's work on antiquity, whereas there are repeated references to Dopsch. In *The Economic and Social Foundations of European Civilization* Dopsch had developed a powerful rebuttal of 'the whole theory of the closed household economy and the "autarchy" of the great estate of the Middle Ages', which, he wrote, 'is clearly based on a very shaky foundation'.[11] This, the arguments of a medievalist, became a central perspective of Mickwitz's own book. Thus the first sense in which we should think of Mickwitz as a modernist is simply that in the great debate or series of debates that dominated German historiography from the 1890s down into the 1930s, when the *geschlossene Hauswirtschaft* was surreptitiously resurrected in Otto Brunner's notion of *das ganze Haus*, but acknowledged to be dead in its primeval form, Mickwitz clearly aligned himself with the camp that was decisively opposed to Bücher's theories. Indeed, the critique of Bücher plays a major role in *Geld und Wirtschaft*, where it spans the whole of chapter 5. Mickwitz saw himself demolishing an orthodoxy – about late antique economic relationships, as he put it – rooted in Bücher's ideas,[12] and there is one fascinating passage in this chapter which gives us a clue to how he positioned himself in the debate. In this he writes, 'It is hard to find sources that actually confirm the theory of the *Oikenwirtschaft* and this is not at all surprising. In other words, Rodbertus' theory was based much less on the actual sources than on an abstract deduction from Book One of Aristotle's *Politics* ... Rodbertus' method was to a great degree constructed on abstractions and logical deductions, and this is generally true of the economists.'[13] German historiography *c.*1930 was dominated by a deep division between the theoretical and purely empirical approaches to economic history. It was, as Stefan Weiß has said in a brilliant recent paper, a terrain studied from two

[10] M. Weber, 'Die sozialen Gründe des Untergangs der antiken Kultur', orig. 1896, repr. in *Gesammelte Aufsätze zur Sozial- und Wirtschaftsgeschichte* (Tübingen, 1924), pp. 289–31; see L. Capogrossi Colognesi, *Economie antiche e capitalismo moderno: La sfida di Max Weber* (Rome, 1990), p. 118, calling this Weber's most 'primitivist' work. R. Marra, *Capitalismo e anticapitalismo in Max Weber: Storia di Roma e sociologia del diritto nella genesi dell'opera weberiana* (Bologna, 2002), pp. 271ff. suggests that it was Meyer's modernist reading of *Die römische Agrargeschichte* that shaped Weber's primitivism in the Freiburg lecture.

[11] Dopsch, *Grundlagen*, p. 405 ('Die ganze Theorie von der geschlossenen Hauswirtschaft der großen Grundherrschaften des Frühmittelalters, ihre Autarkie beruht ... auf sehr schwankendem Boden'), cf. Dopsch, *Economic and Social Foundations*, p. 328.

[12] G. Mickwitz, *Geld und Wirtschaft im römischen Reich des vierten Jahrhunderts n. Chr.* (Helsinki, 1932; repr. Amsterdam 1965), pp. 147–9, 'basiert die herrschende Anschauung über die wirtschaftlichen Verhältnisse der Spätantike auf den Arbeiten Karl Büchers' (the first sentence of ch. 5); p. 162, 'Von der geschlossenen Hauswirtschaft finden wir keine Spur' (about the ecclesiastical sources).

[13] Mickwitz, *Geld und Wirtschaft*, p. 150f.

different directions – 'einer sozialwissenschaftlichen und einer historischen' – and the dominant position on the eve of the *Machtergreifung* was clearly held by the *Sozialwissenschaftler*.[14] Thus Mickwitz's disparaging reference to the *Nationalökonomen* may seem like tacit support for the professional historians who saw themselves shunning theory. But in fact Mickwitz was, like Otto Hintze, one of the few historians who sought to position themselves differently, identifying with neither and defending the need for *both* theory as well as detailed historical research. This ability to transcend the self-diremption of 'economic history' in a new and more powerful synthesis is what gives all of Mickwitz's historical writings such a mesmerising quality.

Mickwitz's middle period work consists chiefly of the superb monograph on the economic significance of the guilds and two fascinating essays on the Byzantine 'influence' in the origins of early capitalism – all of these published in 1936. These writings are already a clear demonstration of Mickwitz's fascination with business organisation and practices, and his attempt to break down the sense of a sharp division, a series of ruptures, in the movement and nature of economic history. Indeed, the essay on 'Economic Rationalism in Graeco-Roman Agriculture' which is generally regarded as a prescient vindication of the kind of positions later identified with Finley – and which of course Finley used – ends with an assertion of the very opposite, namely, the claim that 'it is not impossible to bring ancient and modern economic history into a common system'.[15] Mickwitz saw *Wirtschaftsgeschichte* as a form of universal history, deploying a conceptual apparatus or a set of concepts (a 'common system') that was applicable *across* periods, concepts determined by theory or supplied from economic science, and not drawn from the individual characteristics of each period. The rationalism of this approach could not be further removed from the sort of plea that Finley would make roughly ten years later for a study of the 'ancient economy' grounded in immanent categories, or the reconstruction of economic history as *Geisteswissenschaft*. At any rate, one implication of Mickwitz's view of economic history was his reliance on some of the most advanced work that contemporaries were doing either in modern economic theory or late medieval/early modern history. Mickwitz clearly admired Jacob Strieder's path-breaking study of the origins of capitalism, the second edition of which had been published in 1935, and attended the seminar in Munich conducted by his pupil

14 S. Weiß, 'Otto Brunner und das Ganze Haus, oder Die zwei Arten der Wirtschaftsgeschichte', *Historische Zeitschrift* 273 (2001), 335–69, at p. 348.

15 G. Mickwitz, 'Economic Rationalism in Graeco-Roman Agriculture', *English Historical Review* 52 (208) (1937), 577–89, at p. 589.

Clemens Bauer.[16] Like Heckscher, Strieder was on the editorial board of the *Journal of Economic and Business History*, a mouthpiece of the more modernist economic historians active in the early thirties. The conception of the economic behaviour of the guilds as essentially determined by price fixing between competing suppliers/buyers, i.e. anti-competitive behaviour, was drawn from Robert Liefmann's study of the cartels. Indeed, Mickwitz's definition of the guild was modelled on Liefmann's definition of the cartel. In *Cartels, Concerns and Trusts* Liefmann defined cartels as associations of entrepreneurs formed with the special aim of establishing monopolisation or domination of the market.[17] Mickwitz transposed this definition to the guilds but suggested that Liefmann's cartels were simply one kind or example of a more expansive category of monopolistic associations which could all, loosely, be described as 'cartels'. The modernism of this conception is evident from Liefmann's suggestion that 'cartels, combines and trusts and all that they represent may be regarded as the high point of "modern capitalism"', and his statement that 'The fundamental cause of the formation of cartels lies in the growth of large-scale enterprise … the large-scale plant … has to make sure of keeping its machines going all the time.'[18] In other words, a formation peculiar to the most advanced sectors of capitalist industry in the twentieth century (American oil, German chemicals[19] and steel) was used as the framework for understanding the economic behaviour of the vast range of associations of traders and merchants found in both the medieval and ancient world.

For Mickwitz the guilds were essentially private organisations of a voluntary nature,[20] that is, set up on the initiative of the artisans and merchants themselves and often denounced or regarded with suspicion by the authorities, the way unions were in the nineteenth century.[21] They were economic organisations, primarily,[22] that strove to limit competition

[16] J. Strieder, *Zur Genesis des modernen Kapitalismus: Forschungen zur Entstehung der großen bürgerlichen Kapitalvermögen am Ausgange des Mittelalters und zu Beginn der Neuzeit, zunächst in Augsburg*, 2nd expanded edn (Munich, 1935).

[17] R. Liefmann, *Cartels, Concerns and Trusts* (London, 1932), pp. 4, 7.

[18] Liefmann, *Cartels*, pp. 5, 19.

[19] F. C. Steckel, 'Cartelization of the German Chemical Industry, 1918–1925', *Journal of European Economic History* 19(2) (1990), 329–51.

[20] G. Mickwitz, *Die Kartellfunktionen der Zünfte und ihre Bedeutung bei der Entstehung des Zunftwesens: Eine Studie in spätantiker und mittelalterlicher Wirtschaftsgeschichte* (Helsinki, 1936), p. 33.

[21] Mickwitz, *Kartellfunktionen*, p. 63.

[22] Mickwitz, *Kartellfunktionen*, p. 7, claiming it would be hard to deny that 'die Zünfte … in erster Linie wirtschaftliche Organisationen gewesen sind und deswegen gerade auch vom wirtschaftlichen Standpunkt aus untersucht werden müssen'.

within their respective trades. In short, Mickwitz's model merged three distinct and even conflicting strands of historiography – von Gierke's conception of the guild as a free association, von Below's emphasis on their economic aspects[23] (minus his deeply conservative polemic against von Gierke)[24] and Liefmann's theory of cartels. Of course, the bulk of *Kartellfunktionen* is taken up with a detailed study of the medieval guilds, which Mickwitz believed exemplified each of the criteria just listed. But there are four late antique/early medieval chapters that raise interesting issues. To the question whether we could discern the activity of cartel-like formations in antiquity, Mickwitz's response was complex, and is best understood in terms of a rough chronological layering. About the professional or occupational associations (*collegia*) of the early empire, Mickwitz accepted Waltzing's view that they were not economic organisations. There is no evidence that they set themselves economic goals.[25] Also, they were too heterogeneous in composition to contain the effects of competition and achieve any stable existence as monopolies. So for the early empire medieval-type guild associations were ruled out. The fourth century, the second chronological layer, brought one decisive change. With the government relying on the exaction of goods and services in kind, essential public services were devolved on to corporate-like entities whose transactions with the state were based on a mixture of incentives and compulsion. These organisations, the *corpora*, Mickwitz insisted, were quite distinct from the craft and service associations known as *collegia*, which probably continued to exist in large numbers and were largely unregulated in their own activity. The latter were free, the former were not. Therefore, Mickwitz drew a careful distinction between the *Korporationen* and the *Berufsvereine*.[26] On the other hand, the *corpora* were also quite different from the medieval guilds as Mickwitz understood these, since there was no stipulation that shipowners, for example, could only engage in shipping if they were *corporati*, that is, members of the *corpus naviculariorum*.[27] The absence of a 'closed shop' meant that the *corpora* were not monopolistic

[23] O. G. Oexle, 'Die mittelalterliche Zunft als Forschungsproblem', *Blätter für deutsche Landesgeschichte* 118 (1982), 1–44, at p. 9.

[24] O. G. Oexle, 'Otto von Gierkes "Rechtsgeschichte der deutschen Genossenschaft"', in *Deutsche Geschichtswissenschaft um 1900*, ed. N. Hammerstein (Stuttgart, 1988), pp. 193–217, at 213: 'er [von Below] richtete sich darüber hinaus gegen die liberalen und demokratischen Züge in Gierkes Genossenschaftstheorie, hinter der Below eine "republikanische" Gesinntheit erkannte'.

[25] Mickwitz, *Kartellfunktionen*, p. 168: 'Es fehlt den collegia gerade das, was die Zünfte zu ihrer Machtstellung führte, die wirtschaftlichen Ziele'.

[26] Mickwitz, *Kartellfunktionen*, pp. 174, 177f., 188.

[27] Mickwitz, *Kartellfunktionen*, pp. 174f., 177.

associations, despite the element of corporate personality, and thus totally unlike the medieval guilds. In short, the drive to control competition through cartel-like arrangements was *not* a feature of the fourth century.[28]

The third chronological layer of Mickwitz's analysis continues to deal with late antiquity. The watershed, for Mickwitz, was the fifth century, when a constitution of the emperor Zeno refers explicitly to price cartels (*monopolia*) in a whole range of businesses.[29] *Monopolium exercere* is the term used for operating a price cartel, and the government comes down heavily against it. Thus Mickwitz saw the fifth century bring about a major transformation, a 'complete change in the character of the trade associations', as he put it,[30] towards an economism grounded in the experience *and*, as it turns out, advantages of being forcibly organised. This is a stunning image, for it transforms the element of domination (the compulsion exercised by the late empire) into a mechanism of emancipation. Whatever one thinks of this explanation, it is surely worth pondering the implications for Mickwitz's picture of late antiquity, one that is already more advanced than the dire pessimism that continues to characterise many accounts of late antique social relationships. Even with Marco di Branco's necessary corrections regarding the precise nature and form of the document, the famous Sardis inscription of 459 is a brilliant vindication of Mickwitz's view, suggesting indeed that economic expansion translated into a strong demand for goods and services and the increased bargaining power of a whole range of occupations.[31] At any rate, by the sixth century 'monopolies' had become an established feature of economic life, the government responding this time not with outright bans but with some attempt to *regulate* them.[32] This is a very different image of late antique *dirigisme* to the one that prevailed in Mickwitz's own generation.

The final chapter of *Kartellfunktionen* dealing with the guilds of tenth-century Constantinople known to us from the *Book of the Eparch* adumbrates themes which are more fully and explicitly developed in the two papers of 1936, especially the one published in *Byzantinische*

[28] Mickwitz, *Kartellfunktionen*, pp. 181f.

[29] *Cod. Iust.* 4.59.2 (483), with its fascinating reference to 'illicit agreements' to fix prices: *Iubemus ne quis … monopolium audeat exercere, neve quis illicitis habitis conventionibus coniuraret aut pacisceretur, ut species diversorum corporum negotiationis non minoris, quam inter se statuerint, venumdentur.*

[30] Mickwitz, *Kartellfunktionen*, p. 200.

[31] M. di Branco, 'Lavoro e conflittualità in una città tardo-antica: Una rilettura dell' epigrafe di Sardi *CIG* 3467', *Antiquité Tardive* 8 (2000), 181–208, esp. 190, 192, 193, 198, implying strong demand for labour in the construction industry.

[32] Procop. *HA* 20 (but see *Nov. Iust.* 122 (544), regulating against collusive fixing of prices), and Mickwitz, *Kartellfunktionen*, pp. 202–4.

Zeitschrift. There is by now a huge literature on the internal organisation of the Byzantine silk industry, so Mickwitz's analysis in these writings can be tested against some of these alternative theories. Among the private guilds regulated in the *Book of the Eparch*, the *metaxopratai* or raw silk merchants were clearly the most powerful group. Their monopsony in the purchase of raw silk was well-nigh absolute, thanks to the regulations of the eparch. Regulation 6.10 banned individual members of the guild from acting as fronts or covert agents for the rich and powerful or for the silk manufacturers (*serikarioi*).[33] Regulation 6.12 made pre-emption of raw silk illegal, and 7.4 made it impossible for the yarn producers (*katartarioi*) to buy the raw material except on the invitation of the silk merchants and in partnership (*koinōnia*) with them.[34] Mickwitz concluded, correctly I think, that the regulations reflected the differential economic strength of different groups in the industry and that, for example, the *katartarioi* or yarn twisters who processed the raw silk for resale to the *metaxopratai* were less well placed within this system of regulation.[35] From the regulation forbidding the raw silk merchants from employing workers (*misthētoi*) on contracts exceeding a month (Reg. 6.12), Mickwitz concluded that the *metaxopratai* were entitled to hire *katartarioi* on piece rates and process the raw silk directly.[36] This model places enormous emphasis on hierarchy within the industry, describing the *metaxopratai* as an 'association of entrepreneurs' (*Unternehmerverband* or *corporation d'entrepreneurs*)[37] and the *katartarioi* as a group recruited from the poorer strata of the population and held in subjection to the former.[38] Finally, the *serikarioi* too were a group of entrepreneurs who manufactured woven silks using paid labour.[39] Mickwitz saw them striving to integrate vertically, backward into control over processing and purchase of raw silk and forward into distribution, the domain of the *vestiopratai*.[40] Insofar as the regulations sought to preserve the existing balance of power between the guilds by enforcing a sharp demarcation

[33] J. Koder (ed.), *Das Eparchenbuch Leons des Weisen: Einführung, Edition, Übersetzung und Indices* (Vienna, 1991), p. 98 (6.10).

[34] Koder, *Eparchenbuch*, p. 98 (6.12), p. 102 (7.4).

[35] Mickwitz, *Kartellfunktionen*, p. 212.

[36] G. Mickwitz, 'Die Organisationsformen zweier byzantinischer Gewerbe im x. Jahrhundert', *Byzantinische Zeitschrift* 36 (1936), 63–76, at p. 72.

[37] Mickwitz, 'Organisationsformen', p. 73; G. Mickwitz, 'Un problème d'influence: Byzance et l'économie de l'Occident médiéval', *Annales d'Histoire Économique et Sociale* 8 (1936), 21–8, at p. 25.

[38] Mickwitz, 'Organisationsformen', p. 73 ('Die Katartarier, die ganz darauf angewiesen waren für die Kaufleute gegen Lohn zu arbeiten, müssen arme Leute gewesen sein'), so too in 'Problème', p. 26 ('toute la corporation des catartariens paraît avoir été dans l'étroite dépendance des métaxoprates').

[39] Mickwitz, 'Problème', p. 26.

[40] Mickwitz, 'Organisationsformen', p. 75; 'Problème', pp. 26f.

between businesses, they simply undermined the possibilities of vertical integration and thus destroyed the basis for the emergence of a more integrated and therefore powerful class of capitalists.[41]

The most serious challenge to Mickwitz's description of the industry has come from George Maniatis in a tightly argued paper which, like all his work, is unrelentingly neo-classical in inspiration. Some of Maniatis' arguments against Mickwitz are either weak or unconvincing. The most substantial point he makes against Mickwitz is that the regulations did *not* in fact prevent intra-guild competition. 'The law did not impose price discipline on guild members to thwart intra-guild competition and protect individual members' shares in the total business.'[42] What it did aim to do was 'ensure equal access to commercial opportunities for all members' of a given guild,[43] 'forestall the growth of commercial silk manufacturing outside the guild system'[44] and prevent 'dominance of the market by a few large firms, and weakening or elimination of competitors based on sheer market power – in short, monopolization or lessening of competition'.[45] 'The policy aim was that increased market demand be shared by as many firms as possible and that this demand be channelled through cascaded, close-knit markets at each stage of the production process.'[46] The general drift of this analysis is thus close to Ostrogorsky's view that the chief object of the guild organisation was not to 'serve the interests of the producers and dealers, but rather to facilitate control of economic life by the government in the interests of the state and the consumer'.[47] Mickwitz, on the other hand, had always insisted that the evolution of the guilds reflected a different kind of agency, the needs and initiative of the craftsmen and merchants who founded them.

Mickwitz was fascinated by the general problem of the sense in which Byzantium acted as a repository of late antique forms, transmitting these into the general stream of European culture as this began to emerge in the twelfth and thirteenth centuries.[48] He clearly believed that the rapid advances in banking and maritime trade that occurred then were inconceivable without legacies extending back into antiquity. He accepted the

[41] Mickwitz, 'Organisationsformen', pp. 75f.

[42] G. C. Maniatis, 'Organization, Market Structure and Modus Operandi of the Private Silk Industry in Tenth-century Byzantium', *Dumbarton Oaks Papers* 53 (1999), 263–332, at p. 311.

[43] Maniatis, 'Silk Industry', p. 268. [44] Maniatis, 'Silk Industry', p. 269.

[45] Maniatis, 'Silk Industry', p. 287. [46] Maniatis, 'Silk Industry', p. 298.

[47] G. Ostrogorsky, *History of the Byzantine State*, trans. J. Hussey (Oxford, 1968), p. 254, noting that Mickwitz 'disagrees with this'.

[48] Mickwitz, 'Problème', p. 21.

arguments of Astuti, a young Italian legal historian, that the maritime loan, especially in its transmuted Byzantine form of the *chreokoinōnia*, was the immediate predecessor of the *commenda*, so that a large part of the culture of business partnerships which sustained the expansion of Italian maritime capitalism from the eleventh century was directly descended from antiquity.[49] He also suggested that the revival of banking in the twelfth century was bound up with the 'influence' of Byzantium, that is, the Byzantine ability to preserve and transmit the banking traditions of late antiquity.[50] And he saw the powerful guild organisation of Constantinople in the Macedonian dynasty subsuming the legacy of late antique developments from the later fifth and sixth centuries, and possibly even transmitting these to some of the Italian centres in contact with Byzantium.[51] On the other hand, the organisation of business and that of industry were areas that scholars knew least about. For example, how widespread was the *Verlagssystem* in the ancient economy?[52] And how extensively was it used in the silk industry of the tenth century? Or what kind of internal organisation did the great trading houses of the Roman empire use in pursuit of their commercial activities?[53]

In conclusion, I'd like to take up again the seemingly obsolete and once much vexed question of so-called 'ancient capitalism'. Mickwitz was on the whole careful to avoid the use of the term 'capitalism', because, as he explained, in modern capitalism the striving for profitability presumes the ability to calculate profits in a 'rational' way.[54] He ascribed momentous significance to double-entry bookkeeping, following Sombart's theory that it was indispensable to the rise of capitalism. But his deduction of a general lack of economic rationalism from the absence of double-entry

[49] G. Astuti, *Origini e svolgimento storico della commenda fino al secolo XIII* (Turin, 1933), cf. Mickwitz, 'Problème', pp. 27f. ('dans l'état actuel des documents, on ne peut donner la preuve stricte d'une filiation entre Byzance et l'Occident qu'en matière d'emprunts maritimes'); 'Organisationsformen', p. 70 ('Da die italienischen Städte das byzantinische Seerecht und Seedarlehen übernommen haben, etc.'). So too Lopez, in the late fifties anyway, see R. S. Lopez, 'The Role of Trade in the Economic Readjustment of Byzantium in the Seventh Century', *Dumbarton Oaks Papers* 13 (1959), 67–85, at p. 80 and n. 27, 'I believe ... that Professor Astuti is right in regarding the *chreokoinonia* of the *Nomos Nautikos* and the *Ecloga* as the most important and direct foreign contribution to the origin of the Western *commenda*.'

[50] Mickwitz, 'Organisationsformen', pp. 69–70.

[51] Mickwitz, *Kartellfunktionen*, pp. 207–8, 235 ('Ich habe aber die Möglichkeit aufgezeigt, dass von den antiken Berufsvereinen über die Korporationen von Byzanz zu den abendländischen Zünften *eine Entwicklungslinie gegeben ist*').

[52] Mickwitz, 'Problème', p. 25. [53] Mickwitz, 'Problème', p. 21.

[54] G. Mickwitz, 'Zum Problem der Betriebsführung in der antiken Wirtschaft', *Vierteljahrschrift für Sozial- und Wirtschaftsgeschichte* 32 (1939), 1–25, at p. 25.

seems much less persuasive today.[55] Double-entry was certainly *not* a precondition for the development of capitalism.[56] The vast majority of enterprises used single-entry until well into the nineteenth century, and, as Yamey showed in a famous paper in 1949, most merchants treated double-entry simply as a form of systematic bookkeeping.[57] That is, even when double-entry *was* used, 'There is scant evidence of any attempts at a precise calculation of profits and capital.'[58] In short, Mickwitz's argument is parasitic on a thesis that is now largely untenable. Yet we now know from the presence of some of Finley's papers in the Heichelheim archive that he made Mickwitz's work on economic rationalism the absolute pivot of an argument about the 'ancient economy' as a whole. As he wrote in the draft outline of his projected book on 'Business Practices in the Greek City-States' (1947), 'That the Greeks never progressed to double entry bookkeeping, for example, is a fact of the highest significance not merely for the mechanics of ledgers and journals but equally for the economy as a whole.'[59]

Once we break with the formalism that almost identifies capitalism with the evolution of double-entry, it is easier to go back to the issue and try and reformulate the terms of the problem. When this issue was debated in Italy at the end of the 1920s, Giovanni Sanna argued that Barbagallo had failed to prove 'ch'esso (il mondo antico) fosse già una società capitalistica'.[60] In other words, it was conventional to see the modernists of the period making claims about a characterisation of the workings of the economy, of an overall system, and easy for critics like Salvioli to point to the huge differences between the ancient economy

55 E.g. R. H. Macve, 'Some Glosses on "Greek and Roman Accounting"', in *Crux: Essays in Greek History Presented to G. E. M. de Ste. Croix on his 75th Birthday*, ed. P. A. Cartledge and F. D. Harvey (London, 1985), pp. 233–64; D. Rathbone, *Economic Rationalism and Rural Society in Third-Century A.D. Egypt* (Cambridge, 1991), pp. 331–3.

56 J. R. Edwards, *A History of Financial Accounting* (London, 1989), p. 63.

57 B. S. Yamey, 'Scientific Bookkeeping and the Rise of Capitalism', *Economic History Review*, 2nd ser., 1 (1949), 99–113, at pp. 105, 110.

58 Yamey, 'Scientific Bookkeeping', p. 110.

59 Finley, 'Supplementary statement A', in B. D. Shaw, 'The Early Development of M. I. Finley's Thought: The Heichelheim Dossier', *Athenaeum* 81 (1993), 177–99, at p. 194. Finley's notation for the final chapter reads 'Summary and conclusion: the absence of economic rationalism (Mickwitz)' (p. 192).

60 G. Sanna, 'Intorno all'economia antica e moderna e alla razionalità della storia', *Nuova Rivista Storica* 13(3–4) (1929), 245–54, at p. 246, responding to C. Barbagallo, 'Economia antica e moderna', *Nuova Rivista Storica* 13(1) (1929), 27–44 (part 2 of a longer paper). For the background to this debate, see G. Bandelli, 'Un momento della fortuna di Rostovzev in Italia: Il dibattito su "Economia antica e moderna"', in Marcone, *Rostovtzeff e l'Italia*, pp. 131–59.

and modern capitalism.[61] My feeling is that the way out of this dilemma is to draw a distinction between capitalism in the limited sense of the activity of individual capitalists, which is certainly *well attested throughout antiquity* (defending Mommsen here against Marx), and the more schematic and untenable thesis that ancient society 'was capitalist' or that the economy which was partly shaped by that activity was essentially founded on capital, the way modern economies are.[62] Rostovtzeff himself tended to conflate these positions and sometimes vacillated between them.[63] Within this framework, then, we can speak with perfect equanimity of the predatory and, if you like, 'unproductive' capitalism of the late Republic, as long as we agree this contains a characterisation of the economic activities of particular capitalists or groups of capitalists and not of the economy as a whole. In the late Republic in fact much of Rome's financial system was bound up with the monies invested in Asia.[64] Cicero's description of the *publicani* as *homines honestissimi atque ornatissimi* reflects the respectability of this milieu, against much that has been read into other passages of his work.[65] Cicero's testimony is exceptional, not matched by any written sources from later periods. From these *publicani* and their huge investments in the provinces down to the silk merchants and manufacturers of Macedonian Constantinople, there was surely no period of Republican, imperial or late antique history when *capitalists* were not active in major sectors of the economy or when indeed some of these, or parts of them, were not organised on capitalist lines. In a brilliant and quite unusual paper from 1978, John Drinkwater put together

[61] G. Salvioli, *Il capitalismo antico: Storia dell' economia romana* (Bari, 1929), new edn by A. Giardina (Bari, 1985); e.g. p. 6 (= 7), 'è necessario stabilire se tale sviluppo aveva raggiunto la fase del capitalismo, se le forze motrici della societá romana erano organizzate *su un capitalismo identico al moderno*' (italics mine).

[62] Mommsen's picture of the Republic was influenced by the example of North America where the Southern states were ruled by capitalist interests, e.g. *Römische Geschichte*, 4th edn (Berlin, 1866), vol. III, p. 516. He assumed that *slave* labour could form the basis for (a kind of) capitalist production. It is this assumption that seems to have exasperated Marx (see *Capital Volume One*, trans. B. Fowkes (Harmondsworth, 1976), p. 271, n. 2) – unfairly, since Marx himself would allow for such a possibility, e.g. *Capital Volume Three*, trans. D. Fernbach (Harmondsworth, 1981), p. 940: 'Where the capitalist conception prevails, as on the American plantations, this entire surplus-value is conceived as profit.'

[63] E.g. M. Rostovtzeff, 'Capitalisme et economie nationale dans l'Antiquité', written in 1899, translated in *Pallas* 33 (1987), 19–40; 'The Decay of the Ancient World and its Economic Explanations', *Economic History Review* 2 (1930), 197–214, at pp. 206–8, and M. I. Rostovtzeff, 'The Hellenistic World and its Economic Development', *American Historical Review* 41(2) (1936), 231–52, at p. 250, on which M. Mazza, 'M. I. Rostovtzeff e l'economie antiche', in Marcone, *Rostovtzeff e l'Italia*, pp. 211–56, esp. 246ff.

[64] Cic. *Manil.* 7.19. [65] *Ibid.* 7.17.

a plausible reconstruction of the management and organisation of the Belgian woollen industry in the mid-third century, using the example of the Secundinii, prosperous drapers who celebrated their woollen business on the massive funeral monument south of Trier.[66] He suggested that much of the manufacturing was done by craftsmen working in their own homes, on the model of a capitalistically exploited domestic industry. This is a beautifully Mickwitzian scenario, the full-blown operation, in Roman times, of methods of business organisation that were widely used in the medieval world. Again, in a hugely important and stimulating paper, Andrew Wilson posits the activity of substantial mining companies behind the colossal output of the Spanish mines in the first and second centuries AD.[67] Atmospheric lead pollution levels from Roman-period smelting operations suggest that the mining companies sustained a 'level of activity not paralleled again until the Industrial Revolution'. A fascinating passage in the *Mathesis* of Firmicus Maternus is strong implication of the existence of entrepreneurial families in the Constantinian aristocracy, who appointed agents (*scribae*) to manage a range of financial and commercial enterprises, including banks (*mensae*).[68] In the mid-sixth century, John of Ephesus described the 'great shipowners' of Alexandria as 'the most powerful class in that wealthy city'.[69]

Of course, all of this is sporadic and almost random evidence but, at another level, the whole evolution and sheer pragmatism of Roman commercial law is proof of the existence of such groups. Here the major breakthrough has come with the work of Feliciano Serrao and his school.[70] The governance of liability under Roman law imparted considerable flexibility

[66] J. F. Drinkwater, 'Die Secundinier von Igel und die Woll- und Textilindustrie in Gallica Belgica: Fragen und Hypothesen', *Trierer Zeitschrift* 40–1 (1977 –8), 107–25; see the recent discussion by A. Marcone, 'Tra archeologia e storia economica: Il mausoleo dei *Secundini* a Igel', *Athenaeum* 88 (2000), 485–97.

[67] A. Wilson, 'Machines, Power and the Ancient Economy', *Journal of Roman Studies* 92 (2002), 1–32.

[68] Firmicus, *Math.* 3,10,1 (ed. Monat, Paris, 1994, vol. II, p. 101), *magnorum aut potentium virorum … scribas, rationibus, mensis, apothecis negotiationibusque praepositos*. The date is *c.*334. Like J. Andreau, *Labeo* 42 (1996), 270, I cannot agree with Petrucci's suggestion that this and related passages in the *Mathesis* actually reflect conditions in the first century, A. Petrucci, *'Mensam exercere': Studi sull'impresa finanziaria romana* (Naples, 1991), pp. 46, 51 and 334, arguing this on the grounds that Firmicus copied parts of Manilius' *Astronomica*.

[69] *The Third Part of the Ecclesiastical History of John, Bishop of Ephesus*, trans. R. Payne Smith (Oxford, 1860), p. 69. The reference can be dated to 559/60 from a passage in the 'Chronicle of Zuqnin' (8th cent.), see W. Witakowski, *Pseudo-Dionysius of Tel-Mahre, Chronicle (known also as the Chronicle of Zuqnin), Part III* (Liverpool, 1996), p. 121.

[70] F. Serrao, *Impresa e responsibilità a Roma nell'età commerciale: Forme giuridiche di un'economia-mondo* (Pisa, 1989) brings together some of Serrao's more important essays.

to the way members of the elite could engage in business activities (*negotiationes*). In particular, Di Porto drew attention to forms of indirect agency involving *joint* enterprises with *limited* liability, and to enterprise structures of considerable complexity based on the elements of a coherent legal model.[71] Serrao's modernism is still rooted in conventional assumptions about the late empire, but there is no doubt that the work of this school is path-breaking. It shows the unexhausted potential for reinterrogating existing bodies of material in a spirit thoroughly characteristic of Mickwitz. But the relative modernity of the Roman economy is also beginning to emerge through the publication of new material. A good example is Camodeca's work on the archive of the Sulpicii, which shows, for example, that short-term commercial borrowings were more widespread than we suspected.[72] Against the background of all this new work, Mickwitz's re-evaluation of the economic history of the fourth century is a precocious and remarkable example of the constant *re*interrogation of history which is our only means of making progress in this field.

[71] A. Di Porto, *Impresa collettiva e schiavo 'manager' (II sec. a.C.–II sec. d.C.)* (Milan, 1984); more recently, 'Il diritto commerciale romano: Una "zona d'ombra" nella storiografia romanistica e nelle riflessioni storico-comparative dei commercialisti', in *Nozione formazione e interpretazione del diritto dall'età romana alle esperienze moderne. Ricerche dedicate al Professore Filippo Gallo*, 4 vols (Naples, 1997), vol. III, pp. 413–52.

[72] G. Camodeca, *Tabulae Pompeianae Sulpiciorum (TPSulp.): Edizione critica dell'archivio puteolano dei Sulpicii*, 2 vols (Rome, 1999), with *TPSulp.* 51–3.

CHAPTER 3

State and aristocracy in the economic evolution of the late empire

The chief economic impact of the late Roman state may be identified as the role it played in creating and sustaining the expansion of a powerful monetary economy based on gold. The monetary system of the late empire, as indeed of Byzantium, was a gold monometallism[1] based on a key denomination, the solidus, and a fractional coinage that comprised chiefly tremisses. This denominationally simplified structure worked in the fifth century in the absence of any significant copper coinage, and in the sixth in association with a reformed currency, the follis and its submultiples. However, it is clear that the solidus was the real focus of monetary policy, in the sense that the whole economic and social stability of the regime rested on preserving the purity of this coinage. This policy, implicit till the reign of Valentinian I, was clearly expressed for the very first time in the important monetary reforms of that emperor.[2] The fact that Valentinian I was also the first of the late Roman emperors to reflect and, indeed, consolidate the power of the military elite is obviously significant in this context.[3] The emperor's commitment to gold was symbolic of his commitment to the army, and, in particular, to the decisively important officer corps, and reflects the fact that key sections of the bureaucracy were powerful supporters of monetary economy, the 'social bearers' of – for the fourth century – an entirely new type of monetary and economic regime. Thus to define the crucial impact of the state in terms of its ability to sustain a stable monetary economy (or the system behind it) is to exclude other types of public intervention as candidates for such a role – above all, investments in the economy, that is valorising the resources of the empire – but also to draw attention to the social basis of

[1] So M. Lombard, *Études d'économie médiévale, vol. I: Monnaie et histoire d'Alexandre à Mahomet* (Paris, 1971), p. 138.

[2] M. Amandry *et al.*, 'L'affinage des métaux monnayées au Bas-Empire: Les réformes valentiniennes de 364–368', *Quaderni Ticinesi* 11 (1982), 279–95.

[3] The crucial text is Ammianus 27.9.4.

imperial power and to seeing the state not as an inert (or 'practico-inert') administrative machine (in the tradition of so much late Roman history) but precisely as 'an ensemble of groups'[4] whose interests acquired (or already had) an autonomous social character. The author who expresses this sense of the late Roman state most clearly is Ammianus Marcellinus.[5] His obituaries of Constantius II and Valentinian I leave us in no doubt that Constantius' policy of resisting the aspirations of the military officials (*militares*), and in particular of the commanders called *duces*, in favour of the purely civilian bureaucracy,[6] was finally and permanently abandoned under Valentinian who, in the words of Ammianus, was the 'first of all the emperors to increase the arrogance of the military, to the general detriment of society, with inordinate increases in their gradation and pay' (*dignitates opesque eorum sublimius erigentem*). Thus Valentinian's monetary reform is inseparable from the powers – and pressure – of important groups within the bureaucracy who, exploding the old economic order, had come to identify their interests with gold and were progressively reinterpreting the interests of the empire as a monometallism of gold to the exclusion of: (i) *Naturalwirtschaft*; (ii) a silver-based currency system; and (iii) bimetallism of any form likely to compromise monetary stability.

Thus the perspectives of a Mickwitzian historiography of the late empire are both vindicated and refuted.[7] Mickwitz was right to see the economic evolution of the fourth century as underpinned by a conflict of social forces and to want a history that would discern that conflict in a deeper way. But Mickwitz identified the interests of the bureaucracy – indeed, of the state as a whole – with those of 'natural economy', accepting the dogma that the third century had seen a reversion to payments in kind and that the fiscality of the fourth had not fundamentally modified this trend but in fact, through Diocletian, given it a more systematic and stable expression. The fact is that the Tetrarchic penchant for payments in kind is a myth, as the important *P. Beatty Panopolis* papyri show. The 'disappearance' of gold from the monetary system of the third century had certainly been reversed by the last quarter of that period and there was enough gold in circulation for the higher levels of the bureaucracy to build substantial deposits such as the Arras hoard,[8] and more generally for one

[4] The terminology is borrowed from J.-P. Sartre, *Critique de la raison dialectique, vol. I: Théorie des ensembles pratiques* (Paris, 1960).
[5] See J. Matthews, *The Roman Empire of Ammianus* (London, 1989).
[6] See C. Vogler, *Constance II et l'administration impériale* (Strasbourg, 1979).
[7] G. Mickwitz, *Geld und Wirtschaft im römischen Reich des vierten Jahrhunderts n. Chr.* (Helsinki, 1932).
[8] P. Bastien and C. Metzger, *Le Trésor de Beaurains (dit d'Arras)* (Wetteren, 1977).

numismatist to refer to the 'provision once more of a fairly abundant gold coinage' with reference to Diocletian.[9] Thus the idea that public economy was permanently shaped by the 'crisis' of the third century is untenable, and Mickwitz's peculiar dualism between a private economy geared to a high level of cash transactions and a public sector still rooted in payments in kind has, finally, to be abandoned.[10] Far from pulling in opposite directions, these sectors were dynamically interrelated through mechanisms which we barely understand beyond the simplistic models that impose a 'statist' vision of history and the economy on our perceptions of the late empire. That coinage was a fiscal instrument, as Hendy maintains, may be true,[11] but the economy of the late antique Mediterranean was scarcely the taxation system of that area – except by a huge abstraction – and the assumption that gold circulated for the same reasons for which it entered circulation is a manifest non sequitur.[12]

The economic revival of the late antique period was closely bound up with its monetary history. The idea that the period saw a general impoverishment[13] is just not true. Even the notion of a greater emphasis on the rural aspects of life[14] actually expresses the true fact of an extraordinary flow of capital into the rural sector, not the collapse of urban economy. Of course, Max Weber argued for a structural crisis of the urban sector, the contraction of markets and a 'ruralisation' of the life of the empire.[15] But almost nothing in our actual evidence supports such an idea. The stock of gold currency expanded steadily from the fourth to the seventh centuries, and no sector of late antique society was entirely immune to the grip of the monetary economy. In the thinking of a disillusioned

[9] J. P. C. Kent, 'Gold Coinage in the Later Roman Empire', in *Essays in Roman Coinage Presented to Harold Mattingly*, ed. R. A. G. Carson *et al.* (Oxford, 1956), p. 191.

[10] Cf. S. Mazzarino, *Aspetti sociali del quarto secolo: Ricerche di storia tardo-romana* (Rome 1951) for the first substantial critique of Mickwitz.

[11] M. Hendy, *Studies in the Byzantine Monetary Economy c. 300–1450* (Cambridge 1985), passim.

[12] So also D. M. Metcalf, 'The Mint of Thessalonica in the Early Byzantine Period', in *Villes et peuplement dans l'Illyricum protobyzantin* (Rome, 1984), pp. 111–28, esp. 122.

[13] E.g. M. Rostovtzeff, *The Social and Economic History of the Roman Empire*, 2nd edn (Oxford, 1957), vol. 1, pp. 523–4 : 'The salient trait of the economic life of the late Roman Empire was gradual impoverishment. The poorer the people became, the more primitive grew the economic life of the Empire'; P. Anderson, *Passages from Antiquity to Feudalism* (London, 1974), p. 93: 'Throughout most provinces, urban trade and industry progressively declined: there was a gradual but unmistakeable ruralization of the Empire.'

[14] Rostovtzeff, *Social and Economic History*, vol. 1, p. 506 characterised the late empire as a 'new state based on the peasants and the country'.

[15] The clearest statement of this is in M. Weber, 'Die sozialen Gründe des Untergangs der antiken Kultur', in *Gesammelte Aufsätze zur Sozial- und Wirtschaftsgeschichte* (Tübingen, 1924), pp. 289–311, first published in *Die Wahrheit* 1896.

bureaucrat, the accumulation of vast quantities of gold was the basis of the bureaucratic onslaught of the fourth century, through which a new, 'senatorial' aristocracy was consolidating its position.[16] A fifth-century writer who visited the west saw the wealthier, more traditional, aristocracy of Rome extracting huge revenues in gold.[17] Certainly by the sixth century most ordinary groups of rural labourers were being remunerated in solidi[18] and the circulation of gold was sufficiently common for money changers to be strongly tempted to enforce discounts against older solidi.[19] The Byzantine estates, whose records survive in a fragmentary form, consistently show a 'marked preference for gold'.[20] As Hardy said, 'So far from any tendency to abandon the use of money, the Apion estate seems definitely to have preferred to have its income in cash rather than in kind.'[21] In the seventh century an extensively irrigated medium-sized estate was collecting close to 80% of its income in gold.[22] Ostrogorsky's argument that 'gold issues not only did not diminish in the seventh century, but on the contrary increased significantly'[23] has, of course, been severely criticised,[24] but the fact is that there was a vast amount of gold in circulation in the eastern empire and no sign that the level of circulation declined in the seventh century.[25] By the end of the sixth century the fiscal system was likewise showing a strong tendency to extract the bulk of its revenue in monetary form.

[16] Anon., *De rebus bellicis* 2.1–2 (E. A. Thompson, *A Roman Reformer and Inventor* (Oxford, 1952) pp. 94, 110).

[17] Olympiodorus, fr. 44 (*Fragmenta Historicorum Graecorum*, vol. IV, p. 67).

[18] J. Banaji, *Rural Communities in the Late Empire A.D. 300–700: Monetary and Economic Aspects* (D. Phil. Oxford, 1992), vol. I, p. 89.

[19] E.g. *NVal* XVI (445), cf. Banaji, 'The Circulation of Gold as an Index of Prosperity in the Central and Eastern Mediterranean in Late Antiquity', in *Coin Finds and Coin Use in the Roman World*, ed. C. E. King *et al.* (Berlin, 1996), pp. 41–53.

[20] J. Gascou, 'Les grands domaines, la cité et l'état en Egypte byzantine', *Travaux et Mémoires* 9 (1985), 1–90, at p. 10: 'préférence marquée pour l'or'.

[21] E. R. Hardy, *The Large Estates of Byzantine Egypt* (New York, 1931), p. 100, referring to *P. Oxy*. XVI 1911.209, 1914.5–7.

[22] *P. Bad*. 95 (7c.), from which it is possible to calculate a cash ratio of 77.9%.

[23] G. Ostrogorsky, 'Byzantine Cities in the Early Middle Ages', *Dumbarton Oaks Papers* 13 (1959), 44–66, at p. 51.

[24] Notably by P. Grierson, 'Byzantine Coinage as Source Material', in *Proceedings of the XIIIth* International Congress of Byzantine Stud*ies, Oxford 1966* (London, 1967), pp. 323–4; P. Grierson, *Catalogue of the Byzantine Coins in the Dumbarton Oaks Collection and in the Whittemore Collection*, vol. II : *Phocas to Theodosius III* (Washington, D.C., 1968), pp. 5ff.; P. Grierson, 'Iconografia, circolazione monetaria e tesaurizzazione', in *La cultura bizantina, oggetti e messaggio: Moneta ed economia*, ed. A. Guillou (Rome, 1986), pp. 29–57, at 38–9.

[25] Note the predominance of cash rents in *APEL* II, 77ff., which are leases from the Islamic period; see A. Grohmann, *Arabic Papyri in the Egyptian Library*, vol. I (Cairo, 1936), pp. 29 ff.

In the latter part of Justinian's reign, the Antaeopolite nome paid a total of 10,322 solidi by way of its normal gold assessment.[26] The Antaeopolite was a comparatively small district where one village accounted for as much as 13% of the district's total arable land.[27] In the late sixth century other districts in Middle Egypt were paying money taxes (*chrysika*) to the amount of 20,000 to 25,000 solidi (excluding the commutation of grain shipments, otherwise almost 60,000 solidi!).[28] Again, in *P. Cair. Masp.* 67057, the monies due to the *largitionalia* formed roughly 17% of the total cash intake. If we assume that the *largitionalia* occupied a similar proportion of the Hermopolite's total tax receipts (in money), then *CPR* VII 26 (6c.) shows that the Hermopolite's payments in gold should have been around 60,755 solidi. These are huge sums and the least they imply is that the rural areas from which the bulk of the revenue came must have had access to urban or state markets in which commodities could be sold in bulk for gold.[29] But it seems much more likely that Byzantine fiscality *could* acquire a progressively monetised form because such markets existed than that the dynamic was simply one of 'forced commercialisation'.

The half-monetised fiscality of the fourth century had rested on the precarious base of municipal élites subjected to the double assault of partitioning through inheritance and non-exemption from liturgies.[30] This cumbersome, bureaucratically coercive system emerges clearly in the papyri of the fourth century. But it was destined to be swept away in the great changes which undermined the society and fiscal organisation of the eastern empire. Large and impressive estates like the property of Hyperechius splintered into middle-sized holdings in the early part of the fourth century.[31] The rising landowners of the later fourth century were a formidable group who stemmed directly from various levels of

[26] *P. Cair. Masp.* I 67057.i.3–4, 16–17, ii.32–3, iii.13. The calculation follows A. H. M. Jones in his review of A. C. Johnson and L. C. West, *Byzantine Egypt: Economic Studies*, *Journal of Hellenic Studies* 71 (1951), 271–2, at 271. For the date (*c.*539?) see J. Gascou, 'La table budgétaire d'Antaeopolis (*P. Freer* 08.45 c–d)', in *Hommes et richesses dans l'Empire byzantine, vol. I: IV–VII siècle*, ed. C. Abadie-Reynal *et al.* (Paris 1989), pp. 279–313, at 285–6.

[27] *P. Freer Aphrod.* (*c.*525), 5,200 arouras of arable in Aphrodito, with *P. Cair. Masp.* 167057 for the district figures.

[28] *P. Oxy.* XVI 1909.

[29] P. Spufford, *Money and its Uses in Medieval Europe* (Cambridge 1988), p. 16 notes the decline of these markets in the west in the late sixth century.

[30] On the latter see F. Millar, 'Empire and City, Augustus to Julian: Obligations, Excuses and Status', *Journal of Roman Studies* 73 (1983), 76–96, who emphasises the important social implications of the 'privilege of exemption'.

[31] Banaji, *Rural Communities*, vol. I, p. 146.

the administration, including the army.[32] In his last work Weber argued, 'In the late Roman empire the increasingly important land-owning class of the *possessores* confronted a socially quite distinct stratum of officials, divided into ranks according to the level of benefice-revenues. The same disconnected juxtaposition of landed nobility and patrimonial officialdom can be observed in the early Oriental and the Hellenistic empires.'[33] However, this model is not applicable to the eastern empire, where the dominant landowners of the fifth century were inseparable from the higher echelons of the bureaucracy, and the aristocracy could even be said to be of 'bureaucratic origin'.[34] Of course, large landed proprietors were not equally powerful everywhere and in some sectors, such as the Hauran, rural culture was characterised by an almost exclusive predominance of villages.[35] However, the decisive feature of the fifth to seventh centuries, in the east, is the dominance of a new class which transmitted its properties intact from one generation to the next, avoiding the fragmentation of holdings through inheritance which had drastically undermined the economic strength of the former municipal families,[36] and which, above all, distinguished itself from the previous élite by its close associations with the imperial system. The decisively important changes in fiscal organisation which came about in the course of the fifth century are scarcely comprehensible in abstraction from the rise of this new nobility. What the fifth-century pattern demonstrates is a new, profoundly subtle and infinitely complex set of arrangements between state and aristocracy (or more accurately, between state, aristocracy and church) which neither the traditional model of feudal decentralisation and recalcitrant aristocracies[37] nor

[32] The chief examples have been collected in Banaji, *Rural Communities*, vol. II.

[33] M. Weber, *Economy and Society: An Outline of Interpretive Sociology*, ed. G. Roth and C. Wittich (California, 1978), vol. III, p. 1067.

[34] So R. Rémondon, 'L'Egypte au 5e siècle de notre ère: Les sources papyrologiques et leurs problèmes', in *Atti dell'XI Congresso Internazionale di Papirologia* (Milan, 1966), pp. 135–48, 'C'est vers le milieu du 5e siècle en effet que prend corps la noblesse égyptienne, d'origine bureaucratique' (p. 145); cf. the similar characterisation in I. F. Fikhman, 'Quelques considérations sur les données sociales et économiques des papyrus d'Oxyrhynchus d'époque byzantine', *Jahrbuch der Österreichischen Byzantinistik* 22 (1973), 16–21, at p. 18, 'la nouvelle noblesse issue essentiellement des milieux militaires et burocratiques'.

[35] F. Villeneuve, 'L'économie rurale et la vie des campagnes dans le Hauran antique (Ier siècle av. J.-C.–VIIe siècle ap. J.-C.): Une approche', in *Hauran I: Recherches archéologiques sur la Syrie du Sud à l'époque hellénistique et romaine*, ed. J. M. Dentzer (Paris, 1985–6), pp. 63–136, esp. 115.

[36] See G. Baer, *A History of Landownership in Modern Egypt 1800–1950* (Oxford, 1962), pp. 79ff. for modern examples of this.

[37] M. Gelzer, *Studien zur byzantinischen Verwaltung Ägyptens* (Leipzig, 1909); U. Wilcken and L. Mitteis, *Grundzüge und Chrestomathie der Papyruskunde* (Leipzig and Berlin, 1912); Hardy, *Large Estates* (n. 21); C. Préaux, 'La fin de l'antiquité en Egypte', *Chronique d'Égypte* 24 (1949), 123–32.

the revisionist model of an incorporated aristocracy[38] can at all represent adequately.

The crucial point to grasp is that the new eastern aristocracy owed its existence to the state and was bound to it by a strong sense of patrimonial loyalty.[39] We have no way of quantifying the role of direct grants of land, but legal texts suggest that in certain periods these were substantial.[40] The massive donations through which the church acquired its patrimony[41] must to some extent have been true of the aristocracy. The government also encouraged large landed proprietors to convert public resources (the *fundi patrimoniales*) into private capital (in *ius privatum salvo canone*),[42] and finally, drew members of this class into the management of properties of the *domus divina*.[43] The bulk of these texts date from the late fourth and early fifth century and show how important public intervention of some sort was to the rise of the new nobility. It is equally clear, on the other hand, that this group forced changes on the central authority, which found itself progressively adapting to the social realities of the countryside, but seeking, simultaneously, to circumscribe the power of the new landowners in a pattern of legal responses that involved resistance, concession, new resistance. The state was ultimately unable to do much about the extension of 'patronage' to villages by various levels of the bureaucracy. Its laws were also flouted on the question of whether estates could keep armed retainers. Thus the whole resistance posed to *patrocinia* from at

38 Gascou, 'Les grands domaines', followed by B. Palme, *Das Amt des 'apaitetes' in Ägypten* (Vienna, 1989) and J. Durliat, *Les finances publiques de Dioclétien aux Carolingiens (284–889)* (Sigmaringen, 1990).

39 A. Mócsy, 'Der Name Flavius als Rangbezeichnung in der Spätantike', in *Akte des IV Internationalen Kongresses für griechische und lateinische Epigraphik, Wien 1962* (Vienna, 1964), pp. 257–63, esp. 260, 'Ihr Name Flavius hat diese *persönliche* Verbundenheit ausgedrückt' (my emphasis).

40 Esp. *CJ* 11.62.6 (384), 'hi, quibus patrimoniales possessiones per Asianam ac Ponticam dioecesim vel a nobis vel a divis parentibus nostris sacra largitate donatae sunt, inconcusse possideant atque ad suos posteros mittant'; *CTh.* 11.24.6.8 (415), 'metrocomias possidere nostro beneficio meruerunt, et publicos vicos committere compellantur'; *NVal* x (441), 'omnes quicumque ex iure domus regiae vel a pietate mea vel a qualibet persona sacrarum necessitudinum mearum praedia adepti sunt sive usufructuaria largitate seu donatione directa sive commutationis vel emptionis ratione quaesita...'

41 R. Davis, *The Book of Pontiffs (Liber Pontificalis): The Ancient Biographies of the First Ninety Bishops to A.D. 715* (Liverpool, 1989); T. S. Brown, 'The Church of Ravenna and the Imperial Administration in the Seventh Century', *English Historical Review* 370 (1979), 1–28.

42 R. Delmaire, *Largesses sacrées et res privata: L'aerarium impérial et son administration du IVe au VIe siècle* (Rome, 1989), pp. 671 ff.

43 The most striking example of this is Flavius Strategius, who was appointed general manager of the Oxyrhynchite estates of Aelia Eudocia (Banaji, *Rural Communities*, vol. II, p. 111), who was *comes consistorii* in *P. Oxy.* L 3585 when Theodosius II was still alive, and who is probably also the addressee of *SB* XX 14091. D. Hagedorn, *P. Heid.* IV, pp. 219–20, has argued persuasively that he was the father of Fl. Apion I, and possibly the founder of the *oikos*.

least 360 was finally abandoned in 415,[44] and Leo I's denunciation of landholders who hired mercenary troops[45] was clearly completely disregarded since the *bucellarii* were chiefly used as an escort service for transporting large volumes of cash to receiving centres such as Alexandria.[46]

In short, the aristocracy of the Byzantine period was neither a subaltern group, in the sense of landowners willingly submitting to the liturgy of fiscal and other responsibilities, nor a class of rebellious magnates trying desperately to undermine the foundations of central authority. The relationship between aristocracy and state was one of tension and mutual support. The closest analogy I can think of for the fiscal relationships that evolved under the stamp of this accommodation is Irfan Habib's description of the *ta'alluqdars* of Mughal India. Though analogies can be misleading, it may be useful to try and map the relationship between aristocracy and state in terms of models drawn from better documented systems which afford clear parallels. According to Habib, 'A *ta'alluqdar* was a *zamindar* who contracted to pay revenue not only for his own *zamindari* but also for the *zamindari* of others persons: this arrangement was usually made by the authorities to avoid having to deal with a large number of persons. Thus a *ta'alluqdar* was not necessarily the *zamindar* of the whole area for which he paid the revenue, but only of a part of it; for the rest he was simply an intermediary.' 'The official view seems to have been that he was always an intermediary, who merely rendered to the authorities the service of collecting the land-revenue from the peasants.'[47] This notion of the aristocracy working as an intermediary for the state allows for a greater sense of balance between the private and public domains than Gascou's exaggerated idea of a total integration of the *oikoi* into the fiscal system and of the estates as a simple extension of the public sphere. The ambiguity which allowed private landholders to dominate public taxation[48] was reflected equally in the Mughal ambivalence towards the *zamindars*. 'It is a remarkable fact that general revenue regulations issued in the time of Akbar and Aurangzeb exclude the *zamindars* from the framework of the standard revenue machinery prescribed under them ... On the other hand, there is considerable evidence that the *zamindars* paid the revenue on behalf of whole villages.'[49] Despite the ambiguity, there is no doubt

44 Contrast esp. *CTh.* 11.24.1 (360) and 11.24.3 (395) with 11.24.6 (415), all dealing specifically with Egypt.

45 *CJ* 11.12.10 (476), 'omnibus per civitates et agros habendi bucellarios vel Isauros armatosque servos licentiam volumus esse praeclusam'.

46 This is clearly shown by the Apion accounts.

47 I. Habib, *The Agrarian System of Mughal India (1556–1707)* (London, 1963), pp. 172–3.

48 At first resisted by the state, see *CTh.* 11.22.4 (409).

49 M. Athar Ali, *The Mughal Nobility under Aurangzeb* (London, 1966), p. 84.

that relations proceeded with considerable formality. If Richards's study of Golconda is any indication, there must have been imperial orders, patents of office, appointment fees, percentage allowances on the tax receipts and so on.[50]

If this conception is admitted, then arguments about whether the pressure of taxation stimulated economic activity or crushed the resources of the taxpayers, and so on, should avoid using the fiscal evidence of the Byzantine papyri. In *P. Oxy.* xvi 1912.112 (*c.*570), from the Apion estates, on gross receipts of 3941¼ artabas of wheat, the *embole*, for the same indiction, is 2025¼ artabas, that is 51.38%. In *P. Oxy.* xviii 2195.145 (576/7), on receipts of 4286¼ artabas of wheat for a tenth indiction, the estate pays 3585¼ artabas as *embole*, that is 83.64%.[51] For money taxes, the proportions are lower but still very substantial. Thus in *P. Oxy.* xvi 1918 verso. ii.34ff., the fiscal ratio is 6917 $^{27}/_{28}$ solidi out of gross cash receipts of 20,010 $^{61}/_{96}$ solidi, that is 34.57%. In the seventh century the Catholic church of Ravenna extracted a total of 31,000 solidi from its Sicilian patrimony but paid 15,000 of this (48.39%) directly to Constantinople.[52] To suppose that the state was taxing the private income of landowners at these levels misses the point that the 'bureaucratic' fiscality of the fourth century had disintegrated in favour of a system in which the leading institutions of civil society assumed the characteristics of state agencies without ever being simple appendages of the state.

[50] J. F. Richards, *Mughal Administration in Golconda* (Oxford, 1975), esp. pp. 108ff., on the working relationship between state and regional aristocracy. Thus *hoi tupoi tês pagarchias tou tês endoxou mnêmês humôn patros* in *P. Oxy.* xvi 1829.2–3 were not papers relating to the will of a deceased member of the Apion family, as Grenfell and Hunt maintained (followed by Gascou, 'Les grands domaines', pp. 66–7; J. R. Martindale, *The Prosopography of the Later Roman Empire* (Cambridge, 1992), vol. iiiB, p. 1202, 'probably over a will'), but more likely official, imperial documents which formally acknowledged the Apions' role as intermediaries, probably by conferring a patent of office and including financial details regarding their assumption of the pagarchy. *Tupos* in its Byzantine sense has the more natural meaning of an imperial order, like the Mughal *farman*.

[51] Cf. *P. Oxy.* xvi 1906.ii.14ff, where the proportion is 80.42%.

[52] Agnellus, *Liber pontificalis ecclesiae Ravennatis* iii (*MGH, Scriptores rerum langobard.*, p. 350).

CHAPTER 4

The economic trajectories of late antiquity

Introduction

Michael Rostovtzeff concluded his great history of the early Roman empire by suggesting: 'The catastrophe of the third century dealt a severe blow to the prosperity of the Empire and weakened the creative energies of the better part of the population.'[1] In part, this was a throwback to Weber's thesis about the late empire as a period of expanding natural economy. Yet the distinctiveness of the late empire lies precisely in the fact that *money*, not land, emerged as the general form of wealth. Constantine's restructuring of the monetary system was a major economic watershed in the history of antiquity, inaugurating a period that would see unprecedented levels of monetary circulation. However, for the scholars who made money central to the dynamics of the fourth century, these changes in the monetary system were underpinned by major social transformations. For Mazzarino, the anonymous author of *De rebus bellicis*, a reform tract drafted (probably) in the 350s, had already made the crucial connection by linking the expanding circulation of gold to the consolidation of a new aristocracy, the *clarissimi* of the reigns of Constantine and his sons.[2] Anonymous saw the economic basis of this aristocracy in the rapid accumulation of large masses of gold, and the mechanism of accumulation in Constantine's expansion of the governing class.[3] These are crucial insights into the dramatic transformations of the fourth century, and they offer *one* frame for constructing a more general economic history of late antiquity, based, of course, on a much wider range of sources than either Mickwitz (numismatic, legal, papyrological) or Mazzarino (legal, textual)

[1] M. Rostovtzeff, *The Social and Economic History of the Roman Empire*, 2 vols, 2nd edn, rev. P. M. Fraser (Oxford, 1971), vol. I, p. 530.

[2] S. Mazzarino, *Aspetti sociali del IV secolo*, ed. E. Lo Cascio (Milan, 2002); Mazzarino, *L'Impero romano*, 3 vols, 3rd edn (Bari, 1980), vol. III, pp. 666 ff.

[3] Anon., *De rebus bellicis*, 2.1–4 (Giardina, *Anonimo: Le cose della guerra* (Milan, 1989), p. 12). Cf. R. S. Bagnall, *Currency and Inflation in Fourth Century Egypt* (Atlanta, 1985).

used. In particular, the archaeological revolution of the last, roughly, three decades throws up a huge challenge for historians of late antiquity, since they are now confronted, in an acute way, by the problem of how sources that are so diverse in character can be coherently blended into totalising narratives. Chris Wickham's recent book is probably the most spectacular attempt in this direction, and in the conclusion to this chapter, I shall discuss one or two of its major theses.

Staying with the point about sources for the moment: Anonymous alludes to a process of class formation that was largely true of the western aristocracy. The prosopography of third-century provincial elites (the work of scholars like Pflaum, Alföldy and Jacques) has shown that that process had much deeper roots. The core of the Constantinian elite comprised powerful aristocrats whose roots go back to the huge economic expansion of the western Mediterranean in the second and third centuries and to the ability of some families to survive the savage conflicts that ended in the victory of Septimius Severus. Generalising a model first used by Mario Torelli in prosopographical work on Lepcis Magna, it is possible to see that the booming provincial centres of the western Mediterranean, Africa above all, threw up families who used their wealth to establish a wider network of connections, both matrimonial and political, that could help consolidate their business interests and political ambitions.[4] Clodius Albinus himself is said to have come from Hadrumetum in the heart of the Sahel.[5] The backbone of his support among the provincial upper classes was broken in the fierce reprisals that led to large-scale executions in 197.[6] The Anicii are one family that emerged as strong supporters of Septimius. In 196–7, Q. Anicius Faustus from Uzappa near Mactaris was Septimius' chief military commander in Numidia.[7] His descendants can be traced through the whole of the third century[8] and became, of course, one of the wealthiest families of late antiquity. Thus in this case prosopography provides one context for the deeper understanding of an isolated textual source. Archaeology provides another. The explosion of survey archaeology since the late 1970s has shown just how densely settled the

4 M. Torelli, 'Per una storia della classe dirigente di Leptis Magna', *Atti della Accademia Nazionale dei Lincei, Classe di Scienze Morali, Storiche e Filologiche. Rendiconti* 28 (1973), 377–410.

5 SHA, *Clod. Alb.* 4.1–2; G. Alföldy, 'Herkunft und Laufbahn des Clodius Albinus in der Historia Augusta', in *Bonner Historia-Augusta-Colloquium* 1966/1967 (Bonn, 1968), pp. 19–38.

6 SHA, *Sev.* 12.1, 13.1–7; G. Alföldy, 'Eine Proskriptionsliste in der Historia Augusta', in *Bonner Historia-Augusta-Colloquium* 1968/1969 (Bonn, 1977), pp. 1–11.

7 A. R. Birley, *The African Emperor: Septimius Severus*, rev. edn (London, 1988), p. 195.

8 A. Beschaouch, '*Uzappa* et le proconsul d'Afrique Sex. Cocceius Anicius Faustus Paulinus', *Mélanges de l'École française de Rome. Antiquité* 81 (1969), 195–218; M. Christol, 'À propos des Anicii: Le IIIe siècle', *Mélanges de l'École française de Rome. Antiquité* 98(1) (1986), 141–64.

eastern countrysides were in late antiquity. The expansive energies of the fourth century, of Constantine's empire, found their most durable expression in the *East* Mediterranean of the fifth, sixth and seventh centuries. It was here that gold continued to circulate on a spectacular scale, that the urban traditions of antiquity were at their most resilient and that the economic base existed, clearly, for the survival of a powerful imperial state. Now a major part of this dramatic transformation was the emergence of a new aristocracy in the east, quite different in nature from the kind of aristocracy that Anonymous saw stuffing its 'houses' with gold. Constantius II created a *noblesse de fonction* ('différent de l'aristocratie traditionnelle'), so that the nascent aristocracy of the east was more firmly rooted in the traditions of a bureaucratic state.[9] This remained true of the fifth century, when the Byzantine new aristocracy that emerged in regions like Egypt could reliably be described as 'of bureaucratic origin'.[10]

Thus late antiquity threw up multiple trajectories, and no single formula can do justice to all of them. Even the dissolution of the western aristocracy, when it came, took such different forms and moved in such different ways that the 'fall' of western empire is a mere abstraction unless each context is constructed in its own terms. In particular, the slow erosion of the Gallic aristocracy that proceeded apace with the consolidation of Gothic power in the fifth century stands in sharp contrast to the dramatic and altogether more sudden collapse of the Italian aristocracy in the sixth. And again, the way in which the Merovingian rulers handled the remnants of that class – substantial in southern Gaul – contrasts sharply with the treatment meted out to their north Italian counterparts by the Lombards. There was no unified bloc of 'Barbarians', any more than there was a homogeneous or unified class of late Roman aristocrats, and these differences are what late antique history is largely about.

The late empire

Whatever one thinks of the 'crisis' of the third century, the key consequence of its recurrent monetary instability was the de facto disintegration of bimetallism. The chief expression of this was that *gold came to*

9 C. Vogler, *Constance II et l'administration impériale* (Strasbourg, 1979), pp. 232ff., 239.

10 R. Rémondon, 'L'Égypte au 5e siècle de notre ère', in *Atti del XI Congresso Internazionale di Papirologia, Milano, 2–8 settembre 1965* (Milan, 1966), pp. 135–48, at 145 ('la noblesse égyptienne, d'origine bureaucratique'); so, too, I. F. Fikhman, 'Quelques considérations sur les données sociales et économiques des papyrus d'Oxyrhynchus d'époque byzantine', *Jahrbuch der Österreichischen Byzantinistik* 22 (1973), 16–21, at p. 18 ('La nouvelle noblesse issue essentiellement des milieux militaires et burocratiques').

circulate at a floating rate. As Lo Cascio says, 'With the dissolution of the Roman monetary system in the third century, gold coinage came to occupy a peculiar position within the Roman monetary economy. It was no longer linked through a fixed value relationship to the other denominations and to the unit of account.'[11] Diocletian's attempt to restore a viable bimetallic system ended in failure, and it is no small measure of Constantine's achievement that he was no longer mesmerised by the monetary illusions of the third century and could break so decisively from them. Mazzarino's assessment of Constantine as a 'revolutionary' is thus fully justified. The fourth century began, more or less, with a radically different monetary system based on gold as the measure of value and on a calculated decision not to introduce fixed value relations between the metals. But this monometallism of gold had far-reaching economic and social consequences. The division between gold (the solidus) and the base-metal coinages was in some sense a metaphor for and replicated in a more rampant stratification of society, where the 'abject' strata (*humiliores*) were defined as much by their powerlessness as by economic deprivation or poverty. Thus one way of classifying or dividing up late Roman society was in terms of the contrast, drawn by Ambrose, for example, between the *inopes* and the *potentes*.[12] In one of their several meanings at least, the late antique poor were those who lacked any form of protection and who were thus vulnerable to oppression or more tragic eventualities. They were, in a favourite category of the legal sources, *tenues*, that is, groups vulnerable to domination. The pervasive imagery of power and powerlessness that runs through the discursive worlds of late antiquity reflects the peculiar nature of the Constantinian order, where 'at the highest levels there was no longer any distinction between senators and bureaucracy' (Mazzarino).[13] A purely civilian aristocracy ceased to exist, in the sense that the clans who dominated the City of Rome in the early fourth century could continue to prosper only as part of a much bigger governing class, a class that would in the future, and in the east for centuries, comprise 'the higher officials of the army, the bureaucracy and the

[11] E. Lo Cascio, 'The Function of Gold Coinage in the Monetary Economy of the Roman Empire', in *The Monetary Systems of the Greeks and Romans*, ed. W. V. Harris (Oxford, 2008), pp. 160–73, esp. 172–3. Fluctuations: *P. Oxy*. 3401.7ff. ('everyone is looking for solidi and the price is going up every day'), *P. Oxy*. 1223.31ff., cf. Symmachus, *Rel*. 29.1 (R. H. Barrow, *Prefect and Emperor: The Relationes of Symmachus A.D. 384* (Oxford, 1973), p. 162).

[12] Ambrose, *De fide* 4.81, etc., cited C. Freu, *Les figures du pauvre dans les sources italiennes de l'antiquité tardive* (Paris, 2007), p. 65.

[13] Mazzarino, *L'Impero romano*, vol. III, p. 679: 'Ma nei gradi supremi, non c'è più distinzione tra senatori e burocrazia.'

church'.[14] It was this expanded governing class of the fourth century that formed the powerful social base of a monetary economy based on gold.

The return to a stable, high-value coinage, a single currency that spanned the entire breadth of the empire, had vast economic implications. First, it would mean a sustained increase in the level of monetary activity, which would mean an expansion of the monetised economy. The widespread use of cash payments on rural estates in Egypt (already by the third quarter of the fourth century) is one illustration of this. Second, a growing money supply could match a 'long-term increase in the demand for money' to service a larger volume of transactions in the 'private' sector (among merchants, landowners, monasteries and so on).[15] Third, the solidus was, as Maurice Lombard noted, the sole means of exchange accepted *par le grand commerce méditerranéen*, so that the return of a stable currency was bound to stimulate an expansion of trade as well.[16] Fourth, it would give government flexibility in terms of how much of its own revenue was exacted in money (gold). The 380s were a watershed in this respect, as Theodosius I decided that a larger share of the land tax should be assessed directly in money. Cerati sifted through the constitutions to show that the fiscal system inherited from Constantine was thus 'radically transformed', that is, increasingly monetised.[17] Moreover, late antique taxation was also characterised by widespread commutation of taxes, a movement driven in the first instance by the pressure of the military officers (*militares*) for substantial monetary payments. For example, Valentinian I is said to have made sweeping concessions in this respect.[18] So the result was growing monetisation of the economy, increased liquidity and a tax system based (more and more) on money.

These tendencies reached a sort of climax in the sixth and early seventh centuries. 'The extremely plentiful solidi of Justinian I through to Heraclius would prove, were anyone heroic enough to undertake the formidable task of checking their dies, to be the survivors of a once vast coinage.'[19] Michael Metcalf estimated that Thessalonica alone would have

[14] R. Morris, 'The Powerful and the Poor in Tenth-Century Byzantium: Law and Reality', *Past & Present* 73 (1976), 3–27, at p. 14.

[15] See E. Lo Cascio, 'State and Coinage in the Late Republic and Early Empire', *Journal of Roman Studies* 71 (1981), 76–86, esp. 82ff. on the provision of liquidity.

[16] M. Lombard, *Études d'économie medieval, vol. I: Monnaie et histoire d'Alexandre à Mahomet* (Paris, 1971), p. 138.

[17] A. Cerati, *Caractère annonaire et assiette de l'impôt foncier au Bas-Empire* (Paris, 1975), pp. 71–85.

[18] Ammianus 27.9.4 (Rolfe, vol. III, p. 58).

[19] D. M. Metcalf, 'Monetary Recession in the Middle Byzantine Period: The Numismatic Evidence', *Numismatic Chronicle* 161 (2001), 111–55, at p. 119.

turned out between five and six million solidi a year under Justinian.[20] Assuming, for the sake of argument, that the mint of Thessalonica accounted for a tenth of the total number of solidi struck in his reign, some 50 to 60 million solidi were struck at Constantinople in the main part of the sixth century. This gives us a rough impression of *size* of the sixth-century money supply, which, of course, was substantially greater than that, since the size of a currency (the amount of money in circulation) includes the coins that have stayed in circulation from previous reigns, the average velocity of circulation (the amount of business transacted by the average solidus) *and* the use of credit instruments other than coin. That we are dealing with a *credible* order of magnitude is shown by Procopius' report that Anastasius built up a treasury reserve of 23 million solidi in the course of his reign.[21] The sheer scale of monetary circulation is what is so striking about late antiquity.

'To ensure that terror was universal, provinces too were cut into fragments; many governors and even more officials were imposed on individual regions ... and to these were added numerous accountants, controllers and prefects' deputies.'[22] So wrote Lactantius on Diocletian and the major reforms that overhauled the administration of the empire in the 290s. The proliferation of provinces and the tighter political control and bureaucratic expansion that went with them were, for an unabashedly hostile source, linked to Diocletian's *avaritia*, that is, the drive to tax the expanding wealth of the provinces more effectively. Indeed, the same passage tells us that Africa and Spain were among the wealthiest provinces in the later third century.[23] Spanish olive oil had dominated the Rome market between 140 and 250, and although the massive export drive was now past its peak, the late third century in Spain still absorbed the afterglow of much of that prosperity. The olive oil of North Africa, on the other hand, saw *very* rapid expansion on the Italian market in the middle decades of the third century. So here the ceramic evidence is an even better match for Lactantius' testimony. By the third century, North African producers were bringing vast new areas of the interior into production to sustain this phenomenal drive. Industrial-scale production of the kind exemplified by the villa of Saint-Michel in the commune of La Garde in southern France, still prosperous in the early third century,[24] would have had hundreds of

[20] D. M. Metcalf, 'The Mint of Thessalonica in the Early Byzantine Period', in *Villes et peuplement dans l'Illyricum protobyzantin* (Rome, 1984), pp. 111–28, esp. 119.

[21] Procopius, *Anecd.* 19.7 (Dewing, *Secret History*, p. 228).

[22] Lactantius, *De mortibus persecutorum* 7.4 (Creed, p. 12).

[23] Lactantius, *De mort. persec.* 8.3 (Creed, p. 14).

[24] J.-P. Brun, 'La villa gallo-romaine de Saint-Michel à La Garde (Var)', *Gallia* 46 (1989), 103–62.

counterparts in the African countryside. Olive oil on this scale was clearly an economic sector dominated by the aristocracy, because it required 'massive capital investment' among producers. For Tripolitania alone, Mattingly has surmised a 'potential annual export to Rome in excess of one million litres of oil per year' and suggested, plausibly, that this degree of domination of the countryside was only possible through 'large-scale organisation of the rural economy'.[25] What it implies is a powerful aristocracy backed by the resources of the state, a pattern demonstrated throughout the imperial history of Africa (down to Justin II's laws on the colonate!), and certainly for Tripolitania at least, the amphora stamps are decisive proof (if this were needed) that the senatorial aristocracy of the third century controlled the key enterprises in the region. The same, surely, was true of the areas further west, in Tunisia, where NUM TUS/ CI·ET·ALBin/I·CC Vv on the body of an amphora found at Carthage takes us to the heart of the third-century aristocracy and to a family that had survived the brutal repression of the 190s.[26] Presumably, these were the sons of M. Nummius Senecio Albinus (cos. 227), the first, M. Nummius Tuscus, consul in 258, the second, Nummius Ceionius Albinus, consul in 263, and descended from the brother or half-brother of Didius Julianus, who was executed (most likely) in 193.[27] At any rate, *AE* (1926, 28) pulls together a number of strands in the overlapping histories that led into the late empire. Like the Nummii, the Aradii, the Anicii, the Anullini, the Memmii and so on were all ultimately from provincial backgrounds, wealthy landed families that would form the core of the city's aristocracy under Constantine. They were now among the leading elements of the Italian aristocracy, and under Constantine, the new provinces were carefully ordered in a hierarchy that reflected major concessions to them.[28] His creation of 'consular' provinces affected mainly regions where families like the Caeonii and the Aradii held a substantial part of their assets. Thus Campania, Sicily and Numidia all received consular rank in the 320s, and Byzacena about 330.[29] If, as Jones supposed, 'Diocletian had very little use for senators', in a Constantinian perspective, the proliferation of provinces also allowed tighter control *by aristocratic families* of regions where

[25] D. J. Mattingly, 'The Olive Boom: Oil Surpluses, Wealth and Power in Roman Tripolitania', *Libyan Studies* 19 (1988), 21–42.

[26] *AE* (1926), #28, 'Sur la panse d'une amphore trouvée à Carthage'.

[27] Cf. *PLRE* I, p. 1142 (stemma); G. Alföldy, 'Septimius Severus und der Senat', *Bonner Jahrbücher* 168 (1968), 112–60, at p. 138 (ancestor).

[28] A. Chastagnol, 'Les consulaires de Numidie', in *Mélanges d'archéologie, d'épigraphie et d'histoire offerts à Jérôme Carcopino* (Paris, 1966), pp. 215–28.

[29] W. Kuhoff, *Studien zur zivilen senatorischen Laufbahn im 4. Jhr. n. Chr.* (Frankfurt, 1983), pp. 63–4.

their assets were concentrated – by the Caeonii in Numidia, the Aradii in Byzacena, the Anicii in Campania and so on. No rule barred the aristocracy from governing their home provinces, in other words,[30] and this is surely an important clue to understanding how late Romans themselves understood the distinction between 'public' and 'private'.

Indeed, Rome itself, avoided by the emperors, was almost left to colonisation by the aristocracy! Guidobaldi draws attention to its illicit control of real estate within the city and the expansion of aristocratic *domus* in areas of the city formerly occupied by *insulae* or by commercial buildings.[31] Olympiodorus in the fifth century would describe those *domus* as miniature cities.[32] The 'private' monumentality of the fourth century reflected a major shift in the culture of urban investment, away from the *evergetismo* of the early empire to a more brutal display of power poised ambiguously on a boundary between public and private that was symptomatic of the kind of social order ushered in by Constantine. The great senatorial clans (*gentes*) had multiple residences in the city. The fourth century saw a 'boom in senatorial dwellings of a high standard', with an explosion of new architectural styles and decorative elements.[33] The urban prefecture, controlled by the aristocracy, must have been a key mechanism in the deals that structured the market in real estate. Rufius Volusianus Lampadius, prefect in 365 and notorious for his passion for building, was the owner of a marble workshop (*officina*) in Ostia.[34] Building materials (marble, stone, bricks) were a favourite sphere for the investment of aristocratic capital. The urban aristocracy that effectively ran the city in the 330s was also actively engaged in a range of businesses that included banks (*mensae*) and commercial enterprises (*negotiationes*).[35] One reason there is so little explicit evidence of this side of their economic activities is simply that 'the pose of senatorial disregard for trade'[36] endured and meant that the complex or, better still, mediated patterns of business governance

[30] Kuhoff, *Studien*, p. 77.

[31] F. Guidobaldi, 'Le *domus* tardoantiche di Roma come "sensori" delle transformazioni culturali e sociali', in *The Transformations of Urbs Roma in Late Antiquity*, ed. W. V. Harris (Portsmouth, RI, 1999), pp. 53–68, esp. 58–60.

[32] Olympiodorus, fr. 41.1 (Blockley, *The Fragmentary Classicising Historians of the Later Roman Empire*, vol. II, pp. 204–5).

[33] J. Hillner, 'Domus, Family, and Inheritance: The Senatorial Family House in Late Antique Rome', *JRS* 93 (2003), 129–45, at pp. 135f., 141f. (more than one house), 144f. (boom); Guidobaldi, '*Domus* tardoantiche', pp. 62ff. (architecture).

[34] G. Becatti, *Case ostiense del tardo impero* (Rome, 1948), p. 31.

[35] Firmicus Maternus, *Mathesis* 3.10.1 (Monat, vol. II, p. 101): *magnorum aut potentium virorum ... scribas, rationibus, mensis, apothecis negotiationibusque praepositos*, written *c*.334. Cf. *CTh*. xiii.5.14 (371) for senatorial involvement in commercial shipping.

[36] K. Cooper, *The Fall of the Roman Household* (Cambridge, 2007), p. 93.

discussed by Serrao and Di Porto for a much earlier period were almost certainly still deployed. (The best indication of this is a passage from Firmicus Maternus, with its reference to *praepositi* or agents, who were more properly known as *institores*.) In short, we should be wary of the cliché that sees the late Roman aristocracy as a purely agrarian group, even if in this sector as well there was often rampant speculation (*avara venditio*) and a drive to dominate grain markets. But Ruggini's characterisation of the western aristocracy as *latifondisti speculatori* ignores other dimensions of aristocratic economic behaviour that were inseparable from their wholesaling of food grains and wine.[37]

The fourth century in particular saw a massive wave of investments in rural estates, in the expansion and reorganisation of 'villas' in the archaeological sense. This is probably best documented for the Spanish (or 'Iberian') countryside, where Gorges could count at least 140 villas whose apogee he could date to the fourth century, and where the villas of the Constantinian period were described, nicely if dramatically, as expressions of a 'brutal change in the architectural, artistic, economic and social norms that had governed the countryside till then'.[38] In more recent work, Chavarría has proposed a rudimentary taxonomy dividing the middle-sized estates along the Mediterranean coast of Spain from the monumental villas of the interior, which were mostly abandoned only gradually from the later fifth century.[39] These different sorts of establishments evolved differently in the fourth century: while the smaller establishments in the coastal areas of eastern and southern Spain converted their residential spaces to productive or industrial use – for example, 'mosaics or baths were destroyed and replaced by the installation of agricultural or industrial structures' – the large estates of the interior gained in monumentality and style.[40] Chavarría argues that both movements reflected a common process of rationalisation, as the absorption of the lesser properties by the biggest landowners 'prompted the abandonment of the residential buildings of these "bought out" sites and allowed their re-use for new economic activities'.[41] This is a rare example of the attempt

[37] L. Ruggini, *Economia e società nell' 'Italia annonaria': Rapporti fra agricoltura e commercio dal IV al VI secolo d. C.* (Milan, 1961), p. 230.

[38] J.-G. Gorges, *Les villas hispano-romaines: Inventaire et problématique archéologiques* (Paris, 1979), pp. 48 (apogee), 52 (brutal change).

[39] A. Chavarría Arnau, 'Interpreting the Transformation of Late Roman Villas: The Case of Hispania', in *Landscapes of Change*, ed. N. Christie (Aldershot, 2004), pp. 67–102, esp. 68–75.

[40] Chavarría, 'Transformation', pp. 75–80.

[41] Chavarría, 'Transformation', p. 87; A. Chavarría Arnau, *El final de las villae en Hispania (siglos IV–VII d.C.)* (Turnhout, 2007), pp. 137–8.

to explain the archaeology in terms of a coherent economic movement that is, in any case, reasonably well supported by all the other evidence we have for the aristocratic consolidation of the fourth century. But if true, it would suggest an astonishing degree of concentration of landed assets, which is something we can be much less sure about.

At any rate, there is now a substantial though still largely dispersed bibliography of individual sites, and attention to their specific, individual trajectories demonstrates continuing or renewed vitality in the late fourth century. At the villa of Torre de Palma in Lusitania, the 350s saw a 'burst of building activity [that] created an array of new structures unmatched in number, novelty, and importance since the building campaigns of the late first century'. This included the construction of a new olive press complex with its massive press and a substantial barn in one corner of the old *villa rustica*.[42] A whole clutch of villas in the southern parts of Gaul and Italy show major reconstruction and embellishment towards the end of the fourth century or even late into the fifth. Sometimes an existing villa was demolished and a new, larger one constructed in its place, as at S. Giovanni di Ruoti, where an early first-century villa abandoned in the third, reoccupied in the mid-fourth, was demolished and rebuilt on a 'much more impressive scale and to a coherent plan' in about 400. The large apsidal hall that emerged at this time was emblematic of the new power architecture that characterised the vast majority of the more substantial fourth-century establishments.[43] Elsewhere, and more commonly, major changes were made to existing sites, as villas were redeveloped to underline a new sense of scale and ostentation. This happened at S. Giovanni as well, when the apsidal hall collapsed around 460 and the villa was rebuilt on an even bigger scale till it disappeared in the devastation of the Gothic wars. Many of these 'late' structures, villas built or reconstructed in the late fourth and early fifth centuries, continued in production till well into the main part of the sixth century, showing that large parts of the countryside retained their vitality despite the dissolution of the empire in the west. The huge tuna factory built at Ciudadela de Roses (ancient Rhode) in Catalunya in the late fourth century was abandoned only in the late sixth, probably in the last years of the reign of Leovigild, and then deliberately so.[44] The sumptuous establishment at Faragola in

[42] S. J. Maloney and J. R. Hale, 'The Villa of Torre de Palma (Alto Alentejo)', *Journal of Roman Archaeology* 9 (1996), 275–94, esp. pp. 290ff.

[43] A. M. Small and R. J. Buck, *The Excavations at San Giovanni di Ruoti*, vol. I: *The Villas and Their Environment* (Toronto, 1994).

[44] J. M. Nolla-Brufau, 'Excavaciones recientes en la ciudadela de Roses: El edificio bajo-imperial', in *Papers in Iberian Archaeology*, ed. T. F. C. Blagg *et al.* (Oxford, 1984), pp. 430–59.

Puglia, which saw the construction of a luxurious dining room in the fifth century that used coloured marbles and glass paste in its floors, survived in style into the main decades of the sixth, when it fell into ruin and was eventually abandoned.[45] In Italy, the Gothic wars had a devastating impact on the landscape and the resilience of the countryside, but short of the havoc created by prolonged warfare, there is no compelling reason to see the countrysides of the west enduring a dramatic loss of dynamism in the fifth and sixth centuries. The villas themselves were abandoned only gradually as the aristocracy regrouped or was driven back. Thus Chavarría refers to the 'continued vitality' of Spanish villas in the fifth century,[46] and Balmelle has made a similar point for Aquitania.[47] In Spain, it is the late fifth century that marks a break in terms of the archaeological evidence for the continued presence of an aristocracy.[48] This was a major transformation that I shall come back to shortly.

What *was* the villa? If the archaeological villa just discussed refers to the physical remains of building complexes connected with rural estates where owners may or may not have resided for at least part of the year, in a more purely historical sense, the term *villa* referred to the estates themselves and to some size of estate *with clear boundaries*. In short, the villa was a physically coherent entity. This is a crucial point, as it has an obvious bearing on how we construe the organisation of such estates in terms of their use of labour and the nature of the labour force. The widespread dogma that relations of production in these enterprises were structured as rent tenancies – that is, that the land was broken up into myriad smaller holdings that were simply leased out to peasants who paid some form of rent for them, usually in kind – is simply a cliché transferred to late Roman history from the popular idea of the large landowner (everywhere!) as a landlord. It is quite clear that the *villa* in the Roman sense was a discrete block of land, not a collection of land parcels randomly dispersed through the landscape. Thus in the Llandaff charters, which reflect Roman traditions of landholding and record grants of land of estate size, 'There are boundaries which ran from one villa to another.' Here the areas enclosed 'varied between 125 and 1000 acres, and were, exceptionally, greater'. As

45 G. Volpe, G. De Felice and M. Turchiano, 'Faragola (Ascoli Satriano): Una residenza aristocratica tardoantica e un "villaggio" altomedievale nella Valle del Carapelle', in *Paesaggi e insediamenti rurali in Italia meridionale fra Tardoantico e Altomedioevo*, ed. G. Volpe *et al.* (Bari, 2005) pp. 265–97.

46 Chavarría, 'Transformation', p. 75; Chavarría, *El final de las villae en Hispania*, p. 114.

47 C. Balmelle, *Les demeures aristocratiques d'Aquitaine* (Paris, 2001), p. 119.

48 A. Chavarría Arnau, 'Villas en *Hispania* durante la antigüedad tardía', in *Villas tardoantiguas en el Mediterraneo occidental*, ed. A. Chavarría *et al.* (= *Anejos de AEspA* 39 (2006)) (Madrid, 2006), pp. 17–35, at 25.

Wendy Davies notes, terms like *villa*, *ager* and *terra* referred to 'a coherent unit or estate', an integrated unit.[49] Aristocratic patrimonies may well have been characterised by fragmentation, but not the individual estates of which they were made up. Thus one of the estates (*villae*) owned by the Anicii was the *Casas villa Aniciorum* some twenty-eight miles west of Sabratha on the Libyan coast. This turns up in the Antonine Itinerary in a sequence that lists a series of *villae* along the coastal route between the oasis of Gabes and Lepcis Magna.[50] These must have been *very* substantial estates straddling much of the countryside between the stations listed. The *casas* were almost certainly *mapalia*, settlements typical of the nomadic and transhumant communities throughout the Maghreb from whom the estates drew much of their labour. Procopius described them as καλύβαι ('huts') and called them 'stuffy'.[51] In regions of olive monoculture, landowners would have needed large infusions of labour during the harvest season but practically no permanent workforce otherwise. And since harvests fluctuated, the demand for labour was never constant. Elsewhere, in areas of arable cultivation, estates created more permanent labour settlements, frequently named after the owner, since they lay within or close to the boundaries of the estate. The *vicus Juliani* in Augustine, *Ep.*23A* (from 419), is a good example. As late as the sixth century, estates in Byzantine-controlled Africa contained settlements (*vici*) with labour forces permanently attached to them.[52] Thus, in this crucial respect, there was no substantive difference between the way the biggest estates were organised in the western provinces and in the east, where the documentation is much better. But having said this, it is important to note how little attention scholars have paid to the sheer variety of estates in the western Mediterranean and the empire more generally. The seeming normality of the *villa* is something of an illusion, and this for two reasons. First, there was simply no counterpart to the ubiquitous western villa in the eastern countryside, except for the very rich rural establishments called *proasteia*, which were largely found in suburban countryside, close to urban centres, and nowhere else. More or less consolidated rural estates in the open countryside, such as that of the Apions in the Oxyrhynchite, were run from the nearest urban centre, in this case Oxyrhynchus itself; at least no

49 W. Davies, *An Early Welsh Microcosm: Studies in the Llandaff Charters* (London, 1978), pp. 32–34, 40.

50 *Itin. Ant.* 61.2 (Cuntz, p. 9).

51 Procopius, *Bell.* 4.6.10 (Dewing, *History of the Wars*, vol. II, p. 257).

52 Justin II, *Nov.* 6.1 (570) (*Jus Graecoromanum*, vol. I, p. 10). So, too, in Sicily, cf. Gregory, *Ep.* 9.129 (599).

papyrologist familiar with the Apion material has ever suggested otherwise. This stands in obvious contrast to the substantial managerial role that devolved on the archaeological villa as a complex of buildings from which the surrounding estate was administered. Second, estates differed according to topography. *Saltus* and *castra* are prime examples of this. The *saltus* were vast tracts of woodlands and half-mountainous regions, marshes, lagoons and so on, or any combination of these. In Africa, local communities within these estates had petitioned the authorities for permission to convert wasteland to productive uses.[53] A powerful Antonine family, the Antistii, owned a *saltus* in the region between Thibilis and Bordj Sabath near Cirta.[54] Ammianus' remarkable references to a whole series of *fundi* that were mountain strongholds controlled by a family of tribal chieftains in the Grande Kabylie and the areas to its west are a startling reminder of the same diversity. The most famous of these was, he says, 'built in the style of a city',[55] hence my description of estates of this sort as '*agadir*-type'. None of these estates were remotely like the *villae* controlled by the Anicii on the coast of Libya. One imagines that the *Petra Geminiani* in the Aurès was precisely of this form: the Berber chief Iaudas stored a massive amount of money there, which helped the Byzantines finance much of their fortification programme when it was captured.[56] It is thus fascinating to know that many of the *castra* in Visigothic Spain bore names that suggest they were privately owned strongholds from which a purely local aristocracy dominated the surrounding countryside: *Castrum Liviae*, *Castrum Leonis*, *Castrum Rufiana* and so on.[57] These were the closest counterparts, in the late antique west, to the 'strong, stone-built castles' in which the Armenian aristocracy resided,[58] influenced in part by a Sasanian model, where estates had a very different structure.

The late antique sense of scale triumphed here as well, in the emergence of a form of property that conglomerated individual estates (*fundi*) into massive holdings called *massae*. These are, usually, most widely attested in central-southern Italy and the islands, and not just because these parts

[53] D. Flach, 'Inschriftenuntersuchungen zum römischen Kolonat in Nordafrika', *Chiron* 8 (1978), 441–92.

[54] H. G. Pflaum, 'Glanes épigraphiques dans la région de Constantine', *Recueil de la Société archéologique de Constantine* 71 (1969–71), 59–75.

[55] Ammianus 29.5.13, about the *fundus Petrensis*.

[56] Procopius, *Bell.* 4.20.23; 29 (Dewing, *History of the Wars*, vol. II, p. 390).

[57] J. I. Martínez Melón, 'El vocabulario de los asentamientos rurales (siglos I–IX d.C.): Evolución de la terminología', in *Villas tardoantiguas en el Mediterraneo occidental*, ed. A. Chavarría *et al.* (Madrid, 2006), pp. 113–31, at 124–5, esp. nn. 152–5.

[58] Thomas Artsruni, *History of the House of the Artsrunik'* (Detroit, 1985), p. 143 (trans. Thomson).

of the Mediterranean remained under imperial control. There is a consensus among scholars that the *fundi* that made up the *massa* tended to be more or less contiguous, which would mean that the *massa* itself was a very substantial bloc of land.[59] From the distribution of its brick stamps, Adamesteanu suggested that the *massa Calvisiana*, owned by an early fourth-century (Tetrarchic) governor of Sicily, subsumed much of the countryside east of the Gela, along the southern coast.[60] One of the famous Ravenna papyri (*P. Ital.* 1.58ff.) from the papers of a palatine official at the court of Ravenna shows the amounts of revenue (in solidi) that Sicilian *massae* could yield (445, 500 and 756 solidi in the three instances listed) and suggests also that *massae* were frequently leased to *conductores*, that is, entrepreneurs who, like the more recent Apulian *massari*, 'assumed the management of the estate' for 'short-term financial speculation'.[61] Like the physical monumentality of the villa, the economic dimensions of the *massa* reflected the sheer scale on which the aristocracy accumulated wealth in the late antique west.

What I have tried to do in the preceding pages is convey some sense of the economic power and resilience of the late empire and the scale on which private wealth was accumulated. Catastrophist images of the fall of antiquity use biological metaphors like decay and decline, but the crisis of the western empire and its aristocracy was *not* a reflection of deep-seated economic instabilities or of a loss of dynamism. Italy was the worst-case scenario; the sixth century was traumatic for its aristocracy, which effectively disappeared by the beginning of the seventh. But the dramatic changes that reconfigured Italian history in the sixth century had everything to do with the impact of the Gothic war – a major blow for the aristocracy – and the severity of the Lombard settlement that followed. By contrast, the Ostrogoths chose to rule with the collaboration of the aristocracy, and the senatorial houses were still intact and powerful under them. Aristocrats like Caecina Mavortius Basilius Decius were willing to make substantial investment in the reclamation of marshland if they could

59 Cf. T. S. Brown, *Gentlemen and Officers: Imperial Administration and Aristocratic Power in Byzantine Italy, AD 554–800* (London, 1984), p. 198 ('large blocs'); L. Ruggini, 'La Sicilia fra Roma e Bisanzio', in *Storia della Sicilia,* vol. III, ed. R. Romeo (Naples, 1980), pp. 3–37, esp. 12 ('aggregati di fondi contigui'); A. Castagnetti, 'Le strutture fondiarie ed agrarie', in *Storia di Ravenna, 2/1: Dall'età bizantina all'età Ottoniana*, ed. A. Carile (Venice, 1991), pp. 55–72, esp. 62; D. De Francesco, *La proprietà fondiaria nel Lazio secoli IV–VIII: Storia e topografia* (Rome, 2004), p. 286.

60 D. Adamesteanu, 'Due problemi topografici del retroterra gelese', *Atti della Accademia Nazionale dei Lincei, Classe di Scienze Morali, Storiche e Filologiche. Rendiconti*, ser. viii, 10 (1955), 199–210, cf. *Itin. Ant.* 89.6; 95.7 (Cuntz, p. 12ff.).

61 F. M. Snowden, *Violence and the Great Estates in the South of Italy: Apulia, 1900–1922* (Cambridge, 1986), p. 14.

have the profits.[62] And certainly, southern Italy was still prosperous in the early sixth century. In southern Gaul, where much of the best archaeology has been done, the sixth century emerges as a watershed in the history of the landscape, but the transitions are more complex, subtler than any simple 'end of the villas' model, as Laurent Schneider has shown. Although a new rural geography began to emerge, the key fact is that there was no demographic contraction in southern France in late antiquity.[63] In Spain, the late Roman aristocracy was pushed back more decisively and is much harder to track through the main decades of Visigothic rule. Perhaps the bulk of it migrated to the church. But Chavarría has rejected the idea, argued for Italy, of a desertion of the countryside,[64] which takes us back to the need for more complex transition models than simple catastrophism. There is no doubt that by and large the aristocracy was the chief casualty of the fall of the western empire, as Wickham now argues, but also that aristocratic forms of property survived on a much bigger scale throughout the west, as argued by medievalists like Rouche for Gaul and Modzelewski for Italy.[65] The 'large estate' was one of Rome's chief legacies to the early Middle Ages, certainly in the west, where it had always been a major feature of the landscape.

The eastern Mediterranean

The eastern Mediterranean threw up a rather different formation, much less comprehensively dominated by its aristocracy, with a more complex pattern of stratification and an almost infinite series of gradations between the imperial top and the wage-labouring bottom. To reflect this, the economy was also more complex and ramified, with a stronger urban legacy, a large urban middle class and a substantial layer of commercial capital. Indeed, relations between business and the state, and between the aristocracy and business, were altogether more involved here, completely at odds with conventional dichotomies between 'public' and 'private' or between

62 A. Giardina, 'Pubblico e privato nella bonifica Teodericiana delle paludi pontine', in *Zones côtières littorales dans le monde Méditerranéen au Moyen Âge*, ed. J.-M. Martin (Rome and Madrid, 2001), pp. 35–50.

63 L. Schneider, 'Structures du peuplement et formes de l'habitat dans les campagnes du sud-est de la France de l'Antiquité au Moyen Âge', *Gallia* 64 (2007), 11–56.

64 Chavarría, 'Villas en *Hispania* durante la antigüedad tardía', p. 34; Chavarría, *El final de las villae en Hispania*, p. 139.

65 M. Rouche, *L'Aquitaine des Wisigoths aux Arabes 418–781* (Paris, 1979), pp. 220, 328–9; K. Modzelewski, 'La transizione dall'antichità al feudalesimo', in *Dal feudalesimo al capitalismo: Storia d'Italia, Annali*, vol. 1, ed. R. Romano *et al.* (Turin, 1978), pp. 3–109, esp. 41ff.

'aristocrats' and 'entrepreneurs'. There are several ways of conveying these nuances, but we could just as well start at the bottom. John Chrysostom felt that self-employed artisans were better off than craftsmen in wage employment, since employers often cut a substantial part of the wages of these workers on the pretext that they were fed by the employer.[66] In Egypt, there were rural households who at one extreme could accumulate substantial sums of gold (360 solidi in one will!)[67] and, of course, many more who simply had no land and relied on work as sharecroppers or rural labourers. The Fayyūm sharecroppers of the sixth to seventh centuries are a good example of the latter, since they were easily evictable.[68] For the salaried middle class, late antiquity was an age of comparative affluence. When John the Lydian was taken on as a *chartularius*, he received an annual salary of twenty-four solidi.[69] Senior estate managers were sometimes even better paid,[70] and the local garrisons were remarkably well fed.[71] Where the demand for labour was strong, workers could earn six or seven solidi a year, as in contracts for irrigation work.[72] In a contract dated 588, a goldsmiths' helper was paid three solidi,[73] barely sufficient for a family, but he was lucky to have a regular job at all, since a large proportion of urban wage earners were in casual employment and not even paid in gold but in the copper currency that Anastasius had finally restored to viability. In 553, when Justinian tried to devalue the *follis*, these groups, called πτωχοί (lit. 'the poor'), rioted, and Justinian retreated.[74] The exchange between gold and copper was critical to their ability to defend living standards. Justin II had fewer qualms, and from his reign the undervaluation of the copper coinage effectively condemned it to extinction. A superb analogy for the Byzantine monetary system and its implications for wage earners is Raymond de Roover's description of the way Florence's monetary system affected similar groups in the fourteenth and fifteenth centuries, which is worth citing in full. The Florentines used two currencies,

> the gold florin, which remained more or less stable in weight and fineness, and a silver currency, the *moneta di piccioli*, which was steadily deteriorating

66 John Chrysostom, *In Ep.* I *ad Cor., Hom* xliii, 3 (PG 61.372).
67 *P. Oxy.* I 132, with *BL* 7.127; legacy of a former village headman.
68 E.g., A. Jördens, 'Teilpachtverträge aus dem Arsinoites', *Zeitschrift für Papyrologie und Epigraphik* 65 (1986), 107–22.
69 John Lydus, *De mag.* 3.27 (Bandy, p. 174).
70 *P. Oxy.* XVI 1913.40, thirty solidi and substantial amounts of wheat and barley for an Apion manager.
71 J. Gascou, 'La table budgétaire d'Antaeopolis (*P.Freer* 08.45 c–d)', in *Hommes et richesses dans l'Empire byzantin*, vol. I: *IV–VII siècle* (Paris, 1989), pp. 279–313, esp. 290ff.
72 E.g. *P. Flor.* I 70 (627). 73 *P. Oxy.* LVIII 3933.
74 John Malalas, *Chron.* 18.117 (Thurn, p. 415; Jeffreys, p. 293).

> ... *There was no fixed ratio* as in the bimetallic standard of the classical type; instead the ratio of the florin to the *moneta di piccioli* varied from day to day ... bankers and merchants belonging to the major guilds transacted their business ... in gold florins, but the retail trade was conducted in *piccioli*. While the *lanaioli* bought wool and sold cloth in gold florins, they paid their workers in *piccioli*. As the chronicler Giovanni Villani relates, the *lanaioli*, whenever there was a shortage of money, induced the government to debase the silver currency without disturbing the gold florin ... In other words, they had found the way to reduce real wages without changing nominal wages ... by simply putting less silver into new coins.[75]

Of course, this could work both ways. The strict correlation between the onset of plague in Justinian's empire and his sharp revaluation of the *follis* is surely not accidental and shows how monetary relations could influence the supply of labour.

If the expansion of wage labour was a striking feature of the late antique eastern Mediterranean, the sheer commercial vitality of its urban centres was even more remarkable. Study of the ceramic assemblages at Marseilles, Carthage and elsewhere in the western Mediterranean has clearly established that the fifth century was an absolute watershed in terms of the breakthrough and partial dominance of exports of wine and olive oil from the eastern Mediterranean.[76] The commercial vitality of the eastern Mediterranean urban centres was a vitality backed by a 'widespread late antique boom in the rural economy',[77] with densely populated countrysides. What is not so obvious in the ceramic evidence are the kinds of *networks* that these massive Mediterranean flows presupposed. The penetration of western markets that was especially rapid from the second quarter of the fifth century was bound up, almost certainly, with a diaspora of merchant groups from the Levant. The affluence and business acumen of those groups are repeatedly noted by the author of the mid-fourth-century survey called *Expositio totius mundi*; for example, Tyre, densely populated, was well known for its 'wealthy businessmen', Ashkelon and Gaza 'seethed with business activity' and the Levant in general was characterised by its strong culture of business.[78] These are exceptionally valuable references, as they fill in some of the background to the extraordinary commercial thrust

[75] R. de Roover, 'Labour Conditions in Florence around 1400: Theory, Policy and Reality', in *Florentine Studies: Politics and Society in Renaissance Florence*, ed. N. Rubinstein (London, 1968), pp. 277–313, at 305.

[76] D. Pieri, *Le commerce du vin oriental à l'époque byzantine* (Beirut, 2005).

[77] S. T. Loseby, 'The Mediterranean Economy', in *The New Cambridge Mediaeval History*, vol. I: *c. 500–c. 700*, ed. P. Fouracre (Cambridge, 2005), pp. 605–38, at 631.

[78] *Expositio totius mundi* 24; 29; 33 (Rougé, pp. 158, 162, 166).

that developed in the fifth century by suggesting that eastern merchants were well placed in terms of capital resources to build networks abroad. At Carthage, they may have dominated the commercial and domestic quarter north of the circular harbour[79] and were a major pressure group behind Justinian's decision to invade Africa.[80] And when Guntram entered Orleans in 585, he was 'greeted by acclamations in Hebrew and Syriac as well as Latin'.[81] The dispersion of merchant colonies throughout the Mediterranean *may* imply a transformation of commerce such as that involved in the expansion of Venetian trade from the twelfth century. The famous (Alexandrian) financier in the Muziris contract was bound to have had late antique counterparts, but we know almost nothing about them.[82] John of Ephesus describes the 'great ship-owners' of Alexandria as the 'most powerful class in that wealthy city'. That was about 560.[83] Justinian (*Nov.* 106, 540) shows that there were capitalists who specialised in financing shippers and merchants for an expected return of not less than 10 per cent. Justinian's attempt to instigate an attack on Sasanian commercial interests and the Sasanian occupation of the Yemen in the last years of Khusro I's reign are striking indications of the money to be made by control of or even just access to the Indian Ocean.[84] This was a trading network ruthlessly controlled by the Sasanians, whose merchants would 'buy up whole cargoes [of silk]' by pre-emptive positioning in harbours where it first arrived.[85] On the other hand, a whole swathe of territory in the Fertile Crescent, from Edessa (indeed even further north, from Dvin) down to Bostra on the edge of the desert, prospered on trade with the (non-Roman) east,[86] which may well be one reason that the urban economies of the Levant held up so much better in the crisis that swept through the

79 Procopius, *Bell.* 3.20.3ff., 16 (Dewing, *History of the Wars*, vol. II, pp. 170, 174). Cf. F. M. Clover, 'Carthage and the Vandals', in *Excavations at Carthage 1978, Conducted by the University of Michigan*, vol. VII, ed. J. H. Humphrey (Ann Arbor, MI, 1982), pp. 1–22, at 8.

80 Procopius, *Bell.* 3.20.5–6 (Dewing, *History of the Wars*, vol. II, p. 170).

81 A. H. M. Jones, *The Later Roman Empire 284–602*, 2 vols (Oxford, 1964), vol. II, p. 865.

82 D. Rathbone, 'The "Muziris" Papyrus (*SB* XVIII 13167): Financing Roman Trade with India', in *Alexandrian Studies II in Honour of Mostafa el Abbadi*, ed. M. Abd-el-Ghani *et al.* (Alexandria, 2000), pp. 39–50.

83 John of Ephesus, *Third Part of the Ecclesiastical History*, p. 69 (trans. Payne Smith).

84 John Malalas, *Chron.* 18.56 (Thurn, p. 384–5; Jeffrey, p. 269); Procopius, *Bell.* 1.20.9 (Dewing, *History of the Wars*, vol. I, p. 192); Theophanes of Byzantium *ap.* Photius, *Bibl.*, vol. I, p. 78 (Henry) (explaining Khusro's decision as a *response* to the Byzantine drive to access the Central Asian silk routes via the Türks!).

85 Procopius, *Bell.* 1.20.12 (Dewing, *History of the Wars*, vol. I, p. 192), cf. D. Whitehouse and A. Williamson, 'Sasanian Maritime Trade', *Iran* 11 (1973), 29–49; D. Whitehouse, 'Epilogue: Roman Trade in Perspective', in *Rome and India: The Ancient Sea Trade*, ed. V. Begley *et al.* (Madison, 1991), pp. 216–18.

86 *Expositio totius mundi* 38 (Rougé, p. 176) (Bostra); 22 (p. 156) (Edessa); extrapolating to the sixth century.

Byzantine heartland in the seventh century. Edessa was so prosperous that Khusro I thought he could try to levy 50,000 pounds of gold from its residents,[87] and as late as 622, his grandson could strip 112,000 pounds of silver from its churches![88] And Maurice Sartre explains the wealth of the Hauran in the later sixth century through its contacts with the Ḥijāz, along trade routes whose success depended very largely on a 'network of agreements with local tribes'.[89]

The Hauran was a countryside dominated by *villages*, more typical in this respect of the east than areas with a dense concentration of estates. Indeed, there was no sector of the countryside in the eastern provinces that did not have villages and usually very substantial ones, like the large Negev village south of Elusa (and this in a purely marginal zone!) or Aphrodito in Egypt. Even the Fayyūm, which had an exceptional concentration of aristocratic properties by the seventh century, could boast large villages like Psenyris (still described in the seventeenth century as 'great and very beautiful') or Sele (Saīla), which Nabulsī (d. 1261) claimed had up to forty churches in the past![90] Both the sheer density of settlements in the rural areas of the east and the astonishing prosperity of so many of them reinforce the sense of a world where 'the extraordinary tide of Mediterranean life', which, in Peter Brown's unforgettable image, 'had washed further inland than ever previously' by the second century, had, quite simply, still not receded. The richer villages of the Hauran saw the construction of substantial rural houses in the Byzantine period, *maisons de village* that were linked to rich agricultural holdings and owned essentially by a rich peasantry with a strong sense of its own property.[91] The hill country was dominated by wine growing, and the absence of any trace of the olive suggests considerable regional specialisation. This was *one* countryside, dominated by villages and within them by a substantial peasantry engaged in cash cropping. Villeneuve's inferences are carefully controlled and a model of how far one should go with purely archaeological evidence. Others have been less restrained and characterise the

[87] Procopius, *Bell.* 2.26.39 (Dewing, *History of the Wars*, vol. 1, p. 498).

[88] *Chronicle of AD* 1234, §31 (Palmer, *The Seventh Century in the West-Syrian Chronicles*, pp. 133–4).

[89] M. Sartre, *Bostra: Des origines à l'Islam* (Paris, 1985), pp. 132ff.; M. Sartre, 'Le peuplement et le développement du Ḥawrān antique à la lumière des inscriptions grecques et latines', in *Hauran*, vol. 1: *Recherches archéologiques sur la Syrie du Sud à l'époque hellénistique et romaine*, ed. J.-M. Dentzer (Paris,1985–6), pp. 189–202, at 197–8; H. Kennedy, *The Prophet and the Age of the Caliphates*, 2nd edn (Harlow, 2004), p. 21. The geographer al-Iṣṭakhrī notes that ʿUmar b. al-Khaṭṭāb (the future caliph) had made his fortune trading with Gaza.

[90] al-Nabulsī, *Taʾrīkh al-Fayyūm* 114 (Moritz).

[91] F. Villeneuve, 'L'économie rurale et la vie des campagnes dans le Hauran antique', in *Hauran*, vol. 1, ed. Dentzer (Paris, 1985–6), pp. 63–136.

village populations of the Massif Calcaire farther north in terms like 'une petite paysannerie' and 'a middle class of peasants'.[92] These are meaningless characterisations, since they beg the question of who or what 'peasants' were in the late antique world. None of the numerous terms used (in Greek, for example) to describe people who owned or worked the land maps onto our own (sometimes confused) notions of the peasantry with quite the neatness or symmetry we would like. *Geōrgos* comes closest, but with the caveat that in late antique sources it refers often to a purely landless stratum that worked on large estates on a permanent basis. They certainly were not peasants and had little control of the land they worked. The villagers of Aphrodito described themselves as λεπτοκτήτορες (lit. 'small landowners') when appealing to the authorities, a term that has no obvious connotation of a peasantry.[93] On the other hand, the ownership of villages was a possible form of landholding in the east, not attested in any of the papyri I am familiar with, but certainly referred to by Libanius and John Chrysostom in the later fourth century. Indeed, even very substantial villages could be bought, as a story in Procopius shows.[94] This tradition appears to have been strongest in Armenia. In the pages of the anonymous late fifth-century compilation called *The Epic Histories*, the aristocracy there is depicted as residing in 'inaccessible fortresses protected by the rugged terrain of the country',[95] and it is possible that their 'estates' comprised the villages dominated from these fortresses.

Egypt is the only region where we can track the emergence and evolution of the aristocracy of the eastern Mediterranean with some consistency. The point of saying this is simply that it existed everywhere, from Constantinople to Armenia, and must broadly have reflected the same trends. If the consolidated western aristocracy of the fourth century suffered sustained erosion in the fifth and sixth, in the east by contrast a *new*, 'Byzantine' aristocracy would emerge in the middle decades of the fifth century. This was a *Dienstadel*, quite different in formation from the senatorial clans who dominated the western empire in the fourth and fifth centuries, purely urban in character and with a strong sense of the need to preserve their estates against subdivision and structure those estates as corporate entities that could survive the vagaries of individual fortune. For example, Flavius Apion I, described by Procopius as a man of extraordinary

[92] J.-P. Sodini, 'Archaeology and Late Antique Social Structures', in *Theory and Practice in Late Antique Archaeology*, ed. L. Lavan *et al.* (Leiden, 2003), pp. 29–56, at 46.

[93] *P. Lond.* v 1674.95–6; *P. Cairo Masp.* 67002.

[94] Procopius, *Anecd.* 30.18–19 (Dewing, *Secret History*, pp. 352ff.).

[95] N. G. Garsoïan, *The Epic Histories (Buzandaran Patmut'iwnk')* (Cambridge, MA, 1989), p. 52.

energy,[96] and *praefectus praetorio Orientis* (PPO) in 518, had in fact suffered a major setback in the latter part of Anastasius' reign when he was exiled, ostensibly on religious grounds.[97] Yet there is no evidence that the estate in the Oxyrhynchite suffered unduly. Indeed, when the last known Apion, Flavius Apion III, died in about 619 against the background of the Sasanian invasion of Egypt, the estate (οἶκος) continued to function as an integrated organisation for some years after that.[98] The corporatism of the Byzantine *oikoi* is a remarkable feature of the new aristocracy and reflected in the repeated occurrence of the expression 'the heirs of so-and-so' in the papyri. (When this expression was used, it meant that the estate had remained undivided.)[99] The Apions themselves expanded their holdings through matrimonial alliances, as Azzarello has shown.[100] Indeed, women played a major role in the affairs of the eastern Mediterranean aristocracy. The later papyri are replete with the names of women who presided over major aristocratic households. And at the elite level (the 'patricians'), this was a cosmopolitan aristocracy: Praejecta, the mother of Flavius Apion III, was herself the granddaughter of Justinian's niece of the same name,[101] while Apion III married the daughter of Rusticiana, one of a group of Italian aristocrats who had relocated to Constantinople following the Lombard invasion.

Rentiers? Risk-averse? How do we construe the economic characteristics of the new aristocracy? The French papyrologist Jean Gascou argued that they were content with a 'relative stagnation of revenues', expressed in fixed, long-term, money rents.[102] There are at least two reasons he espoused this odd view. In the first place, he thought that the substantial long-term leases based on what was called *emphyteusis* were a major source of revenue for the Apions. This implies a whole theory of the way estates were organised economically and in terms of their use of labour. At another level, Gascou believed that the Byzantine *oikoi* were semi-public agencies, regulated by government and its drive to enforce a stable exaction of revenue. Neither of these views is plausible. There are very few

96 Procopius, *Bell.* 1.8.5 (Dewing, *History of the Wars*, vol. 1, p. 63).

97 P. Sarris, *Economy and Society in the Age of Justinian* (Cambridge, 2006), pp. 16–17.

98 E.g. *P. Oxy.* LXVIII 4703 dated 22.5.622.

99 N. Gonis, 'Studies on the Aristocracy of Late Antique Oxyrhynchus', *Tyche* 17 (2002), 85–97, at p. 92.

100 G. Azzarello, '*P.Oxy.* XVI 2039 e la nascita della *domus gloriosa* degli Apioni', *Zeitschrift für Papyrologie und Epigraphik* 155 (2006), 207–28, at pp. 210ff., n. 8.

101 J. Beaucamp, 'Apion et Praejecta: Hypothèses anciennes et nouvelles données', *Revue des études byzantines* 59 (2001), 165–78.

102 J. Gascou, 'Les grandes domaines, la cité et l'état en Égypte byzantine', *Travaux et Mémoires* 9 (1985), 1–90, at p. 10.

leases in the Apion archive,[103] and the estate accounts and waterwheel receipts both show that the *ousia* was structured in terms of labour settlements (*epoikia*) rather than dispersed cash tenancies, let alone the very substantial leases that *emphyteusis* involved.[104] This should not be surprising, as Dominic Rathbone's work on the third century likewise shows an aristocratic property managed in terms of the use of a regular, permanent labour force supplemented in this case by casual labourers.[105] The rural workers, usually called *geōrgoi*, were paid in a combination of usufruct plots, estate accommodation and cash wages (paid in gold), and sometimes also allowances in kind. The bureaucratised methods of estate management also suggest a substantial investment in overhead that is hard to reconcile with a model of dispersed tenancies, where the whole point is to minimise the burden of management. As for the view that aristocrats like the Apions had ceased to have an independent economic existence but that, like the church, the aristocracy was effectively a public agency, Roger Rémondon expressed this idea in a more nuanced way than Gascou when he referred to the Byzantine evolution as one based essentially on a 'transfer of public functions to private institutions'.[106] In Egypt, the pagarchy was perhaps the most striking expression of this peculiar fusion of public and private power, because pagarchs were, by and large, leading aristocrats, and the 'office' was an expression of the control they had established over rural taxation. It is not often noticed that in Edict XIII, ostensibly designed to rein in recalcitrant magnates, Justinian in fact removed the authority of the Augustalis over the pagarchs![107]

Behind the fiscal solidarity of aristocracy and state in the eastern Mediterranean lay a more profound evolution, the fact that the state had come to rely on the church and the aristocracy in a fundamental way in the financial management of the empire. If Byzantine Italy, with its rapid dispersion of the former aristocracy, saw a 'clerical take-over of senatorial traditions' and a new, decisively enhanced role for the church (this was true even in the Lombard areas),[108] in the Byzantine east Justinian redrew

[103] As Gascou himself notes! Cf. Gonis, *P. Oxy.* LXVII 4615 intr. (p. 235).

[104] *P. Lond.* II 483 (615 or 616) is a perfectly preserved specimen of an emphyteutic lease. Typically, it involves a monastery, not one of the *oikoi*.

[105] D. Rathbone, *Economic Rationalism and Rural Society in Third-Century A.D. Egypt: The Heroninos Archive and the Appianus Estate* (Cambridge, 1991).

[106] Rémondon, 'L'Égypte au 5e siècle de notre ère', p. 142.

[107] Just., *Ed.* xiii, 12; 25. Most likely date: 539.

[108] Brown, *Gentlemen and Officers* (n. 59), p. 35; W. Pohl, 'The Empire and the Lombards: Treatises and Negotiations in the Sixth Century', in *Kingdoms of the Empire: The Integration of Barbarians in Late Antiquity*, ed. W. Pohl (Leiden, 1997), p. 125.

the map of public and private interests by integrating wealthy individuals, as well as institutions like the church, in the conduct of public business. This was a distinctively Byzantine development, quite different from the way the western senatorial aristocracy had *shared* power with the military and bureaucratic establishment by its own unilateral domination of the civil administration. (Valentinian I hated Petronius Probus but gave him a free hand all the same!) For example, Flavius Anastasius, banker in a famous contract dated 541, was described as καστρησιανὸς τῆς θείας τραπέζης καὶ ἀργυροπράτης [sic]. That τραπέζη should refer to anything other than a bank in this context is unlikely, and the description suggests that Anastasius ran his own banking business and was simultaneously connected with the imperial bank at Constantinople, where he lived.[109] So, too, with the racier and more ambitious Peter Barsymes, who began as a hugely successful banker before Justinian appointed him *comes sacrarum largitionum* (head of the treasury) in 542 and PPO soon afterward. That Peter did not relinquish his own business interests when appointed to those financial posts is clear from Procopius' accusation that 'he established a state monopoly on trade in silk and made for himself a great personal profit thereby'.[110] In fact, it is the Byzantine silk industry that offers the best example of the subtle forms of integration of state and private capital that had evolved by the sixth century, which expressions like 'state monopoly' and 'personal profit' describe in a misleading way. The fact that a whole swathe of exceedingly high-ranking aristocrats were actively involved in the industry as so-called *kommerkiarioi*[111] certainly suggests that, at least down to the main part of the seventh century, they were not simply officials in some purely administrative sense, but, as argued by Oikonomidès, 'wealthy businessmen' who bid for monopolistic control of the trade in silk within wide-ranging regional markets. In Oikonomidès's words, 'We have here a very small number of very wealthy people, who do business with the state and in the name of the state.' Such individuals could form partnerships or business associations when bidding for

[109] *P. Cairo Masp.* II 67126.

[110] *PLRE* IIIb, p. 1001, citing Procopius, *Anecd.* 25.20–6 (Dewing, *Secret History*, pp. 298ff.), which claims that management of the industry was centralised under the *comes sacrarum largitionum*, namely, Peter, who siphoned the bulk of its profits. But in *Anecd.* 20.5 (Dewing, *Secret History*, p. 234) Procopius himself makes it clear that the 'monopolies' were based on competitive bidding.

[111] C. Morrisson and W. Seibt, 'Sceaux de commerciaires byzantins du VIIe siècle trouvés à Carthage', *Revue Numismatique* 24 (1982), 222–41, esp. pp. 226f., 228, 231; J.-C. Cheynet, C. Morrisson and W. Seibt, *Les sceaux byzantins de la Collection Henri Seyrig* (Paris, 1991), pp. 103 (#140), 105 (#143), 105f. (#144); with titles like *paneuphemos* and *endoxotatos*.

contracts, and Oikonomidès even describes them as 'wealthy individuals at the head of powerful economic organizations'.[112]

Scarcely risk-averse, then. The regulation of private commerce by the state can hardly be construed as a sign of 'autocratic centralization'.[113] Those images were popular at a time when the academic imagination was shaped by the imposing conflict between western-style capitalism with supposedly free markets and Soviet bureaucracy. The vibrant economies of the late antique eastern Mediterranean would have had thousands of commercial establishments, well-organised money markets and numerous middle-sized cities like Scythopolis, where a decline in the architectural quality of the town was in part a reflection of the rampant growth of private businesses and a more densely built-up urban environment.[114] Both church and aristocracy owned *ergastēria* – commercial and industrial establishments of various kinds – the cathedral or Great Church of Constantinople owning no fewer than 1,100 of them.[115] Justinian *Nov.* 159 (555), in a document reproducing the will of the aristocrat Hierios and describing a *proasteion* he owned in the suburbs of Constantinople he wanted left to his grandson, shows that these rich suburban estates could include *ergastēria* as well.[116] Čekalova suggested that the aristocracy of Constantinople was not mainly a landed group and held the bulk of its assets in liquid form.[117] Whatever one thinks of this, it certainly suggests a more diversified asset base for the late antique aristocracy than the cliché of a purely landed class. However we characterise the aristocracy of Constantinople itself, it is clear that a vast amount of gold was in circulation in the eastern empire, and the urban economies of the east were sufficiently vibrant to allow for the existence of a wide range of monied groups, such as jewel traders, bankers, silversmiths and silk merchants. Money changers and bankers were among the most prosperous groups in

[112] N. Oikonomidès, 'Silk Trade and Production: The Seals of *Kommerkiarioi*', *Dumbarton Oaks Papers* 40 (1986), 33–53, esp. pp. 39–40, 43.

[113] G. Ostrogorsky, *History of the Byzantine State*, 2nd edn, trans. J. Hussey (Oxford, 1968), p. 253. Marlia Mango refers, with more preciseness, to 'private commerce regulated by the state', M. M. Mango, 'The Commercial Map of Constantinople', *Dumbarton Oaks Papers* 54 (2000), 189–207, at p. 190.

[114] Y. Tsafrir, 'Some Notes on the Settlement and Demography of Palestine in the Byzantine Period', in *Retrieving the Past*, ed. J. D. Seger, (Winona Lake, IN, 1996), pp. 269–83, esp. 276. 'Numerous middle-sized cities' from A. E. Laiou and C. Morrisson, *The Byzantine Economy* (Cambridge, 2007), p. 26.

[115] Just., *Nov.* 43 (536) (*CIC* vol. III, pp. 269ff.); *Vita S. Olympiadis* 6 (*Anal. Boll.* 1896, p. 414).

[116] Just., *Nov.* 159 pr. (*CIC* vol. III, pp. 736ff., at 738).

[117] A. Čekalova, 'Fortune des sénateurs de Constantinople du IVe au début du VIIe siècle', in *ΕΥΨΥΧΙΑ: Mélanges offerts à Hélène Ahrweiler* (Paris, 1998), pp. 119–30.

Ephesus,[118] and the eastern Mediterranean money market functioned with considerable autonomy from government control. In Edict XI, Justinian attacked the coin weighers and dealers (*chrysōnes*) of Alexandria for charging the public an exorbitant commission of 12.5 per cent on transactions involving loose solidi that had lost weight in circulation. This was in 559 during the second prefecture of Peter Barsymes, and Justinian instructed Peter to make sure that the dealers reverted to a rate that would facilitate transactions involving loose coins. As it happens, the papyri show that this particular intervention did bring the commission down to half its former level, 6.25 per cent. In *P. Oxy.* I 144, dated 580, a payment of 720 solidi described as 'in loose coin from the interior districts' attracts a supplement of 45 solidi 'for deficiencies in purity and weight' (*hyper obryzēs kai apokatastatikōn*); in other words, 1.5 carats per solidus or 6.25 per cent. Here is an excellent example of the nature of Byzantine regulation, namely, not quite the dramatic model of 'autocratic centralization' that Ostrogorsky had in mind but a more pragmatic and flexible attempt to encourage the flow of business by eliminating excesses from the market.

The fiscal system of the sixth century was very largely monetised. A detailed tax register from an Egyptian district, Antaeopolis, is one indication of this.[119] Using this document, A. H. M. Jones was able to calculate that 10,322 solidi was the 'normal gold assessment of Antaeopolis' in the reign of Justinian.[120] This works out to a cash ratio of almost 63 per cent; in other words, close to two thirds of the total revenue from this district (one of the lesser ones) was paid in gold.[121] The very high levels of money taxation that the Umayyads could extract from Egypt was thus a development of trends established in the sixth and seventh centuries. Michael Metcalf has shown that the truncated Byzantine state of the later seventh century ran into a severe monetary recession, as the treasury was depleted of fresh inflows following the Arab conquests.[122] But this fiscal crisis and the general deflation bound up with it are *not* a reflection of the state of monetary economy in the eastern Mediterranean in these decades. The Mediterranean remained integrated for much of the sixth and seventh centuries, with Byzantine control of Africa playing a pivotal role in

[118] C. Foss, *Ephesus after Antiquity: A Late Antique, Byzantine and Turkish City* (Cambridge, 1979), p. 8.

[119] *P. Cairo Masp.* I 67057.

[120] A. H. M. Jones, 'Review of Johnson and West, *Byzantine Egypt: Economic Studies*', *Journal of Hellenic Studies* 71 (1951), 271–2, at p. 271.

[121] Contrast Wickham's view: 'It was in general unlikely that most taxation was moved between regions in the form of money in our period', Wickham, *Framing*, p. 768.

[122] Metcalf, 'Monetary Recession'.

preserving the link between its opposite shores. There was an abundance of gold in Africa, Sicily and the Aegean,[123] and much of the continued circulation of solidi and tremisses was undoubtedly due to trade. The very substantial late seventh-century deposit from the Crypta Balbi in Rome[124] is a microcosm of the continued economic vitality of the Mediterranean in this period, despite the huge changes that swept through it politically. The conquests themselves involved no dramatic economic disruption,[125] and the huge sums that cities like Emesa agreed to settle for show just how prosperous the urban Levant remained.[126]

Aftermaths

The transition to the early Middle Ages thus certainly requires the complex and differentiated model that Wickham has developed, minus its minimalism and the obsessive focus on taxation. Catastrophist images of late antiquity were built on the political dissolution of the western empire, coupled with the intensity of the dislocations in sixth-century peninsular Italy. Francovich and Hodges build their model of the Italian transformation on the large-scale desertion of the countryside by the aristocracy and a dramatic shift in the settlement pattern over the later sixth and seventh centuries.[127] For his part, Paolo Delogu refers in Italy's case to the 'great crisis of the sixth and seventh century'.[128] But in Francia, which saw a fairly rapid integration of the surviving aristocracy and the Frankish ruling class, the seventh century was a period of agrarian and demographic expansion, spearheaded by the powerful new nobilities that emerged in the Merovingian *Teilreiche* by the end of the sixth century.[129] The Merovingians inherited the late Roman system of unified estates (*villae*)

[123] R. Guéry, C. Morrisson and H. Slim, *Le trésor de monnaies d'or byzantines: Recherches archéologiques franco-tunisiennes à Rougga 3* (Rome, 1982); Banaji, *Agrarian Change*, pp. 63–4, 83–4.

[124] L. Saguì, 'Roma, i centri privilegiati e la lunga durata della tarda antichità: Dati archeologici dal deposito di VII secolo nell'esedra della Crypta Balbi', *Archeologia Medievale* 29 (2002), 7–42.

[125] Villeneuve, 'L'économie rurale', pp. 64, 128; J. Magness, *The Archaeology of the Early Islamic Settlement in Palestine* (Winona Lake, IN, 2003), p. 215; Loseby, 'Mediterranean Economy', p. 633; A. Walmsley, 'Production, Exchange and Regional Trade in the Islamic East Mediterranean', in *The Long Eighth Century*, ed. I. L. Hansen *et al.* (Leiden, 2000), pp. 265–343, esp. 291–3.

[126] al-Balādhurī, *Futūh al-buldān*, p. 136 (ed. Ridwan).

[127] R. Francovich and R. Hodges, *Villa to Village: The Transformation of the Roman Countryside in Italy c. 400–800* (London, 2003), p. 109.

[128] P. Delogu, 'La fine del mondo antico e l'inizio del medioevo', in *La storia dell'Alto Medioevo italiano (VI–X secolo) alla luce dell'archeologia*, ed. R. Francovich *et al.* (Florence, 1994), pp. 7–29, at 23.

[129] R. Sprandel, *Der merovingische Adel und die Gebiete östlich des Rheins* (Freiburg im Breisgau, 1957).

with their mixed servile labour forces. Slavery was a substantial part of the late antique legacy, but the great movement of manumission that swept through post-Roman societies in the sixth and seventh centuries threw up a less segregated labour force described generically as *mancipia* – not slaves in the rigorous Roman sense but servile all the same, a conglomerate of all the various forms of labour oppression that had survived as part of the debris of the western empire. Manumission entailed the creation of service holdings and the first assaults on the physical integrity of the unified villa.[130] By the *late* seventh century, the Merovingian aristocracy had forged the elements of a new organisation of labour, a further break from antiquity, a further move into the pure Middle Ages. Chris Wickham's rejection of the 'slavery to serfdom' model is unexceptionable and welcome, except that much of that rejection is based on views about late and post-Roman labour organisation that flow more from abstractions than from a closer consideration of the terminology used in sources such as the Merovingian charters. For example, 'Most *servi/mancipia* in our period ... were tenants who *controlled their own holding* and could keep its fruits after rents were paid'.[131] But *mancipia* included former *coloni*, bound tenants, and *servi* were still slaves in Francia, Visigothic Spain and elsewhere, and it is doubtful that these groups in particular were ever thought to 'control their own holdings', whatever other groups may actually have done so. Wickham's thesis of the conversion of slaves into self-managing peasants is really equivalent to the thesis that Roman landowners abandoned direct management, a view I have suggested is implausible.[132]

Farther east, Islam emerged as the dominant economic power in the eighth to eleventh centuries,[133] but much of the prosperity of that period flowed from the legacy of vibrant urban economies inherited from late antiquity by the Umayyads. A key part of that legacy was the monetary economy of the late Roman and Sasanian worlds. The existing coinages (solidi and drahms) continued to circulate for some five decades after the conquests, a fact that is usually little emphasised. The general implication is a strong degree of cultural and economic continuity across the political watersheds of the seventh century, an indication surely of the astonishing resilience of the eastern Mediterranean in this period and the vitality of

130 J. Banaji, 'Aristocracies, Peasantries and the Framing of the Early Middle Ages', *Journal of Agrarian Change* 9(1) (2009), 59–91, at pp. 70ff. See Chapter 7 in this volume, esp. pp. 156ff.

131 Wickham, *Framing*, p. 560; italics mine.

132 See my discussion of Wickham in Chapter 7 in this volume.

133 M. Lombard, 'Les bases monétaires d'une suprématie économique: L'or musulman du VIIe au XIe siècle', *Annales* 2 (1947), 143–60, the classic statement.

its urban sectors. In Egypt, the province of Arcadia could still be assessed for the substantial sum of 200,000 solidi in the early seventh century.[134] Alexandria's population was 300,000 taxable adults at the time of the conquest,[135] which yields a total population of well over a million and puts this great eastern metropolis in the same orbit, demographically, as ninth-century Baghdād, medieval Cordoba and Tang cities like Xi'an and Luoyang. Baṣra, founded in the late 630s, had a population of roughly half a million by the 680s.[136] None of this suggests a demographic fragility any more extreme than the biological precariousness of all ancien régime populations.[137] Of course, the loss of the affluent eastern provinces was a severe financial blow to the Byzantine state and led directly to the prolonged monetary recession I referred to. But the image of imperial crisis that this suggests can scarcely be extended either to the Merovingians, ruling over what was now the richest region of Europe, or to the Muslim Near East, both of which inherited the mantle of late antiquity to become the cutting edge of major new developments.

[134] An estimate based on *P. Oxy.* XVI 1909.

[135] Al-Maqrīzī, *Kitāb al-mawā'iẓ wa-al-i'tibār bi-dhikr al-khiṭaṭ wa-al-āthār*, trans. U. Bouriant, *Description topographique et historique de l'Égypte* (Paris, 1895–1900), p. 226, citing Ibn Lahī'ā. A tradition attributed to the renowned and more reliable Egyptian authority 'Uthmān b. Sālīḥ claimed that Egypt had a total taxable population (meaning a population of adult males) of 'over six million' (Ibn 'Abd al-Ḥakam, *Futūḥ Miṣr*, ed. Torrey, p. 70, lines 10–12), but this would yield an impossibly high figure for the overall demography. Yāqūt cites 'over six million' as the size of the total native population of the country: *Mu'jam al-buldān* (ed. Wüstenfeld), vol. III, p. 895.

[136] G. Rotter, *Die Umayyaden und der Zweite Bürgerkrieg (680–692)* (Wiesbaden, 1982), p. 69; half a million *c.*683.

[137] F. Braudel, *The Mediterranean and the Mediterranean World in the Age of Philip II*, 2 vols, trans. Siân Reynolds (London, 1975), vol. I, p. 413.

PART II

Monetary circulation (rules, rhythms)

CHAPTER 5

Discounts, weight standards and the exchange rate between gold and copper

Insights into the monetary process of the sixth century

Bankers and merchants are among the least well defined groups in ancient history and late antiquity is no exception. We view the ancient world in terms of a sharp and obvious contrast with our own, and it is not plain to us, therefore, that the trading and banking communities of the ancient Mediterranean would have had to organise their affairs with some sophistication to be able to provide the economic and financial infrastructure of the considerable commercial activity which occurred across the length and breadth of that sea, certainly down to the end of the seventh century. That merchants organised the supply of commodities like flax using some form of the 'advance system' shows that they were quite familiar with practices known to us from more recent periods. But who those merchants were, how far they represented commercial firms in Alexandria, and how commercial capital organised its network both domestically and between regions are all largely unknown. Unlike the Geniza records and their profound illumination of the activity of urban groups, the vast bulk of our papyrological evidence comes from the drier, southern districts, which may well have been backwaters in the vibrant commercial economy of cities like Alexandria. On the other hand, it is clear that with the expanding circulation of gold in the middle and later fourth century, bankers diversified into the business of money-dealing. Thus we can view monetary circulation from the perspective of their involvement, and form some impression of the power or influence of such groups. This implies, however, that our picture of the circulation pattern should be broad enough to define its dynamics not just in terms of an abstractly describable monetary 'system' (the physical evolution of coinages), but also, *and essentially*, as a network of rules and institutions without which money may even have ceased to circulate.

This broader view of monetary circulation could start with issues such as the following: if most important transactions were effected in gold, as they were in late antiquity, how worn was the gold coinage in circulation?

How much can we say about the longevity of the main coins in circulation, or about the practices which evolved to handle problems of weight loss? Some light can be thrown on some of these issues by examining the evidence of the hoards, provided we can be certain that the hoards in question are representative of the circulating medium at a given point in time, i.e. are currency hoards and not, say, accumulations which have travelled with their owner.[1] Also, the bigger hoards give us a better impression of the currency in circulation, and, in particular, of the extent to which older solidi continued to circulate in various periods.[2] The hoard from Chatby in Alexandria is an excellent example of this type of hoard. It contained a total of 191 gold pieces including 27 semisses and 71 tremisses, buried in a suburb of that city early in 611.[3] Thus roughly half the number of pieces comprised fractions, while in terms of value around 25 to 30% of the currency was constituted by these smaller denominations. Age-wise, some 38% of the hoard comprised pieces that had been in circulation *for over thirty years*. In other words, the gold currency in circulation in Alexandria *c.*611 contained both a fair number of the fractional gold pieces as well as a significant proportion of coins minted some three, four or five decades earlier. Since fractions circulate at a higher velocity, both features point to an active circulation of gold in the urban centres of the eastern Mediterranean in late antiquity. In a rather different geographical context, a sixth-century hoard with a large proportion of fractions (37% semisses, 8.5% tremisses) – from Afyon (anc. Acroeinos) in Phrygia – included fifteen semisses of Justinian I which had been in circulation for not much more than a decade.[4] Yet the average weight of the semisses in this hoard is said to be 2.15 g, which is an average weight loss of 5.36%, reflecting an annual loss of 0.357%. In two gold hoards of the very early sixth century found in the ancient synagogue of Horvat Rimmon 40 km south-east of Gaza, tremisses account for 58% and 71% of the total number of pieces.

[1] The most detailed discussion of *types* of hoards I know of is John Deyell, *Living without Silver* (New Delhi, 1990).

[2] Cf. T. R. Volk, 'Mint Output and Coin Hoards', in *Rhythmes de la production monetaire de l'antiquité à nos jours*, ed. G. Depeyrot *et al.* (Louvain-la-Neuve, 1987), pp. 141–221, esp. 159: 'The larger the hoard, the better, in general, it is likely to reflect the composition of the currency pool from which it is withdrawn.'

[3] See E. D. J. Dutilh, 'Une trouvaille de 191 monnaies d'or byzantines et de 1 pièce en argent', *Revue Belge de Numismatique* 61 (1905), pp. 155–64, with P. Grierson, 'The Consular Coinage of "Heraclius" and the Revolt against Phocas of 608–610', *Numismatic Chronicle*, ser. vi, 10 (1950), 71–93, esp. p. 77 for the date and a minor correction.

[4] C. Morrisson, A. Ilasli and S. Özgündüz, 'Le trésor de monnaies d'or byzantines d'Afyon, Phrygie (VIe siècle)', *Revue Numismatique*, ser. vi, 31 (1989), 138–44 (discovered in 1984).

The most recent tremisses, of Anastasius, show a weight loss of *c.*4%, five tremisses of Leo I an average loss of *c.*10%.[5]

Of course, the metrology of gold hoards requires a systematic study, and it is not my intention in this chapter to pursue this line of enquiry. My interest is in the implications of a situation where the circulation of gold was both widespread and regular. In a monetary system based on a full-value coinage, the problems posed by weight loss would have required solutions, or at least responses, of a systematic nature. The documentary evidence can throw light on some of these issues and help to build a more complete picture of the circulation process in its 'real' forms. What I shall do in this chapter is attempt to reorganise this evidence (mostly papyrological) into a more coherent account of the sixth-century monetary process than we seem to find in studies such as Hendy's book on Byzantine monetary economy[6] or in the largely outdated work of West and Johnson.[7]

Reinstating metrology: the 'minus carats' system

I shall begin by offering a reinterpretation of the so-called 'minus carats' system against the explanations advanced by West and Johnson in *Currency in Roman and Byzantine Egypt*, which have developed into something of an orthodoxy, judging by the number of scholars who repeat their ideas uncritically. It is well known that the papyri refer to various weight standards (*zyga*) in transactions involving payments in the gold coinage. Different standards were in use in different localities in Egypt and elsewhere, and these were usually, though by no means always, referred to by the name of the locality. Since payments expressed in terms of local standards were in most, though not all, cases formulated as 'so many solidi minus so many carats', e.g. '1 solidus minus 6 carats on the Hermopolite standard (*zygo Hermoupoleos*)', to West and Johnson it seemed that an actual deduction of *value* was involved in these cases, and that the standards in question were 'in official registers, at least, ... bookkeeping devices which enable[d] the local tax-office to determine easily and simply the amount to be deducted or charged on the various accounts'.[8] This theory is manifestly unacceptable for various reasons, not least because it fails to explain why such fiscal deductions, if that is what they were, *varied so*

[5] A. Kloner and T. Mindel, 'Two Byzantine Hoards from the Ancient Synagogue of Ḥorvat Rimmon', *Israel Numismatic Journal* 5 (1981), 60–8 (discovered in 1979).

[6] M. Hendy, *Studies in the Byzantine Monetary Economy c. 300–1450* (Cambridge, 1985).

[7] L. C. West and A. C. Johnson, *Currency in Roman and Byzantine Egypt* (repr. Amsterdam, 1967).

[8] West and Johnson, *Currency*, p. 154.

considerably between districts, and, indeed, West and Johnson repeatedly confessed their inability to explain the nature of the 'deductions' involved in various documents.[9] For example, almost every Byzantine land lease makes it plain that owners, not tenants, paid the taxes accruing on the area leased, yet on p. 155 one reads, 'Leases are frequently given for a solidus or more usually with a deduction of 2 c. per s. This deduction seems to be for the land-tax which was paid by the lessee.'[10] What these authors were clearly reacting against was the notion that the various standards might have something to do with the weight of the actual coins, whether individual pieces or denominations, such as the lightweight solidi which began to be issued, on different standards, in the course of the sixth century.[11] Yet they themselves were aware both that gold circulated in large quantities and that the currency might include worn solidi.[12]

In Hendy's book the problem of weight loss emerges in a more emphatic way.[13] However, Hendy misconstrues the solutions evolved to cope with the problem, as I have argued elsewhere,[14] because he accepts West and Johnson's conception of the local standards as involving actual deductions of value, or, more precisely, as the expression of a system enforcing such deductions. Thus when a solidus is said to be 'minus so many carats', this, for Hendy, implies that it is subject to some process of valuation and that its value is determined as 24–*x* carats. Since this adjustment of values always works downwards, Hendy describes the reduction as a 'discount'. However, he is aware that the local standards applied across the board to a large set of monetary transactions in the individual localities, and also that different localities might have different standards, so he concludes that officials or whoever enforced *general* discounts but also that such 'general'

9 Esp. *Currency*, pp. 151ff. About the Fayum 'deduction' of 6¾–7 carats per solidus, they state (p. 152), 'This deduction is much higher than those found at Oxyrhynchus and *the reason for the difference is unknown*.' About *P. Lond.* II 483, a well-preserved emphyteutic lease dated 616, they write, 'in spite of the clause in this lease which stipulates that the lessee shall not be obligated to pay any *synteleia*, or any other charges, it is possible (!) that a tax of 2 c. per s. was exacted and this he paid to the state (through his emphyteutor)' (p. 151). About *P. Oxy.* 2045, where the *symmachoi* are paid on the 'private' standard, 'The nature of the deduction is unknown' (p. 153). We should also note that the qualification 'in official registers at least' actually suggests that public and private transactions may have used an identical terminology in (possibly) different senses!

10 West and Johnson, *Currency*, p. 155.

11 The best recent discussion of these is J. Smedley, 'Seventh-century Byzantine Coins in Southern Russia and the Problem of Light Weight Solidi', in *Studies in Early Byzantine Gold Coinage*, ed. W. Hahn *et al.* (New York, 1988), pp. 111–30.

12 See esp. West and Johnson, *Currency*, pp. 108 (on *P. Brem.* 83) and 115.

13 Esp. Hendy, *Studies*, p. 346.

14 In my D. Phil., *Rural Communities in the Late Empire*, pp. 104ff.

discounts *could* vary from one district to another.[15] What emerges from this view of the monetary system is an arbitrary, coercive and bureaucratic regime which ended up by disregarding the weight and value of individual pieces by substituting general discounts and presumably forcing people to accept them. Moreover, such discounts are supposed to have varied from a minimum of 8⅓% (on the goldsmith's standard) to as much as 30% (on standards prevalent in the Fayum). Since the main holders of gold assets were the aristocracy and trading classes of the late empire, one has to suppose that they were the chief victims of such a monetary regime!

We can surely rule out the view of Monneret De Villard, Ostrogorsky and others that the minus carats system was related somehow to the circulation of lightweight solidi,[16] since the evolution of the system clearly predates the earliest known issues of such solidi, without discarding the idea that the *zyga* were indeed standards for the weighing of the gold denominations, and that they formed a unified and rational system of adjustments, a sort of conversion table which took one standard (called the 'Alexandrian standard') as the central point of reference. In other words, I shall argue that the 'gold standards' of Egypt (and other parts of the Mediterranean) have nothing to do with the problem of weight loss, whether as accounting devices or as expressions of the circulation of lightweight solidi, and that we have to look elsewhere for the practices which evolved within the eastern Mediterranean banking community to cope with the inevitable problem of worn gold. In more theoretical terms, these were and remained distinct 'form determinations' of the circulation of gold money and it is scarcely helpful to start by confusing them. I shall also suggest that the distinctive feature of the late antique monetary system was that it seemed to lack a legal limit between bullion and coin.

The arguments for a metrological interpretation of the minus carats system rest both on the evidence of actual weights which have survived and on the explicit testimony of the papyri. For the sake of brevity, I shall concentrate only on the most important items of evidence.

Table 5.1 summarises calculations regarding what I call the 'adjusted' weight of the solidus following the various estimates provided for the heavier Egyptian *uncia* or *kharrūbah* (carat).

[15] Cf. his reference to the Arsinoite (or Fayum) standard as a 'general discount or charge of quite scandalous proportions' (Hendy, *Studies*, p. 360).

[16] U. Monneret de Villard, 'Sui diversi valori del soldo bizantino', *Rivista Italiana di Numismatica* 36 (1923), 33–40; G. Ostrogorsky, 'Löhne und Preise in Byzanz', *Byzantinische Zeitschrift* 32 (1932), 293–333, at p. 296, n. 3.

Table 5.1 *Pound weights and the adjusted weight of the solidus*

Source	lb weight	% diff. over Roman lb = 327.45 g	Difference (col. 3) expressed in carats	Adjusted weight of a full-weight solidus (in carats)
Petrie average 1	332.1907	1.4477	0.3475	23.652
Petrie average 2	338.6448	3.4187	0.8205	23.179
Miles p. 84	338.1696	3.2736	0.7856	23.214
Petrie 1918	341.3664	4.2499	1.0199	22.980
Lang	363.83	–	–	–
Grierson's Arabic carat	359.424	6.2851 (see note)	1.5084	22.49

Sources and note: Petrie average 1 = W. M. Flinders Petrie, *Ancient Weights and Measures Illustrated by the Egyptian Collection in University College London* (London, 1926), p. 26, scale box in pl. xvi; Petrie average 2 = Petrie, *loc. cit.*, smaller scale box; G. C. Miles, 'On the Varieties and Accuracy of Eighth-Century Arab Coin Weights', in *L. A. Mayer Memorial Volume (1895–1959)*, ed. M. Avi-Yonha *et al.* (Jerusalem, 1964), p. 84 (Egyptian *kharrubah* = 0.1957 g); Petrie 1918 = W. M. Flinders Petrie, 'Glass Weights', *Numismatic Chronicle* 18, ser. 4 (1918), 111–16, at p. 114 (Ptolemaic *uncia* of 439 grains); M. Lang, 'A Roman Bronze Weight from Egypt', *American Numismatic Society Museum Notes* 7 (1957), 91–3, at p. 93 ('Alexandrian *litra*'); P. Grierson, 'The Monetary Reforms of ʿAbd al-Malik', *JESHO* 3 (1960), 241–64, at pp. 250ff. (Arabic carat = 0.208 g). In the last row of Table 5.1, the % difference is calculated against the Egyptian carat of 0.1957 g (cf. Miles), for reasons that will be obvious in the text.

The two averages quoted by Flinders Petrie are based on late Roman weight sets containing brass weights and dated probably to the latter part of the fourth century. Row 5 gives Lang's estimate of the weight of the 'Alexandrian' pound based on bronze weights of the early empire. The calculation against Miles derives from his recalculation of the weight of the Egyptian *kharrūbah* or carob seed as 0.1957 g. Finally, the last row shows the difference in weight between the Arabic carat of 0.208 g and the Egyptian carat of 0.1957 g (rather than the usual estimate of 0.196 g accepted by Grierson himself in his *JESHO* article) and shows the adjustment (against an Egyptian base) if new scales were introduced into Egypt based on the Arabic carat (see the following text). Except for this last case, the base for adjustment is the heavier Roman pound of 327.45 g. If the estimates of Petrie (rows 1–2 in the table) and Miles reflect the weight range of the Alexandrian pound in the late Roman period, then it is easy to see why a solidus weighed on the 'Alexandrian scale' could be described as 'of 23 carats'. *This description occurs explicitly in at least two papyri*, both of the seventh century, and the important point to note is that in one of them, *BGU* II 367.13ff. from the Fayum, the solidi are described not only as 'each of 23 carats on the Alexandrian scale', but also as *obryza*, that is, of *full* purity and weight.[17] Likewise, in the Nessana papyri, where solidi weighed on the Gaza scale (*zygo Gazes*) are consistently described as 'minus one carat', *P. Ness.* 46.4, dated 605, describes 'pure gold, four-gram weight solidi' (*chrysina ombryza tetragrammiaia*) as minus 1 carat each 'on the Gaza standard'.[18] Again, both in *CPR* VII 47.4 (6c?) and in *SB* I 5320.14–15 (Byz.), solidi 'of 23 carats' are described as *obryza*, and in *SB* VIII 9750 (25.2.642) as *obry(ziaka)*.[19] What mattered in all these instances was a description of the fineness and weight of the coins in question and, often, a reference to the scale or standard on which these had been established. Where no reference was made to the Alexandrian scale but solidi of pure gold were described as 'of 23 carats', we can be certain that the Alexandrian (Gaza, etc.) scale was presupposed.

The least this establishes is that the 'minus carats' expression, when qualified by (implicit or explicit) reference to a standard, did not entail or imply a loss or deduction of value. Also, the description of solidi weighed on the Alexandrian scale as being 'of 23 carats' or 'minus 1 carat' was very clearly a weight adjustment, given the heavier weight of the Alexandrian pound.

The next issue this raises is whether a similar process of reasoning can be applied to the other Egyptian standards. Hypothetically, one might suggest that the most plausible metrological equation to account for the main local standards (the 'public' at minus 6 carats, and the 'private' at minus 4) would be:

$$363.83\text{ g} \times 18 = {}^{*}344.68\text{ g} \times 19 = 327.45\text{ g} \times 20 = 272.875\text{ g} \times 24 = 6548.92\text{ g}$$

In that case, the aristocracy probably introduced the heavier Roman pound into the Oxyrhynchite, which led to the standard being called 'private', since no other district used a pound weight of this type. Indeed, we

17 *BGU* II 367.16ff. ('arabische Zeit'), *chrysiou nomismatia pente obryza hekaston apo keration eikosi trion Alexandreias, P. Flor.* I 70.8–9 (Hermopolite, 27.11.627, cf. *BL* 8.125), *chr[y]sou nomismata he[x] apo keration eikositrion to[u] nom[ism]a(tos) z[y]go Alexandreias.*

18 *P. Ness.* 46.4 (605), the full description is *chrysina despotika ombryza tetragrammiaia protia dokima ton arithmon ennea para keratia ennea zygo Gazes.*

19 These descriptions would be patently contradictory if '23 carats' referred to a lower weight/value of the coins in question.

have more direct evidence that the Apions used the heavier Roman pound on their estates. In *P. Oxy.* XVI 1918 verso line 35, 13092 ½ ⅓ $\frac{1}{24}$ $\frac{1}{48}$ $\frac{1}{96}$ solidi are described as equivalent to 181 lb 10 oz and 3½ ⅛ gr. On the proper weight standard for the solidus, this presumes a pound of 327.45 g.[20] The lighter Roman pound at 272.87 g, which is the 'base' weight, appears to have been the basic silver standard among the Merovingians.[21] The unit marked by an asterisk is not directly attested but Schilbach cites a pound standard of 344.892 g.[22] (A standard of 19 carats is formally attested by *P. Cairo Masp.* III 67299.40–1.) Finally, the 18 carat standard, uncommonly widespread, would correspond to Lang's 'Alexandrian' *litra* of 363.83 g. However, the metrology remains hypothetical, since we have no direct information on the actual pound weights used in different localities.

The papyrological evidence reinforces a metrological interpretation of the minus carats system. (1) In *SB* VIII 9772 (6c.) 2 solidi 'each less 3 carats on the public standard' (ll. 2–4) are re-described a little later as 2 solidi (ll. 11–12). The reference to the 'missing' carats *could* be omitted since no deduction of value was involved. Again, in *SB* 9280 (6c.) a payment of 1 solidus less 5 carats is simultaneously described as a payment of 1 solidus (cf. ll. 9–10 and l. 23), and in *SB* 9459 (Fayum, 7c.) a payment of 1 solidus less 7½ carats is again described, a few lines later, as a payment of 1 solidus (cf. ll. 4–5 and l. 10 *[hy]per tou autou henos nomismatos*). Neither of these documents makes any explicit reference to a standard, unlike *SB* 9772, but it should be obvious that 1 solidus minus *x* carats could be the same as 1 solidus only because a local standard or scale was presupposed, and local scales reflected differences in the weights used to determine the weight of solidi and the value of payments, not actual deductions of value. (2) Loan contracts are strongly suggestive of the same conclusion. Take two sixth-century contracts, from the Fayum and Hermopolis respectively. In the first of these, *SB* VIII 9771 (6c.), the amount loaned is 1 solidus less 7¾ carats. This standard is common in Fayum documents and appears to have been a customary, if unofficial, standard.[23] The interest charged is ¼

[20] That is, converting the specified weight into grams using the traditional Roman pound of 327.45 g yields 59,544.95 g. If this figure is then divided by the number of solidi, 13,092.906, the average weight of the solidus works out to 4.5478 g!

[21] See H. Witthöft, 'Die Rechnung und Zahlung mit Gold und Silber nach Zeugnissen des 6. bis 9. und 13./14. Jahrhunderts', *Hamburger Beiträge zur Numismatik* 30/32 (1976–8), 9–36, esp. pp. 11–17.

[22] E. Schilbach, *Byzantinische Metrologie* (Munich, 1970) p. 178, suggesting comparison with the *argyrika litra* at 335.417 g.

[23] It appears in *BGU* I 303.17–18 (586), *SB* I 4496.13–16 (592), *SB* I 5270.22–4 (610) and a few other documents.

carat per month. Now if the capital sum involved an *actual* deduction of value to the extent of 7¾ carats, the rate of interest would have been

$$\frac{3}{16.25} \times 100 = 18.46\%$$

On the other hand, if we treat the carats deduction as a metrological adjustment and assume a solidus of full value, the interest works out to the perfectly standard rate of 12½%. The same reasoning applies to the second contract, *P. Flor.* III 300 (597). Here, too, the interest is given as ¼ carat per month but the capital value is 1 solidus minus 6 carats (which was the standard followed in the Hermopolite, where this document is from). Assuming a solidus of full weight and value, the interest is again 12½%, otherwise 16⅔%. Since 12½% was a standard rate[24] and figures like 18.46% or 16⅔% are awkward and otherwise unattested, such contracts argue strongly in favour of a metrological theory. (3) The same reasoning applies with respect to price quotations. For example, in *P. Bad.* 95, a long estate account from the seventh century, 15 artabas of barley are priced at 1 solidus minus 6 carats. Again, this is a Hermopolite document and the adjustment of 6 carats was standard in this district. 15 artabas to the solidus would be a perfectly average price for barley, whereas on the value deduction theory, one would have to infer the extraordinarily low price of 20 artabas to the solidus.[25]

Finally, a recently published wooden tablet, *P. Flor.* XVIII 8.5, dated March 669, is particularly fascinating. Here each solidus involved in a certain payment is described as 'of (*apo*) 22½, carats *paganiko zygo*'. No standard of this name is attested from papyri of the Byzantine period, possibly for the following reason. If *paganikos* was a way of referring to the Arabs in the decades after the conquest, then this was clearly a reference to the weight standard introduced by them into Egypt once they conquered the country. In a famous article on the monetary reforms of ʿAbd al-Malik (685–705) Grierson drew attention to the fact that the eastern provinces had carat weights which were considerably *heavier* than the Graeco-Roman carat of 0.189 g. Thus the Egyptian carat weighed 0.196 g and the Arabic carat 0.208 g.[26] Proceeding from these weights, the weight

[24] E.g. *SB* XII 10810 (late 6c), *P. Mich.* XIII 669 (544, *BL* 7.117), *P. Lond.* V 1737 (613).

[25] In *P. Lond.* III 1087 (6/7c), cf. *Tyche* 5 (1990), p. 167, no. 3, the price of barley is 9 artabas to the solidus.

[26] P. Grierson, 'The Monetary Reforms of ʿAbd al-Malik: Their Metrological Basis and their Financial Repercussions', *Journal of the Economic and Social History of the Orient* 3 (1960), 241–64, at pp. 248ff.

difference between the 'Egyptian' carat and the Graeco-Roman carat was 3.7037%, so that a solidus of 23.1 carats on the 'Egyptian' standard equalled a solidus of 24 carats on the Graeco-Roman standard, while the differential between the Arabic carat and the 'Egyptian' carat was 6.122%, so that a solidus of 22.53 carats on the former equalled a solidus of 24 carats on the latter.[27] The evidence of *P. Flor.* XVIII 8 is in perfect accord with this, and I suggest we should see the 'paganikon zygon' as a reference to the introduction of the Arabic weight standard.

To conclude, these are all grounds for rejecting the theory that the minus carats system was devised to express deductions of value for purposes of an official or semi-official nature. In fact, as the last example shows, the system survived well into the Arab period when this whole paraphernalia of semi-licit fees or deductions should have disintegrated conclusively with the large-scale restructuring of fiscal relationships. Metrological practices, on the other hand, were more deeply rooted.

If the equation I have suggested is plausible, then the Alexandrian standard used the lighter of the two Roman pounds and the purpose of the system was to standardise payments by conversion to this central or dominant standard. (By definition, then, payments on the 'Alexandrian standard' could never be expressed as minus so many carats.) Thus in *P. Lond.* III 1006 (p. 261) (555), a cash rent of '1⅓ solidi minus 8 carats on the standard of the village' (*chrysou nomismatia hen triton para keratia okto z[ygo] tes komes*) is equated with '1 solidus on the Alexandrian standard' (ll. 14–16). Bell misunderstood the form of calculation here when he commented, '1⅓ solidi less 8 carats = 1 solidus, and it is so expressed in the repetition in l. 16.'[28] This is wrong, as it makes the exercise a tautology (first a tremiss is added, then eight carats are subtracted). The village in question was in the Hermopolite, where the prevalent standard was 'minus 6 carats' (i.e. the traditional Alexandrian *litra* of 363.83 g) and what the transaction expresses is an adjustment from this standard to the Alexandrian one, that is,

$$\frac{8\ \textit{carats}}{1.33\ \textit{sol.}} = 6\ \textit{carats / sol., 1 solidus - } 6\ \textit{carats}$$
$$= \textit{1 solidus Alexandrian scale}$$

Papyri from the Apion archive suggest that the name for this form of calculation was *parallelismos zygon*.[29] The term *parallelon* appears in

[27] In Table 5.1 I have recalculated these ratios using Miles's estimate of the Egyptian carat as 0.1957 g.
[28] Bell, *P. Lond.* III 1006.15n (p. 261).
[29] *P. Oxy.* XVI 1916.35–6, LV 3805, 1/8 c. in the former.

a law of Anastasius, *CJ* 10.27.2.6, where it means the weight difference between coin of full weight and value and solidi described as *parastathma*, that is, of less than full weight or substantially below weight. Once the weight standardisation system evolved, the dealers or coin weighers would have imposed a small fee for converting payments to the Alexandrian standard. On the Apion estate this seems generally to have been 1/6 carat per solidus (0.69%). The same fee is called *parallage* in an account from the late-seventh century archive of Papas pagarch of Edfu, where Rémondon correctly glossed the term as 'charge pour la conversion de l'étalon local en étalon official'.[30] This might explain why some districts in the sixth century used the term *synallage* as a way of referring to the weight adjustment system, in expressions such as *pros* or *kata ten synallagen tes komes*.[31] These, presumably, were ways of conceptualising a process of standardisation, and since the system was an innovation of the late Roman period, the terminology was understandably fluid.

Discounts

The Anastasian reference to *nomismata parastathma* shows that weight loss clearly was a problem by the latter part of the fifth century, when the minus carats system first evolved. I have tried to show that this system was not devised as a solution to that problem and had nothing to do with it. The balance of our evidence shows that the late Roman state never attempted to define a legal limit between coin and bullion, and that, by default, the market was allowed to intervene to establish a discount policy, if one can call it that. It is a striking fact that whereas imperial legislation refers *repeatedly* to solidi of full weight (*integri ponderis*), no attempt is ever made to define a margin of tolerance within which the solidus would still count as *integri ponderis*. Contrast this with the Mughal situation in India (under Akbar), where detailed regulations were laid down to cope with the erosion of value consequent on weight loss, for both gold and

30 *P. Apol.* 86.4, *(hyper) parall(ag)e(s) (kerat.) etc.*

31 *P. Mich.* XIII 659.340, *BM* 1023.11, *P. Cairo Masp.* III 67299.40–1. The expressions used in *P. Mich.* XIII 662.30ff. (615), 665.44–5 (7c), *P. Hamb.* I 68.33–4 (*c.*519?) and *P. Lond.* 483 (616) are especially interesting, as the reference to 'conversion' or 'adjustment' is successfully disentangled from the reference to local weights, e.g. in *P. Lond.* 483, 1⅔ solidi are described as *te synallage ta poiounta keratia triakonta hex hemisu chrysochoiko stathmo*. See also J. Gascou, 'Papyrus Michigan XIII 665: Complément textuel – notes critiques', *Cahiers de recherches de l'Institut de papyrologie et d'égyptologie de Lille* 7 (1985), 129–35, esp. p. 133 for revised transcriptions in the Michigan papyri.

silver denominations.[32] The situation is even more extraordinary when one considers the fact that not all 24 carat solidi were actually struck to the theoretical weight of 4.5479 g, and that 'Gold coins a little lighter than the solidus were very widely struck during the sixth and seventh centuries',[33] a statement not intended to refer to the lightweight denominations.

One obvious implication of this is that the dealers in money, the *nummularii* or *trapezitai* who controlled the huge volume of transactions involved in money changing, and who acted as professional assayers, late antique ancestors of the medieval *sarrāfs* or Changers, were given considerable latitude in deciding how to deal with worn solidi. It seems likely that by the sixth century most *zygostatai* worked under the control of estate bankers or independent money dealers (Lat. *argentarii*, Gk. *argyropratai*), even if it is certain that the *demosioi zygostatai*, the public or officially appointed coin weighers, survived well into the seventh century.[34] The aristocracy certainly employed *zygostatai*,[35] but they also retained their own bankers[36] and the evidence suggests that within the financial organisation of large estates, the weighers worked directly under the supervision of the *trapezitai*.[37] About the dealers or *sarrāfs* of the late seventeenth century, Tavernier tells us both that 'the great nobles also employ their own', and also that their main source of profit came from the commission charged for the testing of silver. 'This it is which yields such large profits to the Changers, *for whether one receives or makes any payment he must show them the silver*, and they receive for their commission 1/16th of a rupee per cent.'[38] This works out to a commission of 6¼% on each transaction. In late Roman terms, this would mean 4½ solidi to the pound of gold or 1½ carats to the solidus. In the later sixth century, in Alexandria, dealers also charged a commission of 6¼%, as we know from *P. Oxy.* I 144, dated 580. Here a payment of 720 solidi described as *en apolyto Aigyptio kharagmati zygo Alex( )* ('in loose coin from the interior districts, weighed on the

[32] These are described by Abū-l Fazl almost at the start of the *Āʾin-i Akbarī*, see Blochmann's translation of the *Āʾin*, vol. I, pp. 33–6. Cf. I. M. Habib, 'The Currency System of the Mughal Empire (1556–1707)', *Medieval India Quarterly* 4 (1961), 1–21, esp. the statement, 'the official rates of discount were by no means automatically accepted by the market' (p. 6).

[33] P. Grierson, 'Two Byzantine Coin Hoards of the Seventh and Eighth Centuries at Dumbarton Oaks', *Dumbarton Oaks Papers* 19 (1965), 207–29, at p. 227.

[34] See *P. Laur.* III 110 (14.6.615).

[35] *P. Oxy.* XXXVI 2780.22 (553), from the estate of the *patricia* Flavia Gabrielia.

[36] See most recently, *P. Oxy.* LVIII 3935.6–7 (6.3.591), *to aidesimo Iousto trapezite tou endoxou/oikou tou hyperphuestatou Strategiou.*

[37] See especially *P. Daris* inv. no. 1 = *SB* XII 11163 (6c.).

[38] *Travels in India by Jean-Baptiste Tavernier Baron of Aubonne translated from the original French edition of 1676 … by V. Ball*, 2 vols (London, 1925) vol. I, p. 25.

Alexandrian scale') was supplemented by an extra 45 solidi *hyper obryzes kai apokatastatikon* ('for deficiencies in purity and weight'), by contrast with an amount of 1440 solidi which were described as 'coins of pure gold' and which, naturally, attracted no such supplement.[39] Thus deficiencies in weight and purity were covered by a general discount against solidi which were discernibly worn. The same commission (1½ carats to the solidus) appears in *P. Oxy.* XVI 1907 (6c.), where 692 solidi of pure gold are equated with 735¼ solidi 'on the Alexandrian scale'.[40] It is possible, then, that 6.25% had become the standard commission charged by money dealers for handling 'loose' or worn solidi.[41] *P. Oxy.* 144 is our most explicit testimony, in the papyri of the Byzantine period, that much of the coinage in circulation comprised pieces which dealers or the public would only accept at a discount. Despite Edict XI, which tells us that in 559 the dealers had been charging up to 12.5% commission (9 solidi in a pound of gold), and that this rate was unacceptable to the authorities because it was disrupting business, it seems very likely that the money market structured its affairs with minimal interference from the government. (I also interpret *Nov. Val.* 16 (445) to mean that the *collectarii* regularly sold worn solidi to the state, which in that period was willing to buy them at the official rate of 7200 nummi, and that the public which sold such solidi to the changers should avoid selling them for less than 7000 nummi, i.e. at a discount of more than 2.77%.[42] In a sense, this Novel is the closest we ever come to an officially acknowledged rate of discount on coins which were discernibly below weight.)

It is some indication of the scale of monetary transactions in the late antique economy that so much of the gold coinage should have been in a state of obvious or even considerable wear. *P. Oxy.* I 132 from the late sixth or seventh century shows that in largely rural districts such as the Oxyrhynchite, the savings of a village headman could show an average weight loss of 3.797%, that is, a loss of 0.17269 g per solidus or an 'average' solidus of 4.3752 g.[43] The deficiency in weight was made up by

[39] *P. Oxy.* I 144.6–8 (580), wrongly interpreted in West and Johnson, *Currency*, pp. 118, 141.

[40] *P. Oxy.* 1907 is entitled *Log(os) tou kouphism(ou) tou tetart(ou) mer(ous).*

[41] See also *P. Oxy.* I 126 (572), where 22½ carats of pure gold (*keratia obryziaka*) are said to be equivalent to 24 carats 'on the public standard' (ll. 15–16, 27–8).

[42] This is also the interpretation offered by John Kent in his unpublished thesis of 1951, which Dr C. E. King placed at my disposal, for which I am more than grateful; see J. P. C. Kent, *The Office of the Comes Sacrarum Largitionum* (London University Ph.D. thesis, 1951), p. 157.

[43] Cf. C. Carcassone, 'Asymétrie de frai: *Solidi* scandinaves', *Bulletin de la Société Française de Numismatique* (Dec. 1976), pp. 126–8: in hoards from Scandinavia, 4.36–4.39 g generally indicates either 'worn' or 'very worn'.

supplementary payments called *h(yper) parastathm(ias) aut(on).*[44] Late seventh-century papyri, one a bilingual (Greek–Arabic) receipt dated 677, might suggest that the situation became even worse once Egypt passed out of the political control of Byzantium. In these documents,[45] the actual number of coins or nominal value of the payment is contraposed to their intrinsic or 'real' value through the contrast between *arithmia nomismata* and *echonta nomismata.*[46] If *echonta nomismata* may be taken as money of account for solidi of maximum fineness and weight, the average weight of the solidus seems to vary from 4.1871 g in one document (PERF 573, 17.5.677) to 4.3005 g in the other (*P. Apol.* 82). Both weights are well below the averages even of the most worn solidi in a late seventh-century hoard such as Nikertai,[47] and this suggests another possibility. It is also possible that solidi described as *arithmia* often referred to lightweight denominations, for the 23 carat solidus would have weighed 4.358 g and the maximum average weight loss we would be dealing with would then be 3.93% (in our bilingual receipt) rather than 7.93%. If *arithmia* referred to solidi of *all* denominations, there would of course be no way of calculating the average weight loss in cases like these, but this would then explain why the practice of describing coins in this particular way actually evolved as lightweight denominations began to percolate into local circulation and reinforced the habit of determining the weight-value of payments net of depreciation and lower standards. Finally, it is even possible that *arithmia* referred primarily to lightweight denominations.[48]

Gold versus copper

It should be clear by now that gold circulated by weight and that the dealers exerted a primary influence on monetary transactions through their control over the main payments and their ability to enforce discounts on

[44] For the proper resolution of *parastathm( )*, see J. Diethart, 'Dokumentarische Texte aus dem 5.–7. Jahrhundert aus der Wiener Papyrussammlung', *Analecta Papyrologica* 5 (1993), 69–113, at p. 74 = *P. Vindob. G* 16825.5n.

[45] *PERF* 573 (677), re-ed. W. F. Stoetzer and K. A. Worp, 'Zwei Steuerquittungen aus London und Wien', *Tyche* 1 (1986), 195–202, at pp. 198–9, *P. Apol.* 82 (pp. 174f.).

[46] See Stoetzer and Worp, 'Steuerquittungen', p. 201 on the resolution of ἐχ( ), ἐχό( ) and ἐχοᵀ. Bell, *P. Lond.* IV p. 84 describes the *arithmia nomismata* as 'depreciated coins'.

[47] J. Guey, 'Symétrie ou dissymétrie d' émissions', in *Statistics and Numismatics*, ed. C. Carcassone *et al.* (Strasbourg, 1981), pp. 77–105, at 91 (4.37 g as the average weight of the oldest pieces).

[48] See esp. *P. Lond.* V 1907 (Herm., 7c.) where 4 *ar(i)th(mia) no(mismata)* are said to be equal to 3 solidi 8 carats, which suggests that they were solidi of the 20 carat type. *P. Oxy.* XVI 1939 is further proof that the 20 carat denomination circulated in rural areas early in the seventh century. Both documents are from large aristocratic estates.

depreciated coinage. Considering the volume of transactions in gold, an average commission of 6¼% would clearly have meant substantial profits. However, in the Apion accounts, we also encounter a commission called *rhope*, and to see what this might have been we have to expand our vision of the dynamics of monetary economy to include the value relations between the metals.[49] It is clear that under Constantine those relations were restructured to attract gold into circulation. A famous passage in the Anonymous suggests that the new mint valuations had a major impact on the course of circulation and encouraged a large-scale substitution of gold even in the retail trade.[50] The result was an endemic undervaluation of the base currency which must have led to its withdrawal from active circulation and the consequent attempts by the state to respond through short-run readjustments. Stated in a more general form, one might note that the cheaper and overvalued metal is drawn into circulation, the dearer and undervalued one forced out.[51] With gold consistently overvalued relative to the other metals, the circulation of silver almost evaporated in the fifth century,[52] and that of the base metal coinages witnessed a prolonged slump, with a virtual collapse in the 470s and 480s, till Anastasius restructured the subsidiary currency and restored its character as a full-value coinage. On the other hand, gold was abundant throughout the fifth century.[53] Thus the monetary history of the fourth and fifth centuries can in essence be derived from the model proposed by Elio Lo Cascio. Its clear implication is a monetary policy firmly geared to the solidus as a *pure* gold coinage (a stable measure of value) available in sufficient quantity to dominate all but the most trivial exchanges.

What, then, of the sixth century? How far did Constantinople continue 'late Romanism' in the sphere of monetary policy? The idea that there was a *fixed* relationship between the subsidiary currency and the

49 See E. Lo Cascio, 'Teoria e politica monetaria a Roma tra III e IV d.C.', in *Società romana e impero tardoantico*, ed. A. Giardina (Rome and Bari, 1986), vol. I, pp. 535ff., 779ff., for a major contribution to the monetary history of the fourth century, and cf. E. Lo Cascio, 'Aspetti della politica monetaria nel IV secolo', *Atti dell'Accademia Romanistica Costantiniana, X Convegno Internazionale* (Naples, 1995), pp. 481–502.

50 Anonymous, *de rebus bellicis* II.1–2 (Thompson, p. 94), esp. *Constantini temporibus profusa largitio aurum pro aere, quod antea magni pretii habebatur, vilibus commerciis assignavit.*

51 Cf. E. W. Kemmerer, *Money* (New York, 1935), pp. 85ff., and his later book, *Gold and the Gold Standard* (New York and London, 1944) passim.

52 See C. E. King, *Roman Silver Coins*, vol. IV: *Carausius to Romulus Augustus* (London, 1987), pp. 46–50.

53 C. Morrisson, 'La circulation de la monnaie d'or en Afrique à l'epoque Vandale: Bilan des trouvailles locales', in *Mélanges de numismatique offerts à Pierre Bastien*, ed. H. Huvelin *et al.* (Wetteren, 1987), pp. 325–44; S. Bourgey, 'L'evolution du monnayage d'or aux ve et vie siècles', *Numismatics: Witness to History* (Wetteren, 1986), pp. 65–71 both argue this.

solidus can be ruled out immediately and is certainly not supported by any interpretation of *Nov. Val.* 16, as Adelson seemed to think.[54] The base metal coinage circulated by weight, and in the course of the sixth century its exchange against gold also acquired a reasonably structured form. Since the new monetary system presupposed careful regulation of the weights of the copper coins,[55] it has been possible to use the metrology of the follis to reconstruct the ratio over a century or more, as Hahn has done in the various volumes of *MIB*. In addition I would suggest that this reconstruction can be supplemented if we can work out the relationship between the follis and the myriad, since the papyri frequently quote the price of the solidus in myriads of denarii, a money of account used largely in Egypt. It is obvious that there would have had to be a fixed relationship between the follis and this unit of account, as both expressed the same set of fluctuations between coined gold and the subsidiary coinage. I have reproduced this 'expanded' reconstruction in Table 5.2, using the hypothesis that the myriad, a money of account, was embodied in the 6-nummi piece. (1) According to Hahn's reconstruction, in (or rather by) 570, 720 folles of a standard weight of 13.64 g exchanged to the solidus at a gold/copper price of 30 lb.[56] In *noummia* this would yield 28,800 to the solidus, which would equal either 2400 12-nummi coins or 4800 6-nummi ones. In *P. Oxy.* 3804.271, which is dated 566, the exchange rate (in myriads) is 4800 to the solidus. This suggests that fairly soon after Justin II came to power there was a rapid shift in favour of gold and that the aristocracy was exerting a downward pressure on the value of the follis. (2) For 616–18 Hahn gives the value of the follis in terms of gold as 1/1080. That is, 1080 folles of 9.10 g exchanged to the solidus at 30 lb per solidus. This would yield 43,200 *noummia* to the solidus equal to 7200 6-nummi coins. In *P. Oxy.* 1917.59 dated 616/17, the exchange rate is in fact 7200 myriads to the solidus. Again, the equivalence is striking and suggests that at least from the reign of Justin II, if not earlier, the myriad was embodied in the 6-nummi. Finally, a further argument in favour of identifying the myriad with the 6-nummi coin is the fact that where one knows the rate of exchange of the solidus in terms of myriads every *fraction* employed yields

[54] H. L. Adelson and G. L. Kustas, 'A Bronze Hoard of the Period of Leo I', *American Numismatic Society Museum Notes* 9 (1960), 139–88, at pp. 151–3, esp. 'The copper coinage stood in a direct, fixed relationship to the gold solidus' (p. 151).

[55] See H. Pottier, *Analyse d'un trésor de monnaies en bronze enfoui au VIe siècle en Syrie byzantine* (Brussels, 1983), pp. 224–5, 246.

[56] W. Hahn, *Moneta Imperii Bizantini*, vol. II: *Von Justinus II. bis Phocas (565–610)* (Vienna, 1975), p. 15.

Table 5.2 *The gold/copper exchange rate: Hahn's reconstructions and papyrological supplements*

Date	No. of folles/ solidus	Weight of follis (g)	lb of copper/ solidus	Date	Price of solidus in myriads	No. of folles (papyr.)
498–512	360	9.10	20?			
512–38	360	18.19	20		2400?	
538–42	210	24.95	16?			
542–50	180	21.83	12			
550–65	216	18.19	12	556/7	4800	720[Ap]
565	525	15.59	25	566	4800	720[Ap]
570	720	13.64	30	576/7	4800	720[Ap]
579	432	18.19	24			
	(450)		(25)			
580–7	576	13.64	24	581	4500	675
	(600)		(25)			
587–?	600	13.64	25	614	4800	720[Ap]
616–17	1080	9.10	30	616/17	7200	1080[Ap]
				618	7680	1152
				*c.*620		960[Ap]
				624/5		864

Sources and note: W. Hahn, *Moneta Imperii Bizantini*, vol. I: *Von Anastasius I. bis Justinianus I. (491–565)* (Vienna, 1973), pp. 19ff., *Moneta Imperii Bizantini*, vol. II, pp. 15ff., *Moneta Imperii Bizantini*, vol. III: *Von Heraclius bis Leo III.* (Vienna, 1981), pp. 16ff., *CJ* X.29.1, Procopius, *Anecd.* XXV.7–12, *P. Oxy.* XVI 1911.208 (556/7), LV 3804.271 (566), XVIII 2195.48, 143–4 (576/7), *PSI* VIII 963.20–1 (581), *P. Oxy.* LVIII 3958.26 (614), XVI 1917.59 (616/17), 1904.3 (618), 1921.1,7 (*c.*620, cf. *BL* 9.191), *SPP* XX 218.30 (624/5?), Rea, *P. Oxy.* LVIII 3958.26n (p. 115), Rea *P. Oxy.* LV 3804 int (p. 97). [Ap] = Apion archive. Figures in brackets are my suggestions, since Hahn's figures are awkward. On *P. Oxy.* 1911.208, and 2195.48, 143–4, I have followed John Rea's argument for a standard rate of exchange (at 4800 myriads), see *P. Oxy.* LV 3804.272n (pp. 142f.). *PSI* 8, 963.20f. (8 carats = 1000 *lita*) should be read with *P. Prag.* 2, 169 (5 *keratia lita* = 7½ *keratia*). Finally, the conversion in the last column is made on the hypothetical assumption that 1 myriad = 6 nummi.

a sum (in myriads) which is divisible by six. This is the case, for example, in the Apion account *P. Oxy.* 1917 just referred to. Here the fractions used include not only ½, ⅓, ¼, 1/24, but also 1/10, 1/15, 1/20, 1/30, 1/40, 1/60, 1/100, 1/120, all of which break down into sums of myriads divisible by six (so that one would have needed 120, 80, 60, 40, 30, 20, 12 and 10 6-nummi pieces for these respectively). It seems likely that most of these amounts were circulated in purses.

The broad picture is reasonably clear. The aristocracy dominated monetary policy for most of the latter part of the sixth century, and the result was a progressive decline of the subsidiary coinage, with the state unwilling or unable to re-attract copper into circulation. The earlier sixth century, by contrast, had seen a conscious imperial policy of restraining the claims of the aristocracy in favour of those, such as artisans and casual labourers, whose wages were drawn chiefly in the subsidiary coinage.[57] No exchange rates survive from the Apion estate for the early part of the sixth century, but the four rates we do have for the period 557–614 seem to suggest a calculated policy of holding the rate constant in favour of gold in the general region of 4800 myriads to the solidus, or 720 folles. In Hahn's reconstructed series (Table 5.2), this rate was 'standard' only once in the period in question, viz. in 570, when Justin II reduced the value of the follis to its lowest point since 512 and revalued the solidus by a further 20%, on top of the drastic devaluation which had occurred on his accession, when the price of gold was more than doubled.[58] Thus landowners like the Apions seemed to be able to enforce 'internal' rates of exchange which disregarded both the officially favoured rates and those prevailing in the market. The aristocracy's 'preference for gold' could scarcely be more evident. Justinian had been sensitive to public reaction, as we know from a passage in John Malalas,[59] but with the growing influence of the aristocracy in the later sixth century, it becomes hard to disentangle the influence of purely economic factors in shaping the exchange between gold and copper. It is therefore particularly interesting to note that in a passage attacking Justinian for reducing the value of gold in terms of copper (from 210 to 180 folles to the solidus), Procopius strongly implies that the earlier rate of exchange had depended essentially on the money changers (*argyramoiboi*). The 'liberal' policy of the early sixth century had presumably allowed market forces to exert a major influence on the metallic ratio, and Justinian's devaluation of the solidus in 542 may likewise have reflected supply relationships. But this realism was destined to be reversed and to lead, eventually, to a major disintegration of the base metal currency on a pattern familiar from the history of the fourth and fifth centuries. Grierson's suggestion that this occurred because the copper coinage was

[57] The sources are well known: Marcellinus Comes, *Chronicon*, s.a. 498, Procopius, *Anecd.* 25.12 (H. B. Dewing, *The Anecdota or Secret History* (Cambridge, MA, 1935), pp. 294ff.), Malalas, *Chron.*, 486C (Jeffreys, 18.117, p. 293).

[58] Cf. Hahn, *Moneta Imperii Bizantini, vol. II*, p. 15 : 'Justinus II scheint sogleich bei seinem Regierungsantritt das gesamte Währungssystem mit seinen Wertverhältnissen umgebaut zu haben.'

[59] See n. 57, a crucial piece of evidence.

drastically undervalued is eminently acceptable,[60] and takes us back to the model we started with.

Hahn, of course, is strongly tempted to correlate fluctuations in the 'official' rate of exchange with production of the light-weight series, on the quite practical assumption that the follis exchanged against gold in sealed purses or bags on a weight basis.[61] I have just suggested that deeper forces were at work in the determination of the exchange rate. At any rate, the reference back to dealers in a discussion of Justinian's sudden devaluation of the solidus shows that the money market was the constant presupposition of all these movements. Peter Barsymes himself is supposed to have started life as a money changer dealing in the exchange between gold and copper.[62] In conclusion, I would like to suggest that dealers may have charged a commission of 2.083% (i.e. ½ carat in the solidus) in transactions involving the exchange of folles against gold. At any rate, this deduction appears fairly standardly in the Apion accounts in contexts involving estate bankers.[63] There it is called *rhope* and it has usually been seen, somewhat vaguely, as a fee for 'weighing coins', but changing currencies involved weighing in any case,[64] and it seems more likely that it represented a sort of exchange rate commission in an economy which gave such a strong premium to gold.[65]

[60] P. Grierson, 'The Monetary Reforms of Anastasius and Their Economic Consequences', in *The Patterns of Monetary Development in Phoenicia and Palestine in Antiquity*, ed. A. Kindler (Tel Aviv, 1967), pp. 283–302, esp. 290–1, and for supporting evidence from the hoards, see A. I. Dikigoropoulos, 'A Byzantine Hoard from Kharcha, Cyprus', *Numismatic Chronicle*, ser. vi, 16 (1956), 255–65; P. J. Donald and P. D. Whitting, 'A 7th Century Hoard from Cyprus', *Numismatic Circular* 75 (1967), 162–5 (both from Cyprus).

[61] See Metcalf's summary of Hahn in D. M. Metcalf, 'New Light on the Byzantine Coinage System', *Numismatic Circular* 82 (1974), 14–15.

[62] Procopius, *Anecd.* 22.3 (Dewing, *Secret History*, p. 254): ὃς πάλαι μὲν ἐπὶ τῆς τοῦ χαλκοῦ τραπέζης καθήμενος κέρδη αἰσχρότατα ἐκ ταύτης δὴ ἐπορίζετο τῆς ἐργασίας.

[63] E.g. *P. Oxy.* I 143 (535), *P. Lond.* III 780 (535), *P. Oxy.* LV 3804 col. xii. The formulation in *P. Oxy.* XVI 1915.24–5 (555/6) strongly implies that one is dealing with a commission, not a fee. Here the villagers of Pempo seek a collective lease on 38½ arouras for a total rent of 38½ solidi *ekt(os) rhop(es) tou [ge]geouchou kai pro(noetou)*, that is, 'not including the commission paid to the estate and its managers'.

[64] See Symeon Metaphrastes, *Vita Marciani presbyteri, PG* 114.449D.

[65] The money changers who operated under the control of the Dutch East India Company when the latter took Pondicherry from the French in September 1693 charged a commission of 4.167% for converting copper coins into gold *pagodas*. This is equivalent to one carat per solidus, so twice as much as bankers charged on the Apion estate (see Om Prakash, 'Foreign Merchants and Indian Mints in the Seventeenth and the Early Eighteenth Century', in *The Imperial Monetary System of Mughal India*, ed. J. F. Richards (Delhi, 1987), pp. 171–92, at 187–8).

CHAPTER 6

Precious metal coinages and monetary expansion in late antiquity

The currencies of late antiquity were dominated by two substantial if quite distinct and partly competing coinages, the late Roman solidus, the leading gold denomination of the period, and the Sasanian drahm/drachm, the dominant silver one. The solidus and the drahm/drachm were each the exclusive standard of their respective monetary systems, so that, viewed as a whole, the currencies of late antiquity rested on a sort of 'double monometallism' where the subsidiary coinages were simply 'representatives' of the leading metal. This system, if we can call it that, survived for over three centuries till the Arab conquests, when it was subsumed into a new and more expansive empire whose monetary traditions were largely influenced by those of late antiquity.[1]

In this chapter I shall mainly focus on the solidus but argue that its evolution was characteristic of trends in late antiquity as a whole, that is, including the Sasanian Near East, and therefore conclude by looking at the drahm and its wider circulation along the eastern trade routes. The basis of the late Roman monetary system was a gold denomination struck at 72 to the pound. Assuming the conventional figure for the weight of the Roman pound, 327.45 g, is correct, then each full-weight piece would have weighed 4.5479 g.[2] Three features are remarkable about this coinage. First, its prevalence as the exclusive monetary standard broke with centuries of monetary tradition that had sought to run a viable bimetallic system, on the whole without success. Second, it was struck to an exceedingly high standard of fineness, especially after the monetary reform of the late 360s when new regulations were issued for the form in which taxes

[1] 'Double monometallism' is from R. Brunschvig, 'Conceptions monétaires chez les juristes musulmans (VIIIe–XIIIe siècles)', *Arabica* 14 (1967), 113–43, at p. 129: 'un monométallisme double à répartition territoriale'.

[2] The conventional figure is supported by *P. Oxy.* 1918 verso ii 35 (from an estate account). F. Herschend, 'A Case-Study in Metrology: The Szikáncs Hoard', *Tor* 23 (1990–1), 85–104, has now proved that a lighter Roman pound, of 322.3 g, was used in making payments to the Huns in the fifth century.

should reach the Treasury. As the late John Kent noted, 'late Roman gold coins were as fine as it was possible to make them'.[3] Finally, it was struck in substantial quantities and circulated very widely indeed.

For the circulation of the solidus we have not just the testimony of the gold hoards, of which a considerable number survive, though not always in their integral quantities, but also the more local day-to-day evidence contained in the numerous contracts, accounts and other kinds of documentation that survive in the papyri of the fourth to seventh centuries. There is also, of course, the evidence of the historical sources, including numerous references to the very substantial payments made in various contexts – donations to the church, payments to tribal federates, consular largesses and so on. What all of this evidence demonstrates is that there was plenty of gold in the empire, a massive stock of currency, so that *if* it can be shown that the reserves in the state's hands showed a declining trend over time (and I think this is certainly suggested by the Roman/Byzantine evidence), the explanation cannot be found in an *external* flight of gold[4] but has to be sought elsewhere. My own argument will be that much of the gold ended up in private hands, where it was *both* actively used and occasionally hoarded.

Most scholars today would agree that late antiquity was a period of considerable monetary wealth,[5] yet the wider implications of this fact for economic history remain subdued. A major reason for this is that the gold coinage is viewed primarily in fiscal terms, so that even though 'the monetary wealth of the empire … is conceptually a much broader topic than the imperial finances',[6] the two are ultimately conflated in discussions of the late antique Mediterranean. One extreme formulation of this view appears in John Haldon's book on the seventh century where he says, 'the presence of gold coins has very little to do with the existence of a market economy, being a reflection rather of the needs of the state and its military, administrative and fiscal machinery'.[7] By contrast, I want to argue

[3] J. P. C. Kent, *The Roman Imperial Coinage*, vol. VIII: *The Family of Constantine I AD 337–364* (London, 1981), p. 56; also C. Morrisson *et al.*, 'Numismatique et histoire: L'or monnayé de Rome à Byzance, purification et alterations', *Comptes rendus de l'Académie des Inscriptions et Belles-Lettres* (1982), 203–23.

[4] So too P. Veyne, 'Rome devant la prétendue fuite de l'or: Mercantilisme ou politique disciplinaire?', *Annales ESC* 34/2 (1979), 211–44.

[5] E.g. J. P. C. Kent and K. S. Painter, *Wealth of the Roman World: Gold and Silver AD 300–700* (London, 1977).

[6] D. M. Metcalf, 'Monetary Recession in the Middle Byzantine Period: The Numismatic Evidence', *Numismatic Chronicle* 161 (2001), 111–55, at p. 112.

[7] J. F. Haldon, *Byzantium in the Seventh Century: The Transformation of a Culture* (Cambridge, 1990), p. 118.

that late antiquity saw a net expansion in the stock of currency (gold in the Mediterranean, silver in the Near East) and that *this was largely fuelled by an expansion of trade.* Money was needed in circulation as the volume of business expanded. (The theoretical assumption here is that money circulates to 'realise' prices and the quantity of money in circulation is therefore determined by the level of prices, once the volume of transactions and velocity of circulation are given, or by the scale of business – number of transactions × price – if the velocity is taken as fixed. Since late antique prices were generally stable in terms of gold, this equation reduces to the volume of transactions and velocity of circulation.)

Monetary expansion in the fourth to seventh centuries

How would one go about constructing such an argument? Die studies of the gold coinage are few and far between, so we have almost no precise estimates of mint output (one of the variables in the 'stock of currency') and are forced to rely on some combination of a less coherent body of numismatic data with documentary sources (such as the papyri) and the few scraps of textual evidence that can be drawn directly into the argument. Among late Roman texts one of the most valuable is a fascinating passage of the mid-fourth century tract called *De rebus bellicis* ('A Tract on Defence'). The author, perhaps a disillusioned bureaucrat, tells us that Constantine's move to a new monetary standard (the solidus was first issued at Trier *c.*310 and not produced in the eastern mints till 324, after which it was struck at 'almost all the mints throughout the empire')[8] was bound up with a massive dishoarding of gold that led to the (renewed) accumulation of monetary wealth in private hands and sparked a veritable 'passion for spending gold'. The author also links the expanding circulation of gold to powerful social changes. 'This store of gold meant that the houses of the powerful were crammed full and their splendour enhanced to the destruction of the poor …'.[9] The reference here is almost certainly to Constantine's expansion of the governing class of the fourth century, a process continued by his successors that would lead in time, several decades later, to the emergence of a new, more thoroughly Christianised aristocracy in the east, distinct from the older and more traditionalist senatorial families who continued to dominate the central Mediterranean basin.

[8] R. A. G. Carson, *Coins of the Roman Empire* (London and New York, 1990), pp. 149–51, 158–60, 170–1.

[9] Anon., *De rebus bellicis* 2.2 (Thompson, p. 110).

In the modern historiography of the late empire, the perspectives of the 'Anonymous' have had a profound influence in and through the work of Santo Mazzarino, for Mazzarino saw the history of the monetary system as central to the evolution of the late empire.[10] One clue to how this process worked is that if we look at the first batch of Constantine's new gold denomination, it turns out that 'The reverses mainly have a military flavour, such as GLORIA EXERCITVS GALL ...'.[11] The late third century established a tradition of substantial monetary payments to the higher echelons of the late Roman army and within this general movement a strong preference for gold, consolidated by the chaos of third-century bimetallism and the collapse of the silver coinage.[12] By the first decade of the fourth century, high-ranking officials such as the owner of the Beaurains hoard were in regular receipt of substantial sums in gold in the form of military bonuses (*donativa*) and unlikely to be willing to forego these payments.[13] Diocletian's reform of *c.* 294 was the last significant attempt to salvage bimetallism but its whole tendency conflicted with the aspirations of the officer corps (*militares*) and its failure must have been decisive in Constantine's decision to move to a gold standard.

The relative scarcity of Constantine's own solidi in the hoard material coupled with their rarity in the collections and sales catalogues has prompted the view that solidi were not struck on any substantial scale till around the middle of the fourth century, well after his reign.[14] But this is a matter of perspective. It is only true in the limited sense that gold was struck on a truly gigantic scale from the middle decades of the fourth century, dwarfing previous levels of circulation. Constantine produced vastly more gold than the Tetrarchs had ever done,[15] and his donations to the church imply *both* substantial hoards of gold and silver *and* an

[10] S. Mazzarino, *Aspetti sociali del quarto secolo: Ricerche di storia tardo-romana* (Rome, 1951; new edn Milan, 2002).

[11] Carson, *Coins*, p. 151.

[12] E.g. C. E. King, 'The Role of Gold in the Later Third Century A.D.', *Rivista Italiana di Numismatica* 95 (1993), 439–51; R. Bland, 'The Changing Patterns of Hoards of Precious-Metal Coins in the Late Empire', *Antiquité Tardive* 5 (1997), 29–55, at pp. 34–5; C. Katsari, 'Bimetallism and the Circulation of Gold Coins during the Third and Fourth Centuries AD', *Münstersche Beiträge zur antiken Handelsgeschichte* 22(1) (2003), 48–68.

[13] P. Bastien and C. Metzger, *Le trésor de Beaurains (dit d'Arras)* (Wetteren, 1977).

[14] P. Bastien, *Monnaie et Donativa au Bas-Empire* (Wetteren, 1988), p. 35, 'Les monnaies d'or de Constantin sont d'une relative rareté si l'on en juge par les collections et les catalogues de vente'; Bland, 'Changing Patterns', p. 36, 'there is no evidence for a significant increase in the minting of gold coins until the 350s'.

[15] See the data compiled by J.-P. Callu, 'Problèmes monétaires du quatrième siècle (311–395)', in *Transformation et conflits au IVe siècle ap. J.-C.* (Bonn, 1978), pp. 103–25, at 104.

extensive circulation of solidi in his reign.[16] The stocks that third-century emperors had hoarded in the Treasury[17] were rapidly released into circulation, supplemented by other sources such as temple treasures[18] and private hoards.[19] The forces *driving* the expansion of the gold coinage were first dealt with by Mickwitz in his book on the monetary economy of the fourth century. From this it was clear that commutation (*adaeratio*) was a central issue. But Mickwitz saw the mass of landowners (taxpayers) wanting commutation (of taxes) and the bureaucracy resisting commutation (of salaries).[20] For him inflation was the key factor that explained this pattern of behaviour. There was always the possibility that the gold coinage would be subject to debasement, as the silver had, repeatedly, in the third century.[21] Mazzarino's critique of this position developed a more realistic understanding of the late empire. The government was firmly committed to the stability of the solidus precisely because a large and increasing portion of its own revenues and of the emoluments of the bureaucracy were drawn in gold. In fact, officials systematically speculated on the stocks of foodgrains, using commutation and the kinds of arbitrage it allowed.[22] The general implication of Mazzarino's critique is of course that the late Roman bureaucracy was a major standard-bearer of the revitalised monetary economy of the fourth century. Commutation was widespread by the early fifth, despite government resistance, and more and more gold had to be churned out to sustain this system.

Analyses of the trace elements in a sample of solidi suggest that the middle decades of the fourth century saw a *huge* expansion in the volume of coinage struck, sustained by the discovery of fresh mineral sources in the Balkans.[23] In a pathbreaking dissertation, Jacques Poirier suggested

[16] R. Davis (ed.), *The Book of Pontiffs (Liber Pontificalis)* (Liverpool, 2000), pp. 16–27. The assignment of revenues denominated in gold must imply availability of the coinage in the areas where the estates were located.

[17] Veyne, 'Rome', p. 216.

[18] Anon., *De rebus bell.* 2.1 (Thompson, p. 110), 'When the gold and silver and the huge quantity of precious stones which had been stored away in the temples long ago reached the public ...'.

[19] J. R. Rea, 'P.S.I. IV 310 and Imperial Bullion Purchases', *Chronique d'Égypte*, 49 (1974), 163–74.

[20] G. Mickwitz, *Geld und Wirtschaft im römischen Reich des vierten Jahrhunderts n. Chr.* (Helsinki, 1932), ch. 6.

[21] Mickwitz, *Geld und Wirtschaft*, pp. 176–7.

[22] Mazzarino, *Aspetti*, passim (on the bureaucracy's use of *interpretia*); L. Cracco Ruggini, *Economia e società nell 'Italia annonaria': Rapporti fra agricoltura e commercio dal IV al VI secolo d.C.* (Milan, 1961).

[23] J.-P. Callu *et al.*, 'Aureus obryziacus', in *L'or monnayé*, vol. I: *Purification et altérations de Rome à Byzance*, ed. C. Morrisson *et al.* (Paris, 1985), pp. 81–111, esp. 92–5; J.-P. Callu, 'Analyses métalliques et inflation: L'Orient romain de 295 à 361/368', in *Hommes et richesse dans l'Empire byzantin IV–VIIe siècle* (Paris, 1989), pp. 223–33, at 230–2; J.-P. Callu and X. Loriot, *L'or monnayé*, vol. II: *La dispersion des aurei en Gaule romaine sous l'empire* (Juan-les-Pins, 1990), pp. 110 ff.

that the 'monetary mass' (meaning gold) multiplied by a factor of twenty in the years between 346 and 388.[24] Whatever the precise forces it saw itself responding to, it is clear that government saw the *provision of liquidity* as a major monetary objective.[25] All the other evidence suggests that these were decades of significant economic expansion, with a great deal of money flowing into both agriculture and trade. If the stability of the gold coinage mattered for its fiscal objectives and to the stability of contracts, liquidity was crucial to the level of monetary activity in the economy as a whole. The solidus was a 'hard' currency, in the sense that government made sure that it would tend to rise against other currencies.[26] Gold coins were allowed to find their value in the market in the sense that the exchange rate beween solidi and silver or the base metal currency constantly fluctuated.[27] People spoke of 'buying' and 'selling' solidi, much as we do of dollars, pounds and euros. The point to note is that the authorities wanted both consistency and depth in this market. Thus one of the earliest regulations stated that 'All solidi on which Our face and venerability is to be found are to be valued and sold at one price (*uno pretio aestimandi sunt atque vendendi*), however diverse the extent of the image.'[28] The solidus was money, not a piece of metal, and the rejection/discounting of coin on grounds of module or age was strenuously opposed, in part because it undermined the distinction between money and metal.[29] The workings of the economy required a properly functioning market in gold coins of various denominations, and the regulation of such a market was a consistent objective of government policy.

So, how much liquidity? For lack of the kind of numismatic work that alone can yield reliable estimates of the scale on which individual mints, and Constantinople in particular, struck gold at various times in the later fourth to seventh centuries, our next best option is to scour the documentary sources for reasonably reliable estimates of the amount of gold in circulation. Monetary historians are agreed that the stock of currency

[24] J. Poirier, *Contribution à l'analyse de l'or antique: Application aux monnayages du monde méditerranéen du IIe au XIVe siècle* (Thèse de doctorat d'état, l'Université d'Orléans, 1983), p. 178 (platinum not affected by the purification of gold); p. 190 (expansion of the monetary mass); p. 193 (Balkans rich in gold deposits). The increase in platinum was first evident in the coinage of Thessalonica.

[25] This was equally true of earlier centuries, see E. Lo Cascio, 'State and Coinage in the Late Republic and Early Empire', *Journal of Roman Studies* 71 (1981), 76–86, esp. pp. 82–6.

[26] See E. Lo Cascio, 'Teoria e politica monetaria a Roma tra III e IV d.C.', in *Società romana e impero tardoantico*, ed. A. Giardina (Roma/Bari, 1986), vol. 1, pp. 535–7, 779–801.

[27] E.g. *P. Oxy.* 1223, 31ff., 2729, 3401, 3628–36 all attest to fluctuations on a day-to-day or quarterly basis.

[28] *CTh.* 9.22.1 (343?).

[29] On the centrality of this distinction (between *merx* and *pretium*) and the tensions embedded in it, see Lo Cascio, 'Teoria e politica monetaria'.

was 'very large indeed',[30] there was 'plenty' of gold in circulation[31] and that there was a 'vast' coinage in gold.[32] What the documentary sources can do is establish an order of magnitude to give these descriptions a less intuitive feel.

The solidus was used for a very wide range of transactions, in fact for all but the most trivial exchanges.[33] The strongest evidence of this is its use in the East Mediterranean countryside, where, in Egypt for example, the papyri show a regular use of gold in all kinds of transactions from loans, rents and taxes to wage payments and rural fines. By the sixth century, commutation of taxes was widespread, undermining any rigid distinction between the fiscal and the economic functions of the coinage, and most producers would have watched the movement of prices carefully.[34] Anastasius' ability to generate reserves of 23 million solidi[35] was inseparable from the reforms in taxation that encouraged further commutation in his reign. Justinian consolidated this trend, as Khusro I would do in relation to Kavād's seminal reform of Sasanian taxes. In both Byzantium and Persia the main part of the sixth century was the highwater mark of monetary economy, and what is remarkable is how far this was sustained into the seventh century. All of this implies substantial liquidity in both monetary systems, the ability to collect cash revenues in terms of an expanding volume of commercial exchanges. One family of the elite aristocracy, the Apions, generated cash revenues of eighteen to twenty thousand solidi

[30] D. M. Metcalf, 'The Mint of Thessalonica in the Early Byzantine Period', in *Villes et peuplement dans l'Illyricum protobyzantin* (Rome, 1984), pp. 111–28, at 121.

[31] L. C. West and A. C. Johnson, *Currency in Roman and Byzantine Egypt* (Amsterdam, 1967), p. 115.

[32] Metcalf, 'Monetary Recession', p. 119; cf. K. W. Harl, *Coinage in the Roman Economy 300 BC to AD 700* (Baltimore and London, 1996), p. 175, who refers to 'one of the largest gold coinages in Roman history', about the first half of the fifth century.

[33] In what is surely the most detailed study we have of the local circulation of the base metal currency in any part of the empire, Isabel Pereira and her colleagues conclude that (at Conimbriga/Coimbra in Portugal) gold began to replace the bronzes by the late 390s, following the demonetisation of the *maiorina*, till the whole movement was cut short by the invasions of 409: I. Pereira, J.-P. Bost and J. Hiernand, *Fouilles de Conimbriga*, vol. III: *Les monnaies* (Paris, 1974), pp. 300–2. In Egypt the diffusion of the solidus was less belated, e.g. early papyri involving transactions in solidi include: *P. Kell. G* 18 (*c.*350, fragment of a loan of money), *P. Oxy.* 2267 (360, complaint concerning embezzlement of seven solidi), *SB* XX 15096 (363, sale of thirty arouras for 16 solidi) and *P. Vindob G* 25871 (= F. A. J. Hoogendijk, 'Zwei byzantinische Landkäufe', *Tyche* 10 (1995), 13–26, at pp. 13ff., no. 1) (373, sale of 2⅛ arouras for 5 solidi). Circulation was substantial by the 370s, when even minor officials could be entrusted with sums like 238 solidi, cf. *P. Lips.* 34 (*c.*375).

[34] When there is extensive commutation of taxes, the amount of revenue will depend on the state of the market, see al-Maqrīzī, *Description topographique et historique de l'Égypte*, trans. U. Bouriant (Cairo, 1895–1900), pp. 283–4, for the Umayyads in Egypt.

[35] Procopius, *Anecd.* 19. 7.

from their estates in one district alone.[36] Egypt paid 2.6 million solidi a year under Justinian, against an aggregate (cash only?) assessment, for all regions, of over 7 million solidi (100,000 lb of gold).[37] It is particularly remarkable that the papyri show no signs of monetary recession in the early part of the seventh century. It is this that explains why both the Sasanians and the Arabs could still extract huge sums in gold at various times from 620 to 650. Documents from the Oxyrhynchite show the Sasanian official nicknamed Shahrālānyozān (probably Shahrvaraz, Khusro II's commander for the western region)[38] extracting substantial amounts of gold – probably a total of 250 lb from Oxyrhynchus and Cynopolis for the single indiction of 623/4.[39] Again, on the most conservative estimate – that cited by al-Balādhurī – ʿAmr ibn al-ʿĀṣ who governed Egypt in the early 640s was able to impose a tax of 2 million 'dinars' on its people.[40] And in 647, the aristocracy of Byzacena paid the invading forces of ʿAbd Allāh b. Sa'd b.Abī Sarḥ an amount that different traditions variously put at 300 'qintars' of gold (2.16 million solidi) or 2½ million solidi.[41] In this case, the link to large-scale commerce is explicit. In one of the least embellished accounts to survive, ʿUbayd Allāh tells us that following the defeat of Gregory's forces, 'The Muslims saw that their [the Byzantines'] wealth consisted for the most part of gold. They asked them about this gold and how they had come by it. "By selling olive-oil" was the answer.'[42]

[36] *P. Oxy.* XVIII 2196 verso, 31: 18,512 solidi; XVI 1918 verso: 20,010 solidi; with J. Gascou, 'Notes critiques sur quelques papyrus de ve et vie siècles', *Chronique d'Égypte* 47 (1972), 243–53 esp. pp. 243ff.

[37] The figures are from the *Diēgēsis peri tēs oikodomēs tou naou*, c. 25, dealing with the construction costs of St Sophia, see Preger, *Scriptores originum Constantinopolitanarum*, fasc. 1 (Leipzig, 1901), pp. 101f.

[38] This will be argued elsewhere. He was clearly of aristocratic provenance, since his epithet is πανεύφημος in the Greek papyri, and *xwadāy* in the Pahlavi ones.

[39] *P. Oxy.* LI 3637 (Oct. 623); LV 3797 (26.4–25.5.624); XVI 1843 (Nov. 623) list these payments.

[40] Al-Balādhurī, *Kitāb futūḥ al-buldān*, ed. M. J. de Goeje (Leiden, 1863–6), pp. 216, 218; P. K. Hitti, *The Origins of the Islamic State, Being a Translation … of the Kitâb futûh al-buldân* (New York, 1916), pp. 340, 343.

[41] See H. R. Idris, 'Récit d'al-Mālikī sur la conquête de l'Ifrīqiya: Traduction annotée et examen critique', *Revue des Études Islamiques* 37 (1969), 117–49; H. Slim, 'Le trésor de Rougga et l'expédition musulmane de 647 en Ifrīkiya', in *Rougga*, vol. III: *Le trésor de monnaies d'or byzantines*, ed. R. Guéry *et al.* (Rome, 1982), pp. 76–94 on the general consistency of the sources.

[42] E. Lévi-Provençal, 'Un nouveau récit de la conquête de l'Afrique du Nord par les Arabes', *Arabica* 1 (1954), 17–49, at p. 37; cf. Ibn ʿAbd Al-Hakam, *Futûh Ifrîqiya wa'l-Andalus* (*Conquête de l'Afrique du Nord et de l'Espagne*), ed. A. Gateau, 2nd edn (Algiers, 1947) pp. 47–8. Of the 268 solidi that make up the important mid-seventh-century hoard from Rougga (*c.*647), 72% are from the mint of Constantinople, see C. Morrisson in Guéry *et al.*, *Le trésor de monnaies d'or byzantines*, pp. 60–1.

The least one can say on the basis of such figures is that the richest parts of the late antique world had very substantial stocks of gold (and silver) currency running into millions of solidi (and drachms). I want to argue, first, that this was equally true of the Sasanian Near East where the seventh-century trend was in some sense even stronger, and second, that the ageing of the currency probably accounted for much of this accumulating monetary mass, in both Byzantium and Persia. In what follows I shall assume that the theoretical weight of the drachm was 4.2 g of pure silver (or silver of very high fineness, over 95%).[43]

In the early twelfth-century Persian monograph called the *Fārs-nāme* there is a valuable section on the revenues of Fars (south-west Iran) where the author (conventionally called Ibn al-Balkhi) tells us, 'When ... Anushirvan established his land-tax (*kharāj*) in all his kingdoms, the land-tax of Fars amounted to 36 million [silver] dirhams equivalent to 3 million [gold] dinars.'[44] 'Dirham' in this context should be understood to mean *dirham al-wāfī* ('full-weight'), i.e. the Sasanian drachm whose theoretical weight was that of the later Arabic dinar, that is, one 'mithqāl'.[45] The veracity of this figure (36 million drachms) is supported by Ibn Khurradādhbih's corresponding numbers for the Sasanian assessment of Kerman, Khuzistan and Fars. Here we are told that in 'imperial times' (a vague expression but generally used of Khusro I), Fars was assessed at 40 million 'dirhams *mithqāl*', Kerman to its east at 60 million and Khuzistan to its west at 50 million.[46] Since Kerman, Fars and Khuzistan formed the 'southern quarter' of the empire in Khusro I's reign (according to the scheme preserved in al-Thaʿālibī),[47] it seems likely that in the sixth century the region as a whole was assessed for a total of 150 million

[43] On the purity of the Sasanian silver coinage, see J. L. Bacharach and A. A. Gordus, 'The Purity of Sasanian Silver Coins: An Introduction', *Journal of the American Oriental Society* 92/2 (1972), 280–3.

[44] G. Le Strange, *Description of the Province of Fars in Persia ... from the MS of Ibn al-Balkhi in the British Museum* (London, 1912), p. 887 (Eng.); G. Le Strange and R. A. Nicholson (ed.), *The Fársnáma of Ibnu'l-Balkhí* (London, 1921), p. 170 (Pers.).

[45] See al-Maqrīzī in A. Allouche, *Mamluk Economics: A Study and Translation of al-Maqrīzī's Ighāthah* (Salt Lake City, 1994), p. 57.

[46] Ibn Khordâdhbeh, *Kitâb al-masâlik wa'l-mamâlik*, ed. M. J. de Goeje (Leiden, 1889), pp. 35, 42 and 48 (pp. 25, 31 and 34 of the French trans.). The data for Fars and Kerman are supported by a contemporary source, Ibn al-Faqīh al-Hamadhānī, *Kitāb al-buldān = Abrégé du Livre des Pays*, trans. M. Massé (Damascus, 1973), pp. 249–50, while the amount cited for Khuzistan is also found in al-Muqaddasī, *The Best Divisions for Knowledge of the Regions: A Translation of Ahsan al-Taqāsīm fī Ma'rifat al-Aqālīm*, trans. B. A. Collins (Reading, 1994), p. 372.

[47] Al-Thaʿālibī, *Ghurar akhbār mulūk al-Furs wa-siyarihim = Histoire des rois des Perses*, ed. H. Zotenberg (Paris, 1900), p. 609, with al-Ṭabarī, *The History of al-Ṭabarī*, vol. v: *The Sāsānids, the Byzantines, the Lakhmids, and Yemen*, trans. C. E. Bosworth (Albany, 1999), p. 147 (cited as *History*, vol. v).

drachms. As it turns out, the Sawād (Lower Mesopotamia/southern Iraq) was assessed for precisely this amount, 150 million drachms, in (probably) the second reign of Kavād I (498–531), the earlier part of the sixth century.[48] If the Sawād was Khusro's *kust ī xwarvarān* or western quarter, then between them the densely populated south and west, the most developed regions of the empire, would have accounted for a gross revenue of 300 million drachms (assuming Khusro retained Kavād's assessment of the west). Ibn Khurradādhbih also cites a figure for the assessment of the northern provinces. This was substantially less than the figure for the south, only 30 million drachms.[49] Suppose Khurasan, the remaining quarter, contributed at least as much as this, viz. 30 million drachms, the *aggregate* claim may well have been in the region of 360 million drachms, divided, presumably, into three instalments of 120 million each.[50] This of course is hypothetical but it does indicate a broad order of magnitude for the main part of the sixth century that is not totally out of line with the one *exact* estimate we do have from the late Sasanian period for the amount of taxes *actually* collected some decades later, namely, the 420 million drachms (*mithqāls*) that Khusro II collected in the eighteenth year of his reign, i.e. 607/8, before the huge expansion of reserves that characterised the latter part of his rule.[51] According to the figures reported by al-Ṭabarī, the level of reserves stood at 800 million drachms in 602 and had escalated to 1.6 billion drachms by 620, at the end of Khusro II's thirtieth year.[52] The vast quantities of plunder that Khusro II collected in the occupied Byzantine territories of the Near East (120,000 lb of silver from Edessa alone, in 622)[53] is one obvious explanation of this staggering level of reserves, but he is also credited with periodic and sharp increases in taxation which led to a breakdown in his relations with the aristocracy. Even if we suppose that annual tax revenues ran into 400 to 500 million drachms and did not exceed that level, as they probably did, the general conclusion that seems to follow from all this is that both mint output levels (production of currency) and

[48] Ibn Khordâdhbeh, *Kitâb*, p. 14 ℓ.11ff. (p. 11 trans.). Ibn al-Faqīh, *Kitāb al-buldān = Abrégé du Livre des Pays*, p. 249, cites a figure of 123 million drachms. Whatever the true amount, the Sawād's taxes would fall to 100 million drachms by the second quarter of the seventh century, under ʿUmar ibn al-Khaṭṭāb, cf. al-Balādhurī, *Kitāb futūḥ al-buldān*, p. 270, *Origins*, trans. Hitti, p. 428.

[49] Ibn Khordâdhbeh, *Kitâb*, p. 20 (p. 15 trans.).

[50] Al-Ṭabarī, *History*, vol. v, pp. 256–7, for the instalments.

[51] See al-Ṭabarī, *History*, vol. v, p. 377; *Ta'rīkh al-rusul wa'l-mulūk*, ser. i, p. 1042, referring to all taxes (*min al-kharāj wa sā'ir abwāb min al-waraq*); Ibn Khordâdhbeh, *Kitâb*, p. 15, lines 6ff. (p. 12 trans.).

[52] Al-Ṭabarī, *History*, vol. v, pp. 393–4; *Ta'rīkh*, ser. i, p. 1057, for both figures.

[53] *Chronique de Michel le Syrien patriarche jacobite d'Antioche (1166–1199)*, trans. J.-B. Chabot (Paris, 1901; repr. 1963), vol. II, p. 403; A. Palmer, *The Seventh Century in the West-Syrian Chronicles* (Liverpool, 1993), pp. 133–4.

the turnover in agrarian and commercial markets would have had to be enormous to support these levels of taxation.[54]

The Sasanians struck their silver in a far greater multiplicity of mints than the late Romans their gold, most situated in provincial capitals.[55] What is remarkable about Sasanian monetary history is the clearly discernible expansion in mint output that appears to have occurred in the *late sixth and early seventh centuries*. As Sears states, 'Hoards document a staggering increase in the output of drachms during the latter part of the sixth and the beginning of the seventh centuries A.D.'[56] Thus the coins of Hormazd IV (579–90) are 'among the commonest in the whole Sasanian series',[57] and Khusro II's coinage in silver was massive.[58] So the numismatic evidence reinforces the impression culled from the textual sources that the late sixth/early seventh centuries saw considerable monetary expansion, at least in the Sasanian empire.

Justinian is said to have depleted the reserves built up by his predecessors.[59] When Justin II came to the throne, he seems to have used his personal resources to clear the debts that Justinian had run up with a whole throng of private bankers. In the verse panegyric written to celebrate Justin II's accession, there is a dramatic description of this scene, in which Corippus makes the bankers exclaim: 'You know, greatest of rulers, how much benefit your treasury has from business. If our strength fails, whence will come the annual tributes for your resources?'[60] If we believe the bankers, then 'business' was clearly *central* to the monetary wealth of the late empire. However, before coming to this I would like to suggest that the continued circulation of older coin was a major factor in the steady expansion of the stock of currency that took place between the later fourth and seventh centuries.

Now this conflicts radically with the view that the late Roman monetary economy involved an 'incessant recoining of the gold'. According

54 See A. Kolesnikov, 'The Quantity of Silver Coinage and Levels of Revenues in Late Sasanian Iran', in *Matériaux pour l'histoire économique*, ed. R. Gyselen and M. Szuppe (Paris, 1999) pp. 123–30.

55 R. Gyselen, *Arab-Sasanian Copper Coinage* (Vienna, 2000), p. 77.

56 S. Sears, 'Monetary Revision and Monetization in the Late Sasanian Empire', in *Matériaux pour l'histoire économique*, ed. Gyselen and Szuppe, pp. 149–65, at 160.

57 S. Tyler-Smith, 'Sasanian Mint Abbreviations', *Numismatic Chronicle* 143 (1983), 240–7, at p. 243.

58 H. M. Malek, 'A Survey of Research on Sasanian Numismatics', *Numismatic Chronicle* 153 (1993), 227–69, esp. p. 237.

59 Just. *Nov.* 148 pr., 'We found the treasury burdened with many debts and reduced to utter exhaustion.'

60 Corippus, *In laudem Iustini Augusti minoris*, ll. 371–4, 'scis, summe regentum, publica quid vestro prosint commercia fisco, unde tributa tuis succedent annua rebus, deficiet si nostra manus?' (ed. A. Cameron, *Flavius Cresconius Corippus: In laudem Iustini Augusti minoris* (London, 1976), pp. 58–9, text; p. 101, trans.).

to Grierson, 'It is probable that the gold brought in through taxes was melted and re-struck before being reissued ... This incessant recoining of the gold was in large measure responsible for the success of the government in maintaining the standard uniform over so many centuries.'[61] So too Kent who argued in a famous paper, 'The chance of any individual piece circulating for long was slight. If it escaped recoining, it must have gone quickly to ground.'[62] *These views are now largely outdated.* Michael Metcalf has argued, 'Kent's emphasis that gold coins enjoyed a short life in circulation, before being clawed back into the imperial coffers by the ruler's device of insisting that taxes should be paid in gold, may possibly be true of other parts of the Empire, but it would not be an obvious conclusion to draw from the Illyrican finds.'[63] Harl notes that 'Annual reminting would have been wasteful ... Solidi of good weight, regardless of age or the effigy they bore, were the equivalent of new coins.' Moreover, 'the wear on numerous specimens indicates that they had a long circulation life'.[64]

In fact, there is a great deal of evidence to suggest that older coins continued to circulate, and that a considerable if uncertain, and probably fluctuating, portion of the currency comprised such pieces. The emperors repeatedly sought to regulate public responses to the currency in circulation, seeking to combat a widespread public prejudice against older solidi. This is best reflected in Valentinian III's Novel 16, dated 445, from which it is clear that much older coinage was in circulation at that time and that 'buyers' were refusing to accept these pieces except at a discount, obviously because they were perceived to have lost weight through circulation.[65] The same kind of regulation had to be passed by Valentinian and his brother in the mid-fourth century, on the eve of their reform of the coinage,[66] and a famous edict of Justinian I, dated 559, shows that, again in the sixth century, in regions with a large and active circulation of money such as Egypt, the problem persisted, and was clearly disruptive of

61 P. Grierson, 'Coinage and Money in the Byzantine Empire (498–*c.*1090)', in *Moneta e scambi nell'alto medioevo, Settimane di Studio*, 8 (1960), pp. 411–53, at 423.

62 J. P. C. Kent, 'Gold Coinage in the Later Roman Empire', in *Essays in Roman Coinage Presented to Harold Mattingly*, ed. R. A. G. Carson *et al.* (Oxford, 1956), pp. 190–204, at 197.

63 Metcalf, 'Minting', p. 70, pointing out, 'the age structure of the hoards reveals that a significant proportion of the currency consisted of solidi that had remained in circulation for more than ten years'.

64 Harl, *Coinage in the Roman Economy*, p. 160, and p. 428, n. 8.

65 *Nov. Val.* 16 (18/1/445), about repeated complaints that 'solidi stamped with the names of Our ancestors are being refused by buyers'.

66 *CJ* XI.II.I (365–7), enjoining acceptance of older solidi (*solidos veterum principum veneratione formatos*) as long as they were of the requisite weight and alloy.

business activity. Justinian accused the coin-weighers and *chrysones*, probably bankers rather than tax officials, of discounting worn solidi, called ἀπόλυτον χάραγμα, i.e. 'loose coin', by as much as 12½ per cent and described this commission as exorbitant.[67] Papyri survive to show that what the edict did succeed in doing was reducing, not eliminating, the discount to 6¼ per cent.[68] Finally, the stipulation that solidi should be melted down and re-struck[69] only applied to the gold that was actually pulled in through taxation, and was in any case no longer being followed by the early fifth century, when, as Delmaire points out, recoinage was no longer automatic or compulsory.[70]

The coinage itself supports this general counter-argument. The so-called 'circulation' or 'emergency' hoards, that is, those hoards that can plausibly be viewed as random samples of the currency in circulation,[71] tend to show extended age structures (significant numbers of older solidi). At least four of the hoards in Table 6.1 date from the period after the Arab conquests, when the currency must have aged rapidly, but the general situation is sufficiently clear even from the other hoards listed in the table.[72]

[67] See C. Morrisson, 'Alterazioni e svalutazioni', in *La Cultura bizantina: Oggetti e messaggio: Moneta ed economia*, ed. A. Guillou (Rome, 1986), pp. 76–9, 86–8; J. Banaji, *Agrarian Change in Late Antiquity* (Oxford, 2007), pp. 73–5. So too in Italy in the sixth century, see Justinian, *App.* vii.20 (554), where it is said, 'Since we know that the solidi of earlier Roman emperors are easily available in those areas, but have also learned that financiers (*negotiatores*) and others inflict a discount of some sort (*dispendium aliquod*) on our tax payers in transactions that involve solidi (*propter mutationem solidorum*) ...'.

[68] *P. Oxy.* 1144 (580), xvi 1907.6 (7c).

[69] *CTh.* 12.6.13 (367), with M. Amandry *et al.*, 'L'affinage des métaux monnayés au Bas-Empire: Les réformes Valentiniennes de 364–368', *Quaderni Ticinesi* 11 (1982), 279–95.

[70] R. Delmaire, *Largesses sacrées et Res Privata: L'aerarium impérial et son administration du IVe au VIe siècle* (Rome, 1989), p. 259. It may be of some interest to note that in England in the eighteenth century, 'light' gold accounted for as much as 'three-quarters of the total of gold coin in circulation', N. Mayhew, *Sterling: The Rise and Fall of a Currency* (London, 1999), p. 106.

[71] By contrast with sums that travelled with their owner (Beaurains, Sidi-bu-Saïd), or others that were carefully accumulated over time, and still others that were simply one-time payments (Casa delle Vestali, Szikáncs).

[72] Table 6.1 tabulates data for twelve 'circulation' hoards from the early fifth to the late seventh century, which vary in size from 12 to 751 solidi. If we take some arbitrary threshold to indicate the number of *distinctively older solidi* in these hoards (e.g. thirty-three years), and treat each hoard as equally important, that is, calculate a simple, unweighted average of the percentages of older coin (solidi that had circulated for at least thirty-three years before their date of deposition), the overall average percentage of such coin is 44 per cent. Even if we exclude the four post-conquest hoards that are the latest deposits in the sample, the average is still fairly high, namely, 37 per cent. (**Sources**: F. Panvini–Rosati, 'Osservazioni sulla circolazione in Italia nel v sec. d.C. di monete d'oro romane', *Bollettino di numismatica* 4 (1985), 7–14; J. Iluk, 'Skarb solidów znaleziony w 1764 r.w. Xanten (RFN)', *Wiadomości Numizmatyczne* 31 (1987), 76–87; C. Morrisson, 'La circulation de la monnaie d'or en Afrique à époque Vandale: Bilan des trouvailles locales', in *Mélanges de numism. off. à P. Bastien*, ed. H. Huvelin *et al.* (Wetteren, 1987), pp. 325–44, at 336–7; A. Tusa Cutroni, 'La circolazione monetaria nella Sicilia bizantina ed il ripostiglio da Castellana

Table 6.1 *The percentage of older solidi in a sample of circulation hoards (fractions excluded)*

	Gravisca Italy	*Xanten Germany*	*Ain Meddah Algeria*	*Djemila Algeria*	*Castellana Sicily*	*Chatby Alexandria*	*Es-Sermita Tunisia*	*Rougga Tunisia*	*Nikertai Syria*	*South Jordan*	*Bet She'an Israel*	*Yildiz Palace 1 Turkey*
	*c.*408	*c.*428	*c.*496	*c.*496	*c.*538	*c.*611	*c.*615	*c.*647	*c.*681	680*s*	680*s*	685/95
% solidi in circulation for over 33 years	14.9	46.7	33.3	29.6	66.6	17.4	54.5	31.3	65.5	53.5	63.5	51.9
Constantius						1						
Valentinian I	26	47				3						
Valens		33				3						
Gratian						1						
Valentinian II	29	7										
Theodosius I	29	11										
Arcadius	39	38										
Honorius	51	55	3									
Theodosius II		1	19	34	2							
Eudoxia				1								
Pulcheria				1								

Table 6.1 (*cont.*)

	Gravisca Italy	*Xanten Germany*	*Ain Meddah Algeria*	*Djemila Algeria*	*Castellana Sicily*	*Chatby Alexandria*	*Es-Sermita Tunisia*	*Rougga Tunisia*	*Nikertai Syria*	*South Jordan*	*Bet She'an Israel*	*Yildiz Palace 1 Turkey*
Valentinian III		18		1								
Marcian			8	16								
Majorian			1									
Libius Severus			1									
Anthemius			1									
Leo I			26	51	2							
Julius Nepos				1								
Leo II & Zeno				2								
Zeno			29	58	4							
Basiliscus			3	11								
Basiliscus & Marcus				1								
Anastasius I			2	2	2							
Justin I												
Justinian I					2	4	12					1
Justin II						9	2					

	Gravisca Italy	*Xanten Germany*	*Ain Meddah Algeria*	*Djemila Algeria*	*Castellana Sicily*	*Chatby Alexandria*	*Es-Sermita Tunisia*	*Rougga Tunisia*	*Nikertai Syria*	*South Jordan*	*Bet She'an Israel*	*Yildiz Palace 1 Turkey*
Tiberius II						2	4					
Const.												
Maurice						43	8	1	3	1		3
Phocas						21	2	83	57	32	95	41
Heraclius						5	5	121	276	90	382	142
Constans II								63	155	80	219	96
Constantine IV									22	27	55	61
Justinian II												16

The late empire's vast coinage in gold coupled with the tendency for older issues to remain in circulation (subject, of course, to natural wastage) is, I believe, the key to explaining a feature of the monetary history of the seventh century which has not been sufficiently emphasised – the extraordinary fact that an Arab gold coinage did not evolve for some five decades after the conquest of Syria. As Michael Bates points out, 'The remarkable aspect of the matter is not that ʿAbd al-Malik instituted minting, but rather that a half century elapsed after the Arab conquest before a mint was set up in the capital of the caliphate.'[73] Balādhurī's statement that ʿUmar imposed a poll tax on non-Muslims of 4 'dinars' 'on those who had gold' implies that these taxes alone would have involved substantial aggregate payments in gold. Yet we know that a pre-reform gold coinage was rare.[74] It follows that the Arabs relied on the *existing* stock of gold currency, that is, the stock of solidi in circulation in Syria and Egypt, and that this must have been very substantial indeed to allow the early administrations to function *for over fifty years* without fresh stocks of currency, i.e. a regular coinage of their own.[75] For example, under the three-year peace treaty of 659, Muʿāwiya agreed to pay Constantinople 1000 solidi a day, according to the chronicler Theophanes.[76] This payment alone would have come to over a million solidi! In July 685, ʿAbd al-Malik sought a treaty on the same terms,[77] agreeing to an annual payment of 365,000 solidi. This would have lasted till 691 when Justinian II broke the treaty – 'foolishly',

(Palermo)', *Byzantino–Sicula* 1 (1966), 104–10; E. D. J. Dutilh, 'Une trouvaille de 191 monnaies d'or byzantines et de 1 pièce en argent', *Revue Belge de Numismatique* 61 (1905), 155–64; G.-Ch. Picard, *Bulletin Archéologique* (1943–5), pp. 427–8; Guéry *et al.*, *Trésor de monnaies d'or byzantines*, p. 55; C. Morrisson, 'Le trésor byzantin de Nikertai', *Revue Belge de Numismatique* 118 (1972), 29–91; G. Bijovsky, 'A Hoard of Byzantine Solidi from Bet She'an in the Umayyad Period', *Revue Numismatique* 158 (2002), 163–88, esp. p. 183; S. McA. Mosser, *A Bibliography of Byzantine Coin Hoards* (New York, 1935), pp. 91–2.)

73 M. L. Bates, 'History, Geography and Numismatics in the First Century of Islamic Coinage', *Schweizerische numismatische Rundschau* 65 (1986), 231–61, at p. 252.

74 T. Goodwin, 'Arab-Byzantine Coinage', in *Sylloge of Islamic Coins in the Ashmolean, vol. I: The Pre-Reform Coinage of the Early Islamic Period*, ed. S. Album and T. Goodwin (Oxford 2002), pp. 74–112, at 91, 'All pre-reform gold coinage is very rare, and probably never constituted a significant part of the gold coinage in circulation.'

75 Bates, 'History', pp. 251–2, is baffled because he assumes that 'booty' and 'trade' would have been the only sources of supply (into Syria) and fails to consider the possibility that the stock of gold in circulation was sufficiently large to defray the need for currency. S. Heidemann, 'The Merger of Two Currency Zones in Early Islam: The Byzantine and Sasanian Impact on the Circulation in Former Byzantine Syria and Northern Mesopotamia', *Iran* 36 (1998), 95–112, at p. 96, is correct to note that 'the influx of new coins was restricted after 636. It seems that Syria had to rely mainly on the existing stock of gold coins left from the time before the Arab conquest. The coins arriving in Syria later on barely supplemented the existing stock.'

76 Theophanes, *Chronicle*, A.M. 6150, A.D. 657/8; C. Mango and R. Scott, *The Chronicle of Theophanes Confessor: Byzantine and Near Eastern History A.D. 284–813* (Oxford, 1997), p. 484.

77 For the date, see Mango and Scott, *Chronicle*, p. 503.

says Theophanes – because ʿAbd al-Malik now proposed to make the payment in the new gold coinage that began to be struck from the end of 691, and this apparently was unacceptable to the Byzantines.[78]

The solidus vs the drachm?

The most striking feature of the gold coinage of the late empire was its ability to combine a considerable *density* of value with the functions of a *mass* currency. The power of the late Roman state was best encapsulated in both the quality as well as the scale of circulation of its coinage, features paralleled only by the Sasanians. Unlike the Sasanians, however, the Roman state was much less dependent on *external* international trade, and, in any case, unable fully to exploit the potential of that trade, due, in large measure, to a conscious Sasanian policy of controlling access to the east. Whereas the purity of the Sasanian silver coinage was linked to some considerable degree to a far-flung commercial network that used the drachm as a widely accepted means of exchange, the equivalent pressure in the late Roman state was the need to provide a stable monetary basis for the vastly more affluent society that emerged in the Mediterranean in the main part of the fourth and early fifth centuries. This was a society where the aristocracy accumulated enormous sums of money, as Olympiodorus tells us, but also one where the urban economy was largely driven by the monied classes of the empire, that is, those social groups outside the aristocratic elite who drew their incomes from banking, moneylending and trade.

The revival of banking in the fourth century was integrally related to the expanding circulation of gold, as bankers diversified into money changing and began to manage the assets of 'high net worth' individuals through an active deployment of funds.[79] Money changing must have been a hugely lucrative profession,[80] and its integration with banking would mean that vast sums of money were available to finance the expansion

[78] Theophanes, *Chronicle*, AM 6183, AD 690/1 (pp. 509f.). See A. Kaplony, *Konstantinopel und Damaskus: Gesandtschaften und Verträge zwischen Kaisern und Kalifen 639–750* (Berlin, 1996) p. 154, for the argument that this was coinage from the 'imperial images' period ('arabisch–byzantinische Münzen'), viz. 'phase 2' in Bates's subdivision of the earliest gold from Damascus, see Bates, 'History', pp. 238ff., esp. 243. It is possible that in discussing the chronology of the dinar, Bates may have been misled by the translation of Theophanes that he used, where the year in question, AM 6183, is wrongly identified as 691/2 instead of 690/1.

[79] The reference to asset management comes from Basil, *Regulae brevius tractatae*, ccliv (*PG* 31.1251), referring to Alexandria specifically, and based on his personal testimony.

[80] Ambrose, *Expositio evangelii sec. Lucam* 9.18,'Qui sunt nummularii nisi qui de pecunia domini lucrum quaerunt nec bona malaque discernunt?'; Ammianus, 30.9.3, 'nec imperante eo [Valentinian] provinciam nummularius rexit'.

of international trade from the later fourth century. Ambrose depicts the typical merchant of the late fourth century as 'always on the go, day and night, amassing piles of treasure, or accumulating great new stocks of merchandise'.[81] This obviously refers to the more substantial merchants, such as Constantinople's large-scale importers of raw materials such as iron and copper (*to hekastou eidous parektikon, hoion siderοteleis, khalkoteleis*) mentioned in the mid-sixth-century treatise called *Peri stratēgias*,[82] or those who financed and organised trade with the east.[83] There is good textual evidence of the flourishing of this trade in the fourth century – the repeated reference to wealthy traders in the urban centres of the Near East carrying on a substantial business (*negotia maxima*) in goods imported from India and China, some at the great annual fair of Batnae, near the headwaters of the Balikh,[84] others, probably the majority, via Persia,[85] and the interesting reference in the *Hou Han shu*, written *c.*430, to the inhabitants of Ta-Ch'in 'trading with Persia and India and gaining great profit from their dealings'.[86]

What is abundantly clear from the late antique evidence, however, is that by the early sixth century the Indian Ocean trade was largely in the hands of other groups. The formal proof of this is Cosmas' own assertion that because of her location Taprobanē was 'much frequented by ships from all parts of India and from Persia and Ethiopia, and it likewise sends

[81] Ambrose, *De officiis* 1,243 (ed. Davidson, vol. 1, p. 256), and the ref. to their 'relentless quest for profit'.

[82] Anon., *Peri stratēgias*, 1, 11–12; 2, 28ff., ed. G. T. Dennis, *Three Byzantine Military Treatises* (Washington, D.C., 1985), pp. 10, 12; see A. Giardina, 'Modi di scambio e valori sociali nel mondo bizantino (IV–XII secolo)', in *Mercati e mercanti nell'alto medioevo: L'area euroasiatica e l'area mediterranea, Settimane di Studio 40 (1992)*, pp. 523–84, at 532ff., with the correct interpretation of the phrase *to hekastou eidous parektikon*, that is, *supplying* (not producing) every conceivable kind of material.

[83] E.g. (but from an earlier period) the Alexandrian financier in *SB* XVIII 13167, the best discussion of which is D. Rathbone, 'The "Muziris" Papyrus (*SB* XVIII 13167): Financing Roman Trade with India', in *Alexandrian Studies II in Honour of Mostafa El Abbadi*, ed. M. Abd-el-Ghani *et al.* (= *Bulletin de la Société Archéologique d'Alexandrie*, no. 46) (Alexandria, 2000), pp. 39–50, and F. De Romanis, *Cassia, cinnamono, ossidiana: Uomini e merci tra Oceano Indiano e Mediterraneo* (Rome, 1996), pp. 183 ff.

[84] Ammianus, 14.3.3, 'a great crowd of every financial description (*magna promiscuae fortunae multitudo*) gathers to deal in the goods sent from India and China', with F. Millar, *The Roman Near East 31 BC–AD 337* (Cambridge, MA and London, 1993), p. 483 for the location.

[85] *Expositio totius mundi et gentium* xxii (Rougé, p. 156) on Nisibis and Edessa, 'above all, they are both wealthy and equipped with every kind of commodity, for what they import from Persia they sell to the rest of the Roman world and what they buy they export'; so too Bostra at xxxviii (p. 176), from which the reference to 'an exceedingly large volume of business' (*negotia maxima*).

[86] Cited L. Boulnois, *The Silk Road*, trans. D. Chamberlin (London, 1966), p. 131.

many of its own',[87] and the explicit testimony of Procopius that Justinian had to rely on the rulers of Aksum to try and circumvent the Sasanian monopoly of silk.[88] The clear implication of these texts is that *Roman traders were no longer a significant force in the Indian Ocean.*[89] Egeria's fascinating description of Clysma in the later fourth century distinctly implies that Indian merchants controlled a substantial part of the trade directed to the Red Sea.[90] There is a resonance of this in the early fifth-century Pelagian diatribe *De divitiis*, where the author tells his largely aristocratic readership, 'No one coming from India or Arabia or Egypt on business and intending to spend a short time at Rome or in any other place acquires houses or possessions there for himself or other property which seems immovable, but only gold or silver or merchandise of different kinds or anything which he is able to take back with him to his own country.'[91] Here the implication is even stronger, namely, that unlike the Sasanians the late empire did not shut its gates to merchants from the east, and thus, by this stage at least, they could carry gold *back with them*, despite the formal restrictions imposed by Valens some decades earlier. The Arabs too were active traders in the Indian Ocean. From Fa-hsien's account of his travels in India and Sri Lanka, it emerges that in the early fifth century there was a colony of Sabaean merchants settled in the chief city of the island.[92] This reference should be read with Ammianus' description of the flourishing state of the southern coast of Arabia in the latter part of the fourth century, with its 'dense clustering of commercial ports' and 'numerous safe harbours'.[93] The argument is not that Byzantine vessels did not ply these waters but that they must have been a minor part of the traffic.

87 Cosmas, xi, 15 (*Topographie Chrétienne*, ed. W. Wolska-Conus (Paris, 1968–73), vol. III, p. 345), Ἐξ ὅλης δὲ τῆς Ἰνδικῆς καὶ Περσίδος καὶ Αἰθιοπίας δέχεται ἡ νῆσος πλοῖα πολλά, μεσῖτις οὖσα, ὁμοίως καὶ ἐκπέμπει.

88 Procopius, *Bell.* i, 20, 9.

89 I agree with D. Whitehouse, 'Epilogue: Roman Trade in Perspective', in *Rome and India: The Ancient Sea Trade*, ed. V. Begley *et al.* (Madison, 1991), pp. 216–18.

90 J. Wilkinson, *Egeria's Travels* (London, 1971), p. 206, telling us that the port is 'renowned for the Indian merchants who come to it'.

91 Pelagius, *De divitiis* 19.4, in the recent edition by A. Kessler, *Reichtumskritik und Pelagianismus: Die pelagianische Diatribe 'de divitiis': Situierung, Lesetext, Übersetzung, Kommentar* (Freiburg, 1999), p. 324; translation from B. R. Rees, *The Letters of Pelagius and his Followers* (Woodbridge, 1991), p. 208. For the date, 411–14, see Kessler, *Reichtumskritik*, pp. 108ff.

92 Fa-Hsien, *A Record of Buddhistic Kingdoms: Being an Account by the Chinese Monk Fâ-Hien of his Travels in India and Ceylon (A.D. 399–414)*, trans. J. Legge (New York, 1965), p. 104, 'Sabaean merchants whose houses are stately and beautiful'. Now see Chapter 10 in this volume, p. 234.

93 Ammianus, 23.6.46, *Ubi et stationes et portus tranquilli sunt plures, et emporia densa*, and his similar reference, at 23.6.11, to the Persian Gulf, 'All along the coast is a dense network of towns and villages, while ships are constantly sailing to and fro.'

The decisive factor, of course, was the growth of a powerful merchant class in Sasanian Persia, which drew its wealth from the luxury trades (Khusro II's treasures included a 'vast quantity of jewels, gold and silver plate, furs, precious fabrics')[94] and had the strong backing of the state.[95] Sasanian military expansion secured the conditions for the expansion of trade, but less through conquest than a looser, and less stable, system of control. From eastern Arabia to Sind and the Kushan domains to the north, the Sasanians constructed a series of spheres of influence which laid the basis, from the end of the fourth century, for a crushing Sasanian monopoly of the maritime trade[96] and a large-scale circulation of the silver drachm along the terrestrial silk routes. Of 368 drachms in the remarkable Tépé Maranjan hoard near Kabul (date *c.* 385), 326 are of Shāpūr II.[97] Coins of Shāpūr II were *abundant* in the area south of the Hindu Kush,[98] and they are also the earliest Sasanian coins to appear in China or eastern Turkestan.[99] Daibul, Makran and the adjacent parts of Sind were acquired by the Sasanians under Bahrām Gōr (Bahrām V, 421–38) as part of a dowry conferred on him by the local ruler.[100] It was his reign above all that was crucial in consolidating a Sasanian commercial network that led from Sind to Balkh, and from Merv to Bukhara and the desert oases leading to Turfan.[101] Merv churned out huge quantities of Bahrām V's drachms,[102] and these circulated north in sufficient numbers to become the prototype

[94] E. G. Browne, 'Some Account of the Arabic Work Entitled "Niháyatu'l-irab fí akhbári'l-Furs wa'l-ʿArab"', *Journal of the Royal Asiatic Society* (1900), 195–259, at p. 250. In Firdawsī's rendering of Khusro I's circular to state employees, Sasanian merchants are symbolically associated with 'beautiful pearls and musk' (Mohl, *Livre des rois*, VI, p. 131). Pearl fishing flourished under Khusro II, Firdawsī in Mohl, *Livre des rois*, VII, p. 303.

[95] Control of the commercial sea routes was central to Ardashīr's perspectives, see V. F. Piacentini, 'Ardashīr i Pāpakān and the Wars against the Arabs: Working Hypothesis on the Sasanian Hold of the Gulf', *Proceedings of the Seminar for Arabian Studies* 15 (1985), 57–77.

[96] See F. Thierry and C. Morrisson, 'Sur les monnaies byzantines trouvées en Chine', *Revue Numismatique* 36 (1994), 109–45, at p. 137 for the Chinese sources for this.

[97] R. Curiel, 'Le trésor du Tépé Maranjān: Une trouvaille de monnaies sasanides et kušano-sasanides faite près de Caboul', in *Trésors monétaires d'Afghanistan*, ed. R. Curiel and D. Schlumberger (Paris, 1953), pp. 102 f., 104.

[98] Curiel, 'Trésor', p. 119.

[99] J. K. Skaff, 'Sasanian and Arab-Sasanian Silver Coins from Turfan: Their Relationship to International Trade and the Local Economy', *Asia Major*, 3rd ser., 11/2 (1998), 67–115, esp. p. 68; M. Alram, 'Coins and the Silk Road', in *Monks and Merchants: Silk Road Treasures from Northwest China: Gansu and Ningxia 4th–7th Century*, ed. A. L. Juliano *et al.* (New York, 2001), pp. 271–91, at 274, about the Kao-ch'ang hoards from the Turfan area.

[100] Al-Ṭabarī, *History*, vol. V, p. 102; al-Thaʿālibi, *Ghurar*, p. 564; see D. Whitehouse and A. Williamson, 'Sasanian Maritime Trade', *Iran* 11 (1973), 29–49, esp. pp. 43ff.

[101] For Balkh see al-Ṭabarī, *History*, vol. V, p. 99.

[102] E. V. Zeĭmal', 'The Circulation of Coins in Central Asia during the Early Medieval Period (Fifth–Eighth Centuries A.D.)', *Bulletin of the Asia Institute*, new ser. 8 (1994), 245–67, esp. p. 246.

of the Bukhara silver drachms of the sixth century.[103] Merv was the interface of Persian and Sogdian commercial dominance,[104] and a major station in the diffusion of Nestorian Christianity into Central Asia.[105] Even the disastrous closing decades of the fifth century (the losses inflicted by the Hephthalites) did nothing to stop the active trade with Transoxiana, and it is clear that for most of the sixth and early seventh centuries Sogdian merchants used the drachm as an international currency.[106] So entrenched was the circulation of Sasanian silver that, according to Skaff, 'silver coins were still being imported around a decade after the T'ang conquest' of the Kao-ch'ang kingdom in 640.[107]

This is the background against which we have to view the 'intense local competition between Roman and Persian traders'[108] reflected in the story Sopatros told Cosmas. To dismiss the narrative as fiction[109] misses the point that for well over a century the Sasanians had subjected Rome's external trade to what Callu calls a 'tactical blockade'.[110] The Byzantine sources of the sixth century contain some passages of extraordinary value to any reconstruction of events in that period. Justinian's attempt to use the Abyssinians to open a new line of access to the Indian Ocean was a failure, says Procopius, 'for it was impossible for the Ethiopians to buy silk from the Indians, for the Persian merchants always locate themselves at the very harbours where the Indian ships first put in (since they inhabit the adjoining country), and are accustomed to buy the whole cargoes'.[111]

103 *Ibid.*, p. 247, about the Bukhar-khuda series.

104 E. De La Vaissière, *Histoire des marchands sogdiens* (Paris, 2002), p. 178; R. N. Frye, *The Golden Age of Persia: The Arabs in the East* (London, 1975), p. 42.

105 Nestorian Christians would have been among the most active Sasanian traders, for Cosmas, we know, refers to an established community of 'Persian Christians' in Sri Lanka, already by the end of the fifth century: Cosmas, xi, 14. For the date of this reference, see F. De Romanis, 'Romanukharattha e Taprobane: Sui rapporti Roma-Ceylon nel I sec. d.C.', *Helikon* 28 (1988), 5–58, esp. pp. 51–5; for the likely location, J. Carswell, 'The Port of Mantai, Sri Lanka', in *Rome and India: The Ancient Sea Trade*, ed. Begley *et al.*, pp. 197–203, at 199. The East Syrian saint John of Dailam who spent thirty-five years in Fars in the early eighth century built monasteries with the money raised from trade with Sri Lanka, see S. P. Brock, 'A Syriac Life of John of Dailam', *Parole d'Orient* 10 (1981–2), 123–89.

106 De la Vaissière, *Histoire*, pp. 168–70, esp. 'Les monnaies d'argent sassanides ... ont incontestablement connu une vaste circulation liée au commerce des marchands sogdiens.'

107 Skaff, 'Silver Coins from Turfan', p. 99.

108 J. I. Miller, *The Spice Trade of the Roman Empire, 29 BC to AD 641* (Oxford, 1969), p. 240.

109 M. Hendy, *Studies in the Byzantine Monetary Economy c.300–1450* (Cambridge, 1985), pp. 276ff.; cf. F. De Romanis, 'Sul prestigio della moneta aurea romano-bizantina in Oriente (sec. I–VI d.C.)', in *La Persia e Bisanzio* (Rome, 2004), pp. 291–308, at 299–301 for criticism of Hendy.

110 J.-P. Callu, 'I commerci oltre i confini dell'Impero', in *Storia di Roma, III/I: L'età tardoantica: Crisi e trasformazioni*, ed. A. Carandini *et al.* (Turin, 1993), pp. 487–524, at 511.

111 Procopius, *Bell.* i, 20, 12 (ed. Dewing, *History of the Wars*, vol. I, p. 192): τοῖς τε γὰρ Αἰθίοψι τὴν μέταξαν ὠνεῖσθαι πρὸς τῶν Ἰνδῶν ἀδύνατα ἦν, ἐπεὶ ἀεὶ οἱ Περσῶν ἔμποροι πρὸς αὐτοῖς τοῖς

This was in 531, following the last of a series of Abyssinian occupations of Yemen under the *nagaši* Ĕlla Asbĕha but before the coup in which Abrĕha overthrew Sumu-yafa' Ašwa' (Esimphaios).[112] When the Sasanians recovered control of Yemen in the last years of Khusro I's reign (in 575), the real reason, as Theophanes of Byzantium pointed out, was the formidable threat of the emerging Byzantine alliance with the Türks. It was the Türks who approached the Byzantines. The passage in Theophanes documenting this is one of the most coherent in all of Byzantine historiography, for he notes that the Türks were now (in the 560s) in control of the trade with China, having destroyed the monopoly which the Hephthalites had wrested from the Sasanians in the later fifth century.[113] Zemarchus' embassy to the Kaghan was warmly received the following year, in 569. 'It was this', Theophanes says, 'that led Khusro to launch his expedition against' Abyssinian control of the Yemen.[114] What Photius' summary of these parts of this late sixth-century history lacks or leaves out is any reference to the information conveyed by another historian, Menander the Guardsman, that the whole Türk mission to Constantinople arose in the first place as a backlash to the Sasanian refusal to allow the Sogdians access to the Persian and Near Eastern markets for raw silk. It was the Sogdians, says Menander, who instigated the embassy to Byzantium, advising 'Sizabul' (Ishtemi?) 'that it would be better for the Turks to cultivate the friendship of the Romans and send their raw silk for sale to them because they made more use of it than other people'.[115] From this it is clear that in the late sixth century Byzantium was the world's largest market for silk, and since Sasanian merchants charged probably well over 15 solidi per pound of this material,[116] it is easy to see why so much energy was invested

ὅρμοις γινόμενοι οὗ δὴ τὰ πρῶτα αἱ τῶν Ἰνδῶν νῆες καταίρουσιν, ἅτε χώραν προσοικοῦντες τὴν ὅμορον, ἅπαντα ὠνεῖσθαι τὰ φορτία εἰώθασι (showing how commercial strategies were always at work).

112 See Bosworth's commentary on Ṭabarī's description of these events, al-Ṭabarī, *History*, vol. v, pp. 207f., n. 518.

113 Theophanes of Byzantium, in Photius, *Bibliothèque*, vol. 1: *Codices 1–83*, ed. R. Henry (Paris, 1991), p. 78: Οἱ γὰρ Τοῦρκοι τότε τά τε Σηρῶν ἐμπόρια καὶ τοὺς λιμένας κατεῖχον. Ταῦτα δὲ πρὶν μὲν Πέρσαι κατεῖχον, Ἐφθαλάνου δὲ τοῦ Ἐφθαλιτῶν βασιλέως ... Περόζην καὶ Πέρσας νικήσαντος ἀφῃρέθησαν μὲν τούτων οἱ Πέρσαι, δεσπόται δὲ κατέστησαν Ἐφθαλῖται. οὓς μικρῷ ὕστερον μάχῃ νικήσαντες Τοῦρκοι ἀφεῖλον ἐξ αὐτῶν καὶ ταῦτα.

114 Theophanes, *ibid.*, Ἰουστῖνος δὲ Ζήμαρχον ἐς τοὺς Τούρκους πρέσβυν ἀπέστειλεν· ὃς καὶ λαμπρῶς ἑστιάσας τε τοὺς Τούρκους καὶ ἐς τὰ μάλιστα φιλοφρονηθεὶς ἐς τὸ Βυζάντιον ἐπανῄει. Διὸ καὶ ὁ Χοσρόης ἐπ' Αἰθίοπας φίλους ὄντας Ῥωμαίοις ... ἐστράτευσε κτλ.

115 R. C. Blockley (ed.), *The History of Menander the Guardsman: Introductory Essay, Text, Translation (etc.)* (Liverpool, 1985), fr. 10,1 (p. 115).

116 This was the price Justinian asked Byzantine traders to stick to, to avoid competitive bidding, see A. H. M. Jones, *The Roman Economy: Studies in Ancient Economic and Administrative History*, ed. P. A. Brunt (Oxford, 1974), p. 362.

in constructing and retaining their 'monopoly'. Moreover, it is clear from Menander's description of the kind of questions Justin II asked the Türk envoys that the Byzantines knew little about Central Asia *c.* 570.

If the alliance was designed to *contain* Sasanian competition, it was clearly a failure. The late sixth/early seventh centuries saw a veritable explosion of Sasanian trade into Inner Asia.[117] Cosmas had explained the Persian advantage in silk in terms of the differential turnaround times linked to the length of voyages by land and sea,[118] and De la Vaissière in his excellent book on the Sogdian merchants has argued that the terrestrial routes were still dominant in the late sixth century.[119] The 'Turkish consolidation of Inner Asia in the middle of the sixth century' was itself a major factor stimulating revival or further expansion of the silk trade.[120] Secondly, as Skaff argues, the demand for international trade was largely driven by political conditions in China, and the latter part of the sixth century saw the pendulum swinging back to unification.[121] With the T'ang reunification of China in 618, this impact would have been even stronger. At any rate, for the Sasanians the late sixth century was a period of renewed commercial expansion, related perhaps to Hormazd IV's victory over the Türks. Khusro II's coinage of the 610s and 620s represents almost half the surviving coins from Turfan's tombs that have a mint date (eleven out of twenty-five),[122] and his coins were plentiful in various parts of Afghanistan.[123] The hoard from Wuqia in the Xinjiang Uygur Autonomous Region museum, which was never properly published since its discovery in 1959, contains at least 546 drachms of his (96 per cent of the Sasanian coins).[124]

The peak of Sasanian silver circulation in Turfan seems to have occurred later, in the second quarter of the seventh century. It was the purity of the

[117] The Arabic sources overstate the extent of Khusro I's conquests in the east but they also suggest that it was Khusro who sought a matrimonial alliance with Ishtemi, cf. G. Widengren, 'Xosrau Anōšurvān, les Hephtalites et les peuples turcs', *Orientalia Suecana* 1 (1952), 69–94, and M. Grignaschi, 'La chute de l'empire hephthalite dans les sources byzantines et perses et le problème des Avar', *Acta Antiqua Acad. Scient. Hungaricae* 28 (1980), 219–48, assessing the credibility of the sources differently.

[118] Cosmas, ii, 46 (Wolska-Conus, vol. 1, p. 353), who concludes, 'This is the reason why one always finds so much silk in Persia.'

[119] De la Vaissière, *Histoire*, p. 227.

[120] Skaff, 'Silver Coins from Turfan', p. 84–5.

[121] Skaff, 'Silver Coins from Turfan', pp. 85–6.

[122] Skaff, 'Silver Coins from Turfan', p. 86, cf. p. 70, 'almost all of the coins from tombs date to the late sixth and seventh centuries'.

[123] Curiel, 'Trésor', p. 126.

[124] M. Tsumura and K. Yamauchi, *Sasanian and Arab-Sasanian Silver Coins from Xinjiang* (Nara, 2003) (in Japanese), Eng. summary, p. 342.

silver coinage that won general acceptance for it from Bukhara to Turfan,[125] and this must have been a major factor in the state's decision to maintain high levels of purity. On the other hand, late Sasanian silver circulated in other forms equally amenable to trade. The late sixth century also saw an expansion of trade with the regions north of the Caspian.[126] Here, in north-eastern Russia, the chief means of exchange (in the Kama–Perm regions) were the large numbers of silver bowls and other silver objects that have turned up there. A lot of Sasanian silver was recycled to the north by Sogdian merchants,[127] showing that beneath the incessant political fluctuations in this vast landscape, the caravans continued to circulate because traders from different nationalities depended on each other. The late Sasanians had an abundance of silver which they used for both coinage and silverware.

To return to the solidus, Cosmas' story, told to him by Sopatros, about the Sri Lankan king scrutinising the solidus and the drachm is formal proof that both solidi and drahms circulated in the Indian Ocean trade. Since early Roman gold and silver coins had always circulated in the Indian Ocean as bullion, that is, valued for their bullion value,[128] there is no compelling reason to believe that the solidus would have been treated any differently in late antiquity. This contrasts sharply with the export of low-value copper coins to South India and Sri Lanka. Their import into these regions was probably linked to the undervaluation of the Late Roman bronzes[129] and designed to meet a need for local currency.[130] The solidi, by contrast, would have been melted down or holed and used for jewellery. The same was almost certainly true of the few stray solidi that have turned up along the silk routes to China.[131] The scarcity of Byzantine

[125] Cf. R. N. Frye, 'Sasanian–Central Asian Trade Relations', *Bulletin of the Asia Institute*, n.s. 7 (1993), 73–7, at pp. 73–4.

[126] R. N. Frye, 'Byzantine and Sasanian Trade Relations with Northeastern Russia', *Dumbarton Oaks Papers* 26 (1972), 263–9.

[127] De la Vaissière, *Histoire*, pp. 245–8.

[128] D. W. Mac Dowall, 'Indian Imports of Roman Silver Coins', in *Coinage, Trade and Economy: 3rd International Colloquium, 1991*, ed. A. K. Jha (Nasik, 1991), pp. 145–53; and D. W. Mac Dowall, 'The Indo-Roman Metal Trade', in *Foreign Coins Found in the Indian Subcontinent: 4th International Colloquium, 1995*, ed. D. W. Mac Dowall *et al.* (Bombay, 2004), pp. 39–44, arguing that the export of coins as bullion was driven by their relative undervaluation in the Roman monetary system.

[129] Lo Cascio, 'Teoria e politica monetaria', p. 546, and E. Lo Cascio, 'Aspetti della politica monetaria nel IV secolo', in *Atti dell' Accademia Romanistica Costantiniana, X Convegno Internazionale* (Naples, 1995), pp. 481–502, esp. 497–9.

[130] O. Bopearachchi, 'Le commerce maritime entre Rome et Sri Lanka d'après les données numismatiques', *Revue des études anciennes* 94 (1992), 107–21, esp. pp. 116–17.

[131] The best survey is Thierry and Morrisson, 'Sur les monnaies byzantines trouvées en Chine' (n. 96); also see Lin Ying, 'From Portraiture of Power to the Gold Coin of Kaghan: Western Turks and the

gold in this sector of the international trade is not so much an indication of the scale of its circulation as reflective of the fact that these coins had a limited *monetary* use in this part of the world.[132] But gold did circulate in the Central Asian trade, and this could only have come in, initially, as solidi. The evidence here is partly textual. When Qutaiba ibn Muslim conquered Baikand in 706, the Arabs found 'innumerable gold and silver vessels',[133] total assets valued at 150,000 *mithqāls*,[134] so this is some indication that the Sogdians had access to gold from the west. The really crucial pieces of evidence, however, both come from the remarkable early seventh-century history of Theophylact Simocatta. His sources on China were of an exceedingly high quality.[135] Describing the 'realm of Taugast', as he called China, Theophylact says, 'They have a custom, which resembles law, that males should never embellish themselves with gold adornment, even though they have become owners of a great abundance of silver and gold as a result of their large and advantageous trading.'[136] A second passage from the same author states (in the context of Bahrām Čōbīn's campaign against the Türks):

> [T]he Huns [Türks] were subjected to tribute by the Babylonians [Persians], although formerly the *Huns [Türks] levied from the Medes [Persians] forty thousand gold coins* as cause for inactivity. The Turkish realm, then, had been made very rich by the Persians, and this particular nation had turned to great extravagance; for they hammered out gold couches, tables, goblets, thrones, pedestals, horse-trappings, suits of armour, and everything which has been devised by the inebriation of wealth. Subsequently when the Turks broke the treaty and demanded that they be given more than the customary money and that there be a very heavy supplement, the Persians, intolerant of the burden of the imposed tribute, elected to make war. When the Persians won a splendid victory, affairs together with fortune

Eastward Diffusion of Solidi', in *Dal 'denarius' al 'dinar': L'Oriente et la moneta romana*, ed. F. De Romanis and S. Sorda (Rome, 2006), pp. 239–63.

132 Thierry and Morrisson, 'Monnaies', pp. 129–30, citing textual evidence for possible use as currency.

133 Al-Ṭabarī, *The Zenith of the Marwānid House: The Last Years of 'Abd al-Malik and the Caliphate of al-Walīd A.D. 700–715/A.H. 81–96 (The History of al-Ṭabarī, vol.* XXIII*)*, trans. M Hinds (Albany, 1990), p. 137, citing conflicting estimates of the value of the hoard. Ṭabarī also tells us that the stocks of silk warehoused with the Baikand merchants were worth one million dirhams (p. 136).

134 The figure accepted by Narshakhī in his local history, of which only a Persian translation survives, see Narshakhī, *The History of Bukhara, Translated from a Persian Abridgement of the Arabic Original by Narshakhī*, trans. R. N. Frye (Cambridge, MA, 1954), p. 45, 'When he gathered together everything it amounted to 150,000 mithqāls.'

135 See P. A. Boodberg, 'Marginalia to the Histories of the Northern Dynasties', *Harvard Journal of Asiatic Studies* (1938), 223–53, part 1.

136 Theophylact, vii.9.3 (*The History of Theophylact Simocatta*, ed. M. Whitby *et al.* (Oxford, 1988), p. 192).

> reversed their flow, and the Turks were subjected to tribute by the Persians and were also deprived in addition of the wealth which they had previously accumulated.[137]

So the Persians were paying the Türks in gold but conflict erupted and the Türks were defeated, the flows reversed and gold poured into Sasanian coffers. In what form? *Theophylact refers to 'gold coins'.*[138] These are crucially important passages, for they seem to be about the only textual references we have to the actual circulation of solidi in the geographical area covered by Türko-Sasanian interactions, both political (tribute payments) and presumably commercial as well, in the late sixth century.

The coins Theophylact refers to could only have been solidi, since they are not likely to have been Sasanian dinars.[139] Since no solidus hoards have turned up in the former Sasanian territories (at least none I am aware of), we must suppose that these payments, like the plunder the Persians collected in the Levant, were melted down.[140] We can thus visualise two situations for the late Roman/Byzantine gold circulating beyond the eastern boundaries of the empire: one where solidi retained their form of coin but circulated by weight, and did so with other coins such as the drachm, which also circulated by weight. This situation is formally attested by a passage in Balādhurī which says, 'The dînârs of Heraclius used to be current among the people of [Mecca] before Moslem times, but also the baghlîyah [full-weight] dirhams of Persia; but it was not customary to buy and sell with them *except by considering the coins as bullion*.'[141] Both solidi and drachms were used in the Hijaz but they circulated by weight. The second situation, by contrast, was one where the solidi were basically treated as a form of bullion, valued for the purity of their metal content, hence readily melted down, holed, hoarded and so on. The best examples

137 Theophylact, iii.6.10–13 (*History*, pp. 80–1).

138 Τεσσαράκοντα χιλιάδας χρυσῶν, *Theophylacti Simocattae Historiae*, ed. De Boor (Leipzig, 1887), p. 212. The statement in Theophanes that Hormazd 'was able to exact a tribute of 40,000 gold coins from the Turks, whereas previously he had been paying the Turks the same amount', *Chronicle*, AM 6080, AD 587/8 (Mango and Scott, p. 385), looks like an extrapolation from this passage in Theophylact.

139 So too H.-W. Haussig, *Die Geschichte Zentralasiens und der Seidenstrasse in vorislamischer Zeit*, 2nd edn (Darmstadt, 1992), pp. 167, 178.

140 That this is what the Sasanians did with their precious metal plunder is suggested by a passage in Sebeos (or the history attributed to him), see Sebeos, 116 (R. W. Thomson and J. Howard-Johnston, *The Armenian History Attributed to Sebeos, Part I* (Liverpool, 1999), vol. 1, pp. 69–70).

141 Al-Balādhurī, *Kitāb futūḥ al-buldān*, p. 466; F. C. Murgotten, *The Origins of the Islamic State, Being a Translation … of the Kitâb futûh al-buldân, Part 2* (New York, 1924), p. 263; cf. al-Maqrīzī in Allouche, *Mamluk Economics*, p. 56.

of this are surely China, India and Sri Lanka, and of course it is also possible that in these markets the coins were brought in by traders of other nationalities, such as Sogdians, Arabs from the peninsula, Indians and so on. When Cosmas writes that solidi were carefully selected (*eklekta*) for export to Sri Lanka,[142] this must refer, in the first instance, to the fineness of the coins, and to their weight only insofar as there was a demonstrable connection between the weight and fineness of gold coins.[143] Finally, the two situations together would also account for his other assertion that 'all countries use the solidus in their commercial dealing', and that the coin was found from 'one end of the world to the other'.[144]

In the western Mediterranean the Roman monetary system had of course disintegrated by this stage, but the use of Byzantine prototypes shows the profound influence of the solidus in this sector.[145] Like the Arab administrations in Syria and Egypt, and a whole century before them, the Merovingians based their gold coinage largely on existing stocks of solidi.[146] Gold was almost certainly being imported into Italy under the Ostrogoths,[147] and a great deal of Byzantine gold made its way north via the Ostrogoths and transpadana.[148] In the east, one of the most interesting hoards to have turned up is that from al-Madhāriba in Yemen.[149] This contained Aksumite (= 868) and late Roman (= 326) gold coins in a single hoard, but the baffling feature is the considerable gap between the solidi and the Aksumite coins. The bulk of the solidi date between 350 and 367, whereas the hoard stems from the second quarter of the sixth century![150] At any rate, it is always interesting to be able to match a numismatic find with textual or other evidence. In the early sixth century, the wealthier Christian families of Najrān in southern Arabia used solidi in their transactions. The new 'Letter' of Simeon of Bēth-Arshām reports that,

142 Cosmas, xi, 19 (Wolska-Conus, vol. III, p. 351), Ἦν οὖν τὸ νόμισμα ὄβρυζον, λαμπρόν, εὔμορφον· τοιαῦτα γὰρ ἐκλεκτὰ προχωροῦσιν ἐκεῖ.

143 Poirier has tried to show this in his dissertation, *Contribution à l'analyse de l'or antique*, pp. 162–70.

144 Cosmas, ii, 77 (Wolska-Conus, vol. I, pp. 393ff.).

145 J. Lafaurie and C. Morrisson, 'La pénétration des monnaies byzantines en Gaule mérovingienne et visigotique du VIe au VIIe siècle', *Revue Numismatique*, ser. 6, 29 (1987), 38–98, esp. pp. 41–5.

146 *Ibid.*, p. 44: 'Ce sont les monnaies circulant en Gaule ou en Italie qui ont fourni la matière première des nouvelles fabrications.'

147 See S. J. B. Barnish, 'The Wealth of Iulianus Argentarius: Late Antique Banking and the Mediterranean Economy', *Byzantion* 55 (1985), 5–38, esp. pp. 11–12, with the reference to Cassiodorus, *Variae* ix, 3.

148 M. Asolati, 'Considerazioni sulla circolazione di moneta aurea del V e VI secolo d.C.: Materiali inediti da Nerviano', *Quaderni Ticinesi* 25 (1996), 271–86.

149 S. Munro-Hay, 'The al-Madhāriba Hoard of Gold Aksumite and Late Roman Coins', *Numismatic Chronicle* 149 (1989), 83–100.

150 The last coins are those of Kaleb (Ella Asbeha) who died *c.* 536.

following her martyrdom, the princes of Najrān interceded with the king Yuśuf to grant a proper burial to Ruhayma, daughter of Azma', arguing:

> This (woman) has done many good deeds to everyone, to the king, to the notables, and to the poor; and in like manner she formerly treated M'DWKRM <Ma'dī-karib>, who before you has been king in this land. For he was in difficulty and borrowed from her twelve thousand *denarii*, and finally, when she saw that he was in difficulty, she renounced claim to the debt.[151]

Ruhayma's contract can be dated to within a few years. Ma'dī Karib was the last of the Tubba' kings (the Tubba's were the 'ruling house of the kingdom of Himyar')[152] and he seems to have been placed on the throne of Himyar by the Abyssinians in late 518 or early 519.[153] Since he is still attested as ruling in 521–2,[154] Ruhayma's loan can be dated to 518–22. She herself was one of the victims of the great carnage at Najrān, in the autumn of 523,[155] and a superb example of the (largely Monophysite) aristocracy of that town.[156] So we can conclude that solidi were almost certainly legal tender in this highly commercialised sector of the Arabian peninsula, from where, moreover, much of the trade with India and Sri Lanka was conducted.

To conclude, the seventh century was far more vibrant than it has been made out to be from the narrow perspectives of a fragmented western Mediterranean, or even those of Haldon's Byzantium, and much of this was driven clearly by a volume of commercial exchanges that was as substantial as ever. Trade with the Far East saw a new period of expansion coinciding with the T'ang unification of China, and culminating, of course, in the great upsurge of the ninth century. Ibn Ḥabīb describes the international fairs at Sohar and Dibba on the Batinah coast in the last years of Sasanian rule in terms that recall Ammianus' description

[151] I. Shahîd, *The Martyrs of Najrân: New Documents* (Brussels, 1971), p. 60, where Simeon cites the testimony of 'those who came from Najrān'. So too in A. Moberg, *The Book of the Himyarites: Fragments of a Hitherto Unknown Syriac Work* (Lund etc., 1924), p. cxxxiii, which dates from the second quarter of the sixth century and is less well preserved.

[152] Al-Ṭabarī, *History*, vol. v, p. 176.

[153] Bosworth in al-Ṭabarī, *History*, vol. v, p. 194, n. 487.

[154] Bosworth in al-Ṭabarī, *History*, vol. v, pp. 188–9, n. 480.

[155] F. de Blois, 'The Date of the "Martrys of Nagrān"', *Arabian Archaeology and Epigraphy* 1 (1990), 110–28.

[156] See her self-description in Simeon's 'New Letter', Shahîd, *Martyrs of Najrân*, p. 57: 'You know that I am a Christian, and you know my lineage and family and who I am; and that I have gold and silver and slaves and handmaids and field produce and that I lack nothing … And here I am saying to you that on this very day I am in possession of forty thousand *denarii* [solidi], sealed and placed in my treasury apart from the treasury of my husband, and jewelry and pearls and jacinths.'

of Batnae. 'Merchants from Sind, India, China, people of the East and West came to it,' he says about Dibba.[157] Here we have a clear reference to the Chinese sailing to the Gulf, but is the testimony credible? The answer is 'yes'. The Armenian geography now ascribed to Ananias of Širak completely bears it out. This survives in two versions, a long and a short one. The shorter recension, which dates from the late 630s or 640s, says of Yemen (Fortunate Arabia) that 'It produces everything and everything is found there either in the country itself or brought by merchants from China or India.'[158] Baṣra, which was undoubtedly a relatively new foundation at this time, is described as 'filled with merchants and ships coming from India and all parts of the orient'.[159] 'The Sogdians', says Ananias, 'are wealthy and industrious merchants who live between the lands of Turkestan and Ariana.'[160] In short, behind the devastating conflict between Byzantium and Persia, the commercial world of the seventh century lay intact, supported by an abundant circulation of the precious metal coinages.

In terms of *external* trade, the Byzantines were effectively restricted to the 'northern' route (through the Astrakhan steppe or across the Caspian), from where in fact the bulk of solidi moved in other directions – to Scandinavia to finance the trade in Swedish furs,[161] to the Black Sea steppe in political payments.[162] Lombard's famous paper on the three monetary zones saw the late Romans and then the Byzantines progressively exhausting their reserves of gold in a multiple flight that was beyond control.[163] And it is true that measured by the standards of the late Republic[164] or

157 Muhammad b. Ḥabīb, *Kitāb al-Muhabbar*, ed. I. Lichtenstädter (Hyderabad, 1942), p. 265, cf. E. Shoufany, *Al-Riddah and the Muslim Conquest of Arabia* (Toronto, 1972), p. 156, and D. T. Potts, *The Arabian Gulf in Antiquity*, vol. II: *From Alexander the Great to the Coming of Islam* (Oxford, 1990), p. 339. For Persian maritime interests along the Arabian coast and the extent of Persian control, see J. C. Wilkinson, 'Arab–Persian Land Relationships in Late Sasānid Oman', *Proceedings of the Seminar for Arabian Studies* 6 (1973), 40–51.

158 R. H. Hewsen, *The Geography of Ananias of Širak (Ašxarhac'oyc'): The Long and the Short Recensions: Introduction, Translation and Commentary* (Wiesbaden, 1992), p. 72A.

159 *Ibid.*, p. 71A; found only in the shorter recension and crucial for its date. Baṣra was founded between 635–6 and 637–8, cf. F. M. Donner, *The Early Islamic Conquests* (Princeton, 1981), p. 217.

160 Hewsen, *Geography*, p. 74A.

161 D. M. Metcalf, 'Viking-Age Numismatics 1: Late Roman and Byzantine Gold in the Northern Lands', *Numismatic Chronicle* 155 (1995), 413–41, esp. pp. 421, 423, 440.

162 J. Smedley, 'Seventh-Century Byzantine Coins in Southern Russia and the Problem of Light Weight Solidi', in *Studies in Early Byzantine Gold Coinage*, ed. W. Hahn *et al.* (New York, 1988), pp. 111–30.

163 M. Lombard, 'Les bases monétaires d'une suprématie économique: L'or musulman du VIIe au XIe siècle', *Annales ESC* 2 (1947), 143–60, and *Études d'économie médiévale*, vol. I: *Monnaie et histoire d'Alexandre à Mahomet* (Paris, 1971), pp. 133–46.

164 Veyne, 'Rome', p. 215: 530 metric tons of gold in the Temple of Saturn!

even the second century,[165] the reserves of gold in the state's hands had dwindled substantially by the late empire and even more so by the ninth century.[166] But we can certainly rule out an external flight as the chief cause of this. What does seem to have happened is a progressive *dispersal* of the hoard into private hands, through largesse (*profusa largitio*), the vast endowments of the church and, above all, the expansion of private business. In the Sasanian realm, by contrast, the hoard remained largely *concentrated* in the various and numerous treasuries of the shah till it, too, was largely dispersed through the lack of a strong central administration in the Arab conquests.[167]

165 Lo Cascio, 'State and Coinage', p. 79: 675 million denarii *c.*161.

166 W. T. Treadgold, *The Byzantine State Finances in the Eighth and Ninth Centuries* (New York, 1982), pp. 10 ff.

167 See al-Ṭabarī's account of how the Arabs dealt with the so-called 'treasures of al-Nakhīrajān' following the battle of Nihāwand, al-Ṭabarī, *The Conquest of Iraq, Southwestern Persia, and Egypt* (*The History of al-Ṭabarī*, vol. XIII), trans. H. A. Juynboll (Albany, 1989), pp. 182–4.

PART III

Aristocracies and estates

CHAPTER 7

Aristocracies, peasantries and the framing of the early Middle Ages

Introduction

In this chapter I would like to develop a general contrast between the west and the eastern Mediterranean/Near East which has its roots in the classical world, especially the period known as late antiquity. By, say, 600, the west was defined by a tradition of tied labour inherited from the late Roman world and shaped both by the strength of slavery in the post-Roman tradition and by the legacy of the colonate. By contrast, in the east, much of the rural labour force is best described as a landless peasantry that survived on short-term leases or by labour tenancy on the large estates, where these existed. The eastern provinces of the Roman empire were characterised by a disciplined aristocracy, a thriving monetary economy and densely populated countrysides.[1] A new aristocracy emerged in the late fifth century and one of its most striking features was its ability to build substantial estates and ensure that these properties remained intact over generations. Thus the Apion estates in Egypt are attested from the 430s down to the 620s, when the last known member of the family, Flavius Apion III, was killed by the Persians.[2] Both Peter Sarris and I have described the main features of estate organisation characteristic of this late antique aristocracy, viz. the direct management of substantial estates which grouped their workers into settlements that were both structurally and topographically sharply demarcated from the villages (*kōmai*).[3] It is these workers whom I started by defining as a landless peasantry. The usual term for them was *geōrgoi*, but it is important to realise that in their case the term referred not to a smallholding peasantry but to rural

[1] J. Banaji, *Agrarian Change in Late Antiquity*, 2nd edn (Oxford, 2007).

[2] *P. Oxy.* LXIII 4389 (439) for an early document; LVIII 3959 (12.1.620) and LXVIII 4703 (22.5.622) for the latest ones.

[3] P. Sarris, *Economy and Society in the Age of Justinian* (Cambridge, 2006), esp. ch. 2; Banaji, *Agrarian Change*, chs 6–7.

households of whom the majority were clearly dependent on the estate for employment. In the more densely settled eastern provinces, landlessness was endemic, and large estates were major employers of such labour.[4] But the eastern Mediterranean was also characterised by a diversified labour market with considerable fluidity in the forms of employment and types of contracts that wage earners settled for. Sharecropping was widespread, and sustained the expansion of the wine industry, but so was casual labour and a host of more skilled employments/trades, some regulated to impede collusive wage agreements[5] or wage inflation.[6]

Now, some of these features of the late antique eastern Mediterranean would have been true of the west as well. For example, Procopius tells us that the *majority* of Rome's population in the 530s consisted of artisans and casual labourers.[7] Also, there was no dramatic *de*-escalation of monetary economy in the west but a gradual decline. The crucial difference, of course, was that by the sixth century the late Roman aristocracies no longer ruled the state in the various 'kingdoms' that replaced the empire, since the imperial system had ceased to exist and their survival depended on adjustments with the barbarian rulers in the regions where they regrouped. In other words, when the western empire fell apart in the fifth century and the former Roman territories were taken over by the Franks, Burgundians and Goths, the western aristocracy ceased to exist as a unified imperial class, surviving now only as fragmented regional groupings, of which the most substantial, by the sixth century, were those in Rome, southern Italy and the south of France. In Chris Wickham's recent magnum opus, the general weakening and impoverishment of the aristocracy that was bound up with the fragmentation of the late empire is a major theme, rightly so, and a decisive part of the transition to the early Middle Ages.[8] By the *end* of the sixth century the late Roman aristocracy had effectively ceased to exist in the west. Now, Wickham himself identifies this process, that is, the crisis of the western aristocracy, with a certain emancipation of the peasantry, in the sense that the huge fiscal machinery of the late Roman state had disintegrated so that peasants were less intensively taxed or not taxed at all, and the rural population faced a much

[4] J. Banaji, 'Modernizing the Historiography of Rural Labour: An Unwritten Agenda', in *Companion to Historiography*, ed. M. Bentley (London, 1997), pp. 88–102, esp. 93ff.

[5] *CJ* 59.2.1 (483), where the emperor Zeno bans collusive agreements in the skilled building trades, calling such behaviour *monopolium.*

[6] *Nov. Just.* 122.1 (544), clearly reflecting a scarcity of labour of all types in the aftermath of the plague.

[7] Procopius, *BG* 1.25.11 (Dewing, *History of the Wars*, vol. III, pp. 240–2).

[8] C. Wickham, *Framing the Early Middle Ages: Europe and the Mediterranean, 400–800* (Oxford, 2005).

less powerful group of landowners. In other words, the post-Roman west saw a recovery of control by peasants, an advance that was finally only reversed with the reassertion of aristocratic dominance that followed later, and unevenly, between the seventh and the tenth century.[9] As he argued in an earlier work, the peasantry was the 'chief social group that benefited from the fall of the Roman state', and a 'not insignificant class of peasant owners … had survived the wars and patronage agreements of the fifth century'.[10]

Of the two theses just delineated, that of a *crisis of the imperial aristocracy* (in the west) and of a *reassertion of peasant control* during much of the early Middle Ages, the former can scarcely be contested. The late Roman aristocracy disappeared, unevenly but, in the end, with finality. No historian has ever argued the opposite, despite the obsession with continuity peculiar to some historians in France. The second thesis, however, is much less obvious and substantially at odds with my own reading of the evidence. Wickham construes the advance of the peasantry in the earliest Middle Ages as an expansion of the 'peasant mode of production' which came to be juxtaposed with the feudal mode in a vast patchwork of *microregions* that reflected the extreme economic fragmentation of the post-Roman west. The main evidence for this view is the sharp differences in the scale and sophistication of exchange networks reflected in the ceramic evidence, at least as archaeologists currently construe this. This thesis, which I shall call the 'microregionality of modes of production', has its own share of problems, of course (here modes of production become descriptive of a set of local economic structures), but my main interest at this stage is in Wickham's use of the written evidence. Wickham believes that the late Roman and the post-Roman west were both characterised by a feudal mode of production. This is (1) because he defines the feudal mode in a general way as the 'exploitative relationship between tenant and landlord', any tenant and any landlord (a definition that is presumably consciously ahistorical),[11] and (2) because he thinks that 'When the Romans abandoned the slave mode, they went *straight over* to rent-paying tenants',[12] and this long before the advent of the late empire.

[9] Wickham, *Framing*, pp. 576ff.

[10] C. Wickham, 'The Other Transition: From the Ancient World to Feudalism', *Past & Present* 103 (1984), 3–36, at p. 30.

[11] C. Wickham, 'The Uniqueness of the East', in *Feudalism and Non-European Societies*, ed. T. J. Byres *et al.* (London, 1985), pp. 166–96, at 170.

[12] Wickham, 'Other Transition', p. 31.

These are substantial conceptual and historical claims, and I shall come back to them later. To begin with, however, I would like to try and use Wickham's book as a springboard for some reflections of my own about the west, and to start by mapping out a set of contrasts between aristocracies in the late antique world. I shall then propose a hypothesis about the nature of the seventh century, and devote the remaining part of the discussion of the west to a critique of Wickham's model of the transition from late antiquity to the early Middle Ages. Thus the first part of the chapter (about the west) deals with the three separate sets of issues just described, which, though distinct, are clearly interrelated. The third of these levels involves a much closer consideration of the whole issue of the deployment of labour. Wickham's model of the transition is premised on general categories that are unreconstructed or lack any further analysis. One upshot of this is that there is no serious engagement with documentary sources and no analysis of the actual vocabulary used in those sources, of crucial terms like *mancipium*, *mansus*, *colonica*, and so on. When Ganshof wrote in the 1950s and 60s, his confusing description of the Merovingian *villa* as a manor attracted no comment, because the whole issue of the origins of the bipartite estate still awaited the decisive clarification that it received in the work of Adriaan Verhulst.[13] Verhulst, of course, argued, convincingly in my view, that the classic manorial regime was a purely medieval creation, discontinuous with the Roman traditions of Gaul and an expression of the dynamism implicit in the Merovingian economy.[14] One of the theses I would like to propose in this chapter is that much of that dynamism was bound up with the kind of aristocracy that the Merovingians succeeded in establishing – unique for the post-Roman west. To see this, it may be useful to discuss the first of my topics (the contrasting nature and histories of aristocracies) in terms of the three distinct sets of issues that seem to be implicit in it, namely, first, of the *kinds* of aristocracies that dominate the main part of late antiquity, before the decisive evolution of the seventh century (we might call this the problem of morphology); second, of the fate or fortunes of the aristocracy in the huge upheavals that dominate the history of the empire in the fifth and sixth centuries when the Roman imperial state disintegrated bit by bit and eventually ceased to exist except as a pervasive cultural legacy; and third, of the dramatically different ways in which Franks and Visigoths, their

[13] F. L. Ganshof, 'Manorial Organization in the Low Countries in the Seventh, Eighth and Ninth Centuries', *Transactions of the Royal Historical Society*, 4th ser., 31 (1949), 29–59, esp. pp. 33–4, 39.

[14] A. Verhulst, 'La genèse du régime domanial classique en France au haut moyen âge', in *Agricoltura e mondo rurale in Occidente nel Alto Medioevo, Settimane di Studio* 13 (1966), 135–60.

nobilities in particular, reacted to rule by a hereditary monarchy, an issue which surprisingly has received little attention.

Aristocracies

To begin with the morphological problem; take the western empire in the fourth, fifth and early sixth centuries, Egypt or the eastern Mediterranean more generally between the later fifth and early seventh centuries, and Sasanian Iran. Iran under the Sasanids was ruled by powerful regional barons who were firmly wedded to the Sasanian dynasty but also largely in control of royal succession. Among late antique aristocracies, they were the least well integrated into something we might call a state. Their unswerving commitment to dynastic rule is a striking feature and suggests that this was the key factor of cohesion in a class defined otherwise by strongly centrifugal tendencies. When Hormozān, the powerful aristocrat who dominated south-western Iran at the time of the Arab conquest, was asked by ʿUmar, 'From which territory (*'arḍ*) are you?', he replied, 'I am a Mehrajāni.'[15] Regional identities were clearly quite strong even and perhaps precisely at these levels of Sasanian society. At the opposite end of the spectrum to them is the early Byzantine eastern Mediterranean aristocracy that emerges with some vividness in the Egyptian papyri of the later fifth, sixth and early seventh centuries.[16] *This* aristocracy was typically a *Dienstadel*, its roots firmly embedded in service to the late Roman state, a concept for which there is no obvious Sasanian counterpart. Their trajectory runs from the main part of the fifth century to the early seventh, when they were destroyed or dispersed in the Sasanian and Arab invasions that followed in quick succession in the years 610–40. The little we know about the origins of this group suggests that it was the creature of a coherent, culturally sophisticated and economically affluent state, the East Roman empire which reached the pinnacle of its strength under Justinian in the sixth century.[17] Finally, the western aristocracy was an intensely traditionalist group or ensemble of groups more loosely integrated into the imperial state, dominating it as much as it served it and as subversive of imperial unity as the Iranian *bōzōrgān* were of rulers they disliked. An important aspect of this domination was the fact that the leading

[15] Al-Ṭabarī, *Ta'rīkh*, ser. i, pp. 2559 l.13–2560 l.3 = al-Ṭabarī, *The Conquest of Iraq, Southwestern Persia and Egypt* (*The History of al-Ṭabarī*, vol. XIII), trans. G. H. A. Juynboll (Albany, 1989), p. 140; asked through an interpreter.

[16] Banaji, *Agrarian Change*, chs 5–6.

[17] Most recently, Sarris, *Economy and Society in the Age of Justinian*.

senatorial families (or more correctly 'clans') established a significant measure of control over the fiscal system through the offices they monopolised.[18] There is a tradition of late Roman historiography that argues that the Italian aristocracy more than any other sabotaged the coherence of its own state and bears a major share of the blame for the downfall of the empire in the west.[19] Whatever one thinks of this, the fact is that 'western aristocracies long outlived the Imperial government', seeking their own accommodation with barbarian rulers.[20] If the disintegration of the western empire sounded the death knell of an integrated imperial aristocracy of the kind that had emerged under Constantine, transforming the senate into a purely Italian body and choking off the sources of renewal of a living senatorial tradition,[21] it *also* reflected the dispersive tendencies of aristocratic networks that had never been more than loosely integrated into a shifting imperial centre. The rapid consolidation of the western upper classes in the fourth century was followed by their gradual but sustained erosion in the fifth and sixth, as a unified state disintegrated under the pressure of barbarian migrations, settlement and conquest. This crisis was most obvious in sixth-century Italy, but reflected of course throughout the western provinces, to unequal degrees. For the moment the point I wish to make is that late antique aristocracies show major differences in the nature of their integration into the state and that these differences are in some sense more fundamental than the civilian/military divide that Wickham concentrates on in discussing the transformation of the aristocracy.[22]

A quintessential late Roman aristocracy had more or less disappeared by the turn of the sixth century, but its surviving networks followed very different paths into limbo. The Italian aristocracy was decimated by the

[18] This is best illustrated by Petronius Probus' repeated control of the praetorian prefecture in the years 364–83 and the devastating comment by one contemporary (the historian Ammianus Marcellinus) about the powerful lobby behind him and their 'countless instances of avarice', Amm. 27.11.3.

[19] J. Sundwall, *Weströmische Studien* (Berlin, 1915), ch. 5, esp. pp. 158–61, concluding, 'Economic relationships were what drove the western empire to its catastrophe. The State became progressively poorer and the landed aristocracy ever more wealthy'; also E. Stein, *Histoire du Bas-Empire,* vol. 1: *De l'état romain à l'état byzantin (284–476),* trans. J.-R. Palanque (Paris, 1959), pp. 337ff., esp. 341–2.

[20] P. Wormald, 'The Decline of the Western Empire and the Survival of its Aristocracy', *Journal of Roman Studies* 66 (1976), 217–26, at p. 224; K. F. Werner, *Histoire de France,* vol. 1: *Les origines (avant l'an mil)* (Paris, 1984), p. 302; A. Chastagnol, *Le Sénat romain sous le règne d'Odoacre: Recherches sur l'épigraphie du Colisée au Ve siècle* (Bonn, 1966), pp. 48–56.

[21] A. Chastagnol, 'Sidoine Apollinaire et le sénat de Rome', *Acta Antiqua Academiae Scientiarum Hungaricae* 26 (1978), 57–70.

[22] Wickham, *Framing*, pp. 174–7, 200ff., 257.

Gothic wars and the violence of the Lombard invasion that followed.[23] Unlike the Franks and the Burgundians, the Lombards did not seek the collaboration of the Roman aristocracy.[24] Thus large estates survived but the aristocracy was eliminated or fled.[25] By contrast, the Merovingian kingdoms and especially that of Neustria saw the evolution of an ethnically integrated aristocracy based on a fusion of the surviving Roman families and their Frankish counterparts. Bertram, bishop of Le Mans from 586 to 616, is a superb example of the new kind of aristocracy that would dominate the political history of the seventh century, more powerfully and obviously in Francia than elsewhere in the west.[26] My own feeling is that if we want a zone of rupture between late antiquity and the early Middle Ages, it must lie here in the formation of the precocious nobilities that dominated the Frankish *Teilreiche* already by the first quarter of the seventh century.[27] They were the first purely medieval nobilities of Europe, a peculiarly Merovingian achievement, thanks largely to the conscious policy of Chilperic and his son Chlothar II, Neustrian rulers, in seeking the active support of regional elites throughout Francia, in Austrasia, Burgundy and Aquitaine, and integrating them into a pan-Merovingian Frankish ruling class.[28] This evolution is important for the agrarian history of the west,

23 J. Moorhead, 'Totila the Revolutionary', *Historia* 49 (2000), 382–6, esp. pp. 384–6; G. Noyé, 'Économie et société dans la Calabrie byzantine (IVe–XIe siècle)', *Journal des Savants* (Juillet–Décembre 2000), 207–80, at p. 252; G. P. Bognetti, 'La proprietà della terra nel passaggio dal mondo antico al Medioevo occidentale', in *L'età longobarda* (Milan, 1968), vol. IV, pp. 67–89, esp. 75, 78; J. Jarnut, *Geschichte der Langobarden* (Stuttgart, etc., 1982), pp. 49–50; J. Jarnut, 'Aspekte des Kontinuitätsproblems in der Völkerwanderungszeit', in *Herrschaft und Ethnogenese im Frühmittelalter: Gesammelte Aufsätze von Jörg Jarnut*, ed. M. Becher (Munich, 2002), pp. 1–17, esp. 14ff., 323; and G. Tabacco, *The Struggle for Power in Medieval Italy: Structures of Political Rule*, trans. R. B. Jensen (Cambridge, 1989), pp. 94 f. The key passages are in Paul the Deacon, *Hist. Langobardorum* ii, 31; 32 (ed. Waitz., 90), hinting at the liquidation/expulsion of the aristocracy.

24 K. Modzelewski, 'La transizione dall' antichità al feudalesimo', in *Dal feudalesimo al capitalismo (Storia d'Italia: Annali 1)*, ed. R. Romano and C. Vivanti (Turin, 1978), pp. 3–109, at 31: 'Al contrario degli ostrogoti, i conquistatori longobardi non ricercarono la collaborazione dell'aristocrazia romana e non si sforzarono di difendere l'antico ordinamento istituzionale' (Unlike the Ostrogoths, the Lombard invaders did not seek the collaboration of the Roman aristocracy and made no attempt to preserve the old institutional order).

25 Modzelewski, 'Transizione', p. 41: 'la fine dell'aristocrazia romana non abbia comportato la liquidazione fisica dei suoi beni' (the demise of the Roman aristocracy did not entail the physical liquidation of its estates).

26 E.g. in Rome itself the extinction of the old aristocracy left a vacuum in the seventh century, see F. Marazzi, 'Aristocrazia e società (secoli VI–XI)', in *Roma medievale*, ed. A. Vauchez (Rome/Bari, 2001), pp. 41–69, at 46: 'È difficile parlare, per questo periodo (per il VII secolo in particolare), di una nuova aristocrazia urbana in senso stretto ...'.

27 E. Ewig, *Spätantikes und fränkisches Gallien: Gesammelte Schriften (1952–1973)*, ed. H. Atsma, 2 vols (Munich, 1976), vol. I, pp. 169f., 172f.

28 R. Sprandel, *Der merovingische Adel und die Gebiete östlich des Rheins* (Freiburg im Breisgau, 1957), ch. 2.

because it was in Francia that a new kind of enterprise and organisation of labour first emerged.[29] The continuity with Rome lay in the survival of large enterprises; the rupture in the rapid evolution of powerful new aristocracies by the late sixth century, unlike any previous ruling class that had dominated the west. In Spain too the old aristocracy passed rapidly into limbo. A surviving Roman aristocracy is much harder to track than it is in Gaul.[30] But the Visigothic aristocracy itself was deeply divided and permanently embroiled in conflict with the Crown. The repeated assassination of Visigothic rulers is striking testimony to this. The chronicler Fredegar or his seventh-century source called it the *morbum Gothorum*, the 'Visigothic addiction for dethroning their kings'.[31] Here the Merovingian pattern of a strong dynasty and stable aristocratic elites could not have been more radically reversed. This raises a final issue about aristocracies.

I would like to suggest that the dynastic principle favoured the interests of the aristocracy. The weaker the monarchy, the less held together it was by the common bond of a ruling family, the sharper the conflicts *within* the aristocracy. Unregulated succession to the throne reflected lack of cohesion among aristocrats and repeated attempts at usurpation, suggesting unmanageable levels of conflict and considerable fragmentation. This, as I just said, is best exemplified in Spain, where royal succession was characterised by chronic and often violent instability and there was deep factionalism within the aristocracy.[32] A succession of rulers were either deposed or overthrown. Leovigild was the only ruler to be followed on the throne by his son and grandson, and he, characteristically, had the reputation of having executed or exiled much of the aristocracy.[33] The contrast with his late sixth-century Frankish counterparts could scarcely be greater.

[29] Verhulst, 'Genèse du régime domanial'.

[30] K. F. Stroheker, 'Spanische Senatoren der spätrömischen und westgotischen Zeit', *Madrider Mitteilungen* 4 (1963), 107–32 failed to come up with more than a handful. E. A. Thompson, *The Goths in Spain* (Oxford, 1969), p. 115 suggests, 'The class of large Roman landowners had *in some measure* survived the storms of the fifth century.'

[31] Fredegar, iv.82 (J. M. Wallace-Hadrill, *The Fourth Book of the Chronicle of Fredegar with its Continuations* (London, 1960) p. 70): 'One of the magnates named Chindaswinth was chosen king of Spain. When he had dethroned Tulga he had him tonsured; and then, having made sure of his power throughout the Spanish kingdom, and knowing the Gothic weakness for dethroning their kings (for he had been involved with them in such conspiracies), he ordered the killing, one by one, of all those whom he knew to be compromised in rebellion against kings who had been dethroned.'

[32] Thompson, *Goths in Spain*, chs 8–9; L. A. García Moreno, *El fin del reino visigodo de Toledo* (Madrid, 1975), pp. 140ff.; B. F. Reilly, *The Medieval Spains* (Cambridge, 1993), pp. 39ff. García Moreno notes that the cohesion of the aristocracy was a major concern of the Spanish bishops (p. 161).

[33] Thompson, *Goths in Spain*, p. 157; Isidore, *Hist. Goth.* 51 = K. B. Wolf, *Conquerors and Chroniclers of Early Medieval Spain*, 2nd edn (Liverpool, 1999), p. 102.

Chilperic and his son had pursued a far-sighted policy of seeking the support of elites in Austrasia, Burgundy and Aquitaine and the net result was the rapid evolution of powerful aristocracies in the crucial decades around the later sixth and early seventh century. In Francia where the dominance of the Merovingians was never actually contested, the dynastic principle worked in a complex form that necessitated the division and re-division of territories to preserve some balance between the competing Merovingian claimants. Whereas Spain saw an unstable monarchy pitted against a fractious and fragmented aristocracy, in Francia conflict had tended to run between different members or branches of the ruling dynasty, and the division of territory between them almost certainly helped to reduce the level of conflict within the aristocracy. One reason may have been that it allowed for strong regional control, a principle formally embodied in the famous Edict of 614 in which Chlothar explicitly restricted the holding of office to families within the region.[34] This, as Sprandel emphasised repeatedly, was not equivalent to some form of Frankish regionalism.[35] On the contrary, what Chilperic and Chlothar managed to create was a *Reichsaristokratie* with firm local roots. Of the three main Germanic kingdoms that emerged from the ruins of the western empire, the *regnum Francorum* was far and away the most stable, whereas the muted struggle between the Visigothic nobility and the crown that runs through much of the history of Spain in the seventh century culminates of course in the Arab conquest of the peninsula. The final episode in the internal factionalism of the Visigothic aristocracy was also a fatal one. Tradition claims that the sons of the deceased king Witiza actively conspired against Roderic, the last Visigothic king, to ensure his defeat in the decisive battle that ended his reign and the kingdom.[36] These divisions were so obvious to contemporaries that the *Chronicle of 754* links them directly to the success of the Arabs in overthrowing the Visigothic kingdom.[37]

[34] *Chlotharii II Edictum* 12 (*Capit. Merow.* 22) = A. C. Murray, *From Roman to Merovingian Gaul: A Reader* (Peterborough, ON, 1999), pp. 565ff., at 567, cf. R. Sprandel, 'Struktur und Geschichte des merovingischen Adels', *Historische Zeitschrift* 193(1) (1961), 33–71, esp. pp. 61ff.

[35] Sprandel, 'Struktur und Geschichte', esp. 64–5.

[36] E.g. J. Montenegro and A. del Castillo, 'Le règne de Rodéric, Akhila II et l'invasion musulmane de la péninsule ibérique', *Francia (Moyen Âge)* 34 (1) (2007), 1–17.

[37] *Chronicle of 754*, 52; 54 (Wolf, *Conquerors and Chroniclers of Early Medieval Spain*, pp. 131–2) and the reference to Oppas, King Egica's son, collaborating actively with Mūsā b. Nuṣayr as the latter moved against remnants of Toledo's nobility in the summer of 712. A. Barbero de Aguilera, *La sociedad visigoda y su entorno histórico* (Madrid, 1992), p. 216, and A. Barbero and M. Vigil, *La formación del feudalismo en la Península Ibérica*, 1st edn (Barcelona, 1978), pp. 209, 229 argued that the bulk of the Spanish aristocracy came to terms with the Arabs (struck deals with them) and that a substantial section converted to Islam. E. Manzano Moreno, *Conquistadores, emires y califas: Los*

The agrarian watershed of the seventh century

My hypothesis about the seventh century is that it forms an agrarian watershed in the history of the west. The seventh century, in the west, was crucial in two ways. First, it saw a reassertion of aristocratic control, and second it involved, I believe, the beginnings of a new agrarian expansion. These features would of course be linked if a strong case can be made for the view that the aristocracy financed much of that expansion. I don't propose to do that here, but it may be worth indicating briefly some clear signs that such a connection existed. One of the most striking features of the Merovingian charters is the sheer frequency of references to the purchase of land that appears in them. Here is a typical example from the will of Hadoind, bishop of Le Mans, dated 643. Among numerous donations listed in the will, Hadoind says he donates to the church of St Victor of Le Mans 'the estate (*villa*) called Aceruco, which I purchased for money, together with the houses, *mancipia*, vineyards, forests, meadows and pastures' (*dono tibi villa nuncupante Aceruco, quam dato pretio comparavi, cum domibus, mancipiis, vineis, silvis, pratis et pascuis*).[38] There are dozens of references of this kind in the private charters of the Merovingian period and the least this tells us is that the new aristocracy of the seventh century made substantial investments in the acquisition of land, usually whole estates (*villae*). They did the same in the great movement of land clearance that began in the seventh century, the 'vaste mouvement de défrichement' that Verhulst described as a key feature of the 'evolution' from the Merovingian estate to the Carolingian manor;[39] and the same again in the construction of water mills, as Dietrich Lohrmann has pointed out in an important paper on Neustria.[40] Here the crucial point is that the elements of a new organisation of labour began to be laid out as landowners encouraged the expansion of peasant tenures as part of their reclamation of arable. This process must have thrown up hundreds of new settlements and I suggest that one term for these settlements was

omeyas y la formación de al-Andalus (Barcelona, 2006) has the best discussion of those treaties and their role in integrating sections of the Visigothic aristocracy with the (Syrian) Arab military elite of al-Andalus.

38 *Test. Hadoindi Cenomanensis episcopi*, in *Actus Pontificum Cenomannis in Urbe Degentium* (*Archives historiques du Maine*, vol. II), ed. G. Busson and A. Ledru (Au Mans, 1901), pp. 157ff., at 158.

39 Verhulst, 'Genèse du régime domanial', p. 152.

40 See D. Lohrmann, 'Le moulin à eau: Dans le cadre de l'économie rurale de la Neustrie (VIIe–XIe siècles)', in *La Neustrie: Les pays au nord de la Loire de 650 à 850*, ed. H. Atsma (Sigmaringen, 1989), vol. I, pp. 367–104, especially the statement at p. 396 that monasteries were simply adding to or renovating equipment they inherited from previous owners.

colonica. If the term *colonica* could refer *both* to the '"new settlements" located on the fringes, boundaries, or "appendages" of estates, suggesting an origin in the colonization of the wasteland'[41] *and* to the individual tenures that made up those settlements, this would explain why the word shows a mystifying semantic ambiguity, fluctuating between usages that manifestly refer to entire settlements, as in Bertram's will, where Margarete Weidemann explains the term as 'Ausbausiedlung im Bereich einer villa',[42] and other uses where *colonica* is undoubtedly a designation for farms, as when Abbo refers to various freedpeople of his holding *colonicae* 'in beneficio', this in Provence in the early eighth century.[43] One imagines that these new settlements were the first proper signs of the emergence or re-emergence of a peasantry in Europe, and that the *accolae* who appear with increasing frequency from the later seventh century (they are there already in Hadoind's will of 643)[44] were essentially free peasants attracted to estates as part of their drive to expand cultivation. The 'colonization of the wasteland' was the seventh century's major contribution to the history of the countryside in this part of Europe.

By contrast, another key term, *mansus*, which is almost invariably explained in the same way or referred to the same context, in other words, the creation of peasant tenures, may well have had a more complex origin, the proper starting point for which must be our notions of Merovingian estate organisation. New estates for a new aristocracy? The answer, as almost always in history, is yes and no. In a typically fascinating aside, Marc Bloch once suggested that the best historical analogy for the early medieval estate is the Latin American hacienda. What Bloch himself meant by this was that the regime of the hacienda was never so dense that it completely excluded the presence of 'small

41 D. Herlihy, 'The Carolingian *Mansus*', *Economic History Review*, 2nd ser., 13 (1960–1), 79–89, esp. pp. 86–7.

42 M. Weidemann, *Das Testament des Bischofs Berthramn von Le Mans vom 27. März 616* (Mainz, 1986), p. 109. The *colonicae* in Verf. 6, 9, 20, 25 and 35 are all substantial, not just small farms, much less 'tenant plots', as in Wickham, *Framing the Early Middle Ages*, p. 282.

43 P. J. Geary, *Aristocracy in Provence: The Rhône Basin at the Dawn of the Carolingian Age* (Philadelphia, 1985), e.g. 20 (p. 52), 24 (p. 54), 25 (p. 54), etc.; translated 'farms'. The fact that Merovingian *colonicae* often had proper names suggests that many were settlements, e.g. T. Kölzer, *Die Urkunden der Merowinger nach Vorarbeiten von Carlrichard Brühl* (Hannover, 2001), vol. 1, no. 7, pp. 29ff. at 31 (colonica Curtleutachario in Childebert I's donation to the monk Carilephus, dated 515, but 'unecht'); *Test. Remigii*, p. 478 (colonica Passiacus); Weidemann, *Testament*, Verf. 6 (p. 13), 20 (p. 19), 25 (p. 21), 35 (p. 28); *Test. Hadoindi*, in Busson and Ledru, *Actus Pontificum Cenomannis*, p. 160; *Test. de saint Vigile*, ed. M. Quantin, *Cartulaire générale de l'Yonne: Recueil de documents authentiques* (Auxerre, 1854), vol. 1, pp. 17ff., at 20.

44 *Test. Hadoindi*, in Busson and Ledru, *Actus Pontificum Cenomannis*, p. 160. *Accolae* are much commoner in late seventh-century charters, e.g. *CLA* xiii 560 (657/88), estates in the Beauvaisis; 564 (673); 570 (688); *CLA* xiv 577 (694).

independent landowners'.[45] The more general point of the analogy, I take it, is that early medieval estates or let's say the typical Merovingian estate exploited a landless workforce comparable in this respect to the *gañanes* in Mexico. This emphasises continuity with the late Roman world if, unlike Wickham and the ancient historians he follows,[46] we see the late Roman estate as an enterprise still based on direct management and not pulverised into semi-autonomous farms or holdings.[47] And again, that continuity is one of form rather than substance in the sense that the disappearance of the Roman aristocracy and the rise of new medieval nobilities signified a major rupture in the social and economic history of the west. Thus the best context to discuss the meaning of the term *mansus* surely has to be the way we visualise the transition from late Roman to purely medieval forms of organisation in terms of the way landowners structured the management and use of labour and of the kinds of workforces they deployed.

Again, the Merovingian charters are our best clue to the nature of the rural labour force in the sixth and seventh centuries. If the will of Remigius dated *c.*533 is any indication, slavery was still widespread in Gaul in the early sixth century. In fact, Remigius' farms were based on

[45] M. Bloch, 'The Rise of Dependent Cultivation and Seigniorial Institutions', in *Mélanges Historiques* (Paris, 1963), vol. I, pp. 210–58, at 228.

[46] Notably D. Vera, 'Strutture agrarie e strutture patrimoniali nella tarda antichità: L'aristocrazia romana fra agricoltura e commercio', *Opus* 2 (2) (1983), 489–533, who describes the typical late Roman aristocratic estate as a 'latifondo parcellizzato', operated essentially in terms of rent tenancies.

[47] This has to be argued systematically. Cf. Procopius, *BG* 3.6.5 (Dewing, *History of the Wars*, vol. IV, p. 198) which assumes that the incomes of large Italian estates will be in money. Also, Palladius, *Opus agriculturae* 1.6.3 ('A standardised calculation of labour costs isn't possible when soil characteristics vary so much') only makes sense on the premise of direct management. The dominance of tenant labour is one of Wickham's most firmly held beliefs about the organisation of estates in late antiquity and the early Middle Ages. But in one instance at least it involves a manifest misreading of the evidence. The famous passage in the (lost) history of Olympiodorus of Thebes which tells us that the richest senatorial families in the west drew 'a yearly income from their estates of 4,000 lbs of gold apart from grain, wine and other goods in kind the marketable value of which was equal to one-third of the cash income' (trans. E. A. Thompson, 'Olympiodorus of Thebes', *Classical Quarterly* 38 (1944), 43–52, at p. 50) is taken as saying that 'annual income *in rents* for many aristocratic families … in Rome amounted to 5,000-plus pounds of gold … three-quarters of it from *rents in money*' (Wickham, *Framing*, p. 162, repeated at 271, 'major Roman senators got three-quarters of their huge *rents* in money, a quarter in kind'; my emphasis). But Olympiodorus makes no reference to 'rents' anywhere in this passage. He says that the *estates* of the top aristocracy yielded (possibly gross) cash *incomes* of 4,000 lb of gold, apart from the stocks of wine, grain, etc. which they *retained in kind*; had they sold these stocks as well they would have grossed a further third of that amount, bringing the total to just over 5,300 lb of gold. E. A. Thompson's translation captures the sense of the passage exactly and shows that the ratios Olympiodorus cites are those for the break-up of *income* between cash and kind, *not* for the amount of rent received in one form or the other.

a mixed labour force of *servi* and *coloni*, and the *coloni* clearly were tied labourers inherited from the late empire, still called by that name and referring in the will itself to half-free or unfree rural labourers distinct from slaves; for example, they could be bequeathed with the land, transferred between owners, manumitted ('Vitalem colonum liberum esse iubeo'; 'Cispiciolum colonum liberum esse precipio'), and their families could likewise be bequeathed.[48] One of them had even owned a *servus*, and at least one of Remigius' *coloni* was still called *originarius*. Moreover, Remigius' *servi* also had families. Again, in 538 and roughly contemporary with Remigius' will, a Gallic church council legislates that 'no person bound by the *condicio* of a *servus* or *colonus* should be admitted to ecclesiastical office'; the precise expression used is *Nullus servilibus colonariisque conditionibus obligatus*.[49] At any rate neither slaves nor *coloni* disappeared with the disintegration of the western empire; both were present in large numbers and merged indiscriminately into the labour force. The integration of these diverse categories of labour into an increasingly indiscriminate labour force also found a precise expression in the way Latin terminology evolved. The strict Roman legal term for a slave, *mancipium*, became the standard generic description for a labour force now characterised by looser forms of bondage, where the precise legal condition of the workers mattered less and less; for example, Remigius' will is decisive proof that many families were of mixed legal status, that is, members of the same family could be of different legal *condiciones*. These distinctions were not rigid therefore. *Mancipia* included both slaves and freedpeople, but post-classical slaves and freedpeople still subject to domination, and the expression *mancipia quae colonaria appellantur* from the will of Aredius, dated 573 or 591, shows that former *coloni*, tied labourers, were included as well.[50]

Now the Merovingian charters refer standardly to *domus* and *mancipia* among the appurtenances of the estate (*villa*) in formulas such as *cum domibus, mancipiis, agris*, etc. In the will of Bishop Bertram, the most substantial document of its kind from the seventh century, which has a wonderful edition and commentary by Weidemann, *ipsam villam cum domibus, mancipiis* and so on is about the most common expression used. I may be wrong but it is my strong impression that in the

[48] *Test. sancti Remigii (CCSL* 117/2, 473ff.), 474 (bequeathed; transferred), 477, 478 (manumitted).

[49] *Conc. Aur.* (538), *can.* 29.

[50] The will can be found in J.-M. Pardessus, *Diplomata, chartae, epistolae, leges aliaque instrumenta ad res Gallo-Francicas spectantia*, 2 vols, repr. of Paris edn of 1843–9 (Aalen, 1969), vol. I, pp. 136–41, the expression at 139; for the date see Kölzer, *Urkunden der Merowinger*, vol. II, p. 522.

seventh-century charters *domus* are never mentioned without *mancipia*, which suggests that they were the dwellings of the labour force. Bertram had some seventy-four estates (*villae*) and they were almost all equipped in this way, together with land, of course, and land of various descriptions such as vineyards, arable and pasture, as well as more substantial constructions called *aedificia*. There is also repeated reference to forest land. Occasionally, Bertram refers to *colonicae*, but these were on the boundaries of his estates and, as Weidemann suggests, most probably the cutting edge of an expanding regime of arable.[51] At one point Bertram refers to buying a villa or a portion of one, the estate of Brossay, where he 'constructed homes and settled labour' (*ubi domus aedificavi et mancipias stabilivi*).[52] There is a fascinating passage in Gregory of Tours which shows that the drive to expand cultivation in this way was equally true of the first generation of the new Merovingian aristocracy, for Gregory describes a certain Chrodin, 'a man of great virtue and piety', almost certainly a Frank, deceased by 582, 'often creating estates from scratch, laying out vineyards, building homes, and clearing the land' (*Nam sepe a novo fundans villas, ponens vinias, aedificans domus, culturas eregens*).[53] About a century later, Vigilius, bishop of Auxerre, donated vineland to his church *cum mancipiis quos ibidem stabilivi*. The remarkable feature of the will of Vigilius, dated *c.*680, is the repeated reference to *mansi* and *servi*.[54] Medievalists generally agree that the term *mansus* is largely an innovation of the seventh century,[55] but the precise agrarian function they tend to assign to it is as a kind of peasant tenure, the role it has within the economic framework of the bilateral estate.[56] But bilateral estates were not a feature of the seventh century, they were a Carolingian innovation, and we have to explain the Merovingian *mansus* differently. One striking clue to its meaning is that while *mansi* appear repeatedly in the will just mentioned,

51 Weidemann, *Testament*, p. 109.

52 Weidemann, *Testament*, Verf. 1 (8), cf. Verf. 17 (18), *ubi … mancipia posuimus*, 25 (21), *cum servientibus quos inibi posui*.

53 Gregory of Tours, *LH* 6.20.

54 *Test. de saint Vigile*, ed. Quantin, pp. 17ff.

55 F. L. Ganshof, 'Quelques aspects principaux de la vie économique dans la monarchie franque au VIIe siècle', in *Caratteri del secolo VII in Occidente, Settimane di studio* 5 (1958), 73–101, at p. 83; A. Verhulst, 'Genèse du régime domanial', pp. 154–5; G. Duby, *Guerriers et paysans VIIe–XIIe siècle: Premier essor de l'économie européenne* (Paris, 1973), pp. 45–6. *Mansi* appear to have been widespread by 650, cf. the will of Leodebod, abbot of St-Aignan d'Orléans, in M. Prou and A. Vidier, *Recueil des chartes de l'abbaye de Saint-Benoit-sur-Loire*, vol. 1 (Paris, 1900), pp. 5 ff.

56 E.g. Ganshof, 'Quelques aspects', p. 84; A. Verhulst, 'Economic Organisation', in *The New Cambridge Medieval History*, vol. II: *c.700–c.900*, ed. R. McKitterick (Cambridge, 1995), pp. 481–509, at 493: 'From the middle of the seventh century, the term *mansus* is used as a technical term for a holding in a bipartite manor in the region of Paris.'

there is no reference to *domus*! As Tits-Dieuaide suggested in an important paper, '*mansus* est utilisée ici à la place de *domus*'.[57] In other words, the Merovingian *mansi* were not primarily peasant tenures but allotments created for the *mancipia* (= *servi* in Vigilius' testament). Unlike the peasant tenures of a later period, notably the central Middle Ages, these allotments were still an integral part of the Merovingian *Gutswirtschaft* and their occupants a class of workers, both slaves and freedpeople, endowed with service holdings rather than self-sufficient farms.[58] The most substantial argument along these lines is, perhaps paradoxically, Ulrich Weidinger's excellent analysis of the ninth-century inventory material from Fulda, the *Güterverzeichnisse*, whose drafters used vocabulary rather differently from the people who drew up the purely economic documents.[59] Weidinger shows at length that the *mansi* which figure in the Fulda inventories did not include the surrounding fields and meadows. They were *kleine Hofstellenbetriebe* that functioned as reserves of labour for a still largely integrated estate, the *Gutswirtschaftssytem*, and their holders were a class of farm workers, still servile of course, who were subject to almost unlimited exploitation.[60] Weidinger also argues that estate owners would have carved out these plots with a view to preserving or creating some symmetry, either square or rectangular, in their home farms, which is why the *mansi* tended to fluctuate in size.[61] In this sense and all these respects, then, the *mansi* were radically different from the peasant farms known as *hubae* (Bede's 'hide'), which of course did include fields, meadows and the like, and were of a size consciously calculated to yield the normative subsistence of a peasant family, hence more standardised.

There are two points I would like to draw attention to in this analysis. First, Weidinger offers a model, at least implicitly, of the gradual dissolution of the post-Roman *Gutswirtschaft*, if the carving out of service holdings for allotment to the various groups of *mancipia* can, and it surely can, be construed as a mechanism that eroded the integrity of the classic late Roman estate. A passage in the *Vitas sanctorum patrum Emeretensium*, a piece of Spanish hagiography written possibly in the 630s, suggests that

57 M.-J. Tits-Dieuaide, 'Grands domaines, grandes et petites exploitations en Gaule mérovingienne: Remarques et suggestions', in *Le grand domaine aux époques mérovingienne et carolingienne/Die Grundherrschaft im frühen Mittelalter*, ed. A. Verhulst (Gent, 1985), p. 43.

58 Just under 4 acres ('buonaria xv') in a deed dated 639–49/50, the earliest Neustrian document to refer to a *mansus*: Kölzer, *Urkunden*, vol. 1, no. 75, pp. 190ff., at 191, line 4.

59 U. Weidinger, *Untersuchungen zur Wirtschaftsstruktur des Klosters Fulda in der Karolingerzeit* (Stuttgart, 1991), pp. 23–54.

60 Weidinger, *Untersuchungen*, pp. 41ff.

61 Weidinger, *Untersuchungen*, p. 40.

it was standard practice to make such allotments when slaves were freed. When the bishop Masona 'wrote out documents of manumission for the slaves who had given him faithful service', he 'in confirmation of their liberty gave them a little sum of money and even little parcels of land (*exiguas possessiunculas*)'.[62] In Italy such allotments were probably called *casae* or *casales/casalia*,[63] and in the Lombard parts of Italy the *massarii* were initially overwhelmingly of servile origin. They were *servi massarii* and only slightly more exalted than the completely landless slaves.[64] My second comment is that Weidinger's distinction between *mansus* and *huba* chimes remarkably well with the kind of model Ros Faith has developed for the Anglo-Saxon 'inland' and her sharp distinction between worker-tenants and the self-sufficient small peasantry that came to form the true backbone of serfdom in the great feudal reaction of a later period. 'The inland', Faith writes, 'was an area likely to have been crowded with the dwellings of the workers and tenants who lived there,' which reflects a very different topography of power from the bilateral estate.[65] In fact, it is the Anglo-Saxon material that shows us how finely graded the early medieval labour force *could* be, yet bound together by their common condition of landlessness and servility, and Faith's description of the inland workforce as a 'mixed servile labour force' strikes me as the best characterisation we have of the rural labour force in the centuries between the fall of the western empire and the imposition of serfdom in the great feudal transformation of the 'year 1000'. Faith refers to the 'slave and ex-slave farm servants with their cottages huddled on the inland round the curia',[66] which may well be how we should imagine the Merovingian labour force, the *mancipia* in contrast to the *accolae*, that is, as farm workers and a class distinct from the peasantry.

[62] *Vitas sanctorum patrum Emeretensium* 13.4 (J. N. Garvin, *The Vitas Sanctorum Patrum Emeretensium: Text and Translation* (Washington, 1946), p. 249); *Lives of the Visigothic Fathers* 13.4 (A. T. Fear, *Lives of the Visigothic Fathers* (Liverpool, 1997), p. 101).

[63] *Casa*: Pelagius, *Ep.* 84 (*c.*561). The *casales* in the estate lists known as the *Casae Litterarum* (of Italian provenance and late antique) look like land parcels on the boundaries of estates (*fundi*), see E. Migliario, 'Terminologia e organizzazione agraria tra tardo antico e alto medioevo: Ancora su *fundus* e *casalis/casale*', *Athenaeum* 80 (2) (1992), 371–84, calling them *appezzamenti* (pp. 373ff.). A. Roth Congès, 'Nature et authenticité des Casae Litterarum d'aprés l'analyse de leur vocabulaire', in *Les vocabulaires techniques des arpenteurs romains*, ed. D. Conso *et al.* (Besançon, 2005), pp. 71–124 is now the fundamental study of the surveyors' lists.

[64] They were widespread by the mid-seventh century, when Rothari refers to them in his 'Edict' of 643; the best recent edition is C. Azzara and S. Gasparri, *Le leggi dei Longobardi: Storia, memoria e diritto di un popolo germanico*, 2nd edn (Rome, 2005).

[65] R. Faith, *The English Peasantry and the Growth of Lordship* (London, 1997), p. 69.

[66] Faith, *Growth of Lordship*, p. 209.

Critique of Wickham

To turn now to *Framing the Early Middle Ages*, Wickham's image of the transition is completely different in this respect. It is an image dominated by a simple dialectic, the disintegration of something he calls the 'slave mode of production' and its more or less direct replacement by tenancy. This is supposed to have happened well before 400, 'in particular in the second and third centuries', and can, Wickham argues, be construed as an 'economic shift from the slave mode to the feudal mode'.[67] Thus the feudal mode of production is seen as expanding in a gradual, piecemeal fashion, as tenancy expands, and it now covers a vast stretch of history from the second or third century to, presumably, the later Middle Ages, a period of well over one thousand years, a view that should baffle Marxists at least! This model, simple as it is, has several obvious and even massive implications for the way we construct the agrarian history of these periods. In the first place, it implies that Roman landowners gave up direct management when they abandoned the slave mode. Secondly, it denies, ignores or hugely underestimates the persistence of slavery in late antiquity and the early Middle Ages. Thirdly, it construes the *colonatus* of the late empire simply as a system of rent-paying tenancies, with minimal implications for the actual subordination and control of labour. Finally, and most substantially, Wickham sees the tenancy of these historical periods as a type of self-management in which peasants 'controlled the land and their own work process', or '*controlled their own holding* and could keep its fruits after rents were paid'.[68] In other words, there was, as he says, limited landowner control over production, indeed limited interest in it,[69] at least till the emergence of manorialism in the Carolingian period.

I would like to suggest that Wickham's handling of both slavery and the colonate are among the weakest parts of his excellent book. The sheer scale of manumissions that followed in the seventh century (e.g. Spain, England) shows how widespread slavery was, still, in late antiquity. Legal sources, both late Roman and barbarian, provide one indication of this.

67 Wickham, *Framing*, p. 262: 'Actually, plantations had never been frequent outside central Italy, Sicily, and parts of Greece, and even there the basic economic shift from the slave to the feudal mode had already taken place well before 400, in particular in the *second and third centuries*. Throughout our period the slave mode was only a minor survival, everywhere marginal to the basic economic structure, the landlord–peasant relationship (where there were landlords at all)'; my emphasis.

68 Wickham, 'Other Transition', p. 9; Wickham, *Framing*, p. 560; italics mine.

69 C. Wickham, 'Le forme del feudalesimo', in *Il feudalesimo nell'alto medioevo*, 2 vols, *Settimane di studio* 47 (2000), vol. 1, pp. 15–46, at 33.

Wickham's wholesale disregard of the legal evidence is not credible and has rightly been characterised, by Andrea Giardina, as a sort of reductionism.[70] There are *numerous* constitutions in the *Theodosian Code* which either deal with or refer to slavery, both rural and urban, though this clearly is not the place to rehearse the details. The standard legal term for a slave was *mancipium*, the neuter signifying conscious reification. In *CTh.* 2.25.1 (possibly 325) Constantine stipulated that the children of slaves employed on imperial estates in Sardinia should not be separated from their parents when those estates were handed over to private individuals or divided in some way. In *CTh.* 9.42.7 (369) a detailed inventory was prescribed for estates confiscated from private landowners convicted of criminal offences. This *plena describtio* would have to indicate 'how many slaves, either urban or rural, are contained on the seized estate … how many cottagers and *coloni* there are, how many oxen are employed in working the land, etc.'. It is hard to see why the potential evidence of constitutions like these should be discounted on the general prejudice that law has a normative function. In any case, 'Numerous sources refer to rural slaves.'[71] The Greek life of the younger Melania refers to the slaves (*douloi*) on her suburban estates (*proasteia*) near Rome, while the author of the 'Lausiac History', who knew Melania, reports that she manumitted 8,000 of them![72] When Alaric besieged Rome in 408–9, 'many slaves, especially those of barbarian origin, deserted to join him'.[73] Augustine's polemic against the Donatists is full of references to recalcitrant slaves (*servi*), and in the fifth century one chronicle tells us that 'nearly all the slaves of the Gallic provinces (*omnia paene Galliarum servitia*) conspired in [the] Bacaudic movement'.[74] As E. A. Thompson remarked, 'Our sources seem to suggest that these revolts were due *primarily to the agricultural slaves*, or at any rate that slaves played a prominent part in them.'[75] In short, the balance of evidence supports Finley's conclusion that 'Slavery

[70] A. Giardina, 'Marxism and Historiography: Perspectives on Roman History', in *Marxist History-Writing for the Twenty-First Century*, ed. C. Wickham (Oxford, 2007), pp. 15–31, at 28.

[71] C. R. Whittaker, 'Slavery', in *Late Antiquity: A Guide to the Post-Classical World*, ed. G. W. Bowersock *et al.* (Cambridge, MA, 1999), pp. 698–9, at 699.

[72] *Vita Mel. graec.* 11 (*douloi*), Palladius, *Hist. Laus.* 61.5 (*andrapoda*): slaves, not 'unfree dependants', as in M. Innes, *Introduction to Early Medieval Western Europe, 300–900: The Sword, the Plough and the Book* (London, 2007), p. 53. Cf. Symmachus, *Rel.* 28.3 for *mancipia* (strictly slaves) on a suburban estate (*suburbana villa*) of the aristocrat Olybrius, abducted from the holdings of a lesser aristocrat.

[73] Olympiodorus, fr. 7.5 (Blockley, p. 160), Sozomen, 9.6.3.

[74] *Chron. min.* i, 660, s.a. 435.

[75] E. A. Thompson, 'Peasant Revolts in Late Roman Gaul and Spain', *Past & Present* 2 (1952), 11–23, at p. 11.

survived on a considerable quantitative scale.'[76] But this was equally true of the sixth and seventh centuries. According to Tom Brown, 'slaves were widely used in cultivating the patrimony of the Roman Church'.[77] Indeed, in Italy it was not till the ninth century that slavery began to fade away.[78] In Spain the Visigothic legislation is full of references to slavery. Thompson tells us, 'No subject interested the legislators of the sixth and seventh centuries more than the recovery of escaped slaves.'[79] It is not surprising, then, that Werner Rösener should claim, as he has done in a recent paper, 'Slavery was still widespread in the transition from late antiquity to the Middle Ages' and 'The Germanic kingdoms of the early Middle Ages are scarcely different from the late empire in terms of the actual prevalence of slavery.'[80]

Why labour the point, however? First, because slavery was widespread in the post-Roman west and this surely was at least partly a Roman legacy.[81] Second, because the early Middle Ages were not a period of serfdom, if we understand the latter historically, but rather one of *servility*, that is, of *mixed* labour forces where slaves, former *coloni* and freedpeople were conjointly deployed on large estates that were still structured on late Roman lines and indeed designated by an essentially late Roman vocabulary (*villae, mancipia, servi*, etc.). Thus the 'metanarrative' of a transition from slavery to serfdom which Wickham himself rejects, correctly of course, breaks down because it is too much of an abstraction. It simply merges the late Roman world into a medieval one, as Rodney Hilton did when he spoke of 'late ancient society' 'creating the production relations characteristic of feudal society';[82] but, more than that, it eliminates the historical distinction between a Middle Ages dominated by a diversified servile labour force exploited by estates which are not strictly bilateral and one characterised by manorial estates, labour services and a renewed assault on

[76] M. I. Finley, *Ancient Slavery and Modern Ideology* (London, 1980), p. 147.

[77] T. S. Brown, *Gentlemen and Officers: Imperial Administration and Aristocratic Power in Byzantine Italy, A.D. 544–800* (London, 1984), p. 203.

[78] P. Cammarosano, *Storia dell'Italia medievale dal VI all' XI secolo* (Rome, 2001), p. 185.

[79] Thompson, *Goths in Spain*, p. 271.

[80] W. Rösener, 'Vom Sklaven zum Bauern: Zur Stellung der Hörigen in der frühmittelalterlichen Grundherrschaft', in *Tätigkeitsfelder und Erfahrungshorizonte des ländlichen Menschen in der frühmittelalterlichen Grundherrschaft (bis ca.1000): Festschrift für Dieter Hägermann*, ed. Brigitte Kasten (Stuttgart, 2006), pp. 71–89, at 79.

[81] H. Nehlsen, *Sklavenrecht zwischen Antike und Mittelalter* (Göttingen, 1972); H. Grieser, *Sklaverei im spätantiken und frühmittelalterlichen Gallien (5–7 Jh.): Das Zeugnis der christlichen Quellen* (Stuttgart, 1997); P. D. King, *Law and Society in the Visigothic Kingdom* (Cambridge, 1972).

[82] R. Hilton, 'A Comment', orig. *Science and Society* (1953), repr. in *The Transition from Feudalism to Capitalism*, ed. R. H. Hilton (London, 1976), pp. 109–17, at 112.

the peasantry. Without the Roman background of slavery, the servile relations of production of the sixth to ninth centuries would be like Athena emerging from Zeus' head!

The other strand in this argument relates to the heated issue of the *colonatus*. A minor orthodoxy has emerged in late antique studies which consciously seeks to downplay the element of coercion that characterised the subordination of these workers. *Coloni* were a category of permanent farm labour which the government sought to tie to estates in the general interests of fiscal efficiency. They were free persons in the legal sense that they were not slaves,[83] but restricted in their movements and subject increasingly to social downgrading and the control of their employers, e.g. estate owners had automatic rights of control over the progeny of female labourers even if their husbands were free persons unconnected with estates. In the only formal definition to survive, the emperor Justinian in the sixth century defined them as 'farm workers' who were permanently resident on the estates they worked for.[84] The issue here is not how widespread this category of labour was in the imperial territories – it existed presumably wherever large estates did – but what happened to them when the empire disintegrated in the west. On my reading of the evidence, *coloni* continued to exist into the sixth century but were increasingly absorbed into a less and less differentiated labour force that I have characterised as 'servile'. This is why in one of the earliest pieces of post-Roman legislation we have, the Edict of Theoderic, there are repeated references to *servus aut colonus*, 'slaves or coloni', distinct but not vastly different in status (more or less the same legal provisions apply to both groups),[85] whereas in

83 In his recent contribution to *The Cambridge Economic History of the Greco-Roman World*, Andrea Giardina reproaches me with failing to see that the late Roman *coloni* were unfree (A. Giardina, 'The Transition to Late Antiquity', in *The Cambridge Economic History of the Greco-Roman World*, ed. W. Scheidel *et al.* (Cambridge, 2007), pp. 743–63, at 748, n. 19). Surprisingly for a scholar of Giardina's stature, this confuses two totally separate issues: (1) the fact that *coloni* were free individuals under Roman law (not slaves), hence my reference to 'free labour' (i.e. not slave labour; the standard contrast in historical materialism), and (2) the kinds of coercion that the regime of the colonate subjected these particular workers to. If they were 'unfree' to begin with (in some essentialist way), the tensions and paradoxes created by the *gradual* imposition of the laws relating to them would simply evaporate and the fascination of the subject (for scholars anyway) would be a pure enigma.

84 *Nov. Just.* 162, cited Banaji, *Agrarian Change*, p. 182; see n. 119. Savigny assumed that most *coloni* were landless, see F. C. Von Savigny, 'Ueber den römischen Colonat', in *Vermischte Schriften*, vol. II (Berlin, 1850), pp. 1–46, at 32, and certainly landlessness is strongly implied in Justinian, *Nov.* 128.14, which contains the expression, 'Even if [the *coloni*] should happen to have farms of their own'. For the survival/re-emergence of the *colonatus* in the Byzantine parts of Italy, cf. Pelagius, *Ep.* 64 (559); Gregory, *Ep.* 4.21 (594).

85 *Ed. Theod.* (*EIRA*², ii, 684ff.) 21, 84, 98, 104, 109, 121 and 148 all have *servus aut colonus*. In *Ed. Theod.* 80 we have *servus aut originarius*.

barbarian law codes of a later date, such as the Visigothic legislation of the seventh century, there are no references to them as a separate category but to *servi* and *mancipia*, that is, servile classes that undoubtedly included former *coloni*.[86] Indeed, it is fascinating to be able to map this crucially important extension in the meaning of the term *mancipium* from its strict Roman sense of 'chattel slave' to the much looser post-Roman and early medieval meaning of an unfree/servile labourer through the *whole* of the sixth century, when this evolution first begins. Burgundian legislation already subsumes tied labourers under the more general description *mancipia*.[87] And in Theoderic's 'Edict' the expression *servus sive colonus* is used interchangeably with *mancipium*, showing that the latter term could now embrace both groups, slaves as well as *coloni*.[88] By the later sixth century and certainly by the seventh, it was absolutely standard to use *mancipium* as a generic description that included workers descended from former *coloni* who might themselves, still, be called by this name, as, for example, in the will of Aredius which I cited earlier, or in Dagobert's donation of the estate of Etrépagny to the abbey of Saint-Denis, dated 628, which has the expression *cum omni integritate et soliditate, hoc est domibus, edificiis … mancipiis, colonis, inquilinis, accolabus, libertis, servis tam ibidem oriundis quam et aliundis translatis*.[89] Indeed, one will of 632, that of the bishop Eligius, even contains the expression *originarii*.[90]

Wickham disregards all of this evidence to bolster the impression that a more or less self-managing peasantry had emerged from the ruins of the Roman empire and the crisis of its aristocracy, and that words like *servus* and *mancipium* described a purely formal dependence which could barely

[86] King, *Law and Society*, pp. 160–1; Nehlsen, *Sklavenrecht*, pp. 166–7; W. E. Voss, 'Der Grundsatz der "ärgeren Hand" bei Sklaven, Kolonen und Hörigen', in *Römisches Recht in der europäischen Tradition: Symposion aus Anlass des 75. Geburtstages von Franz Wieacker*, ed. O. Behrends *et al.* (Ebelsbach, 1985), pp. 168, n. 239; 170, n. 252.

[87] *LBurg* 54, issued by Gundobad between 501 and 516, refers to the Burgundian elite seizing one third of the labour force on Gallic estates where they had been settled 'by the rule of hospitality'. The term used for these workers is *mancipia* and, as W. Goffart, *Barbarians and Romans A.D. 418–584: The Techniques of Accommodation* (Princeton, 1980), pp. 127ff., esp. 135–6, argues, it is inconceivable that the word should have referred *only* to slaves; so too C. R. Whittaker, 'Circe's Pigs: From Slavery to Serfdom in the Later Roman World', in *Classical Slavery*, ed. M. I. Finley (London, 1987), pp. 88–122, at 109.

[88] Nehlsen, *Sklavenrecht*, p. 131 notes, 'der Kolone, der nunmehr zu den *mancipia* gezählt wird'. Cf. *Ed. Theod.* 142, which has the expression *rustica utriusque sexus mancipia, etiamsi originaria sint*, 'agrarian *mancipia* of either sex, even if they happen to be *originarii*', that is, happen to be the tied labourers technically known as *coloni originarii* because the estate was their *origo*, the place where they were enrolled for tax purposes.

[89] Kölzer, *Urkunden*, vol. 1, no. 31, pp. 85ff. (628); Tits-Dieuaide, 'Grands domaines', p. 32.

[90] *Test. Eligii* 2 (ed. Krusch, *MGH Script, rer. merow.* IV, 746).

counter the economic reality that most rural labourers were now actually tenants who, as he says, 'controlled the land and their own work process'.[91] In *Framing* he endorses the very substantial position that 'Most *servi/mancipia* in our period ... were tenants who controlled their own holding and could keep its fruits after rents were paid.'[92] But the written evidence just does not support this. As I said, in the early sixth-century will of Remigius, bishop of Reims, *colonus* is a term for half-free or unfree rural labourers, distinct from slaves, who could be bequeathed with the land, transferred between owners and even manumitted, and whose families could likewise be bequeathed. These peasants can scarcely be construed as controlling the land. Again, throughout the later sixth and seventh century, the Spanish church fought hard to retain control over the 'services' of freedpeople (*liberti*) who had once been their slaves, and refused to acknowledge their freedom unless it had such control.[93] And Merovingian charters are full of references to *mancipia* who, given the nature of the typical Merovingian estate (*villa*), still rooted in Roman traditions of *Gutswirtschaft*, were not a loose collection or dispersed mass of rent-paying tenancies but at best allotment holders retained by the estate as a captive labour supply and otherwise simply landless slaves domiciled 'in the outbuildings of [their] master's farm'[94] or near the estate centre. The huge wave of manumissions that transformed the landscape of medieval Europe, reassembling what would later and only gradually become a peasantry proper, threw up a vast array of intermediate categories between pure slaves and pure peasants, and it is this mass of servile labour that formed the backbone of elite agriculture down to the feudal reaction of the eleventh to thirteenth centuries and the imposition of serfdom.[95] Thus, on the one hand, slaves and slavery remained a substantial part of Lombard, Anglo-Saxon and other early medieval societies, while on the other hand, large numbers of them were settled on the land with the allotments called *mansi*, described legally

[91] Wickham, 'Other Transition', p. 9.

[92] Wickham, *Framing*, p. 560.

[93] Toledo III, *can.* 6 (J. Vives, *Concilios Visigóticos e hispano-romanos* (Barcelona, 1963), p. 127, Sevilla I, *can.* 1 (151–2), Tol. IV, *can.* 68, 70, 73 (214–16) and Conc. Mérida, *can.* 20 (339–40), dated 589, 590, 633 and 666 respectively, all dealing with *mancipia ecclesiae* who had been 'manumissa' but over whom the church still wanted control (*patrocinium, obsequium*). Also *LV* 4.5.7 (Zeumer, p. 205f.), a law of Wamba that refuses to allow these *liberti* to marry freeborn women.

[94] H. P. R. Finberg, 'Anglo-Saxon England to 1042', in *The Agrarian History of England and Wales, vol. i/ii: A.D. 43–1042*, ed. H. P. R. Finberg (Cambridge, 1972), pp. 383–532, at 431.

[95] The Anglo-Saxon bordars and cottars, German *Tageschalken*, Italian *servi prebendari*, etc. There is a rough analogy in the 'bondsmen' used by modernising Prussian estate owners of the nineteenth century, see W. Conze, 'The Effects of Nineteenth-Century Liberal Agrarian Reforms on Social Structure in Central Europe', in *Essays in European Economic History 1789–1914*, ed. F. Crouzet *et al.* (London, 1969), pp. 53–81, at 67.

as their *peculium*, *peculiaria* or *res peculiares* (the usual vocabulary for the assets managed by a slave).

The general point I wish to make is that the post-Roman/early medieval world was characterised by a great deal more complexity in the structuring and composition of its rural labour force than suggested by Wickham's simplified image of 'tenants who controlled their own holding and could keep its fruits after rents were paid'.[96] The best generic description, as I suggested earlier, might be a 'mixed servile labour force'[97] where families themselves might be of mixed legal status, and where the great movement of manumission was creating reserves of labour still integrated into centralised estates rather than the independent farm complexes called *hubae*, also known, confusingly, as *mansi* when the latter term acquired its more expansive sense in the central Middle Ages. That a more substantial or autonomous peasantry existed or was emerging is incontrovertible (the feudal reaction would be incomprehensible without it), but to understand its emergence we have to describe the context of the relations of production within which it developed with less abstraction and certainly less schematically than either Wickham or an earlier generation of Marxists have tended to do. The metanarrative of the transition from slavery to serfdom which Wickham rejects *cannot* be replaced by the equally abstract idea that 'When the Romans abandoned the slave mode, they went straight over to rent-paying tenants,'[98] or by the notion that the 'economic shift from the slave to the feudal mode had already taken place well before 400'.[99] It is bizarre to call the Roman empire 'feudal' unless one is determined to deplete the category of all historical content. And slavery didn't simply disappear. It would be altogether more correct to refer to its 'mutation', as Georges Duby does.[100] Wickham's simple dichotomy between legal condition and economic form (slavery persisting at the first level, 'tenancy' widespread at the second) lacks the subtlety needed to characterise the transition, *even if* legal status mattered less and less and, as Innes says, 'there was no real social gulf between free and unfree' by the Carolingian period.[101]

96 Wickham, *Framing*, p. 560. 97 Faith, *Growth of Lordship*, p. 252.

98 Wickham, 'Other Transition', p. 31. 99 Wickham, *Framing*, p. 262.

100 Duby, *Guerriers et paysans*, p. 51: 'une lente mutation de l'esclavage'.

101 M. Innes, *State and Society in the Early Middle Ages: The Middle Rhine Valley, 400–1000* (Cambridge, 2000), pp. 78–80. Of course, by the same token, Bonnassie's thesis of the persistence of a slave *economy* down to the 'feudal mutation' of *l'an mil* is equally untenable, P. Bonnassie, *From Slavery to Feudalism in South-Western Europe*, trans. Jean Birrell (Cambridge and Paris, 1991). There is a great deal of value in Bonnassie's work, but the best critiques of his main thesis are P. Freedman, 'La servidumbre catalana y el problema de la revolución feudal', *Hispania* 56 (2) (1996), 425–46; P. Freedman, 'Siervos, campesinos y cambio social', in *Señores, siervos, vasallos en la alta edad*

Now, viewed teleologically, in terms of some inexorable evolution towards the manor and its eventual triumph, the allotment holders of the post-Roman/early medieval countryside may seem like a transitional type, a sort of station between two terminals, one called Antiquity, the other Feudalism; or if you prefer, between Slavery and Serfdom. But this, I suggest, is absolutely the wrong way of approaching the issue. Between the 'demesne slave' or *servi praebendarii* and the peasant families in possession of substantial tenements (viz. 10 acre holdings at the lower end) lay a whole series of intermediate categories who are surely better defined as farm workers than as peasants: the *Tageschalken* in Germany, the geburs, bordars and cottars in Anglo-Saxon England, and so on. They were 'a substantial proportion of the rural population of Anglo-Saxon England'[102] and doubtless the same is true of most countries on the Continent. If we choose to call them tenants, then *worker-tenants* is a better description of these groups than the tenants that Wickham seems to have in mind. Wickham discusses their legal status as largely irrelevant on the grounds that the distinction between free and unfree was typically and increasingly fuzzy. This is true, but the diminished legal condition of most or all of these groups was surely not unrelated to the fact that taken as a whole they formed a tied labour force on a model familiar to late Roman landowners and their free but tied *coloni*. Indeed, the laws on the colonate were themselves a major influence on the social condition of the medieval peasantry, insofar as the successor kingdoms absorbed them selectively and enforced them against their own dependent populations.[103] The *mancipia* who appear in Merovingian charters were certainly not slaves in the strict Roman sense,[104] but the fact that they *were* described in this way was not unrelated to the way large estates saw themselves using the labour of these workers.

To sum up, early medieval relations of production were defined by considerable complexity, not so much in terms of legal status, which mattered less than it did in the Roman world, as economically, in the nature

media = *XXVIII Semana de Estudios Medievales, Estella 16–20 julio 2001* (Pamplona, 2002) pp. 127–46; and Verhulst's discussion of Bois, A. Verhulst, 'The Decline of Slavery and the Economic Expansion of the Early Middle Ages', *Past & Present* 133 (1991), 195–203.

102 Faith, *Growth of Lordship*, p. 85.

103 See W. E. Voss, 'Der Grundsatz der "ärgeren Hand" bei Sklaven, Kolonen und Hörigen', in *Römisches Recht in der europäischen Tradition: Symposion aus Anlass des 75. Geburtstages von Franz Wieacker*, ed. O. Behrends *et al.* (Ebelsbach, 1985) pp. 117–84, the most substantial treatment of the subject.

104 F. Panero, *Schiavi, servi e villani nel'Italia medievale* (Turin, 1999), p. 89.

of the labour force, which was typically mixed but in general characterised by the kind of servility that was distinctive of post-classical slavery[105] and best conveyed by the term *mancipium*. This was a late antique legacy but one which the post-Roman kingdoms transformed, insofar as a common condition of servility now engulfed both slaves and former tied labourers, manumissions were widespread but freedpeople still subject to domination (*obsequium*), and new aristocracies were bringing land into cultivation by creating peasant tenures of a kind previously unknown. Large-scale enterprise and direct management were crucial parts of the legacy late Rome passed on to the Carolingians. Both tied labour and the direct management of estates were integral features of the Carolingian world and of the new energies manifested in the evolution of bilateral estates by the eighth century. *Yet the continuity in traditions of direct management did not imply a continuity of estate structures.* However we construe serfdom, whether economically in terms of labour services or socially in terms of the characteristics Marc Bloch emphasised, it was *not* a feature of the period between 400 and 750 or even 800.[106] The spread of slave tenancies created a captive labour supply in the form of reserves of labour power. As Bloch himself indicated, 'The land that had been granted to them [slaves] … was like their salary.'[107] This was closer in nature to labour tenancies than to the more archetypal feudal institution of labour services. Finally, as Faith writes,

> The freed slave was a worker who in return for selling his labour as a commodity received a 'wage in land' from the lord, who was his employer and sole purchaser of that labour. The lord, in his capacity as employer, was essential to him. By contrast, the serf was a peasant with a holding, which, however small, supported him and his family and provided a surplus which was transferred to the lord in rent paid in cash, kind or labour (or in all these).[108]

What this suggests is the more general distinction between *labour services*, bound up with the expansion of the manorial regime from the eighth century, and *labour tenancies*, still rooted in late antique models of estate organisation.

[105] W. Davies, 'On Servile Status in the Early Middle Ages', in *Serfdom and Slavery: Studies in Legal Bondage*, ed. M. L. Bush, (London, 1996), pp. 225–46, esp. 231.

[106] 900 if serfdom is construed in the full-bodied sense used by Bloch, e.g. M. Bloch, *Slavery and Serfdom in the Middle Ages: Selected Essays*, trans. W. R. Beer (Berkeley, 1975), ch.2.

[107] Bloch, *Slavery and Serfdom*, p. 6.

[108] Faith, *Growth of Lordship*, pp. 69–70, a superb passage.

The east: vulnerability

In his book *The Islamic Law of Land Tax and Rent*, Baber Johansen argues, in a chapter strikingly entitled 'The "death of the proprietors"', that the smallholding peasantry of the Islamic world began to disappear from the second half of the tenth century, with the evolution of the *iqtāʿ* system. (*Iqtāʿ* in this later sense referred of course to the holding of revenue assignments on specified lands in lieu of a cash salary and thus presupposes a more or less centralised state. The system was widely used throughout the Islamic world, including India, where it went by a variety of names, such as *muqasa*, *jāgīr* and so on.) In later centuries, Johansen argues, the trend was consolidated as large estates were formed through the privatisation of these tax assignments, capital investments in the purchase of land and the outright grant of private ownership to members of the elite.[109] Much of the political economy of Islam might be seen as an unstable equilibrium between the fiscal supremacism of the state and the capitalist tendencies of members of the elite who defended claims to private property and the rights of pious foundations (*waqf* rights), especially on arable lands where these were sometimes fiercely contested. In these struggles, the jurists of the Mamluk and Ottoman periods tended to support the latter.[110] In the fifteenth century the Hanafi mufti Ibn al-Humām exclaimed in bafflement, 'Can't you see that the land is not the property of the cultivators (*zurrāʿ*)? This is so in spite of what we said about the lands of Egypt being *kharāj* lands.'[111] In other words, it no longer mattered that the peasants paid taxes (*kharāj*); the legal fiction that the payment of taxes (*kharāj*) was proof of one's title to the land was now effectively defunct. 'For Ibn al-Humām the notion of the "death of the *kharāj* payer" served to explain and legalise the tenant status of peasants and the fact that they no longer enjoyed property rights with regard to their lands in spite of their paying their levies to the *muqta*' and the ruler.'[112] In the following (sixteenth) century, Ibn Nujaym's defence of the property rights of the landed classes against the incipient Ottoman drive to transform all land back into state property rationalised those claims by arguing that peasants too poor to pay taxes or cultivate the land would lose the disposition of their property and that the ruler was entitled to sell such land on their behalf. But once

[109] B. Johansen, *The Islamic Law of Land Tax and Rent: The Peasants' Loss of Property Rights as Interpreted in the Hanafite Legal Literature of the Mamluk and Ottoman Periods* (London, 1988), p. 81.
[110] Johansen, *Islamic Law of Land Tax*, pp. 81ff.
[111] Cited Johansen, *Islamic Law of Land Tax*, pp. 84–5.
[112] Johansen, *Islamic Law of Land Tax*, p. 85.

sold, the government was no longer entitled to an extra payment for the use of the land, that is, such land would count as tax exempt.[113] In an odd piece of reasoning, Ibn Nujaym then went on to argue that whether land was tax exempt or not could be ascertained from how much buyers had paid for it, since no one would pay a high price for land that attracted taxes. Tax exemption was seen as a sign of the status of the landowner as a member of the ruling class. When high prices were paid, the buyer 'becomes an exclusive proprietor (*mālikᵘⁿ lahā 'ala l-khuṣūṣ*) of the land and he is not a sharecropper (*muzāri'*) or a peasant (*fallāḥ*)'.[114]

Now what is interesting in the convoluted argument used to justify the dispossession of the peasantry is not just the conceptual landscape that lies at the back of the argument, viz. that the rural world is divided into landowners and peasants, and that they are sharply distinct classes, but the strong sense of the vulnerability of the peasantry itself. As Johansen notes, 'Private landed property no longer comes into being through the confirmation of the primordial rights of the peasants by the ruler,'[115] referring here to the doctrine that the conquest had confirmed the peasantry in its ownership of the land, in southern Iraq at any rate, and in the general sense that *kharāj* was a tax on private property, so that *kharāj* payers were proprietors in a full-bodied sense.[116] Whatever one thinks of the notion that the conquest entailed a sort of emancipation of the peasantry (to me it seems unlikely), Johansen's book is a good starting point for the general argument I would like to propose in this part of the chapter, namely, that we have to think of the peasantry in the Middle East in very different terms from the situation in the west. I concluded a paper published in 1999 with the claim, it is 'worth emphasising that the Egyptian peasantry in particular has a strangely elusive quality'.[117] I now believe that this is true of the Middle East peasantry as a whole, even if the Egyptian material makes it easier to establish for that country. I would like to lay out *three* arguments for this general thesis, which are, respectively, about class structure, sharecropping and the meaning of 'estate'. Taken together, these arguments suggest that the peasantry in these parts of the world, that is, everywhere from the Maghreb to Sind, lived permanently in a twilight zone of near landlessness. Johansen's discussion of Ibn Nujaym has

[113] Johansen, *Islamic Law of Land Tax*, pp. 88–9.
[114] Cited Johansen, *Islamic Law of Land Tax*, p. 90: *fī hādhihi l-ḥālati mālikᵘⁿ lahā 'alā l-khuṣūṣi laisa bi-muzāriᶜⁱⁿ wa-lā fallāḥ.*
[115] Johansen, *Islamic Law of Land Tax*, p. 91.
[116] Johansen, *Islamic Law of Land Tax*, ch. 1.
[117] J. Banaji, 'Agrarian History and the Labour Organization of Byzantine Large Estates', in *Agriculture in Egypt*, ed. A. Bowman and E. Rogan (Oxford, 1999), pp. 193–216, at 213.

demonstrated one form of this and I shall now look briefly at each of the three topics just mentioned.

By late antiquity there is almost no evidence of a *substantial* stratum that might be called small and middle peasants, except in isolated regions and ecological niches where they were less vulnerable to the depredations of large landowners. In the Byzantine east, summary descriptions of the chief rural classes comprise only two groups, *hoi tōn chōriōn despotai* and *hoi geōrgoi*, or *hoi kyrioi* and *hoi geōrgoi*, or some variation on these couplets such as *hoi ta chōria kektēmenoi* and *hoi geōrgoi*,[118] that is, landowners on one side, peasants on the other. But from the way these terms are deployed, it is clear that the *geōrgoi* were not mainly a landed class. It was not the ownership of land that defined their identity in the eyes of the members of the elite who drafted the laws or wrote histories. What defined them collectively was the fact of rural labour. This is why it was standard to use the term *geōrgos* when referring to *coloni* in the east, although Justinian himself took the trouble to explain that the Latin word designated a class of workers who were 'residents of large estates and farm workers'.[119] On one third-century estate, *geōrgoi* were included among the groups who received monthly wages (in grain),[120] and going even further back, el-Abbadi describes the *dēmosioi geōrgoi* or peasants on former royal (that is, Ptolemaic) land as 'the great mass of landless public peasants', adding that at this time (the first century) the word *geōrgos* 'usually indicate[s] a farmer who owned his own land'.[121] In short, the first thing agrarian historians have to do is reconstruct the meaning of words instead of allowing words to dominate their perception of the flow of history.

In the Sasanian Near East, we know next to nothing about agrarian relations beyond the fact that much Iranian history revolved around the tensions or conflict between the ruler and powerful regional aristocracies. There is one fascinating reference in Ammianus to the Sasanian upper class wielding 'the power of life and death over their slaves and *plebeii obscuri*'.[122] *Bandag* was the standard Middle Persian term for 'slave' or 'servant', but how we should (reverse) translate the latter expression is

[118] Procopius, *HA* 23.16, 26.17ff., *Nov. Just.* 157 (542), *Nov. Tib.* 11 (575), etc. In *Nov. Just.* 8, praef. (535) *ktētores* and *geōrgoi* are the only rural groups listed.

[119] *Nov. Just.* 162.2, *tous oikētoras tōn chōriōn kai tōn agrōn ergatas.* Note that *ergatēs* was the usual Greek term for an unskilled wage earner.

[120] *P. Oxy.* XLII 3048 (246).

[121] M. A. H. El-Abbadi, 'The Edict of Tiberius Julius Alexander: Remarks on its Nature and Aim', *Bulletin de l'Institut français d'archéologie orientale* 65 (1967), 215–26, at p. 219.

[122] Ammianus, 23.6.80: *vitae necisque potestatem in servos et plebeios vindicantes obscuros.* Note that Ammianus had travelled into Sasanian territory with Julian's army.

anyone's guess; perhaps it was Ammianus' Latin equivalent of *driyōšān*.[123] It referred presumably to the mass of commoners who survived through employment for the rich and probably also to the kind of social groups from which the revolutionary priest Mazdak drew his support early in the sixth century. These are described in the (much later!) Arabic sources by a profusion of terms, of which the most telling denote utter destitution.[124] Patricia Crone, in a justly famous paper, argued that Mazdak drew his support from the peasantry, especially in the aftermath of fiscal reforms that introduced a fixed monetary tax.[125] But this, of course, begs the question whether such a group (a peasantry) existed on any substantial scale by the sixth century. What does seem clear is that *if* Mazdak's supporters were rural, they were landless, but on balance it is more likely that Mazdak attracted the urban poor, groups who had no access to food in times of scarcity, *and*, it seems, no access to women and a family life either. At any rate, the picture of late Sasanian society is one of a deeply divided formation where the antagonism between rich and poor was a constant source of anxiety for the ruling groups,[126] and one of the most valuable survivals of an authentic Middle Persian text (via Arabic) shows a ruler, probably Khusrō I, strongly advocating the attachment (*ilḥāq*) of the poor to their closest aristocratic neighbours to reduce class antagonisms and ensure the continued submission of those stricken by poverty.[127] The scale of destitution implied in all this fits remarkably well with the kind of agrarian picture reflected in a major work of agronomy written, almost certainly, in Syriac, in late antiquity, and translated by Ibn Waḥshiyya at the start

[123] W. Sundermann, '*Commendatio pauperum*: Eine Angabe der sassanidischen politisch-didaktischen Literatur zur gesellschaftlichen Struktur Irans', *Altorientalische Forschungen* 4 (1976), 167–94, esp. p. 179.

[124] The most evocative are *al-muqillīn* (the destitute) and *al-fuqarā'* (the poor), both in al-Ṭabarī, *Ta'rīkh*, ser. i, 886 = al-Ṭabarī, *The Sāsānids, the Byzantines, the Lakhmids, and Yemen (The History of al-Ṭabarī, vol. v)*, trans. C. E. Bosworth (Albany, 1999), p. 132. Al-Tha'ālibī, *Ghurar akhbār mulūk al furs* (Zotenberg), p. 600 describes Mazdak's social base as 'the poor (*al-fuqarā'*), the low-class (*al-sifla*) and the rabble (*al-ghaughā'*)'. *Al-ḍu'afā'* (the powerless) was another common description. It seems very likely that the Arabic tradition was trying to render the sense of the Middle Persian terms *driyōš* and *škōh*, on which see Sundermann, '*Commendatio pauperum*', and I. Colditz, *Zur Sozialterminologie der iranischen Manichäer: Eine semantische Analyse im Vergleich zu den nichtmanichäischen iranischen Quellen* (Wiesbaden, 2000), pp. 177ff., 190ff.

[125] P. Crone, 'Kavād's Heresy and Mazdak's Revolt', *Iran* 29 (1991), 21–42, esp. pp. 32ff., repr. in P. Crone, *From Kavād to al-Ghazālī: Religion, Law and Political Thought in the Near East, c.600–c.1100* (Aldershot, 2005); R. N. Frye, *The History of Ancient Iran* (Munich, 1984), p. 323.

[126] E.g. *Dēnkard* 6.147 (Shaked, p. 60), which refers to the poor having contempt (*tarmenišnīh*) for the rich and powerful (*tawānīgān*).

[127] M. Grignaschi, 'Quelques spécimens de la littérature sassanide conservés dans les bibliothèques d'Istanbul', *Journal Asiatique*, 254 (1966), 1–142, at p. 99, with Sundermann, '*Commendatio pauperum*', p. 175.

of the tenth century.[128] Here, as Gunnar Lehmann points out in a review of a recent study of the massive redaction attributed to Ibn Waḥshiyya, 'In the rural masses of the *kitāb al-filāḥa an-nabaṭīya* we are dealing with "free" agricultural workers in Marx's sense. The population depicted there is *employed solely by the large estates, it has no share in landed property.*'[129] That at the time of the conquest of southern Iraq the Arabs did not in fact find a substantial smallholding peasantry but villages ruled by *dehqāns*, a minor gentry, and estates cultivated by mainly Aramaic-speaking 'tenants',[130] is suggested by a tradition reported in Abū Yūsuf's *Kitāb al-kharāj*, viz. ''Umar b. al-Khaṭṭāb first wanted to distribute [the lands of] al-Sawād amongst the Muslims and ordered a census. It was found that each of them would receive two or three tenants (*al-ithnain wa-l-thalātha min al-fallāḥīn*) with their lands' and he decided eventually not to proceed with the division.[131] In short, an independent peasantry was not a major feature of the core regions of the Sasanian empire, and both here and in the Byzantine-controlled eastern Mediterranean landlessness and dependence on large and medium-scale landowners was widespread. Thus, *proletarianisation took very different forms in the east and west*, flowing from the gradual dissolution of bondage and the structured creation of reserves of labour (labour tenancies) in one case, the west, and from the widespread landlessness of the peasantry in the other, the east, where the threat of eviction was a more powerful means of control.

Staying with the east, the second remarkable feature is the kind of sharecropping that prevailed there and its sheer ubiquity. Noting the frequency of indefinite durations in the Egyptian leases of the sixth to seventh centuries, Stefan Waszyński had concluded, correctly in my view, that the Byzantine sharecropper had become a pure and simple wage labourer whom the landowner could evict at any time.[132] No modern papyrologist

[128] For recent studies, see M. El Faïz, *L'Agronomie de la Mésopotamie antique: Analyse du 'Livre de l'agriculture nabatéenne' de Qûtâmä* (Leiden, 1995), and J. Hämeen-Anttila, *The Last Pagans of Iraq: Ibn Waḥshiyya and his 'Nabatean Agriculture'* (Leiden, 2006); on the Arabic translator, see Fahd, 'Ibn Waḥshiyya', *Enc. Islam.*, 2nd ser., vol. III, pp. 963ff.

[129] G. Lehmann, review of El Faïz (n. 128), *Journal of the Economic and Social History of the Orient* 40 (1997), 117ff., at p. 119; my italics. Fahd points out that the Leiden manuscript of the *Kitāb* runs to 1264 pages!

[130] In al-Ṭabarī, *Ta'rīkh*, ser. i, 2426, ll.13ff., Shīrazādh, *dehqān* of Sābāṭ, describes the peasants as *'ulūj* of the Persians, with the general sense, perhaps, of mere servants. Al-Ṭabarī's use of the generic *al-fallāḥīn* for the remnants of the Sasanian peasantry is scarcely a clue to how estates were structured or labour organised, hence the significance of this particular passage!

[131] Abū Yūsuf, *Kitāb al-kharāj*, 21 (1885 edn), trans. A. Ben Shemesh, *Taxation in Islam*, vol. III: *Abū Yūsuf's Kitāb al-kharāj* (Leiden, 1969), p. 97.

[132] S. Waszyński, *Die Bodenpacht: Agrargeschichtliche Papyrusstudien* (Leipzig, 1905), p. 92, esp. 'im Grunde genommen ist dieser demütige *georgos* kein Pächter mehr … er ist zum Mietling,

has registered any serious disagreement with this view, because it is so obvious that tenants-at-will are entirely at the mercy of their landlords. Thus whether the *georgoi* were 'bound' to large estates as *coloni* or permanent farm workers or worked as sharecroppers and tenants-at-will, they were united by their common condition of landlessness and total dependence on the employer. It is *this* feature of eastern Mediterranean sharecropping that comes to the fore in the Islamic period. Here are two passages illustrative of this. Discussing a category of land called the *'arḍ al-ḥauz* or lands that have come into the possession (*ḥauz*) of the ruler and been appropriated by him, the ninth-century Iraqi jurist al-Khaṣṣāf writes, 'the *ḥauz* is something that the Sultan takes possession of (*ḥāzahu*). He brings the sharecroppers (*muzāri'ūn*) to it, so that they may cultivate it. In this way they become farm-hands (*akara*) of the Sultan, whom he may oust at any time he pleases.'[133] And Abū Yūsuf in his discussion of different types of agricultural contracts describes two in particular which are relevant to our theme. One of them is called *muzāra'a* and defined as an agreement where the tenant receives a third or fourth share of the crop.[134] The other, not called *muzāra'a*, is described as follows: 'A landowner hires a peasant to cultivate some land and bears all the expense, promising the peasant a sixth or a seventh of the crop as wages.'[135] From al-Khaṣṣāf it is clear that sharecropping (*muzāra'a*) was widespread on large estates, even though it was rejected by jurists like Abū Ḥanīfa and Shāfi'ī[136] on the substantial legal grounds that the 'rent' was non-existent and unknown at the time the contract was made. The jurists who defended its validity did so on the practical grounds that it was part of the way business (*ta'āmul*) was conducted in their countries. These later Ḥanafī models of sharecropping draw a clear distinction between labour and capital, basing the landowner's claim to a share of the crop on his need to expand his property (i.e. the seed) and the worker's claim on the contract alone.[137] The fact that in most parts of the Islamic world *muzāra'a* typically involved shares varying from one fourth to one seventh is, I suggest, linked to an

zum Lohnarbeiter geworden, den der Grundherr nach Belieben hinauswerfen kann'; about the *eph'hoson chronon boulei* ('for any period you choose') clause.

133 Cited Johansen, *Islamic Law of Land Tax*, p. 14.

134 Abū Yūsuf, *Kitāb al-kharāj*, 52, l.1: *muzāra'a bi-l-thulth wa-l-rub'*, wrongly translated by Ben Shemesh as 'the owner gets a third or fourth of the yield' (*Taxation in Islam*, p. 115), contrast Z. Haque, *Landlord and Peasant in Early Islam: A Study of the Legal Doctrine of Muzāra'a or Sharecropping* (Islamabad, 1977), p. 327.

135 Abū Yūsuf, *K. al-kharāj*, 52, ll.4ff., with Ben Shemesh, *Taxation in Islam*, p. 116, though *fa-yad'uu akkār^{an}* is better translated 'hires a labourer'.

136 Johansen, *Islamic Law of Land Tax*, pp. 52–3.

137 Johansen, *Islamic Law of Land Tax*, p. 63; Haque, *Landlord and Peasant*, p. 325.

underlying conception of these contracts as a hiring of labour. Their sheer tenacity across the most diverse periods of the history of the Middle East is one indication of the peculiarly fragile nature of the peasantry in this part of the world. As Alan Richards says, 'Since the peasants often had little to supply but their labor power, it is not surprising that they usually received only one-fourth or one-fifth of the cotton harvest.'[138] In Nabulsi's Egypt (thirteenth century) the *murābiʿūn* or one-fourth croppers ranked lower than other sorts of tenants, hence Sato's description of them as 'a class of agricultural labourers'.[139] *Murābaʿa* was widespread in the Levant, *khammāsa* more common in North Africa.[140] In his monumental study of Algeria under French occupation, Albert Nouschi included the *khammès* (*khammās*) under 'proletarians'.[141] On the other hand, what the influx of European settlers brought from the 1840s was a different kind of *prolétarisation* of Algerian society, an organised dispossession that disintegrated entire tribes and uprooted wider sections of the peasantry, creating a new kind of landless worker. (Land confiscations affected one third of Algeria's population, once the *colons* decided that impoverishment was the best means of pacification.)[142] The vulnerability I have been at pains to stress is different from the organised creation of labour markets that characterises much nineteenth- and early twentieth-century colonialism. It is better reflected in Iran, which never knew colonialism in this sense and where, as Ann Lambton points out in her book,

> The *vast majority of the peasant population of Persia is … not composed of peasant proprietors, who are a small minority, but of crop-sharing peasants or tenants and 'landless' labourers*. It is with the former that this chapter is concerned. They, too, strictly speaking are landless, but by virtue of a contract, written, or more often merely verbal, a certain area of land is handed

[138] A. Richards, *Egypt's Agricultural Development, 1800–1980: Technical and Social Change* (Boulder, 1982), p. 68, about the period 1890–1914.

[139] T. Sato, *State and Rural Society in Medieval Islam: Sultans, Muqta's and Fallahun* (Leiden, 1997), p. 219.

[140] Y. Firestone, 'Crop-sharing Economics in Mandatory Palestine – Part I', *Middle Eastern Studies* 11 (1975), 3–23, esp. p. 8, who also states, 'in view of the low value attaching to his labour, the cropper cannot really exercise any control in the association. Accordingly, some jurists hold cropping to be a share-wage contract and hence basically illicit.' The *khammès* received a fifth of the crop as his/her share.

[141] A. Nouschi, *Enquête sur le niveau de vie des populations rurales constantinoises de la conquête jusqu'en 1919: Essai d'histoire économique et sociale* (Paris, 1961), p. 154.

[142] Nouschi, *Enquête sur le niveau de vie*, pp. 306, 448–9, 403ff.; *prolétarisation* at 511. See J.-P. Sartre, *Critique de la raison dialectique*, vol. 1: *Théorie des ensembles pratiques* (Paris, 1960), pp. 674–88, arguing that the inert violence of the *system* was rooted in concrete operations (massacres, legal interventions, etc.) designed to shatter an existing society and create (*réaliser*) a mainly agrarian 'sub-proletariat of the destitute and chronically unemployed'.

over to them on a crop-sharing basis for a specified or unspecified period of time, the peasant providing the seed, draught animals, and agricultural implements, or only one or two of these in addition to the labour, whereas the *landless labourer, although he may be also paid by a share of the crop, is differentiated from the crop-sharing peasant by the fact that he provides only labour and can be dismissed at will.* (Lambton, *Landlord and Peasant in Persia*, p. 295; my emphasis)

Since the division between the two groups described here cannot have been a rigid one, this is a lucid summary of the general argument I have made about the nature of the peasantry in the Middle East, conceived historically and in contrast to the west, where the legacies of late antiquity combined a tied labour force with the later expansion of peasant tenures.

The third and final plank of my argument concerns the meaning of the word 'estate' in much of the Near East. Like its sharply polarised agrarian structure, this too is a legacy of late antiquity that survived best in the Muslim world, but one which drew more on Armenian and Sasanian traditions of landholding than on any Byzantine or late Roman equivalents. The form of landholding I have in mind involves the ownership of villages (usually entire villages and often many more than one) and contrasts sharply with the Byzantine large estate that turns up in the papyri of the later fifth to seventh centuries. The latter, as I suggested at the start of this chapter, grouped its workers into estate settlements that were visibly distinct from villages and never confused with them. Since these settlements were called *epoikia*, I have described this kind of estate as '*epoikion*-type'.[143] It corresponds exactly to the *ezba* estates that proliferated in Egypt in the nineteenth century, as land was increasingly re-privatised and the ruling groups invested massively in cotton. The striking feature of the papyrological evidence is the singular absence of anything vaguely resembling the ownership of villages in late antique Egypt. In sharp contrast to this, Procopius refers to an Armenian collaborator persuading the emperor Justinian (in the early 530s) to 'present him with certain villages (*kōmai*) of Armenia'. He became, Procopius says, the 'owner' (*kyrios*) of these estates (*chōriōn*).[144] When this man was assassinated by the pro-Sasanian faction, Justinian handed the same villages over to his nephew Amazaspes.[145] Now this, it seems to me, was primarily a Sasanian tradition, as Michael Morony has argued in a paper that describes this type of landholding as

[143] Banaji, *Agrarian Change*, p. 188.

[144] Procopius, *BP* 2.3.1–2 (Dewing, *History of the Wars*, vol. 1, p. 270).

[145] Procopius, *BP* 2.3.3 and *PLRE* IIIa 54.

'village estates'.[146] Thus Hormozān owned a village which ʿUthmān later granted to Saʿd b. Abī Waqqāṣ as his *iqṭāʿ* (in its classical meaning, any concession of land).[147] In the mid-fifth century, another equally powerful Sasanian figure, Mihr Narseh, is described as 'founding' four villages and laying out orchards around them,[148] and even earlier, in the fourth century, Shāpūr II is described as 'building' the village of Vardāna near Bukhārā.[149] Indeed, in Bukhārā, where a minor Iranian aristocracy survived down to the Sāmānid period, the tradition is abundantly attested in Narshakhī's *History of Bukhara*, a tenth-century work of which the only exemplar is the Persian translation made in the early twelfth century. This refers to the buying and selling of villages, and in one passage to seventy-five 'private' villages (*dīhe khās*) 'on the river of Bukhara and the Upper Farāvāz'.[150] It is *this* tradition, I suggest, that survived both in Iran where, even in the late 1940s, the typical 'large landed proprietors' were described by Lambton as owners of villages, the *'umdeh mālikīn* whose 'estates range from single villages to several villages, the number of which, in certain exceptional cases, is alleged to run into three figures',[151] *and* in those zamindari villages of the Mughal period which, though confusingly also known as *dehāt-i-tāluqa*, were the big zamindars' *private* or exclusive possessions, as opposed to other villages, obviously the majority, over which, technically at least, their rights were essentially fiscal and the model of 'ownership' less full-blooded and closer to a hierarchy of shared claims.[152] Ownership of villages also seems to have been widespread in Egypt in the nineteenth century,[153] and as the term *'uhda* suggests, evolved at least partly from Muhammad Ali's forced restoration of the *iltizām* system (which he had abolished in 1814) and the tendency of the *muta'ahhidūn* or tax farmers

[146] M. G. Morony, 'Landholding in Seventh-Century Iraq: Late Sasanian and Early Islamic Patterns', in *The Islamic Middle East, 700–1900: Studies in Economic and Social History*, ed. A. L. Udovitch (Princeton, 1981), pp. 135–75.

[147] Balādhurī, *Futūḥ al-buldān*, 272 = P. K. Hitti, *The Origins of the Islamic State* (New York, 1916), p. 431; Abū Yūsuf, *K. al-kharāj*, 35, Ben Shemesh, *Taxation in Islam*, p. 77.

[148] Al-Ṭabarī, ser. i, 870 = al-Ṭabarī, *Sāsānids, Byzantines, Lakhmids*, pp. 104–5, which ends, 'These villages, with the gardens and the fire temples, have remained continuously in the hands of his descendants, who are well known till today'; here 'today' is almost certainly taken from al-Ṭabarī's Sasanian source and doesn't refer to his own period.

[149] Narshakhī, *Tārīkh-i Bukhārā*, pp. 44–5, Narshakhī, *The History of Bukhara, Translated from a Persian Abridgement of the Arabic Original*, trans. R. N. Frye (Cambridge, MA, 1954), p. 32.

[150] Narshakhī, *Tārīkh*, pp. 18, 21, 22, 75; Narshakhī, *History*, pp. 13–16, 54.

[151] A. K. S. Lambton, *Landlord and Peasant in Persia: A Study of Land Tenure and Land Revenue Administration* (London, 1953), p. 266, and in fact the whole of ch. 13.

[152] E.g. B. R. Grover, 'Nature of *Dehat-i-Taaluqa* (Zamindari Villages) and the Evolution of the *Taaluqdari* System during the Mughal Age', *Indian Economic and Social History Review* 2(2) (1965), 259–90, esp. pp. 266ff.

[153] G. Baer, *A History of Landownership in Modern Egypt 1800–1950* (London, 1962).

(more correctly, 'tax guarantors')[154] to treat villages whose liabilities they assumed as their private property.[155] Thus Baer points out that 'a number of observers at the time of Muhammad 'Alī simply stated that the system turned the fellahs into labourers working for the *'uhda* recipient. Artin asserts that 'Abbās granted full ownership rights to some *muta'ahhidūn*.'[156] Moreover, the ruling family's *çiftliks* also consisted of villages which the peasantry had abandoned. Some of these were enormous, e.g. 'Sa'īd's at al-Khazzān near Alexandria covered 20,000 feddans.'[157] What the Egyptian example suggests is that a model that was predominantly Iranian/Sasanian was taken over and generalised after the expansion of Islam, almost certainly through the practice of granting *villages* to members of the ruling elite, either as pure land concessions (*iqṭā'āt, qaṭā'i'*) or, later, in lieu of cash salaries, and later still as tax farms.

The general point about this form of landholding is that effectively it abandoned the mass of the peasantry to the arbitrary power and domination of a range of large landowners who came to be called by a wide variety of names. Typically, 'estate' in this Near Eastern/Islamic sense meant control (and often ownership) of villages and not the compact and discrete blocs of land that were inherited from late Rome and transformed into bilateral estates or manors under the Carolingians. Again, this reinforces my general point that in these parts of the world the peasantry, or a considerable part of it, always lived on the verge of dispossession, shadowed by landlessness. A final qualification, however; this model of the elusive boundary between peasants and landlessness doesn't preclude the existence of a wealthy peasantry; on the contrary, it explains why this village elite tended to be a small, highly concentrated group, possibly endogamous and even stable over generations,[158] and, secondly, it allows room for the evolution of estates in the more 'western' sense, as Egypt demonstrates with the *ezbas* and Sasanian Iran with the *dastgird*.

154 G. Alleaume, 'An Industrial Revolution in Agriculture? Some Observations on the Evolution of Rural Egypt in the Nineteenth Century', in *Agriculture in Egypt*, ed. Bowman and Rogan (n. 117), pp. 331–45, at 336.

155 *'Uhda* = contractual obligation of some type; *muta'ahhid* = contractor, guarantor; also, by the evolution just described, estate holder.

156 Baer, *History*, p. 15 discussing *al-'uhda* as a renewed 'basis for the creation of large estates'.

157 Baer, *History*, p. 18.

158 E.g. K. M. Cuno, 'Egypt's Wealthy Peasantry, 1740–1820: A Study of the Region of al-Manṣūra', in *Land Tenure and Social Transformation in the Middle East*, ed. T. Khalidi (Beirut, 1984), pp. 303–32.

CHAPTER 8

Late antique aristocracies
The case of Iran

No one who reads al-Ṭabarī's account of the Sasanians can fail to be struck by the fraught relationship between the Iranian *šahs* or rulers (*šāhān šāhs* as they called themselves) and Iran's aristocracy. Rulers who were hated by the aristocracy were usually overthrown or assassinated by them. Conversely, leading aristocrats were often disgraced or executed. For example, the powerful Karen known to Łazar P'arpets'i as Zarmihr (with the title *hazarawuxt*; Sōkhra, as the Arabic sources call him) was arrested and executed by the young Kavād *c*.494/5 because, says the anonymous author of the *Nihāyat*, Kavād resented his *istibdād*, that is, his high-handedness or tendency to monopolise government.[1] A major aristocrat, Shāpūr Khorbondād, was executed under Hormazd IV. And Queen Azarmidukht had the most powerful aristocrat of her day, Farrukh Hormazd, secretly murdered, ostensibly for seeking to marry her. Indeed, at least seven other high-profile executions can be listed for the four reigns between Kavād I and Khusro II.[2] In part, what this pattern reflected was the emergence from the early part of the fifth century of a series of powerful *leaders* from within the aristocracy, starting with the famous Mihr Narsī under Yazdgird I (399–420).[3] But more fundamentally, what the endemic tension between ruler and ruling class expressed in the Sasanian case was the nature of the aristocracy itself, that is, the fact that the core

[1] *Nihāyat al-'arab fī akhbār al-furs wa-l-'arab*, ed. M. T. Dāneš-Pažūh (Tehran, 1997), p. 295, line 10.

[2] The *artēštārān sālār* (lit. 'leader of the warriors') Siyāvush (Siyavakhsh, Sīāvoš) was executed late in Kavād's reign, thanks to factional intrigue. Kavād's famous diplomat Māhbōdh who secured Khusro's succession against the claims of an elder brother was murdered not long after Khusro came to power. So was the eastern aristocrat Ādhargulbad. Bahrām Ādharmāhān and Yazdan Gošnasp were both killed under Hormazd IV. Bendōy of the Khorbondād family was killed in the early years of Khusro II's reign, and the governor of *nēmrōz* (south) Mardanshah executed towards the end of it.

[3] Mihr Narsī himself, *wuzurg framādār* for the greater part of the early fifth century, was never executed but his career did end in disgrace, see N. G. Garsoïan, 'Une coïncidence supplémentaire entre les sources arméniennes et perses: Le cas du grand vizir Mihr Nersēh', *Revue des Études Arméniennes* 27 (1998–2000), 311–20.

of it did not owe its existence to the new regime and existed largely independently of it. In any case, one way of summarising all this would be to suggest that the *šahs* of the Sasan dynasty could rule only as long as they commanded the support of the aristocracy. On the other hand, the aristocracy itself lacked cohesion and leading aristocrats could be brought down because rulers were able to exploit divisions *within their own ruling class*. This double limitation engendered a recurrent instability and gave whole stretches of Sasanian history the aspect of a state constantly riven by coups.

The aristocracy that forms the subject matter of the present chapter comprised the circle of those families known either as *wuzurgān* or *xwadāyān*. On a descending scale there were first the powerful aristocratic families that dominated entire regions, even if it's not always clear where they were based; then a sort of wider military elite, highly placed military commanders who appear in isolation from any active clan or family networks; and finally, individuals who typified the court-based aristocracy and the intrigues that fermented in that milieu. These layers were quite different from the numerous *local* elites strewn across the countryside in towns like Šuštar, Šuš, Stakhr and Isfahan, or in the rural areas to the east and south of Mosul or in regions like Dailam. Dīnawarī calls the local aristocracy of Dailam that rallied around Besṭām in the 590s *ashrāf al-bilād*, and Balādhurī uses the same term *ashrāf* for the 'nobility of Isfahan', who, exceptionally, agreed to become Muslims.[4] The *shahārija* of the Mosul countryside are a perfect exemplar of these local elites. As Chase Robinson notes, the tenth-century encyclopaedist Bar Bahlūl described them as *a'yan aṣḥāb al-balad*, exact equivalents of the *ashrāf* who figure in Balādhurī and Dīnawarī.[5] They were landholders (Christians in this case) who were said to have 'owned numerous villages',[6] and said by al-Masʿūdī to rank just below the 'three great families of the Sawād', in other words, just below the aristocracy proper.[7] It is some indication of the woeful state of Sasanian scholarship that we still have no idea who those families were, since Masʿūdī doesn't mention them by name. Doubtless, one of the three was the family whose leading figure in the early seventh century was the

[4] Dīnawarī, *Kitāb al-akhbār al-ṭiwāl*, ed. V. Guirgass (Leiden 1888), p. 107, line 12, p. 106, l. 21; Balādhurī, *Futūḥ al-buldān*, ed. R. M. Ridwan (Cairo, 1932), p. 310 = *The Origins of the Islamic State*, vol. 1, trans. P. K. Hitti (New York, 1916), p. 487.

[5] C. F. Robinson, *Empire and Elites after the Muslim Conquest* (Cambridge, 2000), pp. 90ff., esp. 95.

[6] Robinson, *Empire and Elites*, pp. 94–5.

[7] Masʿūdī *Murūj al-dhahab wa-ma'ādin al-jawhar*, ed. Barbier de Meynard and Pavet de Courteille, 9 vols (Paris, 1861–77), vol. II, p. 240; cf. Robinson, *Empire and Elites*, p. 104.

powerful aristocrat known as Hormozān. Another may well have been a branch of the Spāhbad family (one of those seven great families) associated with Narsī who is described in one tradition as the 'son of Khusro's maternal aunt' (Khusro Parvez),[8] that is, a nephew of Besṭām and Bendōy whom we shall turn to shortly. Narsī's estates were concentrated in the fertile region of Kaskar, and his daughter Kamurzad is said to have owned a 'castle' (*qaṣr*) not far from Baṣra.[9]

The landscape of fragmented kingdoms and lordships inherited from Parthian times was never fully obliterated by Ardashir in the third century, and though Ardashir himself is credited with the ruthless subordination/extermination of local rulers (the *mulūk al-ṭawā'if*), both epigraphic and other evidence suggests that next to the purely local elites who formed the true base of Sasanian power, there were numerous local dynasts (rulers of tribes or territories) who continued to exist in all the outlying regions. Their existence is formally acknowledged in Shāpūr I's inscriptions, but they also turn up repeatedly in the literary sources. Thus the famous Letter of Tansar is addressed to 'Gošnasp king of Parišwār and Tabaristān'.[10] His possessions included Dunbāvand,[11] and his descendants used a nomenclature entirely peculiar to themselves. Some of these local dynasts descended from or even intermarried with the ruling family but clearly the vast majority could have had no such connection. Thus the 'Mēšūn xwadāy Mihršah' whom Mani converted some time before 262[12] was a brother of Shapur I and ruler of Mesene, and 'Ādurfarrōbay Mēšān šah' who figures prominently in the Paikuli inscription as an opponent of Narsī son of Bahrām in his struggle with Bahrām III was doubtless a descendant.[13] We do need to mention these

8 Ṭabarī, *Ta'rīkh*, ser. i, p. 2168 = al-Ṭabarī, *The Challenge to the Empires (The History of al-Ṭabarī, vol. xi)*, trans. K. Y. Blankinship (Albany, 1993), p. 182.

9 Yāqūt, *Mu'jam al-buldān*, ed. F. Wüstenfeld, *Jacut's geographisches Wörterbuch* (Leipzig, 1866 –73), vol. IV, p. 844 found Kāmurzād in his copy of Balādhurī, not 'Kāmindār' as in Balādhurī, *Futūḥ al-buldān*, p. 336 = *The Origins of the Islamic State*, part II, trans. F. C. Murgotten (New York, 1924), p. 51. And *qaṣr* is surely better seen as a fortified palatial residence of sorts than a castle. For Narsī's estates see Bal'amī, *Tārīkhnāmah-i Ṭabarī*, ed. M. Raushan (Tehran, 1987–8), p. 433; Ṭabarī, *Challenge to the Empires*, p. 182; M. G. Morony, *Iraq after the Muslim Conquest* (Princeton, 1984), pp. 185–6.

10 M. Boyce, *The Letter of Tansar* (Rome, 1968), p. 29. Mas'ūdī, *Kitāb al-tanbīh wa'l-ishrāf*, ed. M. J. de Goeje (Leiden, 1894), p. 99 (= *Livre de l'avertissement et de la revision*, trans. B. Carra de Vaux (Paris, 1897), p. 142) calls him Māh-Gošnasp, ماجُشْنَس, and ruler (*sāhib*) of 'Dabāvand (= Damāvand), Rayy, Tabaristan, Daylam and Gilan'.

11 M.-L. Chaumont, 'États vassaux dans l'empire des premiers Sasssanides', in *Monumentum H. S. Nyberg*, vol. I (Leiden and Tehran, 1975), pp. 89–137, at 113.

12 M. Boyce, *A Reader in Manichaean Middle Persian and Parthian: Texts with Notes* (Leiden and Tehran), p. 37 (text f), *bid Šābuhr šāhān šāh brād būd Mēšūn xwadāy, ud Mihršāh nām ahāz.*

13 P. O. Skjærvø, *The Sassanian Inscription of Paikuli*, part 3/1: *Restored Text and Translation* (Wiesbaden, 1983), §§34–7 (pp. 44 ff.).

local rulers because in any broader study of the Sasanian aristocracy they would have to count as an obvious sector of the aristocracy, poised between the more powerful aristocrats and the local *ashrāf* and rural elites. There is an explicit reference to them in Khusro Anosharvan's admonition to the ruling class preserved in the *Dēnkard*. 'It is necessary that lords, rulers and men in high authority as well as other people should know each one of these three sayings and should carry them out without fail. One is to know transience; one is humility; one is contentment.'[14] The terms used in this fascinating text are *xwadāyān*, *pādexšāyān* and *tawānīgān*. The *pādexšāyān* were the various territorial rulers who, like Māh-Gošnasp in Tansar's Letter, had claims or pretensions to royalty. The discussion in this chapter leaves them aside to look chiefly at the *xwadāyān*, the aristocracy proper, and the *tawānīgān*, powerful officials, both military and court-based, who were not necessarily from aristocratic backgrounds. The generic term for both these groups was *wuzurgān*.

Three sectors of the aristocracy

The Sasanian aristocracy in the broader sense of the *wuzurgān* is probably best divided into (1) a more traditional aristocracy that comprised a group of powerful *regional barons* and (2) a broader elite of *military governors* that emerged in the sixth century with Khusro I's reorganisation of the Sasanian military command. Among the former, some aristocrats were related to the royal family through intermarriage, notably, the Spāhbads, the clan led by Shapur son of Khorbondād in the late sixth century, while others, possibly the majority, had no special connection of this sort, for example, none is attested for Farrukh Hormazd of Azerbaijan who, as I noted earlier, was executed for presuming to seek a matrimonial alliance with Azarmidukht. The former, royally related subgroup among the regional barons had clearly amassed vast amounts of land by the end of the Sasanian period, for much or all of this passed directly into the holdings set aside as *ṣāfiyah* properties or *ṣawāfī* shortly after the conquest.[15] On the other hand, the spahbeds or military elite were both pivotal figures in the administration and as actively involved in the power struggles of the late sixth and seventh centuries as the great regional barons. The best

[14] Aturpāt-i Ēmētān, *The Wisdom of the Sasanian Sages (Denkard VI)*, trans. S. Shaked (Boulder, CO, 1979), pp. 180–1, *xwadāyan ud pādexšāyān ud tawānīgān*.

[15] Note the reference to these estates in Ṭabarī, *Ta'rīkh*, ser. i, p. 2371 = al-Ṭabarī, *The Battle of Qādisiyyah and the Conquest of Syria and Palstine* (*The History of al-Ṭabarī*, vol. xii), trans. Y. Friedmann (Albany, 1992), pp. 154–5; *Ta'rīkh*, ser. i/5, pp. 2468–9, 2471 = al-Ṭabarī, *The Conquest of Iraq, Southwestern Persia, and Egypt* (*The History of al-Ṭabarī*, vol. xiii), trans. H. A. Juynboll (Albany, 1989), pp. 48–9, 51.

examples of this sector of Iran's aristocracy are the military commanders who turn up on the seals published by Rika Gyselen (for example, Bahrām Ādurmāhān, also known to us from the Greek and Syriac sources)[16] or the generals who led Khusro II's invasion of the west or finally a host of purely military men inducted into the defence of Iran against invading Arab armies in the 630s. If the barons were defined *essentially* by their regional power base and were thus major landed aristocrats as well (a militarised aristocracy with a territorial base, similar to the great Anatolian families of the Middle Byzantine aristocracy), the purely military elite seem mostly to lack any obvious background of this sort, although as the seals show, they certainly thought of themselves as *wuzurgān*, that is, aristocrats. Finally, and at least *partly* distinct from both of the sectors just described, was a court aristocracy, a Sasanian equivalent of the *Kongisnähe* in the west, leading exemplars of which can be tracked throughout the sixth and early seventh centuries, from the major aristocrats who worked as diplomats for Kavād I and his son Khusro I down to Meh-Ādur Gošnasp who ran the empire for Ardashir son of Kavād II a century later, between September 628 and April 630. I say 'at least partly distinct' because the sixth-century Surens are a good example of the otherwise fluid boundaries between some of these aristocratic sectors, as I show later.

The key fact to note about these various sectors of the aristocracy in Iran is that the aristocracy as a whole was completely lacking in cohesion at all levels, both across the diverse formations of which it was composed, from purely local dynasts (rulers of tribes or territories) to the great aristocratic houses (*ahl al-buyutat* in Ṭabarī), the new military elite and the court nobility, *and*, more significantly, within those various groups and categories. The model suggested here is thus the very antithesis of over-generalised notions of the ruling class that give it a coherence and often a cohesiveness that ruling classes in the late antique and early medieval worlds simply did not possess. The clearest case of this is Ostrogorsky's picture of the Byzantine aristocracy as a unified ensemble pitted *collectively* against the state.[17] On the other hand, all of these strata and sectors were clearly unified at some level by a commonality of interest in relation to other groups and classes in society and were viewed as such by the state itself, as a consistent social nomenclature shows.[18] However, before

[16] R. Gyselen, *The Four Generals of the Sasanian Empire: Some Sigillographic Evidence* (Rome, 2001); R. Gyselen, *Sasanian Seals and Sealings in the A. Saeedi Collection* (Louvain, 2007).

[17] See C. S. Sifonas, 'Basile II et l'aristocratie byzantine', *Byzantion* 64 (1994), 118–33 for the alternative view espoused here.

[18] See I. Colditz, *Zur Sozialterminologie der iranischen Manichäer* (Wiesbaden, 2000).

coming to the way this affected the nature of conflicts in Sasanian imperial history, it is worth saying something more about each of the three aristocratic sectors outlined earlier.

At the end of the sixth and in the early seventh centuries the most powerful families in the elite sector were those of Shāpūr son of Khorbondād of the Spāhbad clan and Farrukh Hormazd of Azerbaijan. It is curious that the mid-seventh-century history attributed to Sebeos describes Shāpūr as 'the great Parthian and Pahlaw *aspet*' and again 'the great *asparapet*, the Parthian and Pahlaw' (in both cases meaning *spāhbed* or 'general') but nowhere records his name.[19] For that, both his name and his father's, we are entirely indebted to Dīnawarī.[20] But Sebeos supplies two crucial details that don't seem to be available elsewhere – that Shapur was military governor of Armenia for seven years (in the early 580s, as Howard-Johnston notes),[21] and that he was murdered by Hormazd in the great purge of the aristocracy that dominated the last years of that ruler's reign. Both Ṭabarī and Masʿūdī cite figures for the staggering scale of this purge, the most traumatic in Sasanian history, and even if the numbers seem incredible we have an abundance of early and reliable testimony to support the impression of a massive assault.[22] Indeed, John of Ephesus, who died around 586, could already describe Hormazd as a 'ferocious and savage youth' and claim that he had slaughtered some of his male siblings and blinded the rest.[23] Theophylact who wrote in the late 620s and based his Sasanian material on John of Epiphania decribes Hormazd as a 'violent man' who was 'most hostile towards his subjects, the most powerful of whom he subjected to eternal fetters and chains', hacking some to pieces and drowning others.[24] The Persian source that Sebeos drew on in the mid-seventh century stated that Hormazd 'eliminated all the nobles and ancient lines and original houses from the land of Persia', citing as the

[19] Sebeos, *The Armenian History Attributed to Sebeos*, 2 vols, trans. R. W. Thomson (Liverpool, 1999), vol. 1, 73 (p. 14); 71 (pp. 11–12). (Throughout this chapter, of course, 'Sebeos' is simply shorthand for whoever actually composed the *History*. J. Howard-Johnston, *Witnesses to a World Crisis: Historians and Histories of the Middle East in the Seventh Century* (Oxford, 2010) ch.3 has a careful assessment.)

[20] Dīnawarī, *Kitāb al-akhbār*, p. 107, ll.2–3.

[21] Howard-Johnston in Sebeos, *Armenian History*, p. 166.

[22] Ṭabarī, *Ta'rīkh*, ser. i, p. 990, ll.14–15 = al-Ṭabarī, *The Sāsānids, the Byzantines, the Lakhmids, and Yemen (The History of al-Ṭabarī, vol. v)*, trans. C. E. Bosworth (Albany, 1999), p. 297; Masʿūdī, *Murūj al-dhahab*, vol. 11, p. 211.

[23] John of Ephesus, *The Third Part of the Ecclesiastical History of John Bishop of Ephesus*, trans. R. Payne Smith (Oxford, 1860), pp. 423, 439.

[24] Theophylact, *History*, 3.16.8–9 (Michael and Mary Whitby, *The History of Theophylact Simocatta* (Oxford, 1986), p. 98.)

leading example of this his execution of Shapur Khorbondād.[25] Shapur's daughter was, as Sebeos says, 'mother of the royal prince', that is, the mother of Khusro Parvez.[26] His sons Bendōy and Besṭām were pivotal to the events that led to the coup against Hormazd and to the civil wars that dominated most of the 590s. In Dīnawarī the execution of Hormazd is directly attributed to them, especially Bendōy, who seems to have been the more forceful of the two brothers. But the fate of this family is a stunning illustration of the volatility of aristocratic fortunes. Bendōy and Besṭām were crucial to the success of Khusro's campaigns against Bahrām Čōbīn and the pay-off was substantial. Bendōy became treasurer and grand minister of the state while Besṭām was made governor of Tabaristan, Gorgān, Kōmeš (Kumis) and Khorasan, a wide swathe of territory to the south and east of the Caspian.[27] But Khusro's decision to seek vengeance for the murder of his father would lead to the brutal execution of Bendōy (this, according to Dīnawarī, happened not in Ctesiphon but in Ḥulwān), which then triggered a major rebellion in the course of which Besṭām attracted substantial support throughout the northern provinces, even crowning himself king and issuing coins from Rayy. Again, Dīnawarī provides some fascinating details about the provenance of Besṭām's support, which, he says, included 'a substantial group from the members of his house (*ahl baytihi*) in the region of Iraq',[28] the closest reference we have to the provenance of Shapur's family other than Sebeos' repeated and vague references to their Parthian origins. At any rate, this story ends with the wholesale extermination of some sixty members of the family, a detail we owe to Movsēs Dasxurants'i.[29]

The other powerful family, prominent chiefly in the seventh century, is that of Farrukh Hormazd, or Khořokh Ormizd as the Armenian sources call him. The family's ancestral territory was Azerbaijan (or Atrapatakan), which is why Sebeos repeatedly refers to him and his two famous sons as 'prince of the region of Atrpatakan' or 'the great prince in Atrpatakan' or (in Rustam's case) 'prince in the territory of Atrpatakan' or, finally (of

[25] Sebeos, *Armenian History*, 73 (p. 14). [26] Sebeos, *Armenian History*, 75 (p. 17).
[27] Dīnawarī, *Kitāb al-akhbār*, p. 102, ll.13ff., A. Sh. Shahbazi, 'Besṭām o Bendōy', *Encyclopaedia Iranica* 4 (1990), 180–2, at p. 181.
[28] Dīnawarī, *Kitāb al-akhbār*, p. 107, ll.13–14.
[29] Movsēs Dasxurants'i, *The History of the Caucasian Albanians by Movsēs Dasxuranċi*, trans. C. J. F. Dowsett (London, 1961), p. 107, cf. Bal'amī, *Les prophètes et les rois de Salomon á la chute des Sassanides*, ed. H. Zotenberg (Paris, 1984), p. 379. This had happened before in Sasanian history, cf. the slaughter of the Karen by Ardashir I reported in Moses Khorenats'i, *History of the Armenians*, trans. R. W. Thomson (Cambridge, MA, 1978), p. 219. Also Arshak's massacre of the Kamsarakan family in *History of the Armenians*, p. 287ff.

Khurrazad, his other son), 'prince of the Medes' (this in two passages).[30] It is important to note that these designations (the term used throughout these passages is *išxan*) referred not to their offices or to any formal position they held in the Sasanian administration but to the power they wielded in the region from which the family came and where it was actively based. Thus Abū Manṣūr al-Thaʿālibī even calls Rustam and Farrukhzad 'Azerbaijanis' (الآذرى).[31] Balʿamī tells us that Farrukh Hormazd was a military governor of Khorasan under Khusro Parvez, a position he must have acquired for being one of Khusro's staunchest supporters in his war against Bahrām Čōbīn alongside the uncles Bestam and Bendōy. Since his son Rustam is repeatedly described as his deputy in Khorasan, this suggests that Farrukh himself chose to stay at court, close to the centre of power, and Balʿamī even says so in so many words.[32] The spāhbeds were absolutely pivotal figures in the power structure of the late Sasanian period, and that one of them could choose to have his son depute for him only shows just how confident Farrukh Hormazd felt of his position under Khusro. In the succession crisis of the early 630s he was in fact described as the single most powerful aristocrat in Iran, 'the outstanding great man of Persia at that time', as Ṭabarī calls him.[33] Al-Yaʿqūbī claims that he boasted to Azarmidukht that he was 'a hero of the people and a pillar of the state'.[34] Be that as it may, and whatever the true reasons, Azarmidukht had him murdered, which forced Rustam to return to Ctesiphon and have her killed. The pattern that emerges through a lot of Sasanian history is the unwillingness of rulers to put up with members of the aristocracy who were seen to be either too popular or too powerful or both. Underlying that of course was an endemic tension between rulers and sections of the aristocracy that manifests itself time again from the later third to the seventh centuries. But about the pattern just referred to, recall Kavād's toppling of Sokhra in the first of his two reigns, using the Mihrans against the Karens; Hormazd's covert assassination of Yazdan Gošnasp, which is said to have triggered his own downfall; and Khusro's execution of Mardānshāh, probably spāhbed of the southern region (*kust i nēmrōz*) of whom Ṭabarī says that he (Khusro) grew suspicious of

[30] Sebeos, *Armenian History*, 130 (p. 89), 132 (p. 92).

[31] al-Thaʿālibī, *Ghuraru akhbāri mulūk al-furs wa-siyarihim*, ed. H. Zotenberg, *Histoire des rois des Perses: Texte arabe publié et traduit* (Paris, 1900), p. 738.

[32] Balʿamī, *Tārīkh-i Balʿamī*, ed. M. T. Bahār *et al.* (Tehran, 1974), vol. II, pp. 1202–3; Balʿamī, *Les prophètes et les rois*, p. 388.

[33] Ṭabarī, *Taʾrīkh*, ser. i, p. 1065, ll.2ff. = al-Ṭabarī, *Sāsānids, Byzantines*, p. 406.

[34] Yaʿqūbī, *Taʾrīkh*, 2 vols, ed. M. Th. Houtsma (Leiden, 1883), vol. I, p. 197, ll.12ff.

Mardānshāh on account of his 'great prestige and because *there was no one in that region who could equal him in strength and power*'.[35] It is therefore remarkable that when the succession crisis was finally settled, Yazdgird would go on to appoint Rustam as his chief commander in the fight against the Arabs. These *išxans* of Atrapatakan were much too powerful to dislodge or dispense with by this stage when the armies themselves had disintegrated into regional divisions and Farrukh Hormazd's family controlled the northern troops. When Rustam died at Qādisiyya, his brother Khurrazad emerged as Yazdgird's chief deputy at Ctesiphon, as Yazdgird himself fled to Hulwan. At least that is the tradition reported by Dīnawarī and Ibn Qutayba.[36] Sebeos says that following the massive defeat at Qādisiyya the remnants of the army regrouped in Azerbaijan and installed Khurrazad as their commander, following which he hastened to Ctesiphon to evacuate the royal family and their treasures.[37] And, finally, Thaʿālibī reports that Yazdgird had already deputed Khurrazad to manage affairs in Ctesiphon when he despatched Rustam to Qādisiyya.[38] Whatever the true sequence of these various events, the fact remains that the imperial power was now largely and critically dependent on the progeny of Farrukh Hormazd, *išxan* of the region of Atrapatakan, as Sebeos would describe him.

The third aristocrat worth looking at is Hormozān. Dīnawarī says he was the maternal uncle of Šērōya,[39] that is, of Kavad II, Khusro Parvez's son and unwanted successor who was forced by the aristocracy to sanction the execution of his father and then pressured into slaughtering almost all his male siblings. When news of the Persian defeat at Jalula reached Yazdgird in Ḥulwān and he decided to flee to Qumm and to Kāshān in central Persia, Hormozān was made military commander over Khuzistan and Fars. According to Dīnawarī, he was despatched to Šuštar.[40] But again, as with Farrukh Hormazd, it is important to retain the distinction between the offices members of the elite were appointed to and the dominance they exercised as members of a hereditary aristocracy (a duality that is even more sharply articulated with the Armenian princely houses). The latter, as I said, was marked by a strongly territorial aspect. If Farrukh Hormazd was the great prince of Azerbaijan, as the Armenians described him, Hormozān was the ruler of much of southern Iraq, namely, Ahwāz

[35] Ṭabarī, *Ta'rīkh*, ser. i, pp. 1058–9 = al-Ṭabarī, *Sāsānids, Byzantines*, p. 396.

[36] Dīnawarī, *Kitāb al-akhbār*, p. 133, ll.12–13; Ibn Qutaybah, *Kitāb al-mā'arif*, ed. S. Okacha (Cairo, 1960), p. 667.

[37] Sebeos, *Armenian History*, 137 (p. 99).

[38] Thaʿālibī, *Ghuraru akhbāri*, p. 739.

[39] Dīnawarī, *Kitāb al-akhbār*, p. 136, ll.14–15.

[40] Dīnawarī, *Kitāb al-akhbār*, pp. 136–7.

or Khuzistan. In a remarkable passage that is not a mere replica of Ṭabarī, Balʿami tells us, 'Hormozān was the ruler (*malek*) of Ahwāz. He was a man of the aristocracy (*mardi bozorg*) and sovereignty over Ahwaz lay with him and his family. Ahwaz consists of some seventy towns (*Ahwaz haftād shahr ast*). Hormozān was the ruler (*pādešāh*) of all those towns.'[41] Even more extraordinary, when he was eventually captured (in 642?) and shipped from Baṣra to Medina, ʿUmar is supposed to have asked him, 'Which region are you from?' Hormozān replied, 'I am a Mehrajāni.'[42] As Balādhurī says, Hormozān was a native of Mehrajān-Qadhaq,[43] a fertile district south-west of Media, as Shahbazi notes.[44] This is a fascinating indication of how deeply rooted regional identities were even at these elite levels of Sasanian society. Ṭabarī himself uses the words *qaum* and *ummah* when he refers to Hormozān's home base or his 'territory',[45] as the translator would have it. And of course those terms retain a much stronger social aspect (something more like Hormozān's people, the subjects – *raʿīyat* – he ruled over) than the word 'territory' conveys.

The opposition at Šuštar was fierce.[46] Hormozān himself exemplifies that sector of the Sasanian aristocracy (the bulk of it, in fact) that mounted strong resistance to the Arabs, unlike their Armenian counterparts a decade or two later and certainly quite unlike the *dahāqin* or village landlords. Finally, Ṭabarī notes that Hormozān himself 'was one of the seven noble families among the Persians', though we have no idea which one.

To move on to the military elite, perhaps the best example of the group that I have called highly placed military officers whose family backgrounds are barely known to us is Shahrvaraz. I have dealt with him elsewhere, arguing that we should identify him with the mysterious 'Shahralanyozan' who turns up in the papyri, both Greek and Middle Persian, with the epithets *paneuphēmos* and *xwadāy*.[47] No Greek papyrus from Egypt would have used the term *paneuphēmos* for any personage of less exalted rank than the highest aristocracy, and we have the explicit testimony of Sebeos that it was Shahrvaraz who controlled Alexandria in 629 when

41 Balʿamī, *Tārīkhnāmah-i Ṭabarī*, ed. Raushan, p. 490.

42 Ṭabarī, *Taʾrīkh*, ser. i., p. 2560 = al-Ṭabarī, *Conquest of Iraq*, p. 140.

43 Balādhurī, *Futūḥ al-buldān*, p. 373; Murgotten, *Origins of the Islamic State*, p. 117.

44 A. Sh. Shahbazi, 'Hormozān', *Encyclopaedia Iranica* 12 (2004), 460–1.

45 Ṭabarī, *Taʾrīkh*, ser. i/5, pp. 2534, 2538 = al-Ṭabarī, *Conquest of Iraq*, pp. 114–15, 119 ('territory' in both passages).

46 Balādhurī, *Futūḥ al-buldān*, p. 373; Murgotten, *Origins of the Islamic State*, p. 117.

47 See J. Banaji, 'On the Identity of Shahrālānyōzān in the Greek and Middle Persian Papyri from Egypt', in *Documents and the History of the Early Islamic World*, ed. A. T. Schubert and P. M. Sijpesteijn (Leiden and Boston, 2015), pp. 27–42.

Heraclius opened negotiations with him for the treaty that was concluded at Arabissos in July that year – a view corroborated by reports in the Syriac sources, and also in Tha'ālibī and Ibn Miskawayh, which all attribute the siege and capture of Alexandria in 619 to Shahrvaraz.[48] His rapid ascent to power within the military administration was again due to the decisive support he gave Khusro II in his war with Bahrām Čōbīn, a fact noted by pseudo-Dionysius.[49] His actual name was of course Farrukhan and, like so many of the purely military and court-based aristocracy, he was soon sucked into intrigues whose outcome would determine the fate of the empire in those fateful years from 627 to 632. When the Greek offensive penetrated deep into Sasanian territory towards the end of 627, 'Khoṙeam', Sebeos tells us, 'did not come to the aid of king Khosrov, but remained right where he was in the west.'[50] The decision to *abandon* Khusro at this crucial juncture was an extraordinary one and a powerful factor in the growing rift between Parvez and the military that is consistently attested across a range of sources. Šērōya's famous *risāla* rehearsing charges against Khusro is reported differently in different sources but perhaps most accurately in Dīnawarī, where one of the key accusations is that Khusro actually ordered the execution (fortunately never carried out) of thousands of civilian and military commanders, alleging that they were 'the first to be routed or put to flight in the wars against Rome'.[51] At any rate, in Theophanes' eastern source it was Shahrvaraz who instigated large-scale disaffection among the military commanders.[52] His own bid for power following the intrigues that led to the murder of Kavād's son Ardashir, still a child, in April 630, had, uniquely, no support in the wider aristocracy. He was in fact a hated figure and soon assassinated in another intrigue which, according to Ṭabarī, involved 'a large number of the great men of state and members of leading families'.[53] Among the various traditions recounting the coup against Shahrvaraz the most interesting is Mas'ūdī's. He claims that Azarmidukht was the real author of this putsch, which of course paved the way for the accession of her sister Boran.[54]

[48] Sebeos, *Armenian History*, 129 (p. 88). Al-Zuhrī's account preserved in Ibn 'Abd al-Ḥakam implies the same by noting Shahrvaraz's prolonged absence in Egypt, cf. W. E. Kaegi and P. M. Cobb, 'Heraclius, Shahrbarāz, and al-Ṭabarī', in *Al-Tabari: A Medieval Muslim Historian and his Work*, ed. H. Kennedy (Princeton, NJ, 2008), pp. 95–112.

[49] Palmer, *Seventh Century*, p. 117. [50] Sebeos, *Armenian History*, 127 (pp. 84–5).

[51] Dīnawarī, *Kitāb al-akhbār*, p. 112, ll.16ff.

[52] Theophanes, *Chronicle*, AM 6118, AD 625/6; C. Mango and R. Scott, *The Chronicle of Theophanes Confessor: Byzantine and Near Eastern History AD 284–813* (Oxford, 1997), p. 453.

[53] Ṭabarī, *Ta'rīkh*, ser. i, p. 1063 = al-Ṭabarī, *Sāsānids, Byzantines*, p. 403.

[54] Mas'ūdī, *Murūj al-dhahab*, vol. II, p. 233.

The spāhbeds were the dominant figures in the Sasanian power elite. Bahrām Čōbīn, son of Bahrām Gošnasp (Jushnas) was almost certainly spāhbed of the North under Hormazd, as Shahbazi suggests.[55] His defeat at the hands of Byzantine forces in Albania led to the rapid estrangement of Hormazd and Bahrām and set the stage for the dramatic events that followed. His usurpation of power in 590 and the claim that he was ruling on behalf of Shahriyar, a younger son of Hormazd, split the aristocracy, showing just how uncertain their allegiances were.[56] Bahrām is well known if only because he became a legendary figure but there are a fair number of spāhbeds about whom we know very little indeed. Mihran son of Mihribondad was from Hamadān and is consistently described as 'al-Hamadhāni', suggesting that that was their regional power base. Both Ṭabarī and Balādhurī emphasise his aristocratic background.[57] His defeat at the hands of al-Muthanna opened the way to the invasion of the Sawad. Azādhbih, the Sasanian governor of Ḥīra for some nineteen years, from the reign of Khusro II down to Boran, was, interestingly, from the same family.[58] Namdar Gošnasp, who was governor of Armenia in the early 620s,[59] went on to become spāhbed of the South and held that position when he actively conspired with Shahrvaraz to have the infant Ardashir murdered and bring the former to the throne.[60] What's interesting here is that his father, Meh-Ādur Gošnasp, was the key figure who had held the royal family together when he acted as Ardashir's deputy from late 628 to April 630. Ṭabarī notes that he set about 'fortifying and strengthening the walls and gates of the city of Ctesiphon'.[61] He was hated by Shahrvaraz and would doubtless have died in the massive purge that followed the latter's coup when, as Sebeos tells us, 'All the principal men at court or in the army in whom he (Shahrvaraz) could place no trust he commanded to be put to the sword.'[62] What emerges here is a pattern found repeatedly in the history of the Sasanian aristocracy, namely the deep political divisions that

[55] A. Sh. Shahbazi, 'Bahrām VI Čōbīn', *Encyclopaedia Iranica* 3 (1989), 519–22, at p. 519, cf. Dīnawari, *Kitāb al-akhbār*, pp. 81, l. 20–82, l. 1.

[56] Bal'ami, *Les prophètes et les rois*, pp. 335–6.

[57] Balādhurī, *Futūḥ al-buldān*, p. 336, l. 12; Murgotten, *Origins of the Islamic State*, p. 52; Ṭabarī, *Ta'rīkh*, ser. i, p. 2201, ll.11ff. = al-Ṭabarī, *Challenge to the Empires*, p. 214, where the father's name is given as Bādān.

[58] Ṭabarī, *Ta'rīkh*, ser. i, p. 1038 = al-Ṭabarī, *Sāsānids, Byzantines*, p. 372. For his father's name see Ḥamza al-Isfahani, *Ta'rīkh sinī mulūk al-arḍ*, ed. J. M. E. Gottwaldt (Leipzig, 1848), vol. 1, p. 112, l. 3, ماهبيان

[59] Sebeos, *Armenian History*, 113 (p. 66).

[60] Ṭabarī, *Ta'rīkh*, ser. i, p. 1062, ll.11ff. = al-Ṭabarī, *Sāsānids, Byzantines*, p. 401.

[61] Ṭabarī, *Ta'rīkh*, ser. i, pp. 1061, ll.15ff., 1062, ll.4ff. = al-Ṭabarī, *Sāsānids, Byzantines*, p. 401.

[62] Sebeos, *Armenian History*, 130 (p. 88).

could run *within* families, as if to suggest that the overall lack of cohesion that characterised the aristocracy as a whole was just as true of the individual families that made up the class. Thus Bahrām Čōbīn's immediate family was vertically split in the great conflict following Hormazd's deposition and murder, with his brother siding with Khusro. The struggle between Khusro and his maternal uncles has been mentioned already. And Yazdan Jushnas (Gošnasp), a leading and highly regarded court aristocrat whose murder was blamed on Hormazd,[63] was in fact killed by his own cousin on his father's side, presumably at the behest of the king.[64]

The court aristocracy, finally. Here it is the sixth-century material that throws up the most striking illustrations of this group. The Suren who governed Armenia in the 560s and was eventually assassinated by Vardan Mamikonean in 572, following sharp conflicts with that clan in particular,[65] had also served as a diplomat under Khusro I.[66] He was the son of an even more famous diplomat, the Māhbōdh (Mebodes in the Greek sources) who represented Kavād during the peace negotiations with Justin I in 525/6. Māhbōdh is said by Procopius to have been a *Königsnahe* of Kavād and the key figure in arranging the succession of Khusro I against the claims of Kavād's eldest son, Kavus.[67] His intrigues against Siyavush, a hugely powerful figure under Kavād and more hostile to a settlement with Byzantium than Māhbōdh himself, had led to the former's downfall, and he himself would eventually be executed by Khusro soon after his accession to the throne in 531.[68] This is not all, however. Suren or Čihr Gošnasp as Stephen of Taron calls him, using his actual name,[69] also had a son Māhbōdh who, like both previous generations of this family, worked as a diplomat in the closing years of Khusro's reign. The exalted nature of his position is indicated by the title he is said by both Menander and Theophylact to have borne, viz. *sarnachōragan*, which loosely translated

[63] Bal'ami, *Les prophètes et les rois*, p. 327.

[64] Dīnawarī, *Kitāb al-akhbār*, p. 87, ll.9 (cousin), 14ff. (triggers coup).

[65] *Narratio de rebus Armeniae*, 77 (p. 37) in G. Garitte, *La Narratio de rebus Armeniae: Édition critique et commentaire* (Louvain, 1952), with the invaluable commentary at pp. 175–89. Cf. M. L. Chaumont, 'Armenia and Iran II', *Encyclopaedia Iranica* 2 (1987), 431 : 'The new governor [Čihr-Gušnasp]... took stern measures against *naxarars* suspected of collusion with the Byzantines ...'

[66] Menander, fr. 6.1 (R. C. Blockley, *The History of Menander the Guardsman* (Liverpool, 1985), p. 71).

[67] Procopius, *Bell.* I.21.17ff. (Dewing, *History of the Wars*, vol. I, pp. 198ff.).

[68] Procopius, *Bell.* I.11.31–2 (Dewing, *History*, p. 92), 23.25–9 (Dewing, *History*, pp. 216ff.). On the wider diplomatic/political aspect of this conflict, see H. Börm, *Prokop und die Perser* (Stuttgart, 2007), pp. 318–25, esp. 320, 323.

[69] Stephen of Taron, *Des Stephanos von Taron Armenische Geschichte aus dem altarmenischen übersetzt*, trans. H. Gelzer and A. Burckhardt (Leipzig, 1907), p. 60.

could mean 'chief dignitary'.[70] Then there was Yazd Gošnasp, who went to Constantinople on numerous occasions between the late 540s and 567, in 562 on the same embassy as 'Suren'. He, according to Menander, had the rank of 'sacred chamberlain' (in 561) and was descended from the family or clan named Zikh, so that the Greek historian repeatedly calls him 'the Zikh' as if this was the designation of a rank (*axiōma*) he held rather than his family name.[71] Procopius resented the freedom he enjoyed in moving about freely in the capital and being able apparently to conduct all manner of business transactions there. He describes Yazd Gošnasp 'being followed by a huge throng of retainers' as he moved around the city, with at least two aristocrats in his entourage who wore golden diadems on their heads.[72] The court-based aristocracy played a major role in the intrigues that led to a rapid succession of rulers in 628–32.

The taxonomy suggested earlier does not imply either that the boundaries between these sectors were rigid and impermeable or that the same aristocrat might not assume all three roles. The best late Sasanian example of the latter is Farrukh Hormazd: he was *simultaneously* a powerful regional baron, 'prince of Atrapatakan', as the Armenian sources describe him, military governor of Khorasan *and* court-based (which is why his son Rustam deputed for him in the east). The court in fact is where much of the factionalism of Sasanian aristocratic politics was directly played out, and always the immediate site of major power struggles even when the final outcome of those struggles depended on the command of military force, as with Kavād I's return to power following his removal by the aristocracy or by one faction of it. The ability to influence the course of events or determine the shape of imperial policy depended directly on the aristocracy's access to the court. Striking proof of this is Kavād's desire, during his first reign, to remove the powerful Sokhra *from the court* by appointing him to the governorship of Fars.[73] That unleashed a swirl of factional backbiting against Sokhra and paved the way for Kavād's cynical use of Shapur (from the Mihran clan at Rayy) to engineer his downfall and execution. The execution of powerful aristocrats that I started by referring to would often trigger aristocratic revolts in Sasanian history, and certainly

[70] Theophylact, III.5.14 (M. Whitby, *The History*, p. 79) ('son of Surenas'); Menander, fr. 20.1 (Blockley, *History*, p. 180) and Theophylact, III.15.7; 11 (Whitby, *History*, pp. 96–7) (title).

[71] Menander, fr. 6.1 (Blockley, *History*, p. 64), fr. 6.1 (p. 54); cf. PLRE IIIA, pp. 722–3; wrongly identified by F. Justi, *Iranisches Namenbuch* (Marburg, 1895), p. 149 with the Yazdan Gošnasp executed by Hormazd IV, since Yazd Gošnasp died in 567, cf. Menander, fr. 9.3 (Blockley, *History*, p. 106).

[72] Procopius, *Bell.* VIII. 11.4–6 (Dewing, *History*, vol. V, p. 148), 19–20 (pp. 212ff.).

[73] Thaʿālibī, *Ghuraru akhbāri*, p. 587.

this one did, with the bulk of the aristocracy and army leadership deciding to depose the young ruler in favour of his brother Jamasp.

Struggles within the ruling class

This may be the best place to stand back and look at the struggles within the ruling class in a more direct way. Conflicts between aristocracy and rulers, civil wars and factionalism within the aristocracy[74] were all forms of this, and the decades that ran from the 570s to the early 630s were all replete with dramatic and even spectacular cases of each of these. Relations between ruler and aristocracy became exceptionally violent in the final decades of the sixth century and again in the 620s. Hormazd's purge of the aristocracy seems to have been a traumatic event, unprecedented for its scale and directed at least in part against the *Königsnahe* of his father's regime. Among its known victims were Burz-Mihr and Bahrām Ādurmāhān, both of whom turn up on the seals published by Gyselen as military governors of Khorasan and Nemroz respectively (the latter under Khusro I).[75] Surprisingly, Gyselen herself makes no reference to the passage in Thaʿālibī[76] that *links these figures together* by telling us that when Hormazd set about exterminating the aristocracy, starting with leading members of his father's court, he used Burz-Mihr to try and incriminate Bahrām. We are dealing surely with the same set of individuals. Both figures are described by Thaʿālibī as *min ayān al-daulat al-Anushirvan*, 'from the highest dignitaries of Anushirvan's court'.[77] Ferdowsi also has Bahrām Ādurmāhān play a key role in these intrigues and lose his life under Hormazd.[78] The younger Khusro too engendered considerable resentment

[74] Factions: Skjærvø, *Sassanian Inscription of Paikuli*, part 3/2, p. 10; R. N. Frye, 'The Political History of Iran under the Sasanians', in *Cambridge History of Iran*, vol. III, part 1, ed. E. Yarshater (Cambridge, 1983), pp. 116–77, at 141.

[75] Gyselen, *Four Generals of the Sasanian Empire*, pp. 36–8 (seals 1b–2b) were the first seals to be published. Bahrām now turns up on a seal (bulla) published by D. Akbarzadeh, C. G. Cereti and F. Sinisi, *Glyptic Antiquities from the Museum of Khoy, Western Azerbaijan, Iran* (Rome, 2009), p. 76, no. 116. Gyselen's uncertainty regarding the interpretation of the legend *wahrām ī nām-xwāst-khusrō ādurmāhan* (Gyselen, *Sasanian Seals and Sealings*, pp. 60–1) might have been resolved by a passage in Balādhurī that refers to the royal habit of conferring names like 'Wahman'/Bahman on military commanders, see Balādhurī, *Futūḥ al-buldān*, p. 202 = *Origins of the Islamic State*, trans. Hitti, p. 403.

[76] Cf. her claim that 'It is not certain that the ancient historiographical sources provide any information about the owners of these seals', R. Gyselen, 'Primary Sources and Historiography on the Sasanian Empire', *Studia Iranica* 38 (2009), 163–90, at p. 178.

[77] Thaʿālibī, *Ghuraru akhbāri*, p. 638.

[78] Abolqasem Ferdowsi, *Shahnameh: The Persian Book of Kings*, trans. D. Davis (New York, 2006), pp. 720ff. Thaʿālibī's *History* was composed before 1021, a few years before Ferdowsi died, and used

and hatred among the top army leaders and bulk of the aristocracy in the latter part of his reign,[79] destabilising his own position by contributing to a groundswell of disaffection in the armies stationed outside Iran and actively alienating even those families that had been part of the inner court circle.[80] Both Hormazd and Khusro were toppled in coups that may well have had a wide base of support in the upper classes, and both putsches resulted in civil wars and further rounds of intrigue where rulers were assassinated, armies divided[81] and contending factions of the aristocracy removed in purges. It is extraordinary that Khusro turned against his maternal uncles when they had brought him to power, and eventually exterminated the entire family, not least because the Spāhbads were the clan most closely related to the ruling house by marriage. It is just as extraordinary that he should have executed top military commanders when embroiled in a major war with the west.[82] It was the army that was adamant on Khusro Parvez's execution when Kavād himself was clearly content to have him imprisoned at Stakhr.[83]

Yet for all that, the aristocracy was scarcely a unified force in these major conflicts, since both Bahrām Čōbīn and the Spāhbad brothers commanded considerable support among elites across Iran and the last phase of imperial crisis (628–32) throws up an even more divided establishment, with Shahrvaraz conspiring to seize power with the active connivance of elements close to the court and, following his assassination, different factions opting for different rulers (Azarmidukht/Hormazd V/Yazdgird).[84] Of the various armed struggles that raged in these years, starting with

the same literary prose archetype that Ferdowsi versified, the *Abū manṣūrī shānāma*, which was compiled in 961. This explains why the same traditions survive in both, often to the point of exact textual correspondences, as Omidsalar has noted, M. Omidsalar, 'Could al-Tha'âlibi Have Used the *Shâhnâma* as a Source?', *Der Islam* 75 (1998), 338–46.

79 This is noted especially by Tha'ālibī, *Ghuraru akhbāri*, p. 714, who refers to his 'new habit' (*khulq jadīd*) of shedding blood and terrifying his own top officials.

80 The most obvious case of this is Khusro's treatment of Yazdīn's family and the involvement of Šamta (Yazdīn's son) in the coup against him, cf. Thomas of Marga, *The Book of Governors*, trans. E. A. Wallis Budge (London, 1893), vol. II, pp. 112–15.

81 *Histoire Nestorienne*, 94, ed. A. Scher, *Histoire Nestorienne (Chronique de Séert), seconde partie (II)* (Paris, 1918), pp. 579–80 (three-way split).

82 This at least was the allegation in the famous charge sheet against him, see Tha'ālibī, *Ghuraru akhbāri*, p. 721.

83 Bal'amī, *Chronique de Tabari traduite sur la version persane d'Abou-'Ali Mo'hammed Bel'ami*, trans. H. Zotenberg (Paris, 1871), vol. III, pp. 344–5.

84 Ṭabarī tells us that Yazdagird was installed in power by the aristocracy of Stakhr, Ṭabarī, *Ta'rīkh*, ser. i, p. 1067 = al-Ṭabarī, *Sāsānids, Byzantines*, pp. 409–10. Hormazd V 'held power … in parts of Khuzestan and Fars' (D. Weber, 'Two Pahlavi Letters from the Time of Hormizd V (AD 630–632)', *Bulletin of the Asia Institute*, n.s., 20 (2006), 55–63, at p. 61), hence simultaneously with one or both of the queens.

a war between Shahrvaraz and the wholly mysterious and unknown Kardarigan,[85] the last civil war seems to have pitted the faction (*ṭā'ifa*, as Dinawarī calls it) supporting Azarmidukht and based chiefly in Ctesiphon against the aristocratic supporters of Yazdgird in Iṣṭakhr and the surrounding regions.[86] Yazdgird himself was crowned in the great fire temple at Jur. Dīnawarī states that Azarmidukht was forced to abdicate when Yazdgird was victorious, a tradition that seems to contradict the more dramatic reports in both Yaʿqūbī and Ṭabarī that Rustam returned from Khorasan to avenge the execution of his father, Farrukh Hormazd, when the latter was assassinated by Azarmidukht. In any case, as Nöldeke realised with the acumen that runs through his whole commentary on Ṭabarī,[87] all these various intrigues and struggles for power and the desperate search for a credible ruler were driven by conflicts *within* the aristocracy, which, throughout Sasanian history, had exerted major control over the succession of rulers. Yazdgird was only sixteen at the time of his accession and behind him stood a loose coalition of regional barons, foremost among whom were Farruk Hormazd's sons, the southern aristocrat Hormozan and the aged general or warlord from the Jibāl called Fayruzān.[88]

For its part the aristocracy of Armenia could not help being drawn into these conflicts. In 572 the Mamikonean boss Vardan assassinated the *marzban* of Armenia, the Suren Čihr Gošnasp, in retaliation for the murder or execution of his brother Manuel.[89] He fled to Constantinople along with the *catholicos*, a large number of bishops and 'his family and other noblemen'. His first cousin Musheł Mamikonean, however, fought for Khusro against Bahrām Čōbīn, doubtless under orders from Maurice. Smbat Bagratuni, after a brief but chequered career with the Byzantines,

[85] Dionysius of Tel-Maḥrē in A. Palmer, *The Seventh Century in the West-Syrian Chronicles* (Liverpool, 1993), p. 142; during Shahrvaraz's short-lived reign.

[86] Dīnawarī, *Kitāb al-akhbār*, p. 125, ll.12ff.

[87] T. Nöldeke, *Geschichte der Perser und Araber zur Zeit der Sasaniden* (Leiden, 1879), p. 386, n. 1, noting that all the conflicts following the accession of Ardashir III were driven by struggles within the aristocracy ('sind nur als Kämpfe unter den verschiedenen Grossen zu betrachten'). Thaʿālibī, *Ghuraru akhbāri*, p. 386, lines 6–7 uses the term *al-mutafarriqūn* for the different political factions in these years.

[88] Yaʿqūbī, *Ta'rīkh*, vol. II, p. 162 makes Rustam and Fayruzān look for a male successor in the Sasan line; so too Ṭabarī, *Ta'rīkh*, ser. i, p. 2209 = al-Ṭabarī, *Challenge to the Empires*, pp. 221–2. On Fayruzān's likely provenance cf. Ṭabarī, *Ta'rīkh*, ser. i, p. 2176 = al-Ṭabarī, *Challenge to the Empires*, p. 189; Ṭabarī, *Ta'rīkh*, ser. i, p. 2682 = al-Ṭabarī, *The Conquest of Iran* (*The History of al-Ṭabarī*, vol. XIV), trans. G. Rex Smith (Albany, 1994), pp. 52–3.

[89] Theophanes of Byzantium, *Fragmenta Historicorum Graecorum*, ed. C. Mueller (Paris, 1851), vol. IV, p. 271; see n. 65 above. The Surens may well have had a long-standing connection with Armenia, cf. *Chron. Pasch.* s.a. 363, trans. Whitbys, *Chronicon Paschale 284–628 A.D.* (Liverpool, 1989), p. 42.

switched sides and was made *marzban* of Gorgan by Khusro in the late 590s, spending much of the latter part of his life at the Sasanian court. He died in Ctesiphon in 618/19.[90] His son Varaztiroc', who had been raised at Khusro's court (along with other *naxarar* youth like the Theodore who would become lord of Ṙshtunikʿ), became *marzban* of Armenia under Kavād II till he gathered his troops and fled to Heraclius after the great northern barons of Farrukh Hormazd's family sought unsuccessfully to enforce his continued submission to them and the moribund Sasanian power. In contrast, Musheł Mamikonean son of Dawitʿ would die at Qādisiyya along with Rustam and a considerable part of the Sasan aristocracy.

The *naxarars* and *dynatoi*

Like the *xwadāyān*, the *naxarars* were *regional* barons defined by hereditary territorial lordships rooted in what Tim Greenwood has called the 'fragmented, isolating topography of the central Caucasus region'.[91] Thanks to the relative abundance of Armenian historiography, we know much more about these families and their territorial boundaries than we ever shall know about their Iranian counterparts.[92] Armenia was an essentially aristocratic society dominated by a loose oligarchy of *naxarar* clans of which the foremost throughout late antiquity were the Mamikoneans and the Bagratuni. The *naxarars* were never in favour of a strong central authority and eventually managed to get the Armenian monarchy overthrown and abolished under Bahrām V. They traded the potentially more intrusive controls of a domestic ruler for looser control by an external one. However, if the divisions within Iran's aristocracy stemmed in part from an innate lack of cohesion and persistent factional and economic rivalries, in Armenia these factors were compounded by the division of the country itself between the two main international powers[93] and by Byzantine hostility to the idea of a strong and autonomous aristocratic

[90] Sebeos, *Armenian History*, 96 (pp. 43–4), 104 (p. 54) ('third noble in the palace of king Khosrov'), and P. Boisson-Chenorhokian, *Yovhannēs Drasxanakertc'i Histoire d'Arménie: Introduction, traduction et notes* (Louvain, 2004), p. 131, n. 26 for the date of his demise.

[91] T. Greenwood, 'Armenian Neighbours (600–1045)', in *The Cambridge History of the Byzantine Empire c.500–1492*, ed. J. Shepard (Cambridge, 2008), pp. 333–64, at 335.

[92] See J. Laurent, *L'Arménie entre Byzance et l'Islam depuis la conquête arabe jusqu'en 886* (Paris, 1919), ch. 4; R. Grousset, *Histoire de l'Arménie des origines à 1071* (Paris, 1947), pp. 289–93.

[93] In the division of Armenia under Theodosius I the bulk of the country was absorbed in the 'Persian sector', cf. Khorenats'i, *History of the Armenians*, p. 304, so that the concessions made by Khusro under the terms of his treaty with Maurice produced a balance that was atypical and exceptional.

sector in western Armenia. Indeed, the extinction of an aristocracy in the Byzantine sector (thanks to Justinian's uprooting of the agnatic and corporate traditions that had governed the transmission of estates)[94] would mean that the *naxarars* retained the aspect of a class only in eastern and southern Armenia. This (Persarmenia) was a sector the younger Khusro could describe as late as 591 as the jurisdiction of the *tanutērs*, the family heads or princes (*tanuterakan iškhanut'iwn*), showing that Ctesiphon had always preserved the aristocracy as the instrument of its rule here. By the seventh century, however, Sebeos' lament about the hopeless lack of unity of the *naxarars* in the face of advancing Arab aggression[95] reflected both a continued lack of cohesion in that class and possibly also a growing fragmentation within clans as the lesser branches enjoyed a degree of emancipation in these decades. As the Sasanian state began to disintegrate in the 630s, the Byzantines redoubled their efforts to attract Armenian support,[96] the *naxarars* began to elect their own *išxans* or 'princes',[97] starting with a Ṙštuni (though the Mamikoneans and the Bagratunis would rapidly reassert control), and the aristocracy, like the country as a whole, soon faced an entirely new contender for domination which, through much of the eighth and ninth centuries, would, in the words of Łewond, leave the country 'bereft of its nobles'.[98] The long-standing *rivalry* between the Mamikoneans and the Bagratunis survived into the eighth century, more intense than ever as the Bagratunis established a new-found dominance in the course of the seventh century (given a head start by Khusro Parvez) and emerged as the preferred clients of the later Umayyads. Armenia in the early Middle Ages was a microcosm of the way competition within the aristocracy could come to favour the expansion of some houses to the detriment and even complete destruction of others. On the eve of

[94] C. Toumanoff, *Studies in Christian Caucasian History* (Georgetown, 1963), p. 196; N. Garsoian, 'The Marzpanate (428–652)', in *The Armenian People from Ancient to Modern Times*, vol. I: *The Dynastic Periods* (Basingstoke, 1997), pp. 95–115, esp. 106–7; T. Greenwood, 'Armenia', in *The Oxford Handbook of Late Antiquity*, ed. S. F. Johnson (Oxford and New York, 2012), pp. 115–41, at 131.

[95] Sebeos, *Armenian History*, 134 (p. 94), 'Since all the nobles were disunited, they ruined this land of Armenia'; 138 (p. 99), 'And no one was chosen as general in the land of Armenia, because the princes were disunited and had separated from each other.'

[96] Greenwood, 'Armenian Neighbours', p. 340.

[97] A. Ter-Ghévondian, 'L'Arménie et la conquête arabe', in *Armenian Studies/Études arméniennes in Memoriam Haïg Berbérian*, ed. D. Kouymjian (Lisbon, 1986), pp. 773–92, esp. 776.

[98] Łewond, *History of Łewond the Eminent Vardapet of the Armenians*, trans. Z. Arzoumanian (Philadelphia, 1982), pp. 65–6; cf. Ter-Ghévondian, 'L'Arménie et la conquête arabe', pp. 784–5; N. Garsoïan, 'Esquisse de l'évolution du *naxararut'iuwn* arménien durant l'interrègne (VIIe–IXe siècle)', *Revue des Études Arméniennes* 34 (2012), 41–71, esp. p. 59.

the invasions in the mid-seventh century, the Mamikoneans had controlled roughly a third of the countryside by way of their clan or corporate holdings, much of this along the border with Byzantium,[99] while the Bagratid estates were confined to Sper in north-western Armenia and Vaspurakan in the south. By the ninth century the Artsrunis and Bagratunis between them had grabbed the lion's share of Armenian territory, effecting a large-scale dispossession of the Mamikoneans.[100] The last rebellion ever led by the latter would see them and a host of other families (Amatuni, Ṙštuni, Kamsarakan, etc.) decimated at Bagrewand (in 775) and *bought out* by the two strongest clans.

Thus neither Iran nor Armenia ever had unified ruling classes of the kind widely envisaged in stereotypes that oppose a coherent and united aristocracy to the state (domestic or foreign) as its chief political antagonist. Both Sasanian aristocrats and Armenian *naxarars* were regional barons, the former typified by the 'great families' that Arabic sources call *ahl al-buyutat*, less so by the military elite that originates in the sixth century. The Armenians display no distinction of this sort since the princely houses retained their own military contingents and heads of houses or their brothers often doubled as military commanders. Iran's aristocrats exerted unremitting control over the succession of new rulers, almost never challenging the dynastic basis of Sasanian rule, while the *naxarars* managed to get the monarchy itself abolished. Armenia's aristocracy was unchallenged domestically (in obvious contrast to the *wuzurgān*) but thoroughly *subaltern* in the wider setting of the conflict between the Romans/east Romans and Iran and their struggle for control over Armenian loyalties. *All* late antique aristocracies were riven by internal divisions and factionalism – the western aristocracy of the City of Rome that dominated the civil administration of the fourth-century empire,[101] the aristocratic milieux implicated in the Nika insurrection of 532[102] or the factions around the powerful military families of the Byzantine aristocracy in the tenth and eleventh centuries[103]

99 Laurent, *L'Arménie entre Byzance et l'Islam*, p. 92.

100 M. Canard, '"Les familles féodales d'Arménie et leurs possessions héréditaires" d'A. Ter-Ghévondian', in *Armenian Studies*, ed. Kouymjian (n. 89), pp. 89–104, esp. 92, which adds a third family, the Siwni: 'Trois familles, les Bagratuni, les Arcruni et les Siwni, ont réussi à s'emparer de la plus grande partie des terres d'Arménie.'

101 F. A. Poglio, *Gruppi di potere nella Roma tardoantica (350–395 d.C.)* (Turin, 2007), the senate dominated by two major factions or power blocs of rival families (*gentes*) in the years 350–95.

102 P. Sarris, *Economy and Society in the Age of Justinian* (Cambridge, 2006), p. 216.

103 J.-C. Cheynet, 'Bureaucracy and Aristocracies', in *The Oxford Handbook of Byzantine Studies*, ed. E. Jeffreys *et al.* (New York and Oxford, 2008), pp. 518–26, esp. 520 ('profound rivalries'), 522; P. Stephenson, 'A Development in Nomenclature on the Seals of the Byzantine Provincial Aristocracy

no less than the Merovingian[104] and Visigothic[105] magnates who determined the fate of their respective kingdoms with their own intrigues and struggles. The crucial *difference* lies in the nature of these various aristocratic elites, in other words, their differing relationships to the state. Byzantine aristocrats were inseparable from the state that spawned them in a process of class formation that was largely peculiar to late antiquity. In major contrast to the *xwadāyān*, they were 'not autonomous barons but imperial functionaries who could be dismissed, exiled, or dispossessed at any time' (Kazhdan).[106] Cheynet argues, '[E]ven for the families most solidly established in the provinces, *the emperor's service was the main means of acquiring wealth.*'[107] Despite Ostrogorsky's repeated characterisation of the Byzantine aristocracy as a 'feudal aristocracy' and 'feudal magnates',[108] this aristocracy 'has nothing "feudal" about it, since, until the eleventh century, the imperial authorities always controlled it, forbidding its members any real autonomy in the provinces where they resided'.[109] If, as Ostrogorsky says, the *dynatos* or 'powerful man' was 'at the same time a landholder and a government official',[110] the tendency of the more recent historiography (Rosemary Morris, Oikonomidès, Cheynet) has been to see the aristocracy of the Byzantine empire *essentially* as a bureaucratic elite. Aristocratic wealth 'came mainly from service to the state ... Wealth was intricately bound up with titles and imperial salaries.'[111] Thus even the great military families of Anatolia[112] who most resemble the Sasanian aristocratic houses, not least in their strong regional ties, differed in this crucial respect. Ultimately, it was

in the Late Tenth Century', *Revue des études byzantines* 52 (1994), 187–211, esp. pp. 196–7 (Skleroi vs Phocades).

104 R. A. Gerberding, *The Rise of the Carolingians and the 'Liber Historiae Francorum'* (Oxford, 1987); also S. T. Loseby, 'Marseille and the Pirenne Thesis, I: Gregory of Tours, the Merovingian Kings, and "Un Grand Port"', in *The Sixth Century: Production, Distribution and Demand*, ed. R. Hodges *et al.* (Leiden, etc., 1998), pp. 203–29, at 225–6, for the later sixth century.

105 *The Chronicle of 754*, 54 (trans. K. B. Wolf, *Conquerors and Chroniclers of Early Medieval Spain*, 2nd edn (Liverpool, 1999), pp. 132–3; Ibn al-Qūṭīya, *Ta'rikh*, 1 (trans. D. James, *Early Islamic Spain: The 'History' of Ibn al- Qūṭīya* (London and New York, 2009), pp. 49–50); A. Isla Frez, 'Conflictos internos y externos en el fin del reino visigodo', *Hispania* 62/2 (2002), 619–36.

106 A. P. Kazhdan and A. W. Epstein, *Change in Byzantine Culture in the Eleventh and Twelfth Centuries* (Berkeley, etc., 1985), p. 65.

107 J.-C. Cheynet, 'The Byzantine Aristocracy (8th–13th Centuries)', in J.-C. Cheynet, *The Byzantine Aristocracy and its Military Function* (Aldershot, 2006), no. 1, at p. 25.

108 G. Ostrogorsky, *History of the Byzantine State*, trans. J. Hussey (Oxford, 1968), e.g. pp. 276, 320.

109 Cheynet, 'Byzantine Aristocracy', p. 41.

110 G. Ostrogorsky, 'Observations on the Aristocracy of Byzantium', *Dumbarton Oaks Papers* 25 (1971), 1–32, at p. 7, cf. Ostrogorsky, *History of the Byzantine State*, p. 275.

111 N. Oikonomidès, 'Title and Income at the Byzantine Court', in N. Oikonomidès, *Social and Economic Life in Byzantium*, ed. E. Zachariadou (Aldershot, 2004), no. XVII, at p. 206.

112 Cf. M. Angold, 'Belle Époque or Crisis? (1025–1118)', in *The Cambridge History of the Byzantine Empire c.500–1492*, ed. J. Shepard (Cambridge, 2008), pp. 583–626, at 588.

even possible for the Komnenoi to restructure the aristocracy as an 'enormous extended family', and for Andronikos I Komnenos to decimate it,[113] something no Sasanian ruler could ever do with the 'great families'.

Few traditions of scholarship have had to contend with a more staggering loss of sources than historians and others working on Sasanian Iran. One upshot of this lacuna is the near-invisibility of the economic side of the aristocracy. In some contrast, say, to the Byzantine landowners of the later fifth and sixth centuries and the light thrown on their agrarian assets by the papyri from Egypt, there is simply no coherent body of evidence one can draw on to reconstruct the structure of estates or the management of properties, let alone the extent and forms of their involvement in the commercial economy. What *is* clear is that robust stone-built fortresses were the backbone of the Armenian countryside, and villages were almost certainly scattered *around these epicentres and controlled from them*. Thus Sebeos tells us that as the conflict between the great powers re-emerged in the early seventh century and Armenia became a battleground between them, the Sasanian capture of the fortress of Erginay in 604 entailed the captivity of thirty-three villages around it.[114] The bulk of Armenia's aristocracy lived in these fortresses, and each of the major clans is associated with at least one leading stronghold of this sort. The fort or castle was a major embodiment of the power of the *naxarars* both against invading armies and hostile powers and over the local population. Yovhannes Drasxanakerts'i reports that when Muḥammad b. Marwan, ʿAbd al-Malik's governor in the early 690s, launched a campaign to ensure Armenian submission to the new regime, he completely demolished all the fortresses that he managed to capture.[115] To control the fortresses was to control Armenia. Movses Khorenats'i conveys a vivid picture of what these castles were like in his description of Garni when he writes, 'About that time Trdat completed the construction of the fortress of Garni in hard and dressed blocks of stone cemented with iron [clamps] and lead. Inside, for his sister Khosrovidukht, he built a summer palace with towers and wonderful carvings in high relief.'[116] However, next to villages and fortresses the Armenian countryside included very substantial estates described by the term *dastakert* (< MP *dastagird*). One excavated at Drasxanakert in Širak sprawled over 80 hectares of a mountain plateau

[113] Cheynet, 'Bureaucracy and Aristocracies', pp. 523, 525.
[114] Sebeos, *Armenian History*, 108 (p. 60).
[115] Yovhannes Drasxanakerts'i, *Histoire d'Armenie*, trans. P. Boisson-Chenorokhian (Louvain, 2004), pp. 154–5.
[116] Moses Khorenats'i, *History of the Armenians*, p. 247, with n. 13.

1500 metres high.[117] Drasxanakerts'i also mentions the 'extreme beauty' of a group of church estates (*dastakert*) that the ʿAbbasid governor Khuzayma b. Khāzim was desperate to acquire, and elsewhere describes how the *išxan* Grigor Mamikonean laid the foundations of a superb church in the great *dastakert* of Aruč, also constructing his own palace there on the edge of a rocky gorge.[118] In Ibn Ḥauqal's remarkable description of the wealth of the Armenian aristocracy of the restored kingdom, *dastakert* and *berd* (fortress) are denoted by the distinct Arabic terms *ḍiyāʿ* (pl. of *ḍaiaʿ*) and *qilāʿ* respectively, showing that these were distinct realities, as indeed they were in the Sasanian countryside.[119] In short, the symbiosis of fortress and village was quite distinct from the 'created' estate or *dastagird*, even if there is a strong sense in which both were estates.[120] Ibn Ḥauqal was massively impressed by the wealth of the Caucasian aristocracies, by their 'rich and lavish expenditures' (*al-nafaqāt al-dārrat al-sābigha*). The seventh century in Armenia was arguably an even more prosperous period, going by the sheer scale of building activity[121] and the vibrancy of commercial centres like Dvin[122] and Tiflis.[123] Armenia had been of extraordinary economic value to the Sasanians,[124] but it can scarcely be doubted that the bulk of Armenia's wealth remained inside the country and flowed into the coffers of church and aristocracy. Cash cropping must have been widespread (Łazar's history written *c.*500 claims that the rich plains of Ayrarat grew both raw

[117] F. I. Ter-Martirossov, 'Un "paradis" de l'antiquité classique: Le site de Draskhanakert, à Beniamin', in *Arménie: Trésors de l'Arménie ancienne des origines aux IVe siècle*, ed. J. Santrot (Paris, 1996), pp. 187–9.

[118] Drasxanakerts'i, *Histoire*, pp. 175 (church properties), 151 (Aruč).

[119] Ibn Ḥauqal, *Configuration de la terre (Kitāb ṣurat al-ʾard)*, trans. J. H. Kramers and G. Wiet, 2 vols (Paris, 1964), vol. II, p. 341; a passage not based on al-Iṣṭakhrī but written by Ibn Ḥauqal after his travels there. Sasanian aristocrats also owned fortresses *within* major urban centres. Hormozān possessed a fortress (*qalʿa*, *ḥiṣn*) or fortified area (*qaṣba*) within Tustar where he stored his treasure (*khizāna*) (Balādhurī, *Futūḥ al-buldān*, pp. 373–4; Murgotten, *Origins of the Islamic State*, pp. 117–18) and retired every night with his crack troops (Balʿamī, *Tārīkhnāmah-i Ṭabarī*, ed. Raushan, p. 499; trans. Zotenberg, vol. III, p. 458). It lay, according to *Nihāyat*, ed. Dāneš-Pažūh, p. 471, 'in the centre of' the town (*fī wasṭ al-madīnat*). Its fascinating description as a *qaṣba* occurs in Khalīfa b. Khayyāt's *Taʾrīkh*. Also compare the famous castle or fortress of Farrukhan at Rayy.

[120] A Middle Persian inscription from Bandiān near the Turkmenistan border in Khorasan refers to one Weh-Šapur 'building' or 'creating' the estate that the dedication comes from, cf. P. Gignoux, 'Les inscriptions en moyen-perse de Bandiān', *Studia Iranica* 27 (1998), 251–8, at p. 253: *Weh-Šabuhr brād ēn dastgird kard*.

[121] Garsoïan, 'The Marzpanate', p. 115.

[122] N. Garsoïan, 'The Arab Invasions and the Rise of the Bagratuni (640–884)', in *The Armenian People from Ancient to Modern Times* (n. 94), pp. 117–42, at 124. Cf. Procopius' description of Dvin in the sixth century, Procopius, *Bell.* 2.25.1–3 (Dewing, *History of the Wars*, vol. I, p. 480).

[123] Dasxurants'i, *History of the Caucasian Albanians* (n. 29), p. 85, 'the luxurious, prosperous, famous and great commercial city of Tiflis'.

[124] Menander, fr. 20.2 (Blockley, *The History of Menander the Guardsman*, pp. 184ff.).

silk and sugar cane),[125] Armenia had abundant resources of fish, and at least some major estates contained mineral deposits that included gold and silver. When Vardan Mamikonean fled to Constantinople in 572, he or the group he travelled with brought a 'great store of unwoven silk' with them.[126] Among Sasanian aristocrats Yazdīn's family, Nestorians, were also connected with the trade in silk,[127] and there are other, tantalising references to the links between Iran's aristocracy and the substantial merchant communities of Syria and Iraq. Bahrām Čōbīn is said by one Greek source to have received support from the wealthy Jewish merchants of lower Mesopotamia who had made vast fortunes trading in the Red Sea ports,[128] and Shahrvaraz on his way back from the occupied Byzantine provinces is reported to have been accompanied by 'several merchants from Syria'.[129] Of course, these are no more than sporadic hints but they do support the sort of inferences that should flow from the more general background of an intensive agrarian and urban occupation of core regions like Khuzistan and the Diyala river basin and of the strong Sasanian interest in international trade, including a degree of control of the central and southern Batinah coast where international trade fairs were being held in the early seventh century.[130] Vast amounts of rice and sugar cane were produced in Khuzistan in al-Muqaddasī's day (late tenth century),[131] and it is very likely that sugar cane at least had expanded *already by the seventh century* when Gundeshapur was famous for its sugar industry.[132] In southern Iraq canal-irrigated estates were a major outcome of the large-scale state-financed irrigation schemes that spread across the region in late Sasanian times. The oldest complete Islamic history to survive, Khalīfa b. Khayyāt's *Ta'rīkh*, refers to three estates of this sort in the earliest period of the conquest, one in Maysan/Mēšūn that belonged to

125 Łazar P'arpec'i, *The History of Łazar P'arpec'i*, trans. R. W. Thomson (Atlanta, 1991), p. 43.

126 Gregory of Tours, *A History of the Franks*, trans. L. Thorpe (Harmondsworth, 1976), p. 235.

127 *Vie de Saint Anastase*, 32 (ed. B. Flusin, *Saint Anastase le Perse et l'histoire de la Palestine au début du VIIe siècle* (Paris, 1992), vol. I, p. 77).

128 Theophylact, *History*, 5.7.6 (Whitby, p. 141).

129 *Histoire Nestorienne*, 89, ed. Scher, p. 545.

130 R. Adams, *Land behind Baghdad* (Chicago, 1965), who refers to a 'vast network of new canals' (p. 82), cf. Frye, 'Political History', pp. 131–2, 160–1; D. T. Potts, *The Arabian Gulf in Antiquity*, vol. II: *From Alexander the Great to the Coming of Islam* (Oxford, 1990), pp. 336–40; see pp. 138–9 above.

131 Al-Muqaddasī, *Aḥsan al-taqāsīm fī ma'rifat al-aqālīm*, ed. M. J. de Goeje (Leiden, 1877), pp. 405ff., 416; *The Best Divisions for Knowledge of the Regions: A Translation of Ahsan al-Taqasim fi Ma'rifat al-Aqalim*, trans. B. A. Collins (Reading, 1994), pp. 361–3, 370.

132 R. H. Hewsen, *The Geography of Ananias of Širak (Ašxarhac'oyc'): The Long and the Short Recensions: Introduction, Translation and Commentary* (Wiesbaden, 1992), pp. 74, 74A (*Gundišapurh* where fine sugar is made). B. Laufer, *Sino-Iranica: Chinese Contrbutions to the History of Civilization in Ancient Iran* (Chicago, 1919), p. 377 suggested that in terms of the Chinese evidence 'sugar was known under the Sasanians in the sixth century'.

Ṭamāhīj, a daughter of Khusro Parvez, another called Nahr Tīrā owned by Anūšajān, a cousin of hers and a nephew of Narsī's, and a third named Nahr Besṭām.[133] Canal-irrigated estates of this sort were denoted by the Arabic term for the canals themselves, viz. *nahr*. Ṭamāhīj settled for a tribute of 10,000 drahms.[134] Even supposing this was as much as half the value of the estate's total disposable output, it is still a rough indication of the productivity of these estates. For its part, Nahr Tīrā was situated in what must even then have been the densest concentration of cane plantations anywhere in southern Iraq.[135] In less than two decades of the first shock of the conquest, all of these valuable properties would start being handed out in lavish land grants to the favourites of another regime, as the next chapter will show.

Epilogue: the biological fragility of a class

Ammianus Marcellinus' fascinating reference to the Sasanian upper class wielding 'the power of life and death over their slaves and *plebeii obscuri*' gives us some sense of the texture of ordinary life in Iran for the mass of working people, the *bandagān* and *driyōšān*. But the point worth drawing attention to here is how pervasive a culture of violence was within the circles of the aristocracy itself. Within the ruling family it was almost standard practice to maim or eliminate potentially threatening male siblings, as even Anoshirvan is said to have done with Kāvus and all his brothers.[136] The repeated assassination of individual aristocrats was of course another form of this institutionalised violence, and Hormazd's onslaught on the landed and religious elites only seemed so scandalous for the sheer scale on which it occurred. Anoshirvan's purge of the faction that advanced the claims of Kavus also involved the execution of his maternal uncle from the Spāhbad family.[137] Bendōy's assassination of Hormazd was in part at least retaliation for Hormazd's treatment of his father-in-law, Bendōy's father, Shapur. So too the involvement in the coup against Khusro Parvez of Šamta and Mihr-Hormazd, both sons of fathers who had fallen victim to his rancour. All of this fierce political violence would doubtless have made the continuity of aristocratic lineages a major concern for the aristocracy.

[133] Khalīfa b. Khayyāt al-ʿUṣfurī, *Al-Taʾrīkh*, ed. S. Zakkār (Damascus, 1967), vol. I, p. 114, ll.17ff., p. 119, ll.9–10, p. 120, l.12.

[134] Yāqūt, *Muʿjam al-buldān*, vol. IV, p. 844, line 6.

[135] See Yāqūt, *Muʿjam al-buldān*, vol. IV, p. 837, ll.9ff. on the location, coupled with al-Iṣṭakhrī's description of these parts of Khuzistan, esp. his statement that the cane grown in Masruqān gave the highest yield in sugar, al-Iṣṭakhrī, *Kitāb al-masālik wa-l-mamālik*, ed. M. J. de Goeje (Leiden, 1870), p. 91, ll.6ff.

[136] Procopius, *Bell.* 1.23.6 (Dewing, *History of the Wars*, vol. I, p. 210).

[137] Procopius, *loc. cit.* (*en tois kai Aspebedēs ēn ho tēs Khosroou mētros adelphos*).

Another key factor that would account for high rates of mortality in the Sasanian elite was the practice of going into battle accompanied by whole retinues of kinsmen and dependents. This had a fatal impact in the 630s when, as both Sebeos and Dīnawari tell us, a considerable part of the aristocracy was killed at Qādisiyya. ('All the leading nobles were killed,' as Sebeos says.)[138] At Jalula large numbers of daughters were captured.[139] At Iṣṭakhr the Arab assault wiped out 'most of the noble families', according to Balādhurī.[140] So the conquests decimated the aristocracy thanks largely to the peculiar tradition of having noblemen and their retainers advance into battle. Recall Eutropius' statement that Galerius' victory over Narsī at the end of the third century involved the capture of what, colourfully, he chose to call 'infinitam Persarum nobilitatem'.[141]

In conclusion, Maria Macuch's argument in her seminal paper on ruling-class consolidation and Zoroastrian family law makes perfect sense. She argued that a whole web of institutions with deep religious sanction evolved to buttress the fragile perpetuity of a class plagued by high rates of mortality and low life expectancy.[142] Since the aristocracy was rigorously endogamous, external sources of infusion and growth were stymied. Instead, a peculiar set of rules of marriage and inheritance were pivotal to its reproduction as a class and to the consolidation of property in the main line. Polygamous marriages involving multiple first-degree wives, *čagar* marriages involving subordinate wives and designed solely for the creation of progeny who would count as the legal heirs of the real husband even if the latter was deceased, and *stūrīh* or procreation by proxy, designed again to produce heirs for a childless aristocracy, were all customary and probably had the combined effect of concentrating substantial numbers of women in the major aristocratic households. Childlessness or the lack of legal heirs was a major preoccupation of the aristocracy. And this surely is one of the crucial backgrounds against which we should see Mazdak's radicalism in the early sixth century, the one formidable assault on this whole nexus of institutions and on the class it supported.

138 Sebeos, *Armenian History*, 137 (pp. 98–9).

139 Dīnawarī, *Kitāb al-akhbār*, p. 136, ll.2–3.

140 Balādhurī, *Futūḥ al-buldān*, p. 382, ll.1–3; Murgotten, *Origins of the Islamic State*, p. 133.

141 Eutropius, *Brev.* 9.25.1 (ed. J. Hellegouarch, *Eutrope, Abrégé d'histoire romaine* (Paris, 1999), p. 128.

142 M. Macuch, 'Herrschaftskonsolidierung und zoroastrisches Familienrecht: Zum Verhältnis von Kirche und Staat unter den Sasaniden', in *Iran und Turfan: Beiträge Berliner Wissenschaftler, Werner Sundermann zum 60. Geburtstag gewidmet*, ed. C. Reck *et al.* (Wiesbaden, 1995), pp. 149–67.

PART IV

Beyond the Mediterranean and late antiquity

CHAPTER 9

Late antique legacies and Muslim economic expansion

In a sketch compressed into some fifty pages of *L'Islam dans sa première grandeur*, lectures that he himself never wrote up for publication, Maurice Lombard underlined the rapid economic development of the Muslim world as well as its resulting social tensions. He was especially interested in the way the conquests and the formation of the new state could build on the vast accumulations of gold that had been progressively drained from countries further west and stashed in massive hoards both in the eastern Byzantine provinces and in the treasuries of the Sasanian rulers. What Islam did was release the bulk of this hoard into circulation, with predictable consequences. Moreover, 'the establishment of the Muslim world in the 7th to early 8th centuries created a vast integrated area, a huge common market stretching from central Asia to the Indian Ocean, from the Sudan to the barbarian west and the region of the Russian rivers'.[1] For Lombard, economic integration and the increase in money circulation were thus central parts of the story. Ehrenkreutz's paper of 1972, a contribution to the Pirenne debate, was equally prescient. Like Lombard, he saw the first centuries of Islam as a 'new and dynamic era in the history of Near Eastern economy', which was possible, to start with, because of what he called the 'non-destructive character of the great conquest'.[2] Of course, the ruling elites of the two empires that the Arabs confronted were 'expelled or exterminated',[3] but no substantial losses were inflicted on the tax-paying civilian population, he claimed. For him the most significant features, on the economic side, were 'a powerful injection of ready cash into the Near Eastern economy',[4] the growth of new consumer centres

[1] M. Lombard, *L'Islam dans sa première grandeur (VIIIe–XIe siècle)* (Paris, 1971), p. 123.
[2] A. S. Ehrenkreutz, 'Another Orientalist's Remarks Concerning the Pirenne Thesis', *Journal of the Economic and Social History of the Orient* 15 (1972), 94–104, at p. 99; repr. in *Monetary Change and Economic History in the Medieval Muslim world*, ed. J. L. Bacharach (Aldershot, 1992).
[3] Ehrenkreutz, 'Pirenne Thesis', p. 100.
[4] Ehrenkreutz, 'Pirenne Thesis', p. 101.

in the regions themselves, and the strong economic expansion that offset the potential inflationary effects of the vast supply of money. Ehrenkreutz was hardly a Marxist, far from it, but like Marx he saw the volume of money in circulation as regulated by the state of the economy.[5] 'Although the supply of new coins assumed tremendous proportions, and although their production kept on being expanded during the early Caliphate, no inflationary developments were set off by such a monetary policy.'[6] This, Ehrenkreutz rightly concluded, pointed to the 'great vitality of the Near Eastern market in that period'.

What I want to do in this chapter is build on this model by suggesting the possible way in which the late antique economic background contributed to the vitality Ehrenkreutz speaks of, looking specifically at three issues or sets of issues. The first is the general issue of what happened to the aristocracies of the east Roman and Sasanian empires following the Arab invasions of the 630s and early 640s. Chris Wickham's book *Framing the Early Middle Ages* presents a picture that is remarkably continuitist on this question, much more so for the east than for the west, so it's worth looking at the evidence more closely.[7] Second, if the early Muslim economy can be said to have built on late antique legacies, which ones were those? And finally, how or at what level were those legacies transformed and developed into something new? Where, in other words, can we identify the seeds of a new type of evolution within the social and economic world of the caliphate?

How, to begin with, did the aristocracies respond to the invasions? It is surprising how little attention historians have paid to this issue. It might help to look at the Byzantine and Sasanian aristocracies as a group, ignoring the political distinction between them, and to keep the aristocracy proper distinct from the smaller town or village level elites who may have formed a minor nobility. In that perspective, aristocratic responses can be strung along a spectrum from resistance at one end to flight at the other, with economic bargaining and capitulation wedged between them. The best examples of resistance come from the Iranian side, with both Qādisiyya (638) and Nihāwand (642) decimating the ranks of the

[5] E.g. '[The] decision of the Arab administration to release vast quantities of gold (*dīnār*), silver (*dirham*), and copper (*fals*) coins ... must have been made in response to expanding market conditions', A. S. Ehrenkreutz, 'The Silent Force Behind the Rise of Medieval Islamic Civilization', in *The Islamic World from Classical to Modern Times: Essays in Honor of Bernard Lewis*, ed. C. E. Bosworth *et al.* (Princeton, NJ, 1989), p. 124.

[6] Ehrenkreutz, 'Pirenne Thesis', p. 103.

[7] C. Wickham, *Framing the Early Middle Ages: Europe and the Mediterranean 400–800* (Oxford, 2005).

Sasanian aristocracy, which on the whole simply disappeared.[8] The most dramatic example of flight is Ibn ʿAbd al-Ḥakam's reference to some 30,000 individuals from the Alexandrian governing class (*ahl al-quwwa*) – a substantial number even if not precisely this one – loading their families and moveables onto ships and fleeing.[9] The most successful case of economic bargaining was undoubtedly the ability of the North African aristocracy, especially the large landowners of Byzacena, still formally controlled by Byzantium, to buy off the Arab armies under ʿAbdallāh b. Saʿd b. Abī Sarḥ (this in 647) by coming up with an astonishing sum of money that the sources put between just over 2,000,000 and 2,500,000 solidi.[10] Ibn Abī Sarḥ evacuated Tunisia. Carthage only finally fell *c.*695, and the strong resistance the Arabs encountered here in the intervening decades came not from the landowners but from the Berber tribes in the Aures, led by the Kahena. Finally, the Armenian aristocracy exemplifies both internal divisions and eventual capitulation.[11] To return to Iran, there is an interesting passage in Dīnawarī that suggests a clear division between the *dahāqīn* (the small town or village elite) and the aristocracy proper. He tells us that when the remnants of the Sasanian army fled to Madāʾin/Ctesiphon following the defeat at Qādisiyya and the Arab forces subjected the capital to a protracted siege from the west bank of the Tigris, most of the *dahāqīn* of the surrounding rural areas couldn't take the strain and decided to capitulate.[12] Indeed, the clearest pattern during the conquests is the extremely sharp division between the imperial aristocracies and the

[8] Dīnawarī, *Kitāb al-akhbār al-ṭiwāl*, ed. V. Guirgass (Leiden, 1888), p. 122, listing the groups at Qādisiyya. Note Sebeos' valuable ref. to this battle, 'All the leading nobles were killed, and the general Rostom was also killed', *Armenian History*, 137 (pp. 98–9).

[9] Some time around September 642 when the commander-in-chief Theodore (*PLRE* IIIB, 1280ff.) abandoned the city. Flight: Ibn ʿAbd al-Ḥakam, *Futūḥ Miṣr* (= *The History of the Conquest of Egypt, North Africa and Spain Known as the Futūḥ Miṣr*, ed. C. C. Torrey, New Haven, 1922), p. 82, ll.15–16.

[10] Al-Wāqidī gave both figures, e.g. Ṭabarī, *Taʾrīkh al-rusul waʾl-mulūk*, ed. M. J. de Goeje *et al.*, ser. i, p. 2818, l.2ff. = al-Ṭabarī, *The Crisis of the Early Caliphate (The History of al-Ṭabarī, vol. xv)*, trans. R. Stephen Humphreys (Albany, 1990), p. 23, cf. H. Slim, 'Le trésor de Rougga et l'expédition musulmane de 647 en Ifrīḳiya', in *Recherches archéologiques franco-tunisiennes à Rougga, vol. III: Le trésor de monnaies d'or byzantines*, ed. R. Guéry *et al.* (Rome, 1982). The defeat at Sbeïtla led to a panic dispersal of the Byzantine forces, a major part of which regrouped at Thysdrus, where the treaty was concluded. Ironically, the best material is contained in the latest sources, Ibn al-Athīr, Tidjānī and al-Nuwairī, see Slim, 'Trésor', pp. 84–6.

[11] Yovhannēs Drasxanakertsʿi, *History of Armenia*, trans. K. H. Maksoudian (Atlanta, 1987), pp. 101 (divisions), 103 (capitulation), and the defection of leading aristocrats in Sebeos, *Armenian History*, 169 (142–3), 173 (149). Capitulation in Egypt too, cf. Dionysius of Tel-Maḥrē in A. Palmer, *The Seventh Century in the West-Syrian Chronicles* (Liverpool, 1993), p. 159.

[12] Dīnawarī, *Kitāb al-akhbār*, p. 133; cf. Ṭabarī, *Taʾrīkh*, ser. i, 2427 = al-Ṭabarī, *The Conquest of Iraq, Southwestern Persia, and Egypt (The History of al-Ṭabarī, vol. xiii)*, trans. G. H. A. Juynboll (Albany, 1989), p. 9 for a contrast between the local *dehqāns* and the entourage of the ruler.

local elites. There was scarcely any resistance from the latter, and not just because they lacked the military capability.

Nihāwand broke the resistance of the Sasanian aristocracy and only local concentrations of aristocrats could have survived after that. For example, the assault on Iṣṭakhr by ʿAbdallāh b. ʿĀmir, a cousin of ʿUthmān, some time in the late 640s involved considerable slaughter, 'wiping out most of the noble families (*akhthar ahl al-buyutat*)' in the words of Balādhurī,[13] and recalling the much earlier siege of Šuštar/Tustar, where some 600 (noble?) captives were, reportedly, beheaded.[14] The upshot of all this is that the conquests 'took out' the aristocracy, exterminating or dispersing it, and that only the minor nobility, if one can call it that, survived in any substantial way.[15] In Egypt there is no reference in the surviving seventh-century papyri to the great *oikoi* of the Byzantine period, and the only true aristocrat known to me to have survived into the 650s – clearly as a collaborator – was Flavius Theodorakios, who was *illustris kai pagarchos* in 651 but seems to have started life as the son of a *scholasticus* already in possession of a large estate (*ousia*) in 629.[16] In Iran, claims to descent from the aristocratic families of the Sasanian period only go to highlight the rupture, because if a substantial section of the old aristocracy *had* survived, we would not have remnants of it proclaiming their descent from the old houses.[17]

The decimation/dispersion of the aristocracy in the Arab conquests is simply a way of saying that the Muslim armies smashed the state in those territories. This does not mean that substantial damage was inflicted on the infrastructure, it wasn't – the urban structure was largely unscathed[18] – and there is no archaeological evidence of a major catastrophe in the seventh-century eastern Mediterranean.[19] Nor was the economy of either

[13] Balādhurī, *Futūḥ al-buldān*, ed. R. M. Ridwan (Cairo, 1932), p. 382 = *The Origins of the Islamic State, part II*, trans. F. C. Murgotten (New York, 1924), p. 133.

[14] Balādhurī, *Futūḥ al-buldān*, p. 373 = *Origins of the Islamic State*, trans. Murgotten, p. 117.

[15] See H. Kennedy, *The Prophet and the Age of the Caliphates: The Islamic Near East from the Sixth to the Eleventh Century*, 2nd edn (Harlow and New York, 2004), p. 72 on Fars, 'where the prolonged fighting and the defeat of subsequent rebellions led to the virtual extermination of the ancient aristocracy'.

[16] *CPR* XXIV 32 (4.5.651); *CPR* VII 51 (629) *may* relate to him. In any case, continuity (across the conquest) is established by *P. Lond.* I 113.10 (p. 222) (639/40), *P. Ross.-Georg.* III 50 (21.7.643) and *BGU* I 320 (9.2.644; *BL* xi.17).

[17] A. Tafazzoli, *Sasanian Society. I. Warriors II. Scribes III. Dehqāns* (New York, 2000), p. 43 refers to the 'defeat of the Persian army in the time of ʿUmar and the gradual disappearance of the nobles who administered the country', distinguishing them from the 'local gentry'.

[18] A. Walmsley, 'Production, Exchange and Regional Trade in the Islamic East Mediterranean: Old Structures, New Systems?', in *The Long Eighth Century*, ed. I. L. Hansen *et al.* (Leiden, etc., 2000), pp. 265–343, at 273.

[19] Walmsley, 'Regional Trade', p. 268.

empire substantially affected in a negative way. The most striking proof of this is the continued existence of a monetary economy across the great watershed of the conquests. This was by far the strongest element of continuity between late antiquity and early Islam or between late Roman/Sasanian late antiquity and the late antiquity of Islam and the key factor that allowed for the 'prodigious urban expansion' of the eighth to eleventh centuries. Certainly, at the economic level, the single most enduring legacy of the late antique world was the continued use of money and its availability in substantial quantities. A peculiarly Muslim gold coinage was of course only struck from AH 77 (696/7), so all references to the 'dinar' for transactions before this period were effectively references to the solidus, and the same is true of 'dirhams' and the Sasanian silver coinage based on the drahm. These coins continued to circulate in vast quantities,[20] and certainly there is no indication that the supply of money was a constraint or *any* sort of constraint on the financial system of the emerging Muslim state. Taxes were denominated in money, and so were the salaries/pensions of the *muqātila* settled in the *amsār*. This transition was seamless, and the obvious reason, I suggest, is that from the 640s at least the new regime was controlled by an elite, the Quraysh, who had long been accustomed to using both solidi and drahms in their commercial dealings. There is the well-known passage in Balādhurī which tells us that 'The *dinars* of Heraclius used to be current among the people of Mecca before Muslim times, and also the *baghliyah* dirhams of Persia; but it was not customary to buy and sell with them except by considering the coins as bullion.'[21] Less well known is an equally interesting reference in al-Maqrīzī's *Kitāb al-nizā' wa-t-takhāsum*, which states that in the *jāhiliyya* the Quraysh 'used to vie with each other in supplying the pilgrims with the necessities of life, these being a group of rich men. Each individual of this group might at times send along 100 *mithqāls*' weight of gold coins of the Emperor Heraclius.'[22] The *mithqāl jāhilī*[23] would of course have been

[20] For the continued circulation of solidi, see the late seventh-century hoards published in C. Morrisson, 'Le trésor byzantin de Nikertai', *Revue Belge de Numismatique* 118 (1972), 29–91; W. E. Metcalf, 'Three Seventh-Century Byzantine Gold Hoards', *American Numismatic Society Museum Notes* 25 (1980), 87–108; G. Bijovsky, 'A Hoard of Byzantine Solidi from Bet Sh'ean in the Umayyad period', *Revue Numismatique* 158 (2002), 161–227.

[21] Balādhurī, *Futūḥ al-buldān*, p. 402 = *Origins of the Islamic State*, trans. Murgotten, p. 263.

[22] Maqrīzī, *Kitab al-nizā'*, trans. C. E. Bosworth, *Al-Maqrīzī's 'Book of Contention and Strife Concerning the Relations between the Banū Umayya and the Banū Hāshim'* (Manchester, 1980), p. 49.

[23] Ṭabarī, *Ta'rīkh*, ser. ii, p. 939, l.12ff. = al-Ṭabarī, *The Marwānid Restoration (The History of al-Ṭabarī, vol. xxii)*, trans. E. K. Rowson (Albany, 1989), pp. 91–2.

the weight of the solidus, so the amount mentioned here would have been equal to 100 solidi.[24]

The core of the new political elite that emerged in ʿUthmān's time were the already affluent landed or commercial members of the Quraysh, mostly Umayyad, and their progressive and rapid marginalisation of the so-called theocratic group was a major cause of the tensions that exploded in the 650s.[25] Vast fortunes were accumulated at rapid speed.[26] According to Masʿūdī, ʿUthmān himself left behind liquid assets of 150,000 dinars (read: solidi) and 1 million drahms.[27] There was no restriction on the sale of *kharāj* land,[28] and the sheer scale of liquid assets available to members of the elite, especially Quraysh, would have buoyed an active market in land that was largely driven by speculation and redevelopment.[29] There is little doubt that the acquisition of estates began in a big way with ʿUthmān. He is accused of privatising vast tracts of land in Iraq that had

24 Wāqidī, *The Kitāb al-Maghāzī of al-Wāqidī*, ed. M. Jones (London, 1966), vol. 1, pp. 27–8, cites figures for the amounts of gold (*mithqāl*) invested in the Quraysh-controlled caravan trade to Gaza. The *mithqāl* of '22 carats less a fraction (*kasr*)' (Balādhurī, *loc. cit.*) or '22 carats minus a *ḥabbah*' (Ṭabarī, *loc. cit.*) was the weight of the solidus (4.5479 g), cf. Ṭabarī, ser. ii, p. 940, citing Saʿīd b. al-Musayyab, 'It is by the Syrian [weight] that dīnārs are struck, and that was the weight of the [earlier] dīnārs before [ʿAbd al-Malik's] dīnārs were struck; they were twenty-two *qīrāṭ* minus a *ḥabbah*.' The Syrian carat/*qīrāṭ* of 0.2125 g × 21.4 = 4.547 g, cf. G. C. Miles, 'On the Varieties and Accuracy of Eighth-Century Arab Coin Weights', in *L. A. Mayer Memorial Volume (1895–1959)*, ed. M. Avi-Yonah *et al.* (Jerusalem, 1964), pp. 78–87, at 86, and the slightly different calculation in P. Grierson, 'The Monetary Reforms of ʿAbd al-Malik', *Journal of the Economic and Social History of the Orient* 3 (1960), 241–64, at p. 254.

25 See M. Hinds, 'The Murder of the Caliph ʿUthmān', *International Journal of Middle East Studies* 3 (1972), 450–69 (repr. in M. Hinds, *Studies in Early Islamic History*, ed. Jere Bacharach *et al.* (Princeton, NJ, 1996), pp. 29–55); G. Rotter, *Die Umayyaden und der Zweite Bürgerkrieg (680–692)* (Wiesbaden, 1982), pp. 16ff., 30ff.

26 See esp. Masʿūdī, *Murūj*, iv, 253–5. ʿAbdallāh b. Masʿūd, al-Zubayr b. al-ʿAwwām, Zayd b. Thābit and Saʿd b. Abī Waqqāṣ were among the Companions of the Prophet who left substantial fortunes (Ibn Masʿūd 90,000 *mithqāls*, M. J. Kister, 'Land Property and *Jihād*: A Discussion of Some Early Traditions', *Journal of the Economic and Social History of the Orient* 34 (1991), 270–311, at p. 275, citing al-Dhahabī; al-Zubayr 40 million dirhams, al-Ṭabarī, *Biographies of the Prophet's Companions and their Successors (The History of al-Ṭabarī, vol. xxxix)*, trans. E. Landau-Tasseron (Albany, 1998), p. 27; the last two at least 100,000 dinars, Yaʿqūbī, *Mushākalat al-nās li-zamānihim*, in W. G. Millward (trans.), 'The Adaptation of Men to their Time: An Historical Essay by al-Yaʿqūbī', *Journal of the American Oriental Society* 84 (1964), 329–44, at p. 335, Masʿūdī, *Murūj*, iv. 255). ʿAmr b. al-ʿĀṣ' assets at the time of his death were valued at well over a million 'dinars', cf. Masʿūdī, *Murūj*, v. 61, Maqdisī, *K. al-badʾ*, 6, 3. ʿUthmān's caliphate recalls the reign of Constantine in its rapid enrichment of an emerging elite, except that this one was more tightly structured around kin and close associates, see W. Madelung, *The Succession to Muḥammad: A Study of the Early Caliphate* (Cambridge, 1996), pp. 81ff. and the characterisation in P. Crone, *Slaves on Horses: The Evolution of the Islamic Polity* (Cambridge, 1980), pp. 32, 40, 43, esp. 'the affinal character of the Sufyanid state'.

27 Masʿūdī *Murūj*, iv. 253, so too Yaʿqūbī, *Mushākalat*, trans. Millward, p. 334.

28 A. A. al-Dūrī, 'Landlord and Peasant in Early Islam', *Der Islam* 56 (1979), 97–105, esp. p. 99.

29 Cf. S. A. El-Ali, 'Muslim Estates in Hidjaz in the First Century A.H.', *Journal of the Economic and Social History of the Orient* 2 (1959), 247–61.

been confiscated following the decimation of the aristocracy and the flight of the royal family and clergy, land which was effectively ownerless. But this conflates the build-up of private estates in the Sawad with Muʿāwiya's privatisation of the *ṣawāfī*. 'The setting aside and registration of the *sawāfī* took place during the caliphate of Muʿāwiya,'[30] whereas the issue that badly backfired in ʿUthmān's caliphate was a land exchange scheme that enabled the Madinan elite to buy lucrative estates in Iraq in exchange for properties in the Hijāz and southern Arabia.[31] Al-Māwardī tells us that these 'concessions' yielded some 50 million dirhams, 'some of which he [ʿUthman] offered as gifts and donations'.[32]

ʿAbd al-ʿAzīz Durī's characterisation of the late Umayyad elite as an 'acquisitive aristocracy' is surely true of the whole Umayyad period.[33] Muʿāwiya's massive acquisitions and investments in Madina,[34] his investments in Mecca and al-Ṭā'if,[35] his draining of the marsh land in southern Iraq[36] and the systematic way in which he seems to have gone about establishing the true extent of the former crown lands in Iraq, treating them as a personal fief and massively boosting their revenues, all reflect a kind of political entrepreneurialism rooted in the aristocratic traditions of the late antique eastern Mediterranean and the *jāhilīyya*. In Mecca alone Muʿāwiya must have spent close to a quarter of a million drahms buying up real estate, especially the *diyār* (sing. *dār*, 'mansions', 'courts', 'buildings'), e.g. just one transaction well attested in the sources involved 45,000 dinars (solidi). As Kister notes, 'In some of the courts acquired by Muʿawiya there seem to have been workshops of craftsmen, stores and magazines, which secured income and profit.'[37] Most of these real estate transactions look like straightforward commercial purchases (the verb used is شرى *šarā*, form VIII, 'to buy, purchase; buy up, acquire'), but in Madīna he acquired land through distress sales, the Anṣārīs and others complaining that

[30] Madelung, *Succession to Muhammad*, pp. 372–3.

[31] Ṭabarī, *Ta'rīkh*, ser. i, pp. 2854–5 = al-Ṭabarī, *Crisis of the Early Caliphate*, pp. 59–61, and Hinds, *Studies in Early Islamic History*, pp. 18–19.

[32] Māwardī, *al-Aḥkām as-sultānīya*, trans. W. H. Wahba, *The Ordinances of Government: A Translation of Al-Aḥkām al-Sulṭāniyya wa'l-Wilāyāt al-Dīniyya* (Reading, 1996), p. 211.

[33] A. A. al-Dūrī, 'The Origins of Iqṭāʿ in Islam', *Al-Abhath* 22 (1969), 3–24, at p. 11.

[34] M. J. Kister, 'The Battle of the Ḥarra: Some Socio-Economic Aspects', in *Studies in Memory of Gaston Wiet*, ed. M. Rosen-Ayalon (Jerusalem, 1977), pp. 33–49, esp. 42–3.

[35] M. J. Kister, 'Some Reports Concerning Mecca from *Jāhiliyya* to *Islam*', *Journal of the Economic and Social History of the Orient* 15 (1972), 61–93, esp. pp. 84–6; M. J. Kister, 'Some Reports Concerning al-Ṭā'if', *Jerusalem Studies in Arabic and Islam* 1 (1979), 1–18, esp. pp. 13–14, 17.

[36] Balādhurī, *Futūḥ*, p. 291 = *The Origins of the Islamic State*, vol. 1, trans. P. K. Hitti (New York, 1916), p. 454; Masʿūdī, *Murūj*, i, 225–6.

[37] Kister, 'Mecca', pp. 85–6.

'Muʿāwiya bought (our land) for a hundredth of its (real) value',[38] and in al-Ṭā'if he tried to get ʿAmr b. al-ʿĀṣ to give up his massive vineyard al-Waht, reportedly for no consideration whatever. ʿAmr of course refused.[39] He gave Yazīd his son a village in the Fayyum (*fa-aqṭaʿa Muʿāwiya ayḍan Yazīda qaryatan min qurā al-Fayyūm*), but there were strong protests and the land was returned to *kharāj*.[40] This by the way is one of our first references to the possible private ownership of *villages* in Egypt. The most damaging accusation by far is that Muʿāwiya converted *fay'* land or communal property into his private estates and was the first to do this in a decisive way. Yaʿqūbī writes that Muʿāwiya confiscated the former Sasanian royal estates and 'made them his own *ṣawāfī* and gave land grants from them to all the members of his family'.[41] And later, 'And Mu'āwiya did in Syria, the Jazīra and the Yemen what he had done in Iraq by appropriating the estates of the former rulers and transferring them to himself (*taṣyīrihā li-nafsihi*) as his own and making land grants from them to members of his family and entourage.'[42] Indeed, the conflation between *ṣawāfī* and the ruler's private possessions was so complete that Muʿāwiya's estates in Madīna came to be called *ṣawāfī* though Madīna, obviously, would have had no tradition of crown property.[43]

Muʿāwiya b. Abī Sufyān is thus the prototype of the kind of economic protagonism that was such a pronounced feature of the Marwānid period and associated with powerful elite figures such as Maslama b. ʿAbd al-Malik, Khālid b. ʿAbdallāh al-Qasrī and Yazīd b. al-Muhallab al-Azdī. Maslama was willing to invest three million dirhams (and by now a purely Islamic coinage was in circulation) in repairing the breaches in the *baṭīḥa*, if he could have the land for himself.[44] What we have to ask ourselves is what the reclaimed area would have been used for, and rice growing is one obvious answer. Yazīd had some 4000 buffaloes on his estates in Dijlah and Kaskar,[45] and despite the extermination of the Muhallabid family under Yazīd II[46] he seems to have bequeathed sufficient assets for just half the estates to yield a

[38] Kister, 'Battle of the Ḥarra', p. 47.

[39] Balādhurī, *The Ansāb al-ashrāf of al-Balādhurī, vol. IVA*, ed. Max Schloessinger, rev. M. J. Kister (Jerusalem, 1971), p. 54, l.13ff.

[40] Ibn ʿAbd al-Ḥakam, *Futūḥ*, p. 101, l.15ff.

[41] Yaʿqūbī, *Ta'rīkh*, ed. M. T. Houtsma, 2 vols (Leiden, 1883), vol. II, p. 277, l.12ff.

[42] Yaʿqūbī, *Ta'rīkh*, vol. II, p. 278, l.7ff.

[43] Kister, 'Battle of the Ḥarra', pp. 38–42. ʿUmar II was exceptional in seeking to restrain the alienation of state lands (*ṣawāfī*) as private estates; see the famous 'rescript' in H. A. R. Gibb, 'The Fiscal Rescript of Umar II', *Arabica* 2 (1955), 1–16, esp. pp. 10–11.

[44] Balādhurī, *Futūḥ*, 292 = *Origins*, I, 456. [45] Balādhurī, *Futūḥ*, 172 = *Origins*, I, 259.

[46] ʿAwtabī, *Kitāb al-ansab*, trans. M. Hinds, *An Early Islamic Family from Oman: Al-ʿAwtabī's Account of the Muhallabids* (Manchester, 1991), pp. 73 ff.

daily income of 4000 dinars to his grandson Sufyan b. Muʿāwiya b. Yazīd b. al-Muhallab.[47] And Khālid al-Qasrī's estates yielded not less than ten million dirhams annually.[48] The later seventh and early eighth centuries saw huge investments in reclamation and the revival of 'dead' land.[49] The estates carved out of the reclaimed land were so lucrative that various Marwānid rulers were repeatedly tempted to confiscate them, as Yazīd II did with Yazīd b. al-Muhallab's properties.[50] Using Balādhurī's information on the *iqṭāʿāt* Michael Morony years ago gave us a superb reconstruction of the new landed elite associated with these schemes. Morony argued that their investments triggered massive agrarian development and a new form of agriculture based on 'a more efficient, specialized, market-oriented monoculture on plantation estates'.[51] These were industrial crops such as cotton, sugar and rice, most of them hugely labour-intensive and, since they presupposed reclamation, capital-intensive as well. This Umayyad-sponsored tradition of large-scale commercial agriculture continued into the ʿAbbāsid period, of course. ʿAbd Allāh b. Ṣāliḥ from a powerful Syrian family grew saffron on an irrigated estate near Ḥimṣ.[52] The innovation in contrast to late antiquity is not the emergence of a market-oriented aristocracy but the kind of crops it grew.

Lombard suggested that from the close of the eighth century 'Sudanese gold injected fresh life into the Muslim economy'.[53] Yet even without the 'gold of the Sudan', the scale of monetary circulation was sufficient to sustain a staggering level of money taxes, especially under the Marwānids. Al-Maqrīzī cites a series of useful figures for Egyptian taxes under Hishām. ʿUbaydallāh b. al-Ḥabḥāb, Hishām's director of finance for Egypt, initiated a new land survey and population census soon after his arrival there in 105/724. In what must have been the first fiscal year after that, the gross production of the country was estimated at just over 17 million dinars, a figure that impressed Maqrīzī. Of this, four million or a little under a

47 *Ibid.*, pp. 83–4.

48 Dūrī, 'Origins', p. 10. Ṭabarī, *Taʾrīkh*, ser. ii, p. 1655, ll.5–6 = al-Ṭabarī, *The End of Expansion* (*The History of al-Ṭabarī*, vol. xxv), trans. K. Y. Blankinship (Albany, 1989), p. 184 for 20 million as Khālid's income and for Khālid as an improving landowner, and p. 1658 = al-Ṭabarī, *End of Expansion*, pp. 186–7 for the implied economic rivalry with Hishām.

49 Dūrī, 'Landlord and Peasant', p. 102.

50 Balādhurī, *Futūḥ*, 362 = *Origins*, 2, 96.

51 M. G. Morony, 'Landholding and Social Change: Lower al-'Irāq in the Early Islamic Period', in *Land Tenure and Social Transformation in the Middle East*, ed. T. Khalidi (Beirut, 1984), pp. 209–22, at 210.

52 Yaʿqūbī, *Kitāb al-buldān*, ed. M. J. de Goeje (Leiden, 1967), p. 324, cf. P. M. Cobb, *White Banners: Contention in 'Abbāsid Syria, 750–880* (Albany, 2001), p. 30.

53 Lombard, *L'Islam dans sa première grandeur*, p. 116.

quarter was taken in taxes, and of that amount 2.72 million (as much as 70 per cent!) was despatched to the treasury in Damascus.[54] One has the impression that four million was about the *most* Egypt could yield in taxes even under sound financial management. Contrast that with Iraq. If we take 120 million dirhams as Iraq's average revenue, under the Umayyads (and not including Khuzistan), and divide by twelve to obtain the dinar equivalent, this gives us ten million dinars or two and a half times more than Egypt! In short, Iraq was crucial, the most productive and probably the most heavily taxed province, and this is one background against which we might view both the very substantial investments that went into the Iraqi countryside and the building of a new capital at Baghdād. Fars and Jibāl were the next most heavily taxed regions under Muʿāwiya with tax levels of 70 million drahms each. By contrast, Syria seems to have been under-taxed, perhaps deliberately, since its yield was just 1.88 million dinars.[55]

The money taxation of the Umayyad period was essentially the culmination of a late antique tax system that had its roots in the massive monetary expansion of the fourth to sixth centuries[56] and had formed the backbone of the fiscal systems of both Justinian I and Khusrō I. The essence of this system was a fixed monetary demand on the taxpayer assessed on the area of the holding or the number of trees in the case of tree crops. Abū Yūsuf, who discusses the drawbacks of *misāḥa*, criticised it for lacking the flexibility to match the constant and unpredictable fluctuation of prices. The general implication is that the efficiency of the Umayyad fiscal system depended on the market; in other words, the amount of revenue collected would fluctuate according to the state of the market.[57] But *misāḥa* also worked to the detriment of the peasantry: a system structured to enforce fixed cash payments with no allowance for the season would mean that peasants would *have* to offload stocks in the immediate post-harvest period, thus driving prices down and, especially in good seasons, generating a downward spiral of further disbursements and further deflation.[58] Abū Yūsuf or rather the redactors of the *Kitāb al-kharāj*[59] refer to this

[54] Maqrīzī, *Description topographique et historique de l'Égypte*, trans. U. Bouriant (Paris, 1900), pp. 283–4.
[55] Yaʿqūbī, *Ta'rīkh*, vol. II, p. 277, Māwardī, *Aḥkām*, 192, and Rotter, *Umayyaden*, pp. 61–2.
[56] J. Banaji, *Agrarian Change in Late Antiquity: Gold, Labour and Aristocratic Dominance*, 2nd edn (Oxford, 2007), ch. 3.
[57] E.g. the reason why al-Maqrīzī was so impressed that ʿUbaydallāh b. al-Ḥabḥāb could extract four million dinars from Egypt following his land survey is that *prices* were low at the time.
[58] Banaji, *Agrarian Change*, pp. 84ff., on the 'Wingate effect'.
[59] N. Calder, *Studies in Early Muslim Jurisprudence* (Oxford, 1993), ch. 6.

mechanism in one ḥadīth in which ʿUmar b. ʿAbd al-ʿAzīz is reported as saying: 'My predecessors used to charge the *dhimmīs* with more taxes than they could bear, forcing them thereby to sell their crops at low prices to pay the taxes. However I am not charging anyone with more than he can bear and no one is pressed to sell his crops at cheap prices.'[60]

The upshot of this kind of fiscally induced mechanism was that many peasants (non-Arabs) simply abandoned agriculture and either fled or drifted to the towns. The Marwānid restoration meant a stronger state and the drive to tax more efficiently, so the exodus from the countryside swelled in those years.[61] Ibn Rustah refers to al-Hajjāj b. Yūsuf's 'oppression and despotism' (*li-ẓulmi wa-ʿasfihi*) causing a dramatic collapse of the revenues of the *Sawād* to just 18 million dirhams.[62] In 1938 Lionel Casson collated all the data on Aphrodito's taxes into a time series covering the years 698–722. The staggering feature of the series is the sheer level of *money* taxes the Marwānids wanted from this small district, an annual assessment of almost 7,000 dinars. Aphrodito of course was in Middle Egypt, at some distance from Iraq, but here too the taxes showed substantial arrears, with collections running at an average of some 60 per cent.[63] And of course the papyri from Aphrodito are full of references to a fugitive peasantry whom the governor Qurra b. Sharīk wanted tracked down and returned to their villages. This is a good example of the documentary evidence supporting the *adab* sources.

Now there seem to me to be two reasons why the kind of fiscal narrative that Chris Wickham has recently developed for the later Roman empire won't work for the Islamic world. First, the moment of functionality in Wickham's model resides in the movement of fiscal goods (taxes in kind) between different parts of the Mediterranean (this assumes of course that late Roman taxation was dominated by payments in kind) and the impact this had in terms of integrating the regional economies of the empire. It was the coherence of the tax system that allowed for economic integration at an empire-wide level. Now even if we assume that this is

60 Abū Yūsuf, *Kitāb al-kharāj*, trans. A. Ben Shemesh, *Taxation in Islam*, vol. III: *Abū Yūsuf's Kitāb al-kharāj* (Leiden and London, 1969), p. 90. So too in the later Roman empire, cf. Ammianus Marcellinus 16.5.15: '… since it is universally acknowledged that the poor (*pauperes*) are forced to pay the full burden of their taxes at the very start of the tax year (*inter ipsa indictorum exordia*) without any relief'.

61 H. Cadell, 'Nouveaux fragments de la correspondance de Ḳurrah ben Sharīk', *Recherches de papyrologie* 4 (1967), 107–60, esp. pp. 118ff.

62 Ibn Rustah, *Kitāb al-aʿlāk an-nafīsa*, ed. M. J. de Goeje (Leiden, 1967), p. 105, l.12.

63 L. Casson, 'Tax-Collection Problems in Early Arab Egypt', *Transactions and Proceedings of the American Philological Association* 69 (1938), 274–91, esp. p. 287.

an accurate picture of the late Roman economy and taxation,[64] it cannot be applied to the Umayyad and ʿAbbāsid periods, since, as I have tried to suggest, their tax systems were thoroughly monetised and there was certainly no Islamic-period counterpart to the large-scale movement of fiscal goods between regions. In other words, the key factor in the model is simply missing in the Islamic world. Secondly, Wickham's minimalism, the idea that the fiscal process was 'a major motor for the commercial movement of goods',[65] also doesn't work. There is a brief but striking demonstration of this in Hugh Kennedy's calculation of the likely wage bill of the early Umayyad army, which he estimates at a minimum of 60 million dirhams per year.[66] Even if we double this figure and assume that 120 million dirhams was regularly absorbed by military wage costs, this is still only a fraction of the amount of money in circulation in the caliphate and of the vast amounts that the Muslim political and business elites controlled as part of their private assets.[67] This was not an economy driven by the kind of fiscal dynamic that Wickham posits for the late empire. The cash reserves of some 900 million dirhams in Hārūn al-Rashīd's treasury at the time of his death[68] show just how much wealth the caliphate had come to generate by the end of the second/start of the ninth century. If a fiscal narrative won't work, we need to look elsewhere. Between the late antique and ʿAbbāsid periods, commercial networks were characterised by considerable continuity. This was as true of the Gulf as it was of the Red Sea; for example, Donald Whitcomb has argued (in an unpublished paper) 'The idea of collapse and dramatic cessation of commerce with the Muslim conquest may be discarded in this area as well' (meaning the Persian Gulf).[69]

Indeed, at the economic level, the most remarkable outcome of the expansion of Islam was the evolution of a well-integrated, legally and

64 Cf. Banaji, *Agrarian Change*, app. 5.

65 Wickham, *Framing*, p. 79.

66 H. Kennedy, *The Armies of the Caliphs: Military and Society in the Early Islamic State* (London and New York, 2001), pp. 67–8.

67 E.g. 'The caliph Hishām is said to have reckoned that his property developments in the Jazīra brought in more revenue than the whole of the taxation of the empire', H. Kennedy, 'Elite Incomes in the Early Islamic State', in *The Byzantine and Early Islamic Near East*, vol. VI: *Elites Old and New in the Byzantine and Early Islamic Near East*, ed. J. Haldon *et al.* (Princeton, NJ, 2004), pp. 13–28, at 28, who also notes that 'The ownership of great estates was vastly profitable.'

68 Ṭabarī, *Ta'rīkh*, ser. iii, p. 764 = al-Ṭabarī, *The 'Abbāsid Caliphate in Equilibrium* (*The History of al-Ṭabarī*, vol. xxx), trans. C. E. Bosworth (Albany, 1989), p. 335.

69 D. Whitcomb, 'The "Commercial Crescent": Red Sea Trade in Late Antiquity and Early Islam', paper presented to the Fifth LAEI Workshop on Trade and Exchange in the Late Antique and Early Islamic Near East, 14–16 November 1996.

financially sophisticated business sector that formed the mainstay of economic life throughout the early centuries. That the trade to the east suffered *no* major disruption in the decades of the conquests is strongly implied in Baṣra's rapid evolution as a major commercial centre, attested, remarkably, in the so-called Short Recension of the Armenian Geography now attributed to Ananias of Širak. This recension cannot date from too long after Baṣra itself was founded, and it tells us, 'Baṣra is filled with merchants and ships coming from India and all parts of the orient.'[70] Now one of the most remarkable portions of the Armenian Geography is the passage relating to the limits and four great subdivisions of the Sasanian empire. This exists only in the Long Recension and was clearly taken straight from an official Sasanian document in Middle Persian. For our purposes the most interesting section is the description of *K'usti Nmroj* or the Southern region, which the source says contained nineteen provinces, including *Maazun*, that is, Oman, and *Debuhēl*, that is, Daybul (in Sind).[71] One reason for the continued and rapid expansion of Arab-controlled trade to the east is that the Umayyads simply took over the cosmopolitan maritime empire created over several centuries by the Sasanians,[72] and just as there is a sense in which the late antique model of a monetised tax system reached its climax in the ʿAbbāsid period, because of the role of the Umayyads in preserving it, so too did the commercial infrastructure inherited from the Sasanians reach its most developed and cosmopolitan form in the ninth and tenth centuries, when Ṣuḥār and Sīrāf were flourishing international ports, Sīrāf leading initially, and the cosmopolitanism of the Gulf ports created a religious and intellectual climate conducive to all kinds of progressive tendencies. Al-Iṣṭakhrī, writing in the early tenth century, wrote that the merchants of Fars were driven by their 'passion to accumulate capital' (*maḥabbat jamaʿa al-mal*) and comments on the enormous wealth of the Sirāfī merchants.[73] Ibn Ḥauqal refers to the *ṭirāz* workshops owned by merchants at Jannābā in Arrajān: *wa hiya madīna kāna fīhā ṭuruz li'l-kuttani li'l-tujjāri*.[74] The penetration of merchant

[70] R. H. Hewsen, *The Geography of Ananias of Širak (Ašxarhacʿoycʿ): The Long and the Short Recensions* (Wiesbaden, 1992), p. 71A.

[71] Hewsen, *Geography*, p. 72.

[72] J. C. Wilkinson, 'Ṣuḥār (Sohar) in the Early Islamic Period: The Written Evidence', in *South Asian Archaeology 1977*, ed. M. Taddei (Naples, 1979), vol. II, pp. 887–907, esp. 893, and the background in J. C. Wilkinson, 'Arab–Persian Land Relationships in Late Sasānid Oman', *Proceedings of the Seminar for Arabian Studies* 3 (1973), 40–51.

[73] Iṣṭakhrī, *Kitāb al-masālik wa'l-mamālik*, ed. M. J. de Goeje (Leiden, 1870), p. 138; so too Ibn Ḥauqal, *Kitāb ṣūrat al-ʾarḍ*, ed. J. H. Kramers (Leiden, 1939), p. 290, ll.9–10, elaborating.

[74] Ibn Ḥauqal, *Kitāb ṣūrat al-ʾard*, p. 269; likewise at Jahram, *Kitāb*, p. 268.

capital into production was a far more advanced process in Islam, two or three centuries ahead of the Italians. Certainly, the main Islamic forms of the *commenda*, called *muḍāraba*, *qirāḍ* or *muqāraḍa*, were already developed institutions well before the eleventh century and the subject of an extensive legal literature.[75] The Ḥanafīs were especially sympathetic to the purely productive uses of the *muḍāraba*, creating legal sanction for the merchant's control of manufacturing operations. And that was how Lombard saw the Muslim merchant: 'The merchant-entrepreneur founded industries, provided work, supplied the raw materials, advanced the money, and undertook to find an outlet for the products.'[76] Again, *istiṣnā'* or the supply contracts that merchants struck with craftsmen in control of their own means of production were a prime case of the flexibility and pragmatism that could characterise Ḥanafī law in the economic field, since there was no reference to such contracts in the Qur'ān, and their endorsement implied a victory or *ijmā'* and *istiḥsān* over *qiyās*.[77] The conjunction of various forms of partnership with supply contracts are simply one indication of the complex ways in which businesses could be organised, and suggest a degree of complexity that was considerably beyond anything one finds in late antiquity. In any case, the 'appearance, manufacture and rapid adoption of the Islamic Cream Ware varieties at the expense of existing pottery types' in the later eighth and early ninth centuries[78] presupposes the dominance of this kind of coordination by trading firms, just as the ʿAbbāsid polychrome glazes presume Chinese influence and regular contacts with the Far East, global networks dominated by Iraqi merchants.[79] The precocity of financial instruments is no less striking.

In short, the ʿAbbāsid period elite comprised a substantial layer of 'premodern' capitalists[80] – grain merchants, textile traders, tax farmers,

[75] A. L. Udovitch, *Partnership and Profit in Medieval Islam* (Princeton, NJ, 1970).

[76] Lombard, *L'Islam dans sa première grandeur*, p. 149.

[77] E. Pritsch and O. Spies, 'Der islamische Werklieferungsvertrag (nach al-Kāsānī)', *Zeitschrift für vergleichende Rechtswissenschaft* 56 (1953), 47–75; J. C. Wichard, *Zwischen Markt und Moschee: Wirtschaftliche Bedürfnisse und religiöse Anforderungen im frühen islamischen Vertragsrecht* (Paderborn, 1995), pp. 237 ff.

[78] A. Walmsley, 'Turning East: The Appearance of Islamic Cream Ware in Jordan: The "End of Antiquity"?', in *La céramique byzantine et proto-islamique en Syrie-Jordanie (IVe–VIIIe siècles apr. J.-C)*, ed. E. Villeneuve *et al.* (Beirut, 2001), p. 310.

[79] Anonymous, *Akhbār aṣ-ṣīn*, 12 (7), for Iraqi dominance; 34 (16) for the 'excellent quality' of Chinese ceramics.

[80] P. Crone, 'Weber, Islamic Law and the Rise of Capitalism', in P. Crone, *From Kavād to al-Ghazālī: Religion, Law and Political Thought in the Near East, c.600–c.1100* (Aldershot, 2005), p. 255.

shipowners, moneychangers, the owners of rice and sugar plantations, or the enormously wealthy businessmen who financed the overseas trade, such as Abū Bakr Aḥmad b. ʿUmar Sīrāfī, the Sīrāfī financier whom Ibn Ḥauqal met in Baṣra in 350/961, whose fortune was well over two million dinars, excluding the capital invested in partnerships and the foreign goods warehoused in his *khānbārāt* and *makhāzin*.[81] The fascinating feature of the passage in which Ibn Ḥauqal describes Abū Bakr is the connection he suddenly draws between the wealthy mercantile society of Baṣra and the strength of Muʿtazilī doctrines there. Characterising this remarkable evolution has always generated some uncertainty among historians. Thus Lombard himself was careful to avoid any specific analogies. The most he said was that Muslim merchants 'pooled capital resources and founded trading and banking companies', that they could 'call on great capital reserves' and that 'Capital was constantly ploughed back into ever more ambitious undertakings.'[82] Ashtor claimed, 'there can be no doubt that in the time of the ʿAbbāsids the Near Eastern economy reached the state of pre-capitalism',[83] by which he meant, clearly, the threshold of 'true capitalism' but not the latter, of course. Duri wrote, 'The decisive evolution that came to the fore in the Abbasid period is the expansion of trade and the emergence of a capitalist class among the merchants.'[84] And Patricia Crone states, 'It is well known that premodern capitalism flourished in medieval Islamic society.'[85] The fact remains that however we characterise the evolution that the first two centuries of Islamic economic growth had resulted in, it was sufficiently different from the past to represent a significant advance.

[81] Ibn Ḥauqal, *Kitāb ṣūrat al-'ard*, pp. 290–1.
[82] Lombard, *L'Islam dans sa première grandeur*, p. 150.
[83] E. Ashtor, *A Social and Economic History of the Near East in the Middle Ages* (London, 1976), p. 112.
[84] A. Duri, *Arabische Wirtschaftsgeschichte*, trans. J. Jacobi (Zurich and Munich, 1979), p. 178.
[85] Crone, 'Weber', p. 255.

CHAPTER 10

'Regions that look seaward'
Changing fortunes, submerged histories and the slow capitalism of the sea

All scholars are familiar with the fascinating passage in Procopius where he tells us that 'it was impossible for the Ethiopians to buy silk from the Indians, because Persian merchants would always locate themselves at the very harbours (*hormoi*) where the Indian ships first put in and were used to buying up whole cargoes'.[1] By suggesting that 'the Iranians' near-monopoly in the markets of South India and Ceylon'[2] was a drastic limitation on the Byzantine access to South Asian ports, the least it implies is that by late antiquity trade networks in the Indian Ocean had been radically reconfigured to eliminate any significant Roman/Byzantine presence. Sasanian dominance of the sea lanes in the western Indian Ocean, which was firmly established by the late sixth century, is a major part of the explanation of why Islam was able to expand in the Indian Ocean in the way it did by extending and consolidating links established in the Sasanian centuries.[3] Moreover, Procopius also documents the commercial strategies used by Sasanian traders in buying up whole cargoes, a fascinating allusion to the way merchants worked in the maritime trade. But there are two other features of this passage that have gone largely unnoticed. Procopius tells us that it was *Indian* ships that imported the cargoes that were subsequently bought by Iranian merchants, and he implies that the harbours where these transactions took place were South Asian.

Among classical sources and leaving Ptolemy aside, the most informative accounts of South Asian ports are certainly those in the *Periplus* and in Cosmas. If we disregard Barbarikon (which was in Sind) and start south of the Gulf of Barake (Dwarka?), the following local and major ports are listed: Barygaza, Akabaru, Suppara, Kalliena, Sêmylla, Mandagora, Palaipatmai, Melizeigara, Byzantion, Toparon (?), Tyrannosboas (?),

[1] Procopius, *Bell.* 1.20.12 (Dewing, *History of the Wars*, vol. 1, p. 192).

[2] D. Whitehouse and A. Williamson, 'Sasanian Maritime Trade', *Iran* 11 (1973), 29–49, at p. 44.

[3] E.g. A. Williamson, 'Persian Gulf Commerce in the Sassanian Period and the First Two Centuries of Islam', *Bastan Chenassi va Honar-e Iran* 9–10 (1972), 97–109.

Naura, Tyndis, Muziris, Nelkynda, Bakarê, Balita, Komar, Kolchoi, Kamara, Podukê and Sôpatma.[4] Of the twenty-two ports listed here, roughly half are either known to us or susceptible to identification, while two of the place names are clearly corrupt. In Cosmas (again disregarding 'Sindou') the crucial passage in book XI mentions eleven place names: Orrothâ, Kalliana, Sibôr, Malé, Parti, Mangarouth, Salopatana, Nalopatana, Poudapatana, Marallo and Kaber (with an epsilon).[5] Of these, two are the names of regions: Orrothâ is Saurashtra, i.e. Kathiawar, and Malé is the Malabar coast. Excluding these, Cosmas seems to list a total of nine ports (five of these in Malé/Malabar) of which five are known or can be found. Since Kalliana occurs in both lists, we have a net total of fifteen Indian ports whose locations are either well established or can be surmised with some certainty/probability.

I'd like to start the chapter by looking at some of these uncertain-looking place names whose locations can be mapped with more confidence. In the Cosmas/*Periplus* lists there are six in particular that are worth sorting out. These are Mandagora (*Periplus*), Mangarouth (Cosmas), Sibôr (Cosmas), Poudapatana (Cosmas), Bakarê (*Periplus*) and Kaber (Cosmas). Mandagora was either Mandwa about 12 miles north of Alibag in Raigad district, near its northern tip, or, as Vasant Shinde has suggested, Kuda-Mandad at the head of the Janjira creek a short distance south of Chaul.[6] Since it is listed after Sêmylla in both the *Periplus* and Ptolemy, and Sêmylla was medieval Saimur, that is, Chaul in Raigad (today Revdanda), Shinde's suggestion preserves the sequence of both sources. Mangarouth in Cosmas was almost certainly Mangalore.[7] In Cosmas it is the second Malé (= Malabar) location after Parti (unknown but possibly Barçelore) and before Salopatana and Nalopatana (both unknown). This gives us some idea of how far *up* the west coast Malé = Malabar was thought to extend, at least in the circles Cosmas moved in. In Cosmas Sibôr is sandwitched between Kalliana and Malé and was almost certainly his name for Sindābūr of the Arabic sources, namely, Goa.[8] In

[4] *Periplus Maris Erythraei* 49, 52–60, ed. L. Casson, *The Periplus Maris Erythraei: Text with Introduction, Translation and Commentary* (Princeton, NJ, 1989), pp. 80–9.

[5] Cosmas, *Top. Chrét.* XI.16 (ed. W. Wolska-Conus, *Cosmas Indicopleustès, Topographie Chrétienne* (Paris, 1973), vol. III, p. 347).

[6] V. Shinde, S. Gupta and D. Rajgor, 'An Archaeological Reconnaissance of the Konkan Coast from Bharuch to Janjira', *Man and Environment* 27/1 (2002), 73–82, at p. 78.

[7] H. Yule, *Cathay and the Way Thither: Being a Collection of Medieval Notices of China*, 4 vols, rev.edn by H. Cordier (London, 1915), vol. I, p. 228 n. 1; vol. IV, p. 73.

[8] Yule, *Cathay and the Way Thither*, vol. IV, p. 65: Sindabur 'substantially identical with the port of Goa'; G. R. Tibbetts, *Arab Navigation in the Indian Ocean before the Coming of the Portuguese, Being a Translation of Kitāb al-Fawā'id fī uṣūl al-baḥr wa'l-qawā'id of Aḥmad b. Mājid al-Najdī* (London, 1971), p. 455.

other words, Cosmas' description of the west coast of India divided it into four major segments: Saurashtra or Kathiawar in Gujarat, Kalyan just north of Bombay, Sindābūr or Goa, and the Malabar ports ending with Poudapatana. This last location can be identified with 'Budfattan' in Ibn Baṭṭūṭa[9] or modern Puthupatanam/Puthupanam at Vadakara Beach south of Thalassery. In late medieval times Puthupatanam was a satellite port of Calicut, like Pantalāyini, described by Tomé Pires as one of several 'small ports' that the Zamorin or ruler of Calicut depended on because, as he said, 'The port of Calicut is not good because the land slopes up from the sea'.[10] (In the Lisbon manuscript of the *Suma* the name appears as 'pudy patanam'.) Bakarê in the *Periplus* was Pliny's Becare,[11] described by him as a 'more useful port' than Muziris, though further south in the Pandyan territory. It has usually been identified as Purakkad[12] but the decisive clue to its true identity is the statement in the *Periplus* that 'After Bakarê comes Red Mountain, as it is called, and another region extends …'[13] From this it is certain Bakarê/Becare was Varkala 20 km south-east of Kollam, which the *Rough Guide* describes as backed by 'sheer red laterite cliffs', a unique geological feature of the otherwise flat Kerala coastline and the 'Red Mountain' of the *Periplus*.[14] Pliny tells us that pepper was transported to Becare (Varkala) in country boats from 'Cottonara'. This has to be Kuttanad, the Kottanarikê of the *Periplus*, which the latter wrongly describes as the pepper-growing region par excellence, whereas Pliny simply says it was 'the region from which pepper is conveyed to Becare', implying it may just have been a trans-shipment hub.[15] In that

[9] Muḥammad ibn 'Abdallāh ibn Baṭṭūṭa, *The Travels of Ibn Baṭṭūṭa A.D. 1325–1354*, trans. H. A. R. Gibb (London, 1958–2000), vol. IV, p. 811.

[10] Tomé Pires, *The Suma Oriental of Tomé Pires: An Account of the East, from the Red Sea to Japan, Written in Malacca and India in 1512–1515*, 2 vols, trans. A. Cortesão (London, 1944), vol. I, p. 78.

[11] Pliny, *NH* VI.105 (Rackham, vol. II, p. 418).

[12] E.g. M. L. Dames, *The Book of Duarte Barbosa: An Account of the Countries Bordering on the Indian Ocean and their Inhabitants etc.*, 2 vols (New Delhi, 1989), vol. II, p. 95, n.2

[13] *Periplus* 58, ed. Casson, pp. 86–7.

[14] D. Abram *et al.*, *South India: The Rough Guide* (London, 1999), p. 300.

[15] I borrow the expression from James Michael who notes that Kuttanad itself, as a flat, low-lying, largely coastal region, 'does not have the right kind of climate to grow pepper' (James Michael, pers. comm. dated 14 December 2012). Also see F. De Romanis, 'Comparative Perspectives on the Pepper Trade', in *Across the Ocean: Nine Essays on Indo-Mediterranean Trade*, ed. F. De Romanis *et al.* (Leiden, 2015), but locating Becare-Nelkynda in the southern part of the Vembanad Lake, which would mean that the Pandyas of Madurai had substantially more territory on the west coast than they are likely to have done, since the Pandyas had control of Becare which lay in the territory of the 'Neacyndi'. As Michael pointed out to me, Kollam would be a more natural southern extension of the Vembanad pepper system than Kochi-Thrissur (email, 7 January 2014). In his edition of the *Periplus* Schoff had already remarked that Varkala '*was formerly the southern end of the long line of backwaters*, and a place of considerable commercial importance', W. H. Schoff, *The Periplus of the*

case, Nelkynda would have been somewhere in this vicinity, not far from Varkala, since the *Periplus* reports that 'vessels' (*ta ploia*), the country boats described by Pliny, came downriver from there to Becare on the outbound voyage.[16] That a port so far south was 'active' when the *Periplus* was written shows that by the first century the *whole* of the Kerala coast had been actively drawn into the Red Sea trade orbit.

'Kaber' in Cosmas is clearly Ptolemy's Khaberis,[17] long identified with Kaveripattinam or Poompuhar in Nagai district of Tamil Nadu, a major Sangam-age Chola port[18] which from all accounts seems to have had a quarter for foreign merchants.[19] It is also a rare example of a South Asian port with an actual harbour, judging by the remains of a wharf. Part of Kaveripattinam seems to have been washed away, possibly in the late fifth or early sixth centuries, according to its excavator, K. V. Soundara Rajan.[20] But Rajan is cautious both about the scale of this incursion and its timing, and describes it as a temporary setback. That Cosmas listed Kaber among the major east coast ports is in itself interesting. It suggests that no dramatic incident had been witnessed by the merchant circles from which he gathered his information (in the second or third decades of the sixth century) for the purely geographical book he was writing.[21]

Erythraean Sea: Travel and Trade in the Indian Ocean by a Merchant of the First Century (London, Bombay and Calcutta, 1912), p. 234.

16 No one has identified Nelkynda so far but in Ptolemy's sequence of place names (*Geography* 7. 1.9) it lies south of Bakare (Pliny's Becare), in Āy territory, and the river connecting Nelkynda with Becare is called the 'Barios'.

17 Ptolemy, *Geog.* 7.1.13 (ed. A. Stückelberger and G. Graßhoff, *Klaudios Ptolemaios: Handbuch der Geographie* (Basel, 2006), vol. II, p. 690).

18 J. W. McCrindle, *Ancient India as Described by Ptolemy* (London, 1885), pp. 63ff.; K. A. Nilakanta Sastri, *Foreign Notices of South India: From Megasthenes to Ma Huan* (Madras, 1939), p. 89.

19 R. Champakalakshmi, *Trade, Ideology and Urbanization: South India 300 BC to AD 1300* (New Delhi, 1996), pp. 108, 127, 193. Since this chapter says nothing further about the place names in Ptolemy, it may be worth drawing attention to the following likely or possible identities (in the coastal stretch that runs from Maleo in *Geography* 7.1.4 to Maliarpha in 7.1.14 in the catalogue of locations, Stückelberger and Graßhoff, *Klaudios Ptolemaios*, vol. II, pp. 688–91). Nusaripa = Navsari; Balepatna = Kharepatan in Ratnagiri district (cf. R. Chakravarti, 'Coastal Trade and Voyages in Konkan: The Early Medieval Scenario', *The Indian Economic and Social History Review* 35/2 (1998), 97–123, at pp. 107–8); Bakare = Varkala; Sosikurei = Tuticorin; Cape Kory 'also called Kalligikon' = Valinokkam Point; Salour = Saliyur (the Sangam name of Alagankulam, cf. Champakalakshmi, *Trade, Ideology and Urbanization*, pp. 133, 140); and Maliarpha = Mylapore (K. V. Raman, 'Port Towns of Tamilnadu: Some Field Data and the Prospects of Maritime Archaeology', in *Marine Archaeology of Indian Ocean Countries*, ed. S. R. Rao (Dona Paula, Goa, 1988), pp. 114–18, at 115). The remarkable feature of Ptolemy's list is how easy it is to identify east coast place names from it.

20 K. V. Soundara Rajan, *Kaveripattinnam Excavations 1963–73: A Port City on the Tamilnadu Coast* (New Delhi, 1994), p. 130.

21 The claim that 'it is safe to assume that a major portion of Kavirippompattinam was lost (washed away) during the middle of the sixth century', G. Seshadri, 'New Perspectives on Nagapattinam: The

A final toponym worth examining in some detail is the mysterious BLBQ/B.llin in various manuscripts of Ibn Khurradādhbih and al-Idrīsī. Idrīsī's manuscripts reflect complete uncertainty about this place name, with Jaubert vacillating between two main readings, بلنق (transliterated 'Balanc') and بلبق ('Balabac'; 'Balbak' in Elliot and Dowson),[22] and Maqbul Ahmad printing بليق (Balīq) in his extracts in *India and the Neighbouring Territories as Described by the Sharīf al-Idrīsī* (1954).[23] Now it is clear that part of Idrīsī's information about this 'island', as he calls it, was drawn from a crucial passage in Ibn Khurradādhbih. This, coupled with the fact that the latter's manuscripts show a less dispersed range of readings that fluctuate around the ones that de Goeje published in his edition of 1889, suggests that Ibn Khurradādhbih's manuscripts are our best guide to the name the ʿAbbasid geographer must have used in the original mid-ninth-century version of his work. De Goeje published بَلّين and بلين in his text of Ibn Khurradādhbih[24] and noted بلين, بلن and بلين as variants in the apparatus. Here the strong inference is that the uncertainty regarding where to put the diacritical marks involved not the last letter *nūn* but the first and the third, the *bā'* and the *yā'*. For the moment, let me retain de Goeje's name 'Ballīn' (with the *shadda* on the *lām*) as a rough reading of the port he was referring to.[25]

So where was Ballīn? The crucial fact about it is that this was where 'the maritime route for eastbound ships bifurcated'. As Minorsky says, paraphrasing Ibn Khurradādhbih, 'one branch followed the east coast of India while the other went to Ceylon and China'.[26] Minorsky realised that Ballīn would have to be on the east coast, since 'Generally speaking a

Medieval Port City in the Context of Political, Religious and Commercial Exchanges between South India, Southeast Asia, and China', in *Nagapattinam to Suvarnadwipa: Reflections on the Chola Naval Expeditions to Southeast Asia*, ed. H. Kulke *et al.* (Singapore, 2009), p. 107, is untenable.

[22] Al-Idrīsī, *Kitāb nuzhat al-muštāq fi'khtirāq al-āfāq*, ed. P.-A. Jaubert, *La géographie d'Édrisi*, repr. of Paris edn (Amsterdam, 1836–40; repr. 1975), pp. 73, 175, 178; H. M. Elliot and J. Dowson, *The History of India, as Told by its Own Historians: The Muhammadan Period*, 8 vols (London, 1867 –77), vol. 1, p. 89.

[23] S. Maqbul Ahmad, *India and the Neighbouring Territories as Described by the Sharif al-Idrisi in his Kitāb Nuzhat al-mushtāq fi'khtirāq al-āfāq*: part 1 (Arabic text) (Aligarh, 1954), p. 11 (§29): بليق in the Bodleian and BM manuscripts, بلبق in Paris A; p. 57 (§4): بلنق in Paris A, بلنق in the BM manuscript; at p. 63 (§29) he prints بلبق, following Paris A and BM.

[24] ʿUbayd Allāh b. ʿAbdallāh b. Khurradādhbih, *Kitāb al-masālik wa'l-mamālik (Liber viarum et regnorum)*, ed. M. J. de Goeje (Leiden, 1889), p. 63, ll. 2, 3–4; p. 66, l. 1.

[25] That was how Maqbul Ahmad rendered it in his translation of al-Idrīsī, S. Maqbul Ahmad, *India and the Neighbouring Territories in the Kitāb Nuzhat al-Mushtāq fi'khtirāq al-Āfāq of Sharīf al-Idrīsī: A Translation with Commentary of the Passages Relating to India, Pakistan, etc.* (Leiden, 1960), p. 62.

[26] V. Minorsky, *Hudūd al-ʿĀlam: The Regions of the World: A Persian Geography 372 A.H. = 982 A.D.* (London, 1937), p. 243.

place on the west coast of India is hardly suitable for bifurcation of roads leading further east.'[27] Ibn Khurradādhbih bases his account of the ports and distances in southern India on the testimony of sailors (*al-baḥriyyūn*) and states that Ballīn was roughly equidistant between Malabar (Mulay, ملى) and the 'Great Gulf' (*al-lujjat al-'uẓma*). Since the latter was clearly the Bay of Bengal, Maqbul Ahmad's suggestion that Ballīn was on the Tanjore coast – and may even have been Nagapattinam or a port in its vicinity – seems quite impossible.[28] Ballīn was a day or a little more than a day's journey from Sri Lanka ('Sarandib')[29] and clearly much further south than Nagapattinam, which Ibn Khurradādhbih called 'Bāpattan' (بابتّن) if anything. All the indications are that Ballīn lay in the Palk Bay region or the Gulf of Mannar, not far north or south of Rameshwaram Island. Idrīsī's description of it as located in an estuary makes the Vaigai Delta the most likely candidate for a location.[30]

The key ancient port in this vicinity at the mouth of the Vaigai River was of course Alagankulam, which has thrown up both torpedo jar sherds and late Roman coinage and was without doubt a major international port.[31] If Champakalakshmi is right in suggesting that Nellin was one of the ancient names of Alagankulam,[32] then it is almost certainly this name that lurks behind the mysterious Ballīn of Ibn Khurradādhbeh, with the first diacritical (the *nuqṭa* or dot) displaced from top to bottom to transform the *nūn* into a *bā'*. In short, if this reconstruction is at all plausible, Alagankulam's chronological span can be extended to the ninth century, when, according to Ibn Khurradādhbih, it formed the main east coast port where the eastern shipping lanes bifurcated, with ships bound for China heading for the Nicobars from here. But of course ultimately it is the archaeologists who will have to give substance to this picture.[33]

Let me turn now to the chronological patterns of individual sites and their possible connections to each other. The maritime regions that made up the Indian Ocean and its historical life were of course always more

[27] Minorsky, *Hudūd al-'Ālam*, pp. 243–4, n. 4.
[28] S. Maqbul Ahmad, *Arabic Classical Accounts of India and China* (Shimla, 1989), p. 24.
[29] Ibn Khurradādhbih, *Kitāb al-masālik wa'l-mamālik*, p. 64, ll. 5ff.; al-Idrīsī, *Kitāb nuzhat al-muštāq*, ed. Jaubert, p. 73.
[30] Al-Idrīsī, *Kitāb nuzhat al-muštāq*, ed. Jaubert, p. 73.
[31] E.g. R. Nagaswamy, 'Alagankulam: An Indo-Roman Trading Port', in *Indian Archaeological Heritage: Shri K. V. Soundara Rajan Festschrift*, 2 vols, ed. C. Margabandhu *et al.* (Delhi, 1991), vol. 1, pp. 247–54, at 252, 'profuse Roman contacts in the later period'.
[32] Champakalakshmi, *Trade, Ideology and Urbanization*, p. 134.
[33] The current view is roughly the one stated by V. Begley, *The Ancient Port of Arikamedu: New Excavations and Researches, 1989–1992* (Pondicherry, 1996–2004), vol. 1, p. 290 : 'The site [Alagankulam] seems to have flourished from the third century B.C. to the fourth–fifth century A.D.'

stable than the fortunes of the individual ports within them, and the same could be said of the networks that linked those regions together across vast distances. Thus coastal regions scarcely ever disappeared completely as commercial entities. With our notions of late antiquity radically overhauled in the past four decades, the Red Sea too has come back to life as a zone of more dynamism in the fourth to sixth centuries than formerly suspected. For example, 'The fourth century and later were periods of intense activity at Clysma and Aila,' says one scholar.[34] Ayla in fact enjoyed a renewed lease of life with the founding of a new port in the seventh century and flourished through the ʿAbbāsi and Fatimid periods until it was abandoned in the twelfth century. Adulis, which appears in the *Periplus* as a thriving port, became even more vigorous in the late antique centuries till it declined or was destroyed in the seventh century.[35] Its termination was abrupt compared to Aqaba's slower demise. These are reasonably well-defined patterns but they are the exception. Ports like Clysma (Suez) or Aden have more complex chronologies. Aden had been a major transshipment centre for ships from India to Egypt but was little used in the first century because, as the *Periplus* says, Caesar had sacked it. It reappears in the mid-fourth-century *Arabica* of Uranius as the Yemen's second city (*polis*).[36] By the ninth century Ibn Khurradādhbih could describe it as one of the 'greatest ports' of the Indian Ocean; it was a 'splendid, flourishing, populous town' in al-Muqaddasī's day,[37] and then of course it became a key base of the Indian Ocean shipping industry, as Margariti has shown,[38] still prosperous and rich in the early sixteenth century.[39] Here is an arc of some sixteen centuries, with a long spell of obscurity in between.

The Gulf is another region where continuity was sustained by the reshuffling of ports. As Rougeulle showed in an important paper, the rise of the Fatimids and the great change in the balance of the Islamic world

[34] R. Tomber, *Indo-Roman Trade: From Pots to Pepper* (London, 2008), p. 66. T. Power, *The Red Sea from Byzantium to the Caliphate, AD 500–1000* (Cairo and New York, 2012) is now the best synthesis we have for the Red Sea.

[35] D. W. Phillipson, 'Aksum, the Entrepot, and Highland Ethiopia, 3rd–12th Centuries', in *Byzantine Trade, 4th–12th Centuries: The Archaeology of Local, Regional and International Exchange*, ed. M. M. Mango (Aldershot, 2009), pp. 353–68 argues that Aksum was a major source of the African ivory exported to Mediterranean markets in the Roman period.

[36] Uranius, *Arabica*, fr. 13 (*Fragmenta Historicorum Graecorum*, ed. C. Müller (Paris, 1868), vol. IV, p. 524).

[37] Muḥammad b. Aḥmad al-Muqaddasī, *The Best Divisions for Knowledge of the Regions: A Translation of Aḥsan al-Taqāsīm fi Ma'rifat al-Aqālīm*, trans. B. A. Collins (Reading, 2001), p. 76.

[38] R. E. Margariti, *Aden and the Indian Ocean Trade: 150 Years in the Life of a Medieval Arabian Port* (Chapel Hill, 2007).

[39] Pires, *Suma Oriental*, vol. I, p. 17.

that came about in the later tenth century did not mean the end of the Gulf networks. Cairo and the Red Sea could now access markets in the Far East and did so on a substantial scale, but 'the Gulf area never lost the part it played in the international trade of the Indian Ocean to the Red Sea merchants. Only the nature of the Gulf trade changed, in the eleventh century, from a free economy handled by private traders ... to a monopoly economy concentrated in the hands of some local rulers.'[40] Here the 'transfers' between ports were abrupt and often dramatic. Ubulla, the Apologos of the *Periplus* and the main international port of the Sasanid rulers,[41] declined to the level of a village, certainly by the tenth century, replaced by Baṣra, which, founded in the late 630s, developed with astonishing speed. Barely two decades after its foundation it was described by Ananias of Širak as 'filled with merchants and ships coming from India and all parts of the East'.[42] Sīrāf, a substantial Sasanian port, known apparently as 'Sūriyānj' (?), expanded rapidly in the ʿAbbāsid commercial boom, reached a peak in the early tenth century and was then dramatically hit, first by a succession of earthquakes in 978 and 1008 and then by the economic recession that spread through the Gulf in the eleventh century. The author of the *Fārs Nāmah* claimed that merchants boycotted Sīrāf because the rulers of Kīsh finally gained control of it. Hamdollah Mostowfi, writing later, stated more simply, 'during the Buyid supremacy the sea trade was transferred from here to Kish'.[43] Sohar was closely linked with the Omani overseas community living in Baṣra,[44] flourished in tandem with Siraf and was a major international port in the ninth century – a thoroughly cosmopolitan centre, until it lost its status in the thirteenth century.[45] Kīsh cornered the Persian Gulf trade in the second half of the eleventh century[46] and was the leading entrepot till its dominance was finally destroyed in the 1330s. The history of the struggle between Kish

40 A. Rougeulle, 'Medieval Trade Networks in the Western Indian Ocean (8th–14th Centuries)', in *Tradition and Archaeology: Early Maritime Contacts in the Indian Ocean*, ed. H. P. Ray *et al.* (Delhi, 1996), pp. 159–80, at 175.

41 Dīnawarī, *Akhbār al-ṭiwāl*, ed. Guirgass, p. 123, ll. 9ff.

42 R. H. Hewsen, *The Geography of Ananias of Širak (Ašxarhac'oyc'): The Long and the Short Recensions* (Wiesbaden, 1992) p. 71 A (short recension).

43 G. Le Strange, *Description of the Province of Fars in Persia at the Beginning of the Fourteenth Century A.D. from the MS. of Ibn al-Balkhi in the British Museum* (London, 1912), pp. 322–3; G. Le Strange, *The Geographical Part of the Nuzhat al-Qulūb Composed by Hamd-Allah Mustawfi of Qazwin*, 2 vols (London, 1915–19), vol. II, p. 116.

44 J. C. Wilkinson, 'Ṣuḥār (Sohar) in the Early Islamic Period: The Written Evidence', in *South Asian Archaeology 1977* (Naples, 1979), p. 889.

45 Wilkinson, 'Ṣuḥār (Sohar) in the Early Islamic Period', pp. 903, 899, 890.

46 R. R. Di Meglio, 'Arab Trade with Indonesia and the Malay Peninsula', in *Islam and the Trade of Asia: A Colloquium*, ed. D. S. Richards (Oxford, 1970), p. 107.

and Hormuz is conceivably the most dramatic instance of commercial rivalry in the Indian Ocean prior to the expansion of the Portuguese, and illustrates both the fluidity of ports and the mobility of merchant families within broadly integrated coastal regions. The growth of Hormuz was largely due to the migration of Sirafi merchant families,[47] and Hormuz itself was a port that moved from the mainland to Jarun Island in 1300.[48]

A rapid survey, it is true, but this exercise can of course be extended to *all* the main sectors and micro-regions of the Indian Ocean, in more detail no doubt, and with greater precision. For example, among the Tamil ports, Arikamedu fades after the second century but resurfaces in the Chola period.[49] Puhar/Kaveripattinam to its south was a thriving Coromandel port down to the fifth century, when part of it was washed away by a tidal wave, an event reflected in the legend that the goddess Manimekhalai had cursed this grand port to engulfment by the sea. In fact, Kaveripattinam retained its vitality down to the tenth/eleventh centuries, once the Imperial Cholas had wrested Thanjavur from the local chieftains who ruled it for the Pallavas of Tondaimandalam and made it their capital. There is a profusion of Rajaraja I's coinage.[50] Nagapattinam emerged by the seventh century and was the main Chola port by 1000, still thriving in the thirteenth and fourteenth centuries.[51] Kayal further south replaced Korkai (the Kolchoi of the *Periplus*)[52] but seems to have flourished only in the thirteenth century,[53] when the waters around it silted up and 'traders had to seek new harbour sites large enough to accommodate ocean-going ships'.[54] New Kayal and Kayalpatnam emerged

[47] V. F. Piacentini, *Merchants, Merchandise and Military Power in the Persian Gulf (Sūriyānj/Shahriyāj-Sīrāf)* (Rome, 1992), p. 170.

[48] P. Morgan, 'New Thoughts on Old Hormuz: Chinese Ceramics in the Hormuz Region in the Thirteenth and Fourteenth Centuries', *Iran* 29 (1991), 67–83; J. Aubin, 'Les princes d'Ormuz du XIIIe au XVe siècle', *Journal Asiatique* 241 (1953), 77–138, at p. 94.

[49] Begley, *The Ancient Port of Arikamedu*, vol. 1, pp. 31ff. R. Nagaswamy, *Roman Karur* (Madras, 1995), pp. 24–5 notes a substantial third-century hoard some forty miles west of Puducherry, 'A huge treasure of over 200 Roman gold coins found' in 1992 at Sorayapattu near Tirukoyyilur.

[50] Soundara Rajan, *Kaveripattinnam Excavations 1963–73*.

[51] John Carswell suggested that Nagapattinam 'probably supplanted Mantai as the chief South Asian trading centre' soon after the end of the tenth century, following the Chola conquest of Sri Lanka, J. Carswell, 'Sri Lanka and China', in *Festschrift 1985: James Thevathasan Rutnam*, ed. A. R. B. Amerasinghe *et al.* (Colombo, 1985), pp. 57–60, at 58.

[52] J. Hornell, *The Sacred Chank of India: A Monograph of the Indian Conch (Turbinella Pyrum)* (Madras, 1914), p. 45.

[53] N. Karashima, *Ancient to Medieval: South Indian Society in Transition* (New Delhi, 2009), pp. 240 ff.

[54] R. Ptak, 'Yuan and Early Ming Notices on the Kayal Area in South India', *Bulletin de l'École française d'Extrême-Orient* 80 (1993), 137–56, at p. 139. (My thanks to Sanjay Subrahmanyam for this reference.)

as replacements, demonstrating the essential resilience of the seaside villages. K. Rajan has pointed out that

> Ports like Kaveripattinam (Poompuhar), Alagankulam and Korkai were affected either by sea-level variations or changes in river courses. The ports Korkai and Alagankulam are now located away from the present sea coast on the rivers Tambaraparni and Vaigai respectively. At Kaveripattinam too, the present river Kaveri flows about two kilometres south of the ancient port.[55]

In Kerala it was K. P. Shajan's work on the geomorphology of the central Kerala coast that proved decisive to the identification of Muziris as Pattanam some 3.5 km east of the present coast.[56] Muziris (Murachipattanam) saw 'intense occupation' in the Roman period (the Tamil 'Early Historic'), extending down to the fourth century. It was obviously a thriving port when the substantial cargoes in *SB* XVIII 13167 were contracted by an Alexandrian firm in the late second century,[57] and saw continued occupation in the 'early medieval' period.[58] But since large-scale excavations at Pattanam have only just begun (since 2007), the chronological pattern is still fuzzy. What *doesn't* seem credible is Tomber's inference that since Cosmas fails to mention Muziris, it no longer functioned by the mid-sixth century.[59] Kollam (Quilon) may well have emerged by the ninth century to fill the void left by Pattanam's decline, battening on the Gulf networks and attracting a cosmopolitan community of traders who were literate in Arabic, Hebrew and Pahlavi[60] – Nestorians, Jews, Muslims and Zoroastrians.[61] It was dominant down to the twelfth century when it was (momentarily) destroyed by the Chola armies[62] and its place

[55] K. Rajan, 'Early Maritime Activities of the Tamils', in *Tradition and Archaeology*, ed. Ray *et al.* (n. 40), pp. 97–108, at 99.

[56] K. P. Shajan, R. Tomber, V. Selvakumar and P. J. Cherian, 'Locating the Ancient Port of Muziris: Fresh Findings from Pattanam', *Journal of Roman Archaeology* 17 (2004), 313–20, esp. pp. 313–16.

[57] D. Rathbone, 'The "Muziris" Papyrus (SB XVIII 13167): Financing Roman Trade with India', *Bulletin de la Société d'Archéologie d'Alexandrie* 46 (2000), 39–50, esp. pp. 43ff., calculating the staggering value of the cargo.

[58] V. Selvakumar, K. P. Shajan and R. Tomber, 'Archaeological Investigations at Pattanam, Kerala: New Evidence for the Location of Ancient Muziris', in *Migration, Trade and Peoples*, part 1: *Indian Commerce and the Archaeology of Western India*, ed. R. Tomber *et al.* (London, 2010), pp. 29–41, at 34.

[59] Tomber, *Indo-Roman Trade*, p. 143.

[60] M. Abraham, *Two Medieval Merchant Guilds of South India* (New Delhi, 1988), pp. 21 ff.

[61] On the last of these communities see C. G. Cereti, 'Le croci di San Tommaso e la letteratura cristiana in lingue medioiraniche', in *Studi in onore di Umberto Scerrato*, ed. M. V. Fontana *et al.* (Naples, 2003), pp. 193–206, esp. 202.

[62] G. Bouchon, 'Un microcosme: Calicut au 16e siècle', in *Marchands et hommes d'affaires asiatiques dans l'Océan Indien et la Mer de Chine 13e–20e siècles*, ed. D. Lombard *et al.* (Paris, 1988), pp. 49–57, at 50.

taken by Calicut. Calicut, founded in 1042, became the 'great country of the Western Ocean', as the Chinese described it,[63] and reached its own apogee in the mid-fifteenth century. Like Kollam, it was a late development – a port for which no late antique evidence exists, while Kochi of course emerged even later, becoming prosperous after the arrival of the Portuguese, as Pires said.[64] The excavations at Pattanam may throw up a more vibrant 'late antique' phase, but until that happens Kerala is a perfect example of what I've called a 'submerged' history – the gap between Cosmas' listing of five ports along the coast and the current state of the archaeology. In any case, the sheer density of ports along the Malabar coast that Tomé Pires documented for the early sixteenth century (he listed no fewer than twenty-nine)[65] was the more or less permanent background from which the cosmopolitan ports emerged. The reshuffling of ports that went on throughout the life of the Ocean drew on a huge reservoir of informal harbours that moved back and forth between their stellar moments (if they were lucky) and their unrecorded or submerged histories.[66] And clearly the vast mass of these lesser ports survived on coastal trading.

Now Hermann Kulke has argued that the late tenth century ushered in a major break in the constellation of forces that had shaped the destinies of the Indian Ocean. The Fatimids, Cholas and Northern Song emerged more or less simultaneously and redrew the economic map of the Ocean for the next two or three centuries – indeed, in a sense down to the advent of the Portuguese.[67] A key upshot of this conjuncture was the further dramatic expansion of the trade with China as well as the more aggressive role played by Indian merchants, *both* Hindus and Muslims, in contrast to the Omani and other Gulf communities that had dominated long-distance voyages till then. All the major coastal regions of India by now had substantial settlements of Muslim traders, both natives and foreigners – an expat elite, the *pardesis*, who dominated the trade of the western Indian Ocean, and indigenous groups like the Marakkar Muslims of the east coast who controlled the coastal trade between Malabar and Coromandel. That the Portuguese

[63] Ma Huan, *Ying-yai sheng-lan: 'The Overall Survey of the Ocean's Shores' [1433], Translated from the Chinese Text etc.*, ed. J. V. G. Mills (Cambridge, 1970), p. 137.

[64] Pires, *Suma Oriental*, vol. 1, p. 79.

[65] Pires, *Suma Oriental*, vol. 1, p. 74.

[66] F. Braudel, *The Mediterranean and the Mediterranean World in the Age of Philip II*, 2 vols, trans. Siân Reynolds (London, 1975), vol. 1, p. 148.

[67] H. Kulke, 'Rivalry and Competition in the Bay of Bengal in the Eleventh Century and its Bearing on Indian Ocean Studies' in *Commerce and Culture in the Bay of Bengal 1500–1800*, ed. Om Prakash *et al.* (New Delhi, 1999), pp. 17–36.

set out to break the power of Muslim-dominated commercial networks on both coasts of India and across the Indian Ocean shows the amazing tenacity of networks that had first emerged in the eighth century and evolved patiently and gradually through a pattern of migration that is best described by Mark Horton in his work on Shanga. This was, Horton writes, 'not a large-scale migration of Arabs to East Africa, but often single individuals who settled and established substantial lineages'.[68] Horton dates the 'beginnings' of Swahili Islam to *c.*780–850.[69] These were precisely the decades when the Rashtrakutas controlled much of Gujarat, and Masʿūdī was especially struck by the Rashtrakuta reception of Arab traders – the respect and tolerance shown to 'Arabs and Muslims' in a kingdom that often seemed to roughly contemporary Arabic sources the only one worth mentioning![70]

Among the Hindu trading communities, the most important were the Gujarati *baniyas* and the Tamil-speaking Chettis. The Gujaratis were the most powerful expat community in Malacca on the eve of its capture by the Portuguese,[71] but so too were the Coromandel Chettis, described by Barbosa as 'men of great estates and owning many great ships which they call *juncos*'.[72] These groups controlled a substantial part of the trade between India and the Far East, especially the trade in textiles. Pires reported that 'There used to be a thousand Gujarat merchants in Malacca, besides four or five thousand Gujarat seamen, who came and went,'[73] which gives us some sense of the scale of this business. He also claimed that the Gujaratis had 'larger ships and more men to man them'.[74] Indeed, Gujarat vessels were built to a thousand tons and upwards, according to one scholar,[75] and to me it seems certain that the 'massive' Indian ships that Egeria saw at Clysma in the 380s, over ten centuries earlier,[76]

[68] M. C. Horton, 'Islam, Archaeology, and Swahili Identity', in *Changing Social Identity with the Spread of Islam: Archaeological Perspectives*, ed. D. Whitcomb (Chicago, 2003), pp. 67–88, at 79.

[69] M. Horton, *Shanga: The Archaeology of a Muslim Trading Community on the Coast of East Africa* (London, 1996), pp. 397 ff.

[70] Masʿūdī, *Les prairies d'or*, vol. I, p. 382; K. A. Nizami, 'Early Arab Contact with South Asia', *Journal of Islamic Studies*, 5(1) (1994), 52–69, esp. p. 59.

[71] L. F. Thomaz, 'Malaka et ses communautés marchandes au tournant du 16e siècle', in *Marchands et hommes d'affaires asiatiques*, ed. Lombard (n. 62), pp. 31–48, at 36: 'la communauté la plus puissante de Malaka'.

[72] Dames, *The Book of Duarte Barbosa*, vol. II, p. 172.

[73] Pires, *Suma Oriental*, vol. I, p. 45.

[74] Pires, *Suma Oriental*, vol. I, p. 45.

[75] H. P. Ray, *The Archaeology of Seafaring in Ancient South Asia* (Cambridge, 2003), p. 73.

[76] *Itinerarium Egeriae*, ed. Weber, p. 101 (Y6): 'Naves autem ibi et multe et ingentes sunt; quia portus famosus est pro advenientibus ibi mercatoribus de India'; trans. J. Wilkinson, *Egeria's Travels* (London, 1971), p. 206: 'the ships there are numerous and massive because the port is famous for the Indian merchants who come there'.

were Gujarati *baniya*-controlled vessels of substantial tonnages, possibly 300–600 tons.[77] The other classical reference to the sheer size of Gujarati vessels is of course the *Periplus*, with its statement that the merchants of Barygaza (Bharuch) would send out 'big vessels' (*ploia megala*) to Omana (ed-Dur?) and Apologos (Ubulla) with supplies of copper, teakwood and beams. And of course Bharuch also exported textiles of all kinds including silk from China.[78]

So, if Procopius was right, the import of silk into the Byzantine markets depended not just on the Sasanian merchants buying up whole cargoes in the South Asia ports but on Indian merchants shipping those cargoes in vessels that they owned or chartered. The *sa-po* or *sārthavāha* who turn up in Fa-hsien owning 'stately and beautiful' homes in Anuradhapura in the early fifth century were surely neither Sabaeans, as Samuel Beals suggested, nor Sogdians, as Paolo Daffina argued, but simply South Asian traders, possibly including big merchants from the Gujarat ports where *sārthavāha* was a generic term for merchants but referred especially to the wealthier merchant princes active in the long-distance trade.[79] But how do we characterise merchants at this level? The Alexandrian financier whose investment was secured by commodities worth well over seven million sesterces in the famous shipment from Muziris? Or Abu Bakr b. ʿUmar as-Sirāfī, whom Ibn Ḥauqal was desperate to meet in 961 and who operated from Baṣra with a whole fleet of ships, agents (*wakīl*), business partners, warehouses and so on, trading to India, China and East Africa?[80] Or the 'merchant millionaire' Rāmisht of Siraf who came back from China with merchandise worth half a million dinars?[81] Rāmisht was a *nākhudā*, as he was described on his tombstone in Mecca, a ship-owning merchant of the kind that 'ran both shipping and trading enterprises'.[82] Margariti has suggested that he was based in Aden,[83] and, if so, he would certainly have interacted closely with the Jewish India traders who operated out of there. Or finally how do we characterise the great business firms that dominated

[77] Cf. M. N. Pearson, *The Indian Ocean* (London, 2007), pp. 68–9, on the size of Gujarati ships, 'on average 300 to 600 tons'.

[78] *Periplus* 49 (ed. Casson, p. 81).

[79] V. K. Jain, *Trade and Traders in Western India, A.D. 1000–1300* (New Delhi, 1990), pp. 221ff. (discussing Gujarat).

[80] Ibn Ḥauqal, *Kitāb Ṣurat al-'arḍ*, ed. J. H. Kramers (Leiden, 1938), pp. 290–1 = *Configuration de la terre (Kitāb ṣurat al-'ard)*, trans. J. H. Kramers and G. Wiet, 2 vols (Paris, 1964), vol. II, pp. 284–5.

[81] S. M. Stern, 'Rāmisht of Sīrāf, a Merchant Millionaire of the Twelfth Century', *The Journal of the Royal Asiatic Society of Great Britain and Ireland* 1/2 (Apr.1967), 10–14.

[82] Margariti, *Aden and the Indian Ocean Trade*, pp. 144–5.

[83] Margariti, *Aden and the Indian Ocean Trade*, p. 148.

Chinese shipping in the Song–Yuan periods? Lo Jung-pang tells us that the heads of these joint-stock companies 'employed factors (*kang-shou*) to take charge of the merchant fleets and to transact business abroad'.[84] In China shipbuilding, like the silk, pottery and iron industries, was based on industrial-scale production. Chuimei Ho has suggested that one reason why Quanzhou superseded Guanzhou as the busiest seaport in China was the spectacular growth of the ceramic industry in the Quanzhou area starting in the late eleventh century, when factories sprawled over entire valleys, churning out stoneware and porcelains for the South Seas trade.[85]

As we move into the early modern period, historians become progressively less reluctant to recognise in these various groups and the networks and practices bound up with them the signs of a precocious capitalism. In her excellent monograph on the Coromandel merchants, Kanakalatha Mukund has no hesitation describing the Chettis as 'merchant capitalists'.[86] In the seventeenth century, they were large-scale export merchants who owned their own ships and traded extensively with the South-east Asian ports. 'The trade links of these merchants radiated from the ports to the hinterland, giving them a very large sphere of influence.'[87] Jeyaseela Stephen has used the same description of the Tamil-speaking Mudaliars of the early sixteenth century.[88] Braudel's pages on the Mediterranean are replete with references to this capitalism of the sea, of the big merchants and the financiers connected with them. In a classic study Giorgio Cracco reduced this 'Mediterranean capitalism'[89] to an early microcosm, that of the Venetian *Duecento*, suggesting that by then the evolution of Venice's mercantile economy had generated a sharper demarcation between the capitalists and the merchants, that is, between the *big* merchants (*il grande imprenditore mercantile*) and the mass of merchant workers (*mercanti lavoratori*), as he called them.[90] This, I suggest, was one strand of

[84] Lo Jung-pang, 'Chinese Shipping and East–West Trade from the Tenth to the Fourteenth Century', in *Sociétés et compagnies de commerce en Orient et dans l'Océan Indien*, ed. M. Mollat (Paris, 1970), pp. 167–75, at 173.

[85] Chuimei Ho, 'The Ceramic Boom in Minnan during Song and Yuan Times', in *The Emporium of the World: Maritime Quanzhou, 1000–1400*, ed. A. Schottenhammer (Leiden and Boston, 2001), pp. 237–81, esp. 268ff. where she accepts the notion of 'some kind of quasi-capitalistic investment' for the early phase of Minnan's ceramic industry, viz. 1050–1150.

[86] K. Mukund, *The Trading World of the Tamil Merchant: Evolution of Merchant Capitalism in the Coromandel* (London, 1999), ch. 5.

[87] Mukund, *Trading World of the Tamil Merchant*, p. 60.

[88] S. Jeyaseela Stephen, *The Coromandel Coast and its Hinterland: Economy, Society and Political System, A.D. 1500–1600* (New Delhi, 1997), p. 134.

[89] Braudel, *Mediterranean*, vol. 1, p. 445.

[90] G. Cracco, *Società e stato nel Medioevo veneziano (secoli xii–xiv)* (Florence, 1967), esp. pp. 38ff., 86, 189, 193ff.

an ancient Mediterranean tradition, the distinction between the *nauklēroi* and the *daneistai* that runs through Justinian's attempt to regulate the system of maritime loans in the year 540.[91] The former were shipmasters and smaller-scale merchants (they are also called *emporoi*), the latter big financiers who had no intrinsic connection with the maritime means of production, even when they specialised in financing voyages across the Mediterranean or possibly further afield. By contrast, the Indian Ocean networks typically seem to have involved merchant capitalists who owned their own ships, like the Aden merchants described by Ibn Baṭṭūṭa[92] or the Tamil Naina Suryadeva who was the richest merchant in Malacca around 1511.[93] In the Mediterranean this type, too, was well known. Indeed, when the fourth-century senator-cum-astrologer Firmicus Maternus refers to *potentes navicularii*,[94] he is clearly describing shipowners who were also powerful merchants, on a pattern exemplified later by the *nākhudās* of a bigger and different kind of sea.

91 Justinian, *Nov.* cvi (540).
92 Ibn Baṭṭūṭa, *Travels in Asia and Africa 1325–1354*, trans. H. A. R. Gibb (London, 1929), p. 110; *Riḥlat Ibn Baṭṭūṭa* (Beirut, 1960), p. 251. Cf. S. D. Goitein and M. A. Friedman, *India Traders of the Middle Ages: Documents from the Cairo Geniza: 'India Book', Part One* (Leiden and Boston, 2007), p. 155, 'Shipowners were wealthy merchants', about the Aden-based Jewish shipowners.
93 Thomaz, 'Malaka', p. 37.
94 Firmicus Maternus, *Mathesis* 8.20.10 (ed. Monat, vol. III, p. 278).

Select bibliography

Allouche, A., *Mamluk Economics: A Study and Translation of al-Maqrīzī's Ighāthah* (Salt Lake City, 1994)

Balard, M., 'Les hommes d'affaires occidentaux ont-ils asphyxié l'économie byzantine?', in *Europa medievale e mondo bizantino*, ed. G. Arnaldi and G. Cavallo (Rome, 1997), pp. 255–65

Banaji, J., *Agrarian Change in Late Antiquity: Gold, Labour and Aristocratic Dominance*, 2nd edn (Oxford, 2007)

Bates, M. L., 'Coins and Money in the Arabic Papyri', in *Documents de l'Islam médiéval: Nouvelles perspectives de recherche*, ed. Y. Rāġib (Cairo, 1991), pp. 43–64

Bell, P., *Social Conflict in the Age of Justinian: Its Nature, Management, and Mediation* (Oxford, 2013)

Bessard, F., 'The Urban Economy in Southern Inland Greater Syria from the Seventh Century to the End of the Umayyads', in *Local Economies? Production and Exchange of Inland Regions in Late Antiquity*, ed. L. Lavan (Leiden and Boston, 2015), pp. 377–421

Bianchini, M., 'Controllo dei prezzi e autonomia delle associazioni di mestiere in *Nov. Iust.* 122', in *Studi in memoria di Giovanni Tarello,* vol. I*: Saggi storici* (Milan, 1990), pp. 117–40

Bijovsky, G., 'A Hoard of Byzantine Solidi from Bet She'an in the Umayyad Period', *Revue Numismatique* 158 (2002), 161–227

Blackledge, P. (ed.), Symposium on Chris Wickham's *Framing the Early Middle Ages*, *Historical Materialism* 19(1) (2011), 37–231

Bognetti, G. P., 'La proprietà della terra nel passagio dal mondo antico al Medioevo occidentale', in *L'età longobarda,* vol. IV (Milan, 1968), pp. 67–89

Bridbury, A. R., 'The Dark Ages', *Economic History Review*, 2nd ser., 22 (1969), 526–37, repr. in *The English Economy from Bede to the Reformation* (Woodbridge and Rochester, 1992), pp. 43–55

Britnell, R. H. and Campbell, B. M. S., *A Commercialising Economy: England 1086 to c. 1300* (Manchester and New York, 1995)

Brown, P., 'The Later Roman Empire', *Economic History Review*, 2nd ser., 20 (1967), 327–43; repr. in *Religion and Society in the Age of Saint Augustine* (Eugene, OR, 2007), pp. 46–73

Through the Eye of a Needle: Wealth, the Fall of Rome, and the Making of Christianity in the West, 350–550 AD (Princeton and Oxford, 2012)

Bruand, O., *Voyageurs et marchandises aux temps carolingiens: Les réseaux de communication entre Loire et Meuse aux VIIIe et IXe siècles* (Brussels, 2002)

Cameron, A., 'Anician Myths', *Journal of Roman Studies* 102 (2012), 133–71

Camodeca, G., '[Puteoli]: La società e le attività produttive', in *Puteoli*, ed. F. Zevi (Naples, 1993), pp. 31–50

Campbell, J., *The Anglo-Saxon State* (London and New York, 2000)

Carandini, A., *L'anatomia della scimmia: La formazione economica della società prima del capitale* (Turin, 1979)

'Il mondo della tarda antichità visto attraverso le merci', in *Società romana e impero tardoantico,* vol. III: *le merci, gli insediamenti*, ed. A. Giardina (Rome and Bari, 1986) pp. 3–19

Carla, F., *L'oro nella tarda antichità: Aspetti economici e sociali* (Turin, 2009)

Carswell, J., Deraniyagala, S. and Graham, A., *Mantai: City by the Sea* (Aichwald, 2013)

Cheynet, J.-C. (ed.), *Le monde byzantin, t.2: L'Empire byzantin, 641–1204* (Paris, 2006)

Cheynet, J.-C., 'Bureaucracy and Aristocracies', in *The Oxford Handbook of Byzantine Studies*, ed. E. Jeffreys, J. Haldon and R. Cormack (New York and Oxford, 2008), pp. 518–26

Cosentino, S., 'Le fortune di un banchiere tardoantico. Giuliano argentario e l'economia di Ravenna nel VI secolo', in *Santi banchieri re. Ravenna e Classe nel VI secolo*, ed. A. Augenti and C. Bertelli (Milan, 2006), pp. 43–8

Cracco, G., *Società e stato nel Medioevo veneziano (secoli xii–xiv)* (Florence, 1967)

Dark, K., 'Proto-industrialization and the Economy of the Roman Empire', in *L'artisanat romain: Évolutions, continuités et ruptures (Italie et provinces occidentales)*, ed. M. Polfer (Montagnac, 2001), pp. 19–29

Davies, W., 'On Servile Status in the Early Middle Ages', in *Serfdom and Slavery: Studies in Legal Bondage*, ed. M. L. Bush (London and New York, 1996), pp. 225–46

Day, J., 'The Levant Trade in the Middle Ages', in *The Economic History of Byzantium from the Seventh Through the Fifteenth Century*, vol. II, ed. A. E. Laiou (Washington, D.C., 2002), pp. 807–14

de la Vaissière, E., *Histoire des marchands sogdiens* (Paris, 2002)

Dopsch, A., 'Frühmittelalterliche und spätantike Wirtschaft', in *Verfassungs- und Wirtschaftsgeschichte des Mittelalters: Gesammelte Aufsätze von Alfons Dopsch*, 2 vols, ed. E. Patzelt (Vienna, 1928; repr. Aalen, 1968), vol. I, pp. 219–34

Drinkwater, J. F., 'The Wool Textile Industry of Gallia Belgica and the Secundinii of Igel: Questions and Hypotheses', *Textile History* 13 (1982), 111–28

Duri, A., *Arabische Wirtschaftsgeschichte*, trans. J. Jacobi (Zurich and Munich, 1979)

El Abbadi, M., 'The Grain Supply of Alexandria and its Population in Byzantine Times', in *Proceedings of the XVIIIth International Congress of Papyrology, Athens 25–31 May 1986* (Athens, 1988), vol. II, pp. 317–23

Faith, R., *The English Peasantry and the Growth of Lordship* (London and New York, 1997)

Finley, M. I., *The Ancient Economy* (London, 1975); updated edn (Berkeley, etc., 1999)

Foote, R. M., 'Commerce, Industrial Expansion, and Orthogonal Planning: Mutually Compatible Terms in Settlements of Bilad al-Sham during the Umayyad Period', *Mediterranean Archaeology* 13 (2000), 25–38

Fowden, G., 'The Umayyad Horizon', *Journal of Roman Archaeology* 25 (2012), 974–82

Before and After Muḥammad: The First Millennium Refocused (Princeton, 2013)

Frederiksen, M. W., 'Theory, Evidence and the Ancient Economy', *Journal of Roman Studies* 65 (1975), 164–71

Fulford, M. G., 'Byzantium and Britain: A Mediterranean Perspective on Post-Roman Mediterranean Imports in Western Britain and Ireland', *Medieval Archaeology* 33 (1989), 1–6

Fulford, M. and Durham, E., *Seeing Red: New Economic and Social Perspectives on 'Terra Sigillata'* (London, 2013)

Garnsey, P., 'Les travailleurs du bâtiment de Sardes et l'économie urbaine du Bas-Empire', in *L'Origine des richesses dépensées dans la ville antique*, ed. P. Leveau (Aix-en-Provence, 1985), pp. 147–60

Gascou, J., 'Les grandes domaines, la cité et l'état en Égypte byzantine', *Travaux et Mémoires* 9 (1985), 1–90; repr. in *Fiscalité et société en Égypte byzantine* (Paris, 2008), pp. 125–213

Un codex fiscal hermopolite (P. Sorb. II 69) (Atlanta, 1994)

Gelichi, S., 'The Eels of Venice: The Long Eighth Century of the Emporia of the Northern Region along the Adriatic Coast', in *774: Ipotesi su una transizione*, ed. S. Gasparri (Turnhout, 2008), pp. 81–117

Giardina, A., 'Mazzarino e Rostovtzeff', in *Rostovtzeff e l'Italia*, ed. A. Marcone (Naples, 1999), pp. 117–29

Grabar, O., 'Umayyad "Palace" and the ʿAbbasid "Revolution"', *Studia Islamica* 18 (1963), 5–18

Greene, K., 'Roman Pottery and the Economy; Part I', in *Roman Pottery Research in Britain and North-West Europe: Papers Presented to Graham Webster*, ed. A. C. Anderson and A. S. Anderson, 2 vols (Oxford, 1981), vol. 1, pp. 1–8

Greenwood, T., 'Sasanian Echoes and Apocalyptic Expectations: A Re-evaluation of the Armenian History Attributed to Sebeos', *Le Muséon* 115 (2002), 323–97

Grierson, P., 'The Monetary Reforms of ʿAbd al-Malik: Their Metrological Basis and their Financial Repercussions', *Journal of the Economic and Social History of the Orient* 3 (1960), 241–64

Guéry, R., Morrisson, C. and Slim, H., *Recherches archéologiques franco-tunisiennes à Rougga*, vol. III: *Le trésor de monnaies d'or byzantines* (Rome, 1982)

Guidobaldi, F., 'Le *domus* tardoantiche di Roma come "sensori" delle trasformazioni culturali e sociali', in *The Transformations of 'Urbs Roma' in Late Antiquity*, ed. W. V. Harris (Portsmouth, RI, 1999), pp. 53–68

Haider, N., 'Standardization and Empire: A Study of the Exchange Rates of Mughal Currencies', in *Mind over Matter: Essays on Mentalities in Medieval India*, ed. E. Vanina and D. N. Jha (New Delhi, 2009)

Haldon, J., *The State and the Tributary Mode of Production* (London, 1993)

Halsall, G., 'From Roman *Fundus* to Early Medieval *Grand Domaine*: Crucial Ruptures between Antiquity and the Middle Ages', *Revue Belge de Philologie et d'Histoire* 90 (2012), 273–98

Harper, K., *Slavery in the Late Roman World AD 275–425* (Cambridge, 2011)

'The Transformation of Roman Slavery: An Economic Myth?', *Antiquité Tardive* 20 (2012), 165–72

Heck, G., 'Gold Mining in Arabia and the Rise of the Islamic State', *Journal of the Economic and Social History of the Orient* 42 (1999), 364–95

Hendy, M., *Studies in the Byzantine Monetary Economy c. 300–1450* (Cambridge, 1985)

Hickey, T. M., *Wine, Wealth, and the State in Late Antique Egypt: The House of Apion at Oxyrhynchus* (Ann Arbor, 2012)

Hillner, J., *Jedes Haus ist eine Stadt: Privatimmobilien im spätantiken Rom* (Bonn, 2004)

Ho, Ping-ti, *Studies on the Population of China, 1368–1953* (Cambridge, MA, 1959)

Horden, P. and Purcell, N., *The Corrupting Sea: A Study of Mediterranean History* (Oxford, 2000)

Jacoby, D., 'Silk in Western Byzantium before the Fourth Crusade', *Byzantinische Zeitschrift* 84/5 (1991–2), 452–500; repr. in *Trade, Commodities and Shipping in the Medieval Mediterranean* (Aldershot, 1997)

Johansen, B., 'Le contrat *salam*: Droit et formation du capital dans l'Empire abbasside (XIe–XIIe siècle)', *Annales HSS* 61 (2006), 863–99

Jones, A. H. M., 'Over-Taxation and the Decline of the Roman Empire', *Antiquity* 33 (1959), 39–43; repr. in *The Roman Economy: Studies in Ancient Economic and Administrative History*, ed. P. A. Brunt (Oxford, 1974), pp. 82–9

Kajava, M. (ed.), *Gunnar Mickwitz nella storiografia europea tra le due guerre* (Rome, 2007)

Kehoe, D., 'Aristocratic Dominance in the Late Roman Agrarian Economy and the Question of Economic Growth', *Journal of Roman Archaeology* 16 (2003), 711–21

Kingsley, S., 'Late Antique Trade: Research Methodologies and Field Practices', in *Theory and Practice in Late Antique Archaeology*, ed. L. Lavan and W. Bowden (Leiden and Boston, 2003), pp. 113–38

Kolesnikov, A., 'The Quantity of Silver Coinage and Levels of Revenues in Late Sasanian Iran', in *Matériaux pour l'histoire économique du monde iranien*, ed. R. Gyselen and M. Szuppe (Paris, 1999), pp. 123–30

Kuhn, D., *The Age of Confucian Rule: The Song Transformation of China* (Cambridge, MA, and London, 2009)

Labib, S. Y., 'Capitalism in Medieval Islam', *Journal of the Economic and Social History of the Orient* 29 (1969), 79–96

Laiou, A., *Economic Thought and Economic Life in Byzantium*, ed. C. Morrisson and E. Dorin (Aldershot, 2013)

Lemerle, P., 'Byzance au tournant de son destin', in *Cinq études sur le XIe siècle byzantin* (Paris, 1977), pp. 251–312

Lo, Jung-pang, 'Chinese Shipping and East–West Trade from the Tenth to the Fourteenth Century', in *Sociétés et compagnies de commerce en Orient et dans l'Océan indien*, ed. M. Mollat (Paris, 1970), pp. 167–75

Lo Cascio, E., 'Teoria e politica monetaria a Roma tra III e IV d.C.', in *Società romana e impero tardoantico*, ed. A. Giardina (Rome and Bari, 1986), vol. 1, pp. 535–57, 779–801

Lombard, M., 'Les bases monétaires d'une suprématie économique: L'or musulman du VIIe au XIe siècle', *Annales ESC* 2 (1947), 143–60

Espaces et réseaux du haut moyen âge (Paris and The Hague, 1972)

Lopez, A. G., *Shenoute of Atripe and the Uses of Poverty: Rural Patronage, Religious Conflict, and Monasticism in Late Antique Egypt* (Berkeley and London, 2013)

Loseby, S. T., 'Marseille and the Pirenne Thesis, I: Gregory of Tours, the Merovingian Kings, and "Un Grand Port"', in *The Sixth Century: Production, Distribution and Demand*, ed. R. Hodges and W. Bowden (Leiden, etc., 1998), pp. 203–29

'The Mediterranean Economy', in *The New Cambridge Medieval History*, vol. 1, ed. P. Fouracre (Cambridge, 2006), pp. 605–38

Luzzatto, G., *Storia economica di Venezia dall'XI al XVI secolo* (Venice, 1961)

Magness, J., *The Archaeology of the Early Islamic Settlement in Palestine* (Winona Lake, IN, 2003)

Maiuro, M., *'Res Caesaris': Ricerche sulla proprietà imperiale nel Principato* (Bari, 2012)

Malek, H. M., 'Late Sasanian Coinage and the Collection in the Muzeh Melli Iran', *Numismatic Chronicle* 173 (2013), pp. 457–99

Mattingly, D. J., 'The Olive Boom: Oil Surpluses, Wealth and Power in Roman Tripolitania', *Libyan Studies* 19 (1988), 21–41

Mauro, F., *Le XVIe siecle européen: Aspects économiques*, 2nd edn (Paris, 1970)

Mazza, M., 'Economia naturale ed economia monetaria nel dibattito tra le due guerre: Brevi note di ordine storiografico su GUNNAR MICKWITZ, *Geld und Wirtschaft im römischen Reich des vierten Jahrhunderts n. Chr.*', in *Gunnar Mickwitz nella storiografia europea tra le due guerre*, ed. M. Kajava (Rome, 2007), pp. 63–83

Mazzarino, S., *Aspetti sociali del quarto secolo: Ricerche di storia tardo-romana* (Rome, 1951); new edn, ed. E. Lo Cascio (Milan, 2002)

Mertens, H.-G., *Wirtschaftliche und soziale Strukturen zentralmexikanischer Weizenhaciendas aus dem Tal von Atlixco (1890–1912)* (Wiesbaden, 1983)

Metcalf, D. M., 'Monetary Recession in the Middle Byzantine Period: The Numismatic Evidence', *Numismatic Chronicle* 161 (2001), 111–55

Mickwitz, G., *Geld und Wirtschaft im römischen Reich des vierten Jahrhunderts n. Chr.* (Helsinki, 1932; repr. Amsterdam, 1965)

Miles, G. C., 'On the Varieties and Accuracy of Eighth-Century Arab Coin Weights', in *L. A. Mayer Memorial Volume (1895–1959)*, ed. M. Avi-Yonah *et al.* (Jerusalem, 1964) pp. 78–87
Miquel, A., *La géographie humaine du monde musulman jusqu'au milieu du XIe siècle*, 4 vols (Paris, 1967–88)
Morel, J.-P., 'La produzione artigianale e il commercio transmarino', in *La repubblica imperiale* (*Storia di Roma,* vol. II/1), ed. G. Clemente, F. Coarelli and E. Gabba (Turin, 1990), pp. 399–412
Morony, M. G., 'Landholding and Social Change: Lower al-ʿIraq in the Early Islamic Period', in *Land Tenure and Social Transformation in the Middle East*, ed. T. Khalidi (Beirut, 1984), pp. 209–22
'Economic Boundaries? Late Antiquity and Early Islam', *Journal of the Economic and Social History of the Orient* 47 (2004), 166–94
Morris, R., 'The Powerful and the Poor in Tenth-Century Byzantium: Law and Reality', *Past & Present* 73 (1976), 3–27
Morrisson, C. (ed.), *Trade and Markets in Byzantium* (Washington, D.C., 2012)
Muthesius, A., 'The Byzantine Silk Industry: Lopez and Beyond', *Journal of Medieval History* 19 (1993), 1–67
Naismith, R., *Money and Power in Anglo-Saxon England: The Southern English Kingdoms 757–865* (Cambridge, 2014)
Oikonomidès, N., 'Byzantium between East and West (XIII–XV Cent.)', *Byzantinische Forschungen* 13 (1988), 319–32
Social and Economic Life in Byzantium, ed. F. Zachariadou (Aldershot, 2004)
Ostrogorsky, G., 'Observations on the Aristocracy in Byzantium', *Dumbarton Oaks Papers* 25 (1971), 1–32
Picard, G.-Ch., 'Deux sénateurs romains inconnus', *Karthago* 4 (1953), 119–35
Picon, M., 'Production artisanale et manufacturière à l'époque romaine: À propos de *L'Histoire brisée* d'Aldo Schiavone', in *L'économie antique: Une économie de marché?*, ed. Y. Roman and J. Dalaison (Paris, 2008), pp. 191–214
Planhol, X. de, *Les fondements géographiques de l'histoire de l'Islam* (Paris, 1968)
Poglio, F. A., *Gruppi di potere nella Roma tardoantica (350–395 d.C.)* (Turin, 2007)
Purcell, N., 'Wine and Wealth in Ancient Italy', *Journal of Roman Studies* 75 (1985), 1–19
Rathbone, D., 'The Financing of Maritime Commerce in the Roman Empire', in *Credito e moneta nel mondo romano*, ed. E. Lo Cascio (Bari, 2003), pp. 197–229
'Economic Rationalism and the Heroninos Archive', *Topoi* 12 (2005), 261–9
Richards, D. S. (ed.), *Islam and the Trade of Asia: A Colloquium* (Oxford, 1970)
Robinson, D., 'Re-thinking the Social Organisation of Trade and Industry in First Century AD Pompeii', in *Roman Working Lives and Urban Living*, ed. A. Mac Mahon and J. Price (Oxford, 2005), pp. 88–105
Rogers, G. B., 'Analyse statistique de deux trésors de monnaies romaines en or', *Gallia* 33 (1975), 257–65
Rostovtzeff, M., *The Social and Economic History of the Roman Empire*, 2 vols, 2nd edn (Oxford, 1957)

Rostovtzeff, M. I., *Per la storia economica e sociale del mondo ellenistico-romano: Saggi scelti*, ed. T. Gnoli and J. Thornton, intro. M. Mazza (Catania, 2002)
Rubin, U., 'Meccan Trade and Qur'ānic Exegesis (Qur'ān 2: 198)', *Bulletin of the School of Oriental and African Studies* 53 (1990), 421–8
Ruffini, G. R., *Social Networks in Byzantine Egypt* (Cambridge, 2008)
Russell, B., *The Economics of the Roman Stone Trade* (Oxford, 2013)
Saguì, L., 'Roma, i centri privilegiati e la lunga durata della tarda antichità: Dati archeologici dal deposito di VII secolo nell'esedra della Crypta Balbi', *Archeologia Medievale* 29 (2002), 7–42
Sarris, P., *Economy and Society in the Age of Justinian* (Cambridge, 2006)
'Large Estates and the Peasantry in Byzantium *c.* 600–1100', *Revue Belge de Philologie et d'Histoire* 90 (2012), 429–50
Shaw, B. D., 'The Early Development of M. I. Finley's Thought: The Heichelheim Dossier', *Athenaeum* 81 (1993), 177–99
Bringing in the Sheaves: Economy and Metaphor in the Roman World (Toronto, etc., 2013)
Sifonas, C. S., 'Basile II et l'aristocratie byzantine', *Byzantion* 64 (1994), 118–33
Skaff, J. K., 'Sasanian and Arab-Sasanian Coins from Turfan: Their Relationship to International Trade and the Local Economy', *Asia Major*, 3rd ser., 11 (1998), 67–115
Skinner, A., 'Political Mobility in the Later Roman Empire', *Past & Present* 218 (2013), 17–53
Steinby, M., 'I senatori e l'industria laterizia urbana', in *Epigrafia e ordine senatorio,* vol. 1 (Rome, 1982), pp. 227–37
Strobel, K., 'Zwischen Primitivismus und Modernismus: Die römische Keramikindustrie und die Suche nach einem Kategorisierungsmodell der römischen Wirtschaft', in *Forschungen zur römischen Keramikindustrie: Produktions-, Rechts- und Distributionsstrukturen*, ed. K. Strobel (Mainz, 2000), pp. 1–8
Swain, S., *Economy, Family, and Society from Rome to Islam: A Critical Edition, English Translation, and Study of Bryson's 'Management of the Estate'* (Cambridge, 2013)
Torelli, M., *Tota Italia: Essays in the Cultural Formation of Roman Italy* (Oxford, 1999)
Walmsley, A., *Early Islamic Syria: An Archaeological Assessment* (London, 2007)
Ward-Perkins, B., *The Fall of Rome and the End of Civilization* (Oxford, 2005)
'Jones and the Late Roman Economy', in *A. H. M. Jones and the Later Roman Empire*, ed. D. M. Gwynn (Leiden and Boston, 2008), 193–211
Whitehouse, D. and A. Williamson, 'Sasanian Maritime Trade', *Iran* 11 (1973), 29–49
Whittow, M., 'The Middle Byzantine Economy (600–1204)', in *The Cambridge History of the Byzantine Empire c.500–1492*, ed. J. Shepard (Cambridge, 2008), pp. 465–92
'Early Medieval Byzantium and the End of the Ancient World', *Journal of Agrarian Change* 9 (2009), 134–53

Wichard, J. C., *Zwischen Markt und Moschee: Wirtschaftliche Bedürfnisse und religiöse Anforderungen im frühen islamischen Vertragsrecht* (Paderborn, etc., 1995)

Wickham, C., *Framing the Early Middle Ages: Europe and the Mediterranean 400–800* (Oxford, 2005)

The Inheritance of Rome: A History of Europe from 400 to 1000 (London, 2009)

Wilson, A., 'Machines, Power and the Ancient Economy', *Journal of Roman Studies* 92 (2002), 1–32

Wilson, A. I., 'Large-scale Manufacturing, Standardization, and Trade', in *The Oxford Handbook of Engineering and Technology in the Classical World*, ed. J. P. Oleson (Oxford, 2008), pp. 393–417

Zuckerman, C., *Du village à l'Empire: Autour du Registre fiscal d'Aphroditô (525/526)* (Paris, 2004)

Index